The Network +
Cram Sheet

This Cram Sheet contains the distilled, key facts about the CompTIA Network+ exam. Review this information as the last thing you do before you enter the testing center, paying special attention to those areas where you feel that you need the most review. You can transfer any of these facts from your head onto a blank sheet of paper immediately before you begin the exam.

MEDIA AND TOPOLOGIES

- Peer-to-peer networks are useful for only relatively small networks. They are often used in small offices or home environments.
- Client/server networks, also called server-centric networks, have clients and servers. Servers provide centralized administration, data storage, and security. The client system requests data from the server and displays the data to the end user.
- The bus network topology is also known as a linear bus because the computers in such a network are linked together using a single cable called a trunk, or backbone.
- If a terminator on a bus network is loose, data communications might be disrupted. Any other break in the cable will cause the entire network segment to fail.
- In a star configuration, all devices on the network connect to a central device, and this central device creates a single point of failure on the network.
- In the ring topology, the network layout forms a complete ring. Computers connect to the network cable directly or, more commonly, through a specialized network device.
- Breaking the loop of a ring network disrupts the entire network.
- The mesh topology requires each computer on the network to be individually connected to every other device. This configuration provides maximum reliability and redundancy for the network.
- Wireless networks use a centralized device kn... as a wireless access point (W...
- 802.2, the LLC sublayer, defi... the Logical Link Control (LLC... standard series.

- 802.3 defines the carrier-sense multiple-access with collision detection (CSMA/CD) media access method used in Ethernet networks. This is the most popular networking standard used today.
- 802.5 defines Token Ring networking.
- 802.11 defines standards for wireless LAN communication.
- Many factors cause EMI, including computer monitors and fluorescent lighting fixtures.
- Copper-based media are prone to EMI, whereas fiber-optic cable is resistant to it.
- Data signals may also be subjected to something commonly referred to as *crosstalk*, which occurs when signals from two cables, or from wires within a single cable, interfere with each other.
- The weakening of data signals as they traverse the media is referred to as *attenuation*.
- Half-duplex mode allows each device to both transmit and receive, but only one of these processes can occur at a time.
- Full-duplex mode allows devices to receive and transmit simultaneously. A 100Mbps network card in full-duplex mode can operate at 200Mbps.

CABLES AND CONNECTORS

- Thin coax is only .25 inches in diameter and has a maximum cable length of 185 meters (approximately 600 feet).
- Thick coax networks use a device called a tap to connect a smaller cable to the thick coax backbone. Thick ... x has a 500-meter cable length.
- ... nterface (AUI) ports are network ... t are often associated with thick ... se5) networks. The AUI port ... o which a transceiver is

- SC and ST connectors are associated with fiber cabling. ST connectors offer a twist-type attachment and SC connectors are push-on connectors.
- RJ-45 connectors are used with UTP cable.

10BASEX, 100BASEX, AND 1000BASEX STANDARDS

- 10Base2, sometimes called Thinnet or Thin Ethernet, is the 802.3 specification for a network that uses thin coaxial cable (that is, RG-58 cable).
- 10Base2 specifies a maximum speed of 10Mbps and uses BNC barrel and BNC T connectors to connect the cable and computers. At the physical ends of each cable segment, a 50-ohm terminator absorbs the signal, thus preventing signal reflection.
- The 10Base2 standard specifies a limit of 185 meters per segment (approximately 600 feet).

NETWORK DEVICES

- Token Ring networks use special devices called multistation access units (MSAUs) to create the network.
- A straight-through cable is used to connect systems to the switch or hub using the MDI-X ports.
- In a crossover cable, Wires 1 and 3 and Wires 2 and 6 are crossed.
- Bridges are used to divide networks and thus reduce the amount of traffic on each network.
- Routing Information Protocol (RIP) is a distance-vector routing protocol for both Transmission Control Protocol (TCP) and Internetwork Packet Exchange (IPX).
- A MAC address is a 6-byte address that lets a NIC be uniquely identified on the network. The first three bytes (00:D0:59) identify the manufacturer of the card; the last three bytes (09:07:51) are the Universal LAN MAC address, which makes the interface unique.

OSI MODEL

- As data is passed up or down through the OSI model structure, headers are added (going down) or removed (going up) at each layer—a process called *encapsulation* (when added) or *decapsulation* (when removed).
- The Application Layer provides access to the network for applications and certain end-user functions. It displays incoming information and prepares outgoing information for network access.
- The Presentation Layer converts data from the Application Layer into a format that can be sent over the network. It converts data from the Session Layer into a format that can be understood by the Application Layer. It also handles encryption and decryption of data and provides compression and decompression functionalities.

- The Session Layer synchronizes the data exchange between applications on separate devices. It handles error detection and notification to the peer layer on the other device.
- The Transport Layer establishes, maintains, and breaks connections between two devices. It determines the ordering and priorities of data. It also performs error checking and verification and handles retransmissions, if necessary.
- The Network Layer provides mechanisms for the routing of data between devices across single or multiple network segments and handles the discovery of destination systems and addressing.
- The Data-link Layer has two distinct sublayers: LLC and MAC. It performs error detection and handling for the transmitted signals. It also defines the method by which the medium is accessed and defines hardware addressing through the MAC sublayer.
- The Physical Layer defines the physical structure of the network. It also defines voltage/signal rates and the physical connection methods, as well as the physical topology.
- Mapping network devices to the OSI model:

Hub	Physical (Layer 1)
Switch	Data-link (Layer 2)
Bridge	Data-link (Layer 2)
Router	Network (Layer 3)
NIC	Data-link (Layer 2)

PROTOCOLS

- A Class A TCP/IP address uses only the first octet to represent the network portion, a Class B address uses two octets, and a Class C address uses three octets.
- Class A addresses span from 1 to 126, with a default subnet mask of 255.0.0.0.
- Class B addresses span from 128 to 191, with a default subnet mask of 255.255.0.0.
- Class C addresses span from 192 to 223, with a default subnet mask of 255.255.255.0.
- The 127 network ID is reserved for the local loopback.
- Application protocols map to the Application, Presentation, and Session layers of the OSI model. Application protocols include AFT, FTP, TFTP, NCP, and SNMP.
- Transport protocols map to the Transport layer of the OSI model and are responsible for transporting data across the network. Transport protocols include ATP, NetBEUI, SPX, TCP, and UDP.
- The NetBEUI protocol uses names as addresses.
- Network protocols are responsible for providing the addressing and routing information. Network protocols include IP, IPX, and DP.

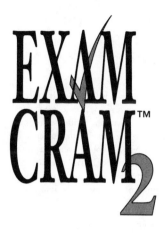

Network+

Mike Harwood

CERTIFICATION

Network+ Exam Cram2 (Exam N10-002)

Copyright © 2003 by Que Certification

International Standard Book Number: 0-7897-2865-6

Library of Congress Catalog Card Number: 2002113785

Printed in the United States of America

First Printing: November 2002
Second Printing with corrections: March 2003

05   04   03   4   3

Trademarks

Warning and Disclaimer

Publisher
Paul Boger

Executive Editor
Jeff Riley

Development Editor
Ginny Bess Munroe

Managing Editor
Thomas F. Hayes

Project Editor
Tonya Simpson

Copy Editor
Kezia Endsley

Indexer
Ken Johnson

Proofreader
Juli Cook

Technical Editors
Dave Bixler
Bill Ferguson

Team Coordinator
Rosemary Lewis

Multimedia Developer
Michael Hunter

Interior Designer
Gary Adair

Cover Designer
Charis Ann Santille

Page Layout
Stacey Richwine-DeRome

Taking You to the
Network+ Finish Line!

Network+ Training Guide
Mike Harwood and Drew Bird
ISBN 0-7897-2830-3
$49.99 US/$77.99 CAN/£36.50 Net UK

Before you walk into your local testing center, make absolutely sure you're prepared to pass your exam. In addition to the Exam Cram2 series, consider our Training Guide series. Que Certification's Training Guides have exactly what you need to pass your exam:

- Exam Objectives highlighted in every chapter
- Notes, Tips, Warnings, and Exam Tips advise what to watch out for
- Step-by-Step Exercises for "hands-on" practice
- End-of-chapter Exercises and Exam Questions
- Final Review with Fast Facts, Study and Exam Tips, and another Practice Exam
- A CD that includes PrepLogic Practice Tests for complete evaluation of your knowledge
- Our authors are recognized experts in the field. In most cases, they are current or former instructors, trainers, or consultants – they know exactly what you need to know!

CERTIFICATION

Que Certification • 201 West 103rd Street • Indianapolis, Indiana 46290

A Note from Series Editor Ed Tittel

You know better than to trust your certification preparation to just anybody. That's why you, and more than two million others, have purchased an Exam Cram book. As Series Editor for the new and improved Exam Cram2 series, I have worked with the staff at Que Certification to ensure you won't be disappointed. That's why we've taken the world's best-selling certification product—a finalist for "Best Study Guide" in a CertCities reader poll in 2002—and made it even better.

As a "Favorite Study Guide Author" finalist in a 2002 poll of CertCities readers, I know the value of good books. You'll be impressed with Que Certification's stringent review process, which ensures the books are high-quality, relevant, and technically accurate. Rest assured that at least a dozen industry experts—including the panel of certification experts at CramSession—have reviewed this material, helping us deliver an excellent solution to your exam preparation needs.

We've also added a preview edition of PrepLogic's powerful, full-featured test engine, which is trusted by certification students throughout the world.

As a 20-year-plus veteran of the computing industry and the original creator and editor of the Exam Cram series, I've brought my IT experience to bear on these books. During my tenure at Novell from 1989 to 1994, I worked with and around its excellent education and certification department. This experience helped push my writing and teaching activities heavily in the certification direction. Since then, I've worked on more than 70 certification-related books, and I write about certification topics for numerous Web sites and for *Certification* magazine.

In 1996, while studying for various MCP exams, I became frustrated with the huge, unwieldy study guides that were the only preparation tools available. As an experienced IT professional and former instructor, I wanted "nothing but the facts" necessary to prepare for the exams. From this impetus, Exam Cram emerged in 1997. It quickly became the best-selling computer book series since "*...For Dummies*," and the best-selling certification book series ever. By maintaining an intense focus on subject matter, tracking errata and updates quickly, and following the certification market closely, Exam Cram was able to establish the dominant position in cert prep books.

You will not be disappointed in your decision to purchase this book. If you are, please contact me at etittel@jump.net. All suggestions, ideas, input, or constructive criticism are welcome!

Ed Tittel

About the Author

. . . .

Mike Harwood (MCSE, A+, Network+, Server+, Linux+) has held a number of roles in the computer world starting with PC repair to the more current tasks of being the manager of a multisite network and independent consultant. Mike is the co-author of numerous computer books, including the *Network+ Training Guide* from Que Publishing and a regular technology presenter for CBC Radio. When not working, Mike stays as far away from keyboards as possible.

About the Technical Reviewers

Bill Ferguson (MCT, MCSE, MCP+I, A+, Network+) has been in the computer industry for more than 15 years. Originally in technical sales and sales management with Sprint, Bill made his transition to Certified Technical Trainer in 1997, with ExecuTrain. Bill now runs his own company as an independent contractor in Birmingham, Alabama, teaching classes for most of the national training companies and some regional training companies. In addition, Bill writes and produces technical training videos for Virtual Training Company, Inc. He currently has certifications in A+, Network+, Windows 2000 management, Windows XP management, and Windows 2000 security. Bill keeps his skills sharp by reviewing books and sample tests. He says, "My job is to understand the material so well that I can make it easier for my students to learn than it was for me to learn."

Dave Bixler (MCSE, MCNE, PSE, CCSE) is the technology services manager for one of the largest systems integrators in the United States. He has been working in the industry for the past 15 years, working on network designs, server implementations, and network management. Dave has focused on Internet technologies, including DNS and Web servers, information security, firewalls, and Windows 2000. Dave has also worked on a number of titles as an author, a technical editor, and a book reviewer. Dave's industry certifications include Microsoft's MCPS and MCSE, as well as Novell's CNE for NetWare versions 3.x, 4.x, and IntranetWare, ECNE, and MCNE. Dave lives in Cincinnati, Ohio, with his wife, Sarah, and his sons, Marty and Nicholas.

Acknowledgments

. . . .

I would like to thank Drew Bird for all his help and support on this project. Without it, the book would not have seen the light of day.

I would also like to say a huge thanks to the folks at Que Publishing—Ginny Bess, Kezia Endsley and Tonya Simpson—for their input and keeping everything on track despite the lure of the summer sun!

Let's not forget the technical editors—Dave Bixler and Bill Ferguson—who kept the project technically on target and taught me a few things along the way. Who knew NetWare 1.0 didn't support TCP/IP? And finally, thanks to Jeff Riley for overseeing the project with enthusiasm.

Dedication

This book is dedicated to life outside the office window.

❧

Contents at a Glance

Table of Contents

Chapter 4

We Want to Hear from You!

As the reader of this book, *you* are our most important critic and commentator. We value your opinion and want to know what we're doing right, what we could do better, what areas you'd like to see us publish in, and any other words of wisdom you're willing to pass our way.

As an executive editor for Que, I welcome your comments. You can email or write me directly to let me know what you did or didn't like about this book—as well as what we can do to make our books better.

Please note that I cannot help you with technical problems related to the *topic* of this book. We do have a User Services group, however, where I will forward specific technical questions related to the book.

When you write, please be sure to include this book's title and author as well as your name, email address, and phone number. I will carefully review your comments and share them with the author and editors who worked on the book.

Email: feedback@quepublishing.com

Mail: Jeff Riley
          Que Certification
          201 West 103rd Street
          Indianapolis, IN 46290 USA

For more information about this book or another Que title, visit our Web site at www.quepublishing.com. Type the ISBN (excluding hyphens) or the title of a book in the Search field to find the page you're looking for.

Introduction

Welcome to the *Network+ Exam Cram*. This book is designed to prepare you to take—and pass—the CompTIA Network+ exam. The Network+ exam has become the leading introductory-level network certification available today. It is recognized by both employers and industry giants (such as Microsoft and Novell) as providing candidates with a solid foundation of networking concepts, terminology, and skills. The Network+ exam covers a broad range of networking concepts to prepare candidates for those technologies they are likely to be working with in today's network environments.

About *Network+ Exam Cram*

Exam Crams are specifically designed to give you the "what-you-need-to-know" information to prepare for the Network+ exam. They cut through the extra information, focusing on the areas you need to get through the exam. With this in mind, the elements within the *Exam Cram* titles are aimed directly at providing the exam information you need in the most succinct and accessible manner.

In this light, this book is organized to closely follow the actual CompTIA objectives. As such, it is easy to find the information required for each of the specified CompTIA Network+ objectives. The objective focus design used by this Exam Cram is an important feature, because the information you need to know is easily identifiable and accessible. To see what we mean, compare the CompTIA objectives to the book's layout and you will see that the facts are right where you would expect them to be.

Within the chapters themselves, potential exam hotspots are clearly highlighted with *Exam Alerts*. Exam Alerts have been carefully placed to let you know that the surrounding discussion is an important area for the exam. To further help you prepare for the exam, a Cram Sheet is included that can be used in the final stages of test preparation. Be sure to pay close attention to the bulleted points provided in the Cram Sheet, as they pinpoint the technologies and facts you are likely going to encounter on the test.

Finally, great effort has gone into the end-of-chapter questions and practice tests to ensure that they accurately represent the look and feel of the ones you will have on the real Network+ exam. Be sure, before taking the exam, that you are comfortable with both the format and content of the questions provided in this book.

About the Network+ exam

The Network+ N10-002 exam is a revised version of the original exam. The original Network+ objectives were targeted for candidates with 18 to 24 months experience working in IT, whereas the new Network+ objectives are aimed toward those who have nine months experience in network support and administration. CompTIA believes that new Network+ candidates will require more hands-on experience in network administration and troubleshooting, but this should not discourage those who do not. Quite simply, the nature of the questions on the new exam is not dissimilar to the old and you can get by without the actual hands-on experience. Still, a little hands-on experience never hurt anyone and will certainly add to your confidence going into the exam.

You will have a maximum of 90 minutes to answer the 72 questions on the exam. The allotted time is quite generous and, by the time you are finished, you are likely going to have time to double-check a few of the answers you are unsure of. By the time the dust settles, you will need a minimum score of 646 to pass the Network+ exam. This is on a scale of 100 to 900.

One of the best things about the Network+ certification is that after you pass the exam, you are certified for life. There is no need to ever recertify. This fact can make the cost of taking the Network+ exam a little easier to swallow. For more information on the specifics of the Network+ exam, refer to CompTIA's main Web site at http://www.comptia.org/certification/.

Booking and taking the Network+ certification exam

Unfortunately, testing is not free. You'll be charged $199 for each test you take, whether you pass or fail. In the United States and Canada, tests are administered by Sylvan Prometric or VUE testing services. To book a test with Prometric or locate a Prometric testing center near you, refer to the Web site at www.2test.com or call directly at 800-776-4276. To access the VUE contact information and book an exam, refer to the Web site at www.vue.com or call directly at 877-551-7587. When booking an exam, you will need to identify the following information:

➤ Your name as you would like to have it appear on your certificate.

➤ Your Social Security or Social Insurance number.

➤ Contact phone numbers (to be called in case of a problem).

➤ Mailing address, which identifies the address at which you would like your certificate to be mailed.

➤ Exam number and title.

➤ Email address, once again for contact purposes. This often is the fastest and most effective means of contacting you. Many clients require it for registration.

➤ Credit-card payment to pay online. Vouchers can be redeemed by calling the respective testing center.

What to expect from the exam

For those who have not taken a certification test, the process can be a little unnerving. For those who have taken numerous tests, it is not much better. Mastering the inner mental game often can be as much of the battle as knowing the material itself. Knowing what to expect before heading in can make the process a little more comfortable.

Certification tests are administered on a computer system at a Prometric or VUE authorized testing center. The format of the exams is straightforward: Each question has several possible answers to choose from. In fact, the questions in this book provide a very good example of the types of questions you can expect on the actual exam. If you are comfortable with them, the test should hold few surprises. Many of the questions vary in terms of length; some of them are longer scenario questions, whereas others are short and right to the point. Read the questions carefully; the longer questions often have a key point in them that will lead you to the correct answer.

Most of the questions on the Network+ exam require you to choose a single correct answer, but a few will require multiple answers. When there are multiple correct answers, a message at the bottom of the screen prompts you to "choose all that apply." Be sure to read the messages.

A few exam-day details

It is recommended to get to the examination room at least 15 minutes early, although a few minutes earlier certainly would not hurt. This is good strategy used to prepare yourself and to allow the test administrator time to answer any questions you might have before the test begins. Many people suggest that you review the most critical information about the test you're taking just before the test. (*Exam Cram* books provide a reference—the Cram Sheet, located inside the front of this book—that lists the essential information from the book in distilled form.) Arriving a few minutes early will give you some time to compose yourself and to mentally review this critical information.

You will be asked to provide two forms of ID, with one of those being a photo ID. Both of the identifications you choose should have a signature. You also might need to sign in when you arrive and sign out when you leave.

Be warned, the rules are very clear about what you can and cannot take into the examination room. Books, laptops, note sheets, and so on, are not allowed in the examination room with you. The test administrator will hold these items, to be returned after you complete the exam. You might receive either a wipe board or a pen and a single piece of paper for making notes during the exam. The test administrator will ensure that no paper is removed from the examination room.

After the test

Whether you want it or not, as soon as you finish your test, your score is displayed on the computer screen. In addition to the results appearing on the computer screen, a hard copy of the report is printed for you. Like the onscreen report, the hard copy displays the results of your exam and provides a summary of how you did on each section of the exam and on each technology. If you were unsuccessful, this summary can help you determine the areas that you need to brush up on.

When you pass the Network+ exam, you will have earned the Network+ certification and your certificate will be mailed to you within a few weeks. Should you not receive your certificate and information packet within five weeks of passing your exam, please contact CompTIA at `fulfillment@ comptia.org` or call 630-268-1818 and ask for the fulfillment department.

Last-minute exam tips

Studying for a certification exam really is no different from studying for any other exam, but a few hints and tips can give you the edge come exam day:

➤ **Read all the material**—CompTIA has been known to include material not expressly specified in the objectives. This book has included additional information not reflected in the objectives in an effort to give you the best possible preparation for the examination.

➤ **Watch for the Exam Tips and Notes**—The Network+ objectives include a wide range of technologies. Exam Tips and Notes found throughout each chapter are designed to pull out exam-related hotspots. These can be your best friends when preparing for the exam.

➤ **Use the questions to assess your knowledge**—Don't just read the chapter content; use the exam questions to find out what you know and what you don't. If you are struggling, study some more, review, and then assess your knowledge again.

➤ **Review the exam objectives**—Develop your own questions and examples for each topic listed. If you can develop and answer several questions for each topic, you should not find it difficult to pass the exam.

Remember, at the end of the day, the primary object is not just to pass the exam—it is to understand the material. After you understand the material, passing the exam should be simple. Knowledge is a pyramid; to build upward, you need a solid foundation. This book and the Network+ certification are designed to ensure that you have that solid foundation.

Good luck!

Self-Assessment

We included a self-assessment in this *Exam Cram* to help you evaluate your readiness to tackle the Network+ certification. It is also designed to assist you in understanding the skills and experience needed to successfully pass the CompTIA Network+ certification exam.

Network+ professionals in the real world

The next section describes an ideal Network+ candidate, although we know full well that not all candidates will meet this ideal. In fact, the description of that ideal candidate might seem downright scary. But take heart: Increasing numbers of people are attaining CompTIA certifications, so the goal is within reach. You can get all the real-world motivation you need from knowing that many others have gone before you, so you will be able to follow in their footsteps. If you're willing to tackle the process seriously and do what it takes to obtain the necessary experience and knowledge, you can take—and pass—the certification test required to obtain an Network+ certification. In fact, we've designed this *Exam Cram* to make it as easy on you as possible to prepare for the exam. But prepare you must!

The same, of course, is true for other CompTIA certifications, including:

➤ *A+ certification*—A testing program that certifies the competency of entry-level service technicians in the computer industry. It consists of a Core exam and a DOS/Windows exam. It is targeted at computer technicians with six months of experience.

➤ *Certified Document Imaging Architech*—A testing program that is divided into sections within one test that correspond to an imaging professional's areas of responsibility. The technologies include Input/Capture, Display, Storage, Communications, Output, Standard Computing Environment, Integration, and Management Applications, as well as areas such as pre-processing and paper handling.

➤ *Server+*—The Server+ certification is designed to test a candidate's knowledge of server hardware, server best practices, and server maintenance. Some of the technologies covered include upgrading and repairing server hardware and software, troubleshooting hardware configurations, and best practices when working in the server room.

The ideal Network+ candidate

The following list describes some relevant statistics about the background and experience an ideal individual might have. Don't worry if you don't meet these qualifications or don't come that close—this is a far from ideal world, and where you fall short is simply where you'll have more work to do.

➤ Academic or professional training in network theory, concepts, and operations. This includes everything from networking media and transmission techniques to network operating systems, services, and applications.

➤ Between 9 and 24 months of professional networking experience, including experience with Ethernet, routers, and modems, with particular emphasis on the TCP/IP suite. This must include installation, configuration, upgrading, and troubleshooting experience.

➤ Two-plus years in an internetwork environment that includes hands-on experience with Web servers, email servers, database servers, and DHCP and DNS servers. A solid understanding of each system's architecture, installation, configuration, maintenance, and troubleshooting is also essential.

➤ Experience with the Internet, intranets, and extranets.

➤ Familiarity with client and network operating systems.

➤ Experience working with networking protocols, specifically TCP/IP.

If you were to review all of the criteria that goes into making an ideal Network+ candidate, you will find that it boils down to practical experience in a technical position involving installation, configuration, and maintenance of networks. We believe that well under half of all certification candidates meet these requirements, and that, in fact, most meet fewer than half of these requirements—at least, when they begin the certification process. But because others who already have been certified have survived this ordeal, you can survive it, too—especially if you heed what our self-assessment can tell you about what you already know and what you need to learn.

Put yourself to the test

The following series of questions and observations is designed to help you determine how much work you must do to pursue CompTIA Network+ certification and what kinds of resources you may consult on your quest. Be absolutely honest in your answers, or you'll end up wasting money on an exam you're not yet ready to take. There are no right or wrong answers, only steps along the path to certification. Only you can decide where you really belong in the broad spectrum of aspiring candidates.

Two things should be clear from the outset, however:

➤ Even a modest background in computer science will be helpful.

➤ Hands-on experience using network technologies is an important ingredient to certification success.

Educational background

1. Have you ever taken any networking concepts or technologies classes? [Yes or No]

   If Yes, proceed to Question 2; if No, you may want to augment the material in the *Exam Cram* with a book that approaches the topic of networking from an independent point of view and not from a certification point of view. When looking for a suitable title, look for those that explain technologies such as TCP/IP, routing, network design and others, in a clear and concise manner.

2. Do you have experience using and working with a network? [Yes or No]

   If Yes, you will probably be able to better understand CompTIA's Network+ objectives. Even being around networks as a user makes you familiar with how they are designed to function. If you're rusty, brush up on basic networking concepts and terminology, especially networking media as it relates to the TCP/IP suite, network security, dial-up fundamentals, and remote connectivity. Then, proceed to Question 3.

   If No, you may need to delve a little deeper into networking concepts. This is as simple as taking a trip to the local book store and getting an easy-to-read, up-to-date networking basics title.

3. Do you have experience working with network and client operating systems? [Yes or No]

   If Yes, you are on the right track. Network+ requires knowledge of working with both client-side operating systems such as Windows 98/Me and network-operating systems such as Windows 2000. Knowing how to navigate such OSs can be a benefit when configuring and troubleshooting network connectivity from within an operating system.

If No, crank up a computer with an OS on it and start going through it. Look for the network configuration screens. Look to the help file within the OS for quick tutorials and for help in configuring the client system for network connectivity.

If this sounds like a lot, it isn't. Perhaps the single most important element for the successful completion is a desire to learn all about networking. It is, after all, really quite interesting. Once the desire to learn kicks in, the test becomes that much easier.

Hands-on experience

CompTIA sites hands-on experience as a key to success on the CompTIA Network+ test. This is true, because hands-on experience reinforces what is written in the book. However, Network+ covers a broad range of networking technologies, some of which you may never see in your networking career. In such a case, all you can do is rely on the book knowledge. So can you pass the exam without reinforcing knowledge with practical hands-on experience? Yes. Is it advised? No. Bottom line—the more experience the better. If we leave you with only one realization after taking this self-assessment, it should be that there's no substitute for time spent installing, configuring, and using the various networking products upon which you'll be tested repeatedly and in depth. If you have never worked with any of the networking products or operating systems mentioned earlier, you would be well advised to review this work at least three or four times.

Testing your exam readiness

Whether you attend a formal class on a specific topic to get ready for an exam or use written materials to study on your own, some preparation for the CompTIA certification exam is essential. At $199 a try ($145 for CompTIA members), pass or fail, you want to do everything you can to pass on your first try. That's where studying comes in.

For any given subject, consider taking a class if you've tackled self-study materials, taken the test, and failed anyway. The opportunity to interact with an instructor and fellow students can make all the difference in the world, if you can afford that privilege.

If you can't afford to take a class, try the Training Resources link at www.comptia.com for any pointers to free practice exams. And even if you can't afford to spend much at all, you should still invest in some low-cost practice exams from commercial vendors, because they can help you assess your readiness to pass a test better than any other tool.

We have included practice questions at the end of each chapter, plus two practice exams at the end of the book. If you don't do that well on the questions at the end of the chapters, you can study more and then tackle the practice exams. From there, feel free to surf the Web and do a little research on the Network+ exam. Newsgroups are a good place to look, because there are a number of people willing to chat about their experiences studying and taking the Network+ exam.

If you take the practice tests and score 85 percent or better, you're probably ready to tackle the real thing. If your score isn't above that crucial threshold, obtain all the free and low-budget practice tests you can find and get to work. Keep at it until you can break the passing threshold comfortably.

When it comes to assessing your test readiness, there is no better way than to take a good-quality practice exam and pass with a score of 85 percent or better. When we're preparing ourselves, we shoot for 90-plus percent, just to leave room for the "weirdness factor" that sometimes shows up on CompTIA exams.

Because the Internet is the most rapidly changing segment of Information Technology (IT), the test may change, but this book's material is sufficiently comprehensive that it will be a good preparation tool regardless. Also, you should be aware that CompTIA and other certifications reserve the right to a function known as *slipstreaming*, in which questions are removed and new ones are added without announcement. We scoured the latest trends and interviewed many industry veterans in an attempt to prepare you for the inevitable changes that will occur.

Onward, through the fog!

Once you've assessed your readiness, undertaken the right background studies, obtained the hands-on experience that will help you understand the technologies at work, and reviewed the many sources of information to help you prepare for a test, you'll be ready to take a round of practice tests. When your scores come back positive enough to get you through the exam, you're ready to go after the real thing. If you follow our assessment regime, you'll not only know what you need to study, but when you're ready to make a test date at Prometric or VUE.

Good luck!

Introduction to Networking

Objectives

1.1 Recognize the following logical or physical network topologies given a schematic diagram or description:

✓ Star/hierarchal

✓ Bus

✓ Mesh

✓ Ring

✓ Wireless

1.2 Specify the main features of 802.2 (LLC), 802.3 (Ethernet), 802.5 (Token Ring), 802.11b (wireless), and FDDI network topologies, including

✓ Speed

✓ Access method

✓ Topology

✓ Media

What you need to know

✓ Understand the differences between Local Area Networks (LANs) and Wide Area Networks (WANs)

✓ Identify the characteristics between peer-to-peer and client/server networking

✓ Identify the characteristics of various network topologies

✓ Understand the characteristics of the following IEEE standards, 802.2, 802.3, 802.5, and 802.11b

✓ Identify the characteristics of Fiber Distributed Data Interface (FDDI)

Introduction

There are a variety of physical and logical network layouts in use today. As a network administrator you may find yourself working on these different network layouts or topologies and as such will require knowledge of how they are designed to function.

This chapter reviews general network considerations such as the various topologies used on today's networks, LANs and WANs, and the IEEE standards.

LANs and WANs

Networks are classified according to their geographical coverage and size. The two most common network classifications are local area networks (LANs) and wide area networks (WANs).

LANs

A *LAN* is a data network that is restricted to a single geographical location and typically encompasses a relatively small area such as an office building or school. The function of the LAN is to interconnect workstation computers for the purposes of sharing files and resources. Because of its localized nature, the LAN is typically high speed and cheaper to set up than a WAN. Figure 1.1 shows an example of a LAN.

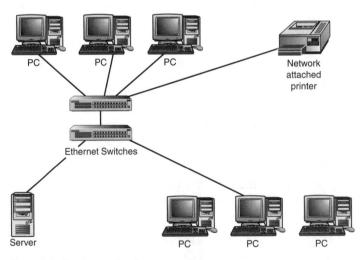

Figure 1.1 Local area network.

WANs

A *WAN* is a network that spans more than one geographical location often connecting separated LANs. WANs are slower than LANs and often require additional and costly hardware such as routers, dedicated leased lines, and complicated implementation procedures. Figure 1.2 shows an example of a WAN.

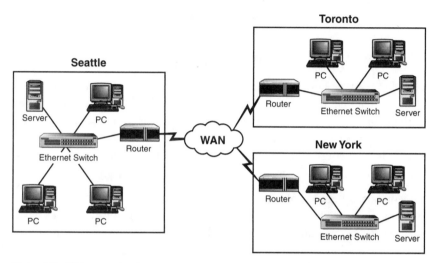

Figure 1.2   Wide area network.

Network models

There are two basic network models from which to choose, the peer-to-peer network model and the client/server model. The model used for a network is determined by several factors, including how the network will be used, how many users will be on the network, and budgetary considerations.

Peer-to-peer networking

A *peer-to-peer network* is a decentralized network model offering no centralized storage of data or centralized control over the sharing of files or resources. All systems on a peer-to-peer network can share the resources on their local computer as well as use resources of other systems.

Peer-to-peer networks are cheaper and easier to implement than client/server networks, making them an ideal solution for environments where budgets are a concern. The peer-to-peer model does not work well with large numbers of computer systems. As a peer-to-peer network grows, it becomes increasingly complicated to navigate and access files and resources connected to each computer because they are distributed throughout the network. Further, the lack of centralized data storage makes it difficult to locate and back up key files.

Peer-to-peer networks are typically found in small offices or in residential settings where only a limited number of computers will be attached and only a few files and resources shared. A general rule of thumb is to have no more than 10 computers connected to a peer-to-peer network.

Client/server networking model

The client/server networking model is, without question, the most widely implemented model and the one you are most likely to encounter when working in real-world environments. The advantages of the client/server stem from the fact that it is a centralized model. It allows for centralized network management of all network services, including user management, security, and backup procedures.

A client/server network often requires technically skilled personnel to implement and manage the network. This and the cost of a dedicated server hardware and software increase the cost of the client/server model. Despite this, the advantages of the centralized management, data storage, administration, and security make it the network model of choice. Table 1.1 summarizes the characteristics of the peer-to-peer and client/server network models.

 The role of the client computer in the client/server model is to request the data from the server and present that data to the users.

Table 1.1	Comparison of Networking Models	
Attribute	**Peer-to-Peer Network**	**Client/Server Network**
Size	Restricted to a maximum of 10 computers	The size of the network is limited only by server size and network hardware, and it can have thousands of connected systems.
Administration	Each individual is responsible for the administration of his or her own system. A dedicated administrator is not needed.	A skilled network administrator is often required to maintain and manage the network.

(continued)

Table 1.1 Comparison of Networking Models *(continued)*		
Security	Each individual is responsible for maintaining security for shared files or resources connected to the system.	Security is managed from a central location but often requires a skilled administrator to correctly configure.
Cost	Minimal startup and implementation cost.	Requires dedicated equipment and specialized hardware and administration, increasing the cost of the network.
Implementation	Easy to configure and set up.	Often requires complex setup procedures and skilled staff to set up.

Centralized and distributed computing

The terms centralized and distributed computing are used to describe where the network processing takes place. In a *centralized computing model*, one system provides both the data storage and the processing power for client systems. This networking model is most often associated with computer mainframes and dumb terminals, where no processing or storage capability exists at the workstation. These network environments are rare but they do still exist.

A distributed network model has the processing power distributed between the client systems and the server. Most modern networks use the distributed network model where client workstations share in the processing responsibilities.

Network topologies

A *topology* refers to both the physical and logical layout of a network. The *physical* topology of a network refers to the actual layout of the computer cables and other network devices. The *logical* topology of a network, on the other hand, refers to the way in which the network appears to the devices that use it.

There are several topologies in use for networks today. Some of the more common include the bus, ring, star, mesh, and wireless topologies. The following sections provide an overview of each.

Bus topology

A *bus network* uses a trunk or backbone to which all of the computers on the network connect. Systems connect to this backbone using *T connectors* or taps. To avoid signal reflection, a physical bus topology requires that each end of the physical bus be terminated. Figure 1.3 shows an example of a physical bus topology.

Loose or missing terminators from a bus network will disrupt data transmissions.

Figure 1.3 Physical bus topology.

The most common implementation of a linear bus is the IEEE 802.3 standard.

Table 1.2 Advantages and Disadvantages of the Bus Topology	
Advantages	**Disadvantages**
Compared to other topologies, a bus is cheap and easy to implement.	There might be network disruption when computers are added or removed.
Requires less cable than other topologies.	Because all systems on the network connect to a single backbone, a break in the cable will prevent all systems from accessing the network.
Does not use any specialized network equipment.	Difficult to troubleshoot.

Ring topology

The *ring topology* is actually a logical ring, meaning that the data travels in circular fashion from one computer to another on the network. It is not a physical ring topology. Figure 1.4 shows the logical layout of a ring network.

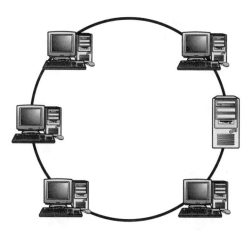

Figure 1.4   Logical design of the ring network.

In a true ring topology, if a single computer or section of cable fails, there is an interruption in the signal. The entire network becomes inaccessible. Network disruption can also occur when computers are added or removed from the network, making it an impractical network design in environments where there is constant change to the network.

Ring networks are most commonly wired in a star configuration. In a Token Ring network, a multistation access unit (MSAU) is equivalent to a hub or switch on an Ethernet network. The MSAU performs the token circulation internally. To create the complete ring, the Ring In (RI) port on each MSAU is connected to the Ring Out (RO) port on another MSAU. The last MSAU in the ring is then connected to the first, to complete the ring. Table 1.3 summarizes the advantages and disadvantages of the ring topology.

Table 1.3 Advantages and Disadvantages of the Ring Topology	
Advantages	**Disadvantages**
Cable faults are easily located, making troubleshooting easier.	Expansion to the network can cause network disruption.
Ring networks are moderately easy to install.	A single break in the cable can disrupt the entire network.

Star topology

In the *star topology*, all computers and other network devices connect to a central device called a *hub* or *switch*. Each connected device requires a single cable to be connected to the hub, creating a point-to-point connection between the device and the hub.

Using a separate cable to connect to the hub allows the network to be expanded without disruption to the network. A break in any single cable will not cause the entire network to fail. Figure 1.5 provides an example of a star topology.

 Among the network topologies discussed in this chapter, the star topology is the easiest to expand in terms of the number of devices connected to the network.

Figure 1.5 Star topology.

The star topology is the most widely implemented network design in use today but it is not without its shortcomings. Because all devices connect to a centralized hub, this creates a single point of failure for the network. If the hub fails, any device connected to it will not be able to access the network. Because of the number of cables required and the need for network devices, the cost of a star network is often higher than other topologies. Table 1.4 summarizes the advantages and disadvantages of the star topology.

Table 1.4 Advantages and Disadvantages of the Star Topology	
Advantages	**Disadvantages**
Star networks are easily expanded without disruption to the network.	Requires more cable than most of the other topologies.
Cable failure affects only a single user.	A central connecting device allows for a single point of failure.
Easy to troubleshoot and isolate problems.	More difficult than other topologies to implement.

Mesh topology

The *mesh topology* incorporates a unique network design in which each computer on the network connects to every other, creating a point-to-point connection between every device on the network. The purpose of the mesh design is to provide a high level of *redundancy*. If one network cable fails, the data always has an alternative path to get to its destination. Figure 1.6 shows the mesh topology.

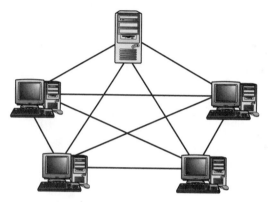

Figure 1.6   Mesh topology.

As you can see from Figure 1.6, the wiring for a mesh network can be very complicated. Further, the cabling costs associated with the mesh topology can be high and troubleshooting a failed cable can be tricky. Because of this, the mesh topology is rarely used. A variation on a true mesh topology is the hybrid mesh. It creates a redundant point-to-point network connection between only specific network devices. The hybrid mesh is most often seen in WAN implementations. Table 1.5 summarizes the advantages and disadvantages of the mesh topology.

Because of the redundant connections, the mesh topology offers better fault tolerance than other topologies.

Table 1.5   Advantages and Disadvantages of the Mesh Topology

Advantages	Disadvantages
Provides redundant paths between devices.	Requires more cable than the other LAN topologies.
The network can be expanded without disruption to current users.	Complicated implementation.

Wireless networking

As the name suggests, wireless networks do not require physical cabling to connect computers. The benefits of such a configuration are clear; remote access to files and resources can be achieved without cabling. Wireless technology is particularly useful for remote access for laptop users. In addition, wireless networking eliminates cable faults and cable breaks. It does however introduce its own issues—namely signal interference and security. Figure 1.7 shows a possible configuration for a wireless network.

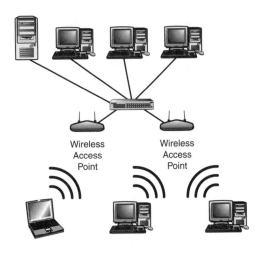

Computer

Figure 1.7   Wireless network.

Unfortunately, the speed of wireless networking is slower than traditional wired topologies and there are security concerns over wireless access. Many of these concerns have been addressed, but its reputation as an insecure transmission method still lingers. Table 1.6 identifies the advantages and disadvantages of the wireless topology.

Wireless devices use a wireless access point (WAP) to connect to the network.

Table 1.6　Advantages and Disadvantages of the Wireless Topology

Advantages	Disadvantages
Allows for wireless remote access.	Potential security issues associated with wireless transmissions.
Network can be expanded without disruption to current users.	Limited speed in comparison to other network topologies.

IEEE and networking standards

The Institute of Electrical and Electronic Engineers (IEEE) developed a series of networking standards to ensure that networking technologies developed by respective manufacturers are compatible. This means that the cabling, networking devices, and protocols are all interchangeable when designed under the banner of a specific IEEE standard. Table 1.7 summarizes the IEEE 802 networking standards.

Table 1.7　IEEE 802 Networking Standards

Specification	Name
802.1	Internetworking
802.2	The LLC (Logical Link Control) sublayer
802.3	CSMA/CD (Carrier Sense Multiple Access with Collision Detection) for Ethernet networks
802.4	A token passing bus
802.5	Token Ring networks
802.6	Metropolitan Area Network (MAN)
802.7	Broadband Technical Advisory Group
802.8	Fiber-Optic Technical Advisory Group
802.9	Integrated Voice and Data Networks
802.10	Standards for Interoperable LAN/MAN Security (SILS) (Network Security)
802.11	Wireless networks
802.12	100Mbps technologies, including 100BASEVG-AnyLAN

Only a few of the standards listed in Table 1.7 are tested on the CompTIA exam. The standards that are specifically included in the CompTIA objectives are 802.2, 802.3, 802.5, and 802.11b. Each of these IEEE specifications outlines specific characteristics for LAN networking including the speed, topology, cabling, and access method. The following sections outline the key features of these IEEE specifications and the specific characteristics of each.

802.2 IEEE standard

The 802.2 standard, referred to as the Logical Link Control (LLC), manages data flow control and error control for the other IEEE LAN standards. Data flow control regulates how much data can be transmitted in a certain amount of time. Error control refers to the recognition and notification of damaged signals. The LLC layer is discussed more in Chapter 4, "OSI Model and Network Protocols."

802.3 IEEE standard

The IEEE 802.3 standard defines the characteristics for Ethernet networks. Ethernet networking is by far the most widely implemented form of local area networking. There are several Ethernet LAN characteristics identified in the 802.3 standard.

Since the development of the original 802.3 standards there have also been several additions that have been assigned new designators. These standards are often referred to as the 802.3x standards. Some of the newer standards include 802.3u for Fast Ethernet and 802.3z for Gigabit Ethernet. The features for 802.3 are listed here:

➤ **Speed**—The original IEEE 802.3 standard specified a network transfer rate of 10Mbps. There have been modifications to the standard, the result being Fast Ethernet (802.3u), which can transmit network data up to 100Mbps and higher, as well as Gigabit Ethernet (802.3z), which can transmit at speeds up to 1000Mbps.

➤ **Topology**—The original Ethernet networks used a bus or star topology because the original 802.3 standard included specifications for both twisted pair and coaxial cabling. The IEEE 802.3u and 802.3z specify twisted pair cabling and use a star topology. Remember that even when Ethernet uses a physical star topology, it uses a logical bus topology.

➤ **Media**—The media refers to the physical cabling used to transmit the signal around the network. The original 802.3 specifications identified co-axial and twisted pair cabling to be used. The more modern standards specify twisted pair and fiber optic cable.

➤ **Access method**—The access method refers to the way that the network media is accessed. Ethernet networks use a system called *Carrier Sense Multiple Access with Collision Detection (CSMA/CD)*. CSMA/CD works by monitoring the computers that are sending data on the network. If two computers transmit data at the same time, a data collision will occur. To prevent collisions, the systems sending the data will be required to wait a period of time and then retransmit the data to avoid the collision.

One of the shortcomings of CSMA/CD is that as more systems are added to the network, the likelihood of collisions increases and the network becomes slower.

802.5 IEEE standard

The IEEE 802.5 standard specifies the characteristics for Token Ring networks. Token Ring was introduced by IBM in the mid 1980s and quickly became the network topology of choice until the rise in popularity of Ethernet. It is unlikely that you will encounter a ring network in your travels and even more unlikely that you will be implementing a ring network as a new installation. For what it's worth, Token Ring is a solid network system but Ethernet has all but eliminated it.

The following is a list of the specific characteristics specified in the 802.5 standard:

➤ **Speed**—The 802.5 Token Ring specifies network speeds of 4 and 16Mbps.

➤ **Topology**—Token Ring networks use a logical ring topology and most often a physical star. The logical ring is often created in the Multistation Access Unit (MSAU).

➤ **Media**—Token Ring networks use unshielded twisted pair cabling or shielded twisted pair. More information on the specific characteristics of twisted pair cabling is covered in Chapter 2, "Cabling and Connectors."

➤ **Access method**—802.5 specifies an access method known as *token passing*. On a Token Ring network, only one computer at a time can transmit data. When a computer has data to send, it must use a special type of packet known as a *token*. The token travels around the network looking for computers with data to send. The computer's data is passed along with the token until it gets to the destination computer, at which point the data is removed from the token and the empty token placed back on the ring.

 All network cards on a Token Ring network must operate at the same speed.

802.11b IEEE standard

The 802.11b standard specifies the characteristics of wireless LAN Ethernet networks. The 802.11b standard can be implemented many ways, but the most common is to have special devices called *wireless access points* that allow multiple wireless devices to communicate. In addition, these wireless access points can connect to wired networks to create wireless portions of entire networks. Wireless access points can cover distances up to several hundred feet, but the actual range depends on the location of the receiver and the local conditions.

The following list summarizes the characteristics of the 802.11b standard:

➤ **Speed**—802.11b specifies transmissions speeds of 11Mbps.

➤ **Media**—The media specified in the 802.11b standard is 2.4Ghz radio waves.

➤ **Topology**—802.11b uses a physical wireless topology and because it is based on Ethernet standards it uses a logical bus topology.

➤ **Access method**—802.11b uses Carrier Sense Multiple Access/Collision Avoidance (CSMA/CA). CSMA/CA is a variation on the CSMA/CD access method.

FDDI

The American National Standards Institute (ANSI) developed the *Fiber Distributed Data Interface (FDDI)* standard in the mid 1980s to meet the growing need for a reliable and fast networking system to accommodate distributed applications. FDDI uses a ring network design but, unlike the traditional 802.5 standard, FDDI uses a dual ring technology for fault tolerance. Because of the dual ring design, FDDI is not susceptible to a single cable failure like the regular 802.5 IEEE standard. Figure 1.8 shows an FDDI network with a dual ring configuration.

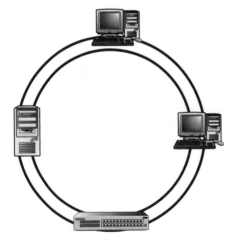

Figure 1.8 FDDI network.

As with any of the other standards, FDDI has specific characteristics:

➤ **Speed**—FDDI transmits data at 100Mbps and higher.

➤ **Topology**—FDDI uses a dual ring topology for fault-tolerant reasons.

➤ **Media**—FDDI used fiber optic cable that allows data transmissions that exceed two kilometers. Additionally, it is possible to use FDDI protocols over copper wire known as the Copper Distributed Data Interface (CDDI).

➤ **Access method**—Similar to 802.5, FDDI uses a token-passing access method.

Table 1.8 summarizes each of the standards discussed in the previous sections.

Table 1.8	IEEE 802 Network Standards				
Standard	**Speed**	**Physical Topology**	**Logical Topology**	**Media**	**Access Method**
802.3	10Mbps		Bus and Star	Coaxial and twisted pair	CSMA/CD
(802.3u)	100Mbps (Fast Ethernet)	Star	Bus	Twisted pair	CSMA/CD
(802.3z)	1000Mbps	Star	Bus	Twisted pair	CSMA/CD
802.5	4Mbps and 16Mbps	Star	Ring	Twisted pair	Token passing
802.11b	11Mbps	Wireless	Bus	Radio waves	CSMA/CA
FDDI	100Mbps	Dual ring	Ring	Fiber-optic Twisted pair (CDDI)	Token passing

Pay close attention to the information provided in Table 1.8. You can expect questions on the Network+ exam based on the details provided in the table.

Review and test yourself

The following sections provide you with the opportunity to review what you learned in this chapter and to test yourself.

The facts

For the exam, don't forget these important key concepts:

➤ In a star topology, each device on the network connects to a centralized device via a single cable.

➤ Computers in a star network can be connected and disconnected from the network without affecting any other systems.

➤ In a star configuration, all devices on the network connect to devices that act as connectivity points for the network, and these devices create a single point of failure on the network.

➤ The most common implementation of the physical star topology is the Ethernet 10BaseT standard, although most new installations are 100BaseT, at a minimum.

➤ In the ring topology, the network layout forms a complete ring. Computers connect to the network cable directly or, far more commonly, through a specialized network device.

➤ Breaking the loop of a ring network disrupts the entire network. Even if network devices are used to create the ring, the ring must still be broken if a fault occurs or the network needs to be expanded.

➤ The mesh topology requires each computer on the network be connected to each device. This configuration provides maximum reliability and redundancy for the network.

➤ Wireless networks use a centralized device known as a *wireless access point (WAP)*, which transmits signals to devices with wireless NICs installed in them.

➤ 802.3 defines the Carrier Sense Multiple Access with Collision Avoidance Detection (CSMA/CD) media access method used in Ethernet networks. This is the most popular networking standard used today.

➤ 802.5 defines Token Ring networking.

➤ All cards in a Token Ring network must operate at the same speed.

➤ Ring networks are most commonly wired in a star configuration. In a Token Ring network, a multistation access unit (MSAU) is equivalent to a hub or switch on an Ethernet network.

➤ To connect MSAUs, the ring in and ring out configuration must be properly set.

➤ FDDI uses a dual-ring configuration for fault tolerance.

Key terms

➤ LANs and WANs

➤ Peer-to-peer and client/server networking models

➤ Physical topology

➤ Logical topology

➤ Bus

➤ Ring

➤ Star

➤ Mesh

➤ Wireless

➤ IEEE 802.2, 802.3, 802.5, and 802.11b

➤ FDDI

Practice exam

Question 1

> Which of the following standards uses a dual ring configuration for fault tolerance?
>
> ○ A. 802.3
> ○ B. FDDI
> ○ C. 802.5
> ○ D. 802.2

The correct answer is B. FDDI uses a ring network design but uses dual rings for fault tolerance. If there is disruption in one of the rings, network traffic can use the other ring. Answer A is incorrect, as the 802.3 specifies Ethernet networks and does not use a ring design. Answer C is incorrect, as 802.5 only defines a single ring. Answer D is incorrect, as 802.2 is the IEEE standard for the Logical Link Layer.

Question 2

> Which of the following access methods is associated with Ethernet networks?
>
> ○ A. CSMA/CD
> ○ B. CSMA/CA
> ○ C. Token Passing
> ○ D. Demand Polling

The correct answer is A. CSMA/CD works by monitoring the computers that are sending data on the network. If two computers transmit data at the same time onto the network, a data collision will occur. Answer B is incorrect; CSMA/CA uses collision avoidance as an access method. Answer C is incorrect; token passing is associated with ring networks. Demand polling is an access method based on priority and is not used on Ethernet networks; therefore, answer D is incorrect.

Question 3

You have been asked to install a network that will provide the network users with the greatest amount of fault tolerance. Which of the following network topologies would you choose?

○ A. Star

○ B. Ring

○ C. Mesh

○ D. Bus

The correct answer is C. A mesh network uses a point-to-point connection to every device on the network. This creates multiple points for the data to be transmitted around the network and therefore creates a high degree of redundancy. The star, ring, and bus topologies do not offer fault tolerance.

Question 4

Which of the following access methods is associated with the 802.11b standard?

○ A. CSMA/CD

○ B. CSMA/CA

○ C. Token Passing

○ D. Radio Waves

The correct answer is B. 802.11b specifies CSMA/CA as the access method for wireless networks. CSMA/CD is the access method associated with the IEEE 802.3 standards and is therefore incorrect. Token passing is an access method but is not used for wireless networks making answer C incorrect. Answer D is incorrect as radio waves represent the media used by wireless, not the access method.

Question 5

Which of the following topologies allow for network expansion with the least amount of disruption for the current network users?

○ A. Bus

○ B. Ring

○ C. 802.5

○ D. 802.4

○ E. Star

The correct answer is E. On a star network, each network device uses a separate cable to make a point-to-point connection to a centralized device such as a hub. With such a configuration, a new device can be added to the network by attaching the new device to the hub with its own cable. This process does not disrupt the users who are currently on the network. Answers A, B, C, and D are incorrect because the addition of new network devices on a ring or bus network can cause a disruption in the network and cause network services to be unavailable during the installation of a new device. 802.5 is the IEEE specification for a ring network and 802.4 is the IEEE specification for a token bus.

Question 6

Which of the following are functions of the LLC? (Choose all that apply.)

❑ A. Data flow control

❑ B. Data fault tolerance

❑ C. Error control

❑ D. Token passing

The correct answers are A and C. The LLC manages both the data flow control and error control for LAN networking standards such as 802.3, 802.5, and 802.11b. The function of the LLC is not to provide fault tolerance; therefore, answer B is incorrect. Similarly, the function of LLC is not associated with token passing.

Question 7

Which of the following statements are associated with a bus LAN network? (Choose all correct answers.)

- ❏ A. A single cable break can cause complete network disruption.
- ❏ B. All devices connect to a central device.
- ❏ C. Uses a single backbone to connect all network devices.
- ❏ D. Uses a dual ring configuration.

The correct answers are A and C. In a bus network, a single break in the network cable can disrupt all of the devices on that segment of the network, a significant shortcoming. A bus network also uses a single cable as a backbone to which all networking devices attach. A star network requires networked devices to connect to a centralized device such as a hub or MSAU. Therefore answer B is incorrect. A dual ring topology is associated with FDDI, not a bus network.

Question 8

Which of the following is associated with 802.3u?

- ○ A. Gigabit Ethernet
- ○ B. Fast Ethernet
- ○ C. FDDI
- ○ D. 802.2

The correct answer is B. 802.3u is the specification for Fast Ethernet under the original 802.3 IEEE standard. 802.3z is the specification for Gigabit Ethernet; therefore, answer A is incorrect. FDDI is not associated with 802.3u; FDDI uses a dual ring network design. 802.2 is the IEEE standard for the LLC sublayer.

Question 9

What is the maximum speed for the 802.11b IEEE standard?

- ○ A. 100Mbps
- ○ B. 40Mbps
- ○ C. 11Mbps
- ○ D. 32Mbps

The correct answer is C. 802.11b allows for a transfer rate of 11Mbps.

Question 10

As a network administrator, you are called in to troubleshoot a problem on a token ring network. The network uses two MSAUs connected using the ring in ports on both devices. All network cards are set at the same speed. What is the likely cause of the problem?

○ A. Bad network card

○ B. Faulty cabling

○ C. MSAU configuration

○ D. Network card configuration

The correct answer is C. To create the complete ring, the Ring In (RI) port on each MSAU is connected to the Ring Out (RO) port on another MSAU. The last MSAU in the ring is then connected to the first, to complete the ring.

Want to know more?

Bird, Drew and Harwood, Mike. *Network+ Training Guide*, Que Publishing, 2002.

Sheldon, Thomas. *McGraw-Hill's Encyclopedia of Networking and Telecommunications.* McGraw-Hill Professional Publishing, 2001.

Tulloch, Mitch. *Microsoft Encyclopedia of Networking* (with CD-ROM). Microsoft Press, 2000.

Cabling and Connectors

Objectives

1.3 Specify the characteristics (for example, speed, length, topology, and cable type) of the following IEEE 802.3 (Ethernet) standards:

✓ 10BaseT

✓ 100BaseTX

✓ 10Base2

✓ 10Base5

✓ 100BaseFX

✓ Gigabit Ethernet

1.4 Recognize the following media connectors and describe their uses:

✓ RJ-11

✓ RJ-45

✓ AUI

✓ BNC

✓ ST

✓ SC

1.5 Choose the appropriate media type and connectors to add a client to an existing network.

What you need to know

✓ Identify common media considerations

✓ Understand the relationship between media and bandwidth

✓ Identify the two signaling methods used on networks

✓ Understand the three media dialog methods

✓ Identify the characteristics of IEEE standards 802.3, 802.3u, and 802.3z

✓ Identify the various connectors used with network media

Introduction

When it comes to working with an existing network or implementing a new network, you need to be able to identify the characteristics of network media and their associated cabling. This chapter focuses on the network media and connectors used in today's networks.

In addition to media and connectors, this chapter identifies the characteristics of the IEEE 802.3 standard and the modified standards 802.3u and 802.3z.

General media considerations

In addition to identifying the characteristics of network media and their associated cabling, the Network+ exam requires knowledge of some general terms and concepts that are associated with network media. Before looking at the individual media types, it is a good idea to first have an understanding of some general media considerations.

Broadband versus baseband

Networks employ two types of signaling methods: baseband and broadband. *Baseband transmissions* use digital signaling over a single wire. Communication on baseband transmissions is bidirectional, allowing signals to be sent and received but not at the same time. To send multiple signals on a single cable, baseband uses something called *Time Division Multiplexing (TDM)*. TDM divides a single channel into time slots.

Broadband transmissions, on the other hand, use analog transmissions. For broadband transmissions to be sent and received, the media has to be split into two channels. Multiple channels are created using Frequency Division-Multiplexing (FDM).

Simplex, half duplex, and full duplex

Simplex, half duplex, and full duplex are referred to as dialog modes, and they determine the direction in which data can flow through the network media.

Simplex allows for one-way communication of data through the network, with the full bandwidth of the cable being used for the transmitting signal. One-way communication is of little use on LANs, making it unusual at best for network implementations. Far more common is the *half-duplex* mode, which accommodates transmitting and receiving on the network but not at the same time. Many networks are configured for half-duplex communication.

The preferred dialog mode for network communication is the *full-duplex* mode. To use full duplex, both the network card and the hub or switch must support full duplexing. Devices configured for full duplexing are able to transmit and receive simultaneously. This means that 100Mbps network cards are able to transmit at 200Mbps using full-duplex mode.

Media interference

Depending on where network cabling is installed, *interference* can be a major consideration. Two types of media interference can adversely affect data transmissions over network media: electromagnetic interference (EMI) and crosstalk.

EMI is a problem when cables are installed near electrical devices, such as air conditioners or fluorescent light fixtures. If a network media is placed close enough to such a device, the signal within the cable might become corrupt. Network media vary in their resistance to the effects of EMI. Standard UTP cable is susceptible to EMI, whereas fiber cable with its light transmissions is resistant to EMI. When deciding on a particular media, consider where it will run and the impact EMI can have on the installation.

A second type of interference is *crosstalk*. Crosstalk refers to how the data signals on two separate media interfere with each other. The result is that the signal on both cables can become corrupt. As with EMI, media varies in its resistance to crosstalk, with fiber-optic cable being the most resistant.

 For the Network+ exam, remember that fiber-optic cable offers the most resistance to EMI and crosstalk.

Attenuation

Attenuation refers to the weakening of data signals as they travel through a respective media. Network media varies in its resistance to attenuation. Coaxial cable is generally more resistant than UTP, STP more resistant than UTP, and fiber more resistant than all of them.

It's important to understand attenuation and the maximum distances specified for network media. Exceeding a media's distance without using repeaters can cause hard-to-troubleshoot network problems. Most attenuation-related difficulties on a network require using a network analyzer to detect them.

Bandwidth

One of the more important media considerations is its *bandwidth* capacity. Bandwidth refers to the transmission capacity of a media (the amount of data that a cable can carry). Data throughput is measured in bits per second (bps). Today's networks are measured in Mbps and Gbps (gigabytes per second).

The different network media vary greatly in the bandwidth capacity they support. Many of today's application-intensive networks require more than the 10Mbps offered by the older Ethernet standards. In some cases, even 100Mbps, which is found in many modern LANs, is simply not enough to meet current network needs. In others it offers more than enough bandwidth.

Network media

Whatever type of network is used, some type of network media is needed to carry signals between computers. Two types of media are used in networks: cable-based media, such as twisted pair, and the media types associated with wireless networking, such as radio waves.

In networks using cable-based media, there are three basic choices:

➤ Coaxial

➤ Twisted pair

➤ Fiber-optic

Coaxial and twisted-pair cables both use copper wire to conduct the signals electronically; fiber-optic cable uses a glass or plastic conductor and transmits the signals as light.

For many years coaxial was the cable of choice for most LANs. Today however, twisted pair has proved to be far and away the cable media of choice, thus retiring coax to the confines of storage closets. Fiber-optic cable has also seen its popularity rise but—due to cost—has been primarily restricted to use as a network backbone where segment length and higher speeds are needed. Fiber is however becoming increasingly common in server room environments as a server to switch connection method. The following sections summarize the characteristics of each of these cable types.

Coaxial

Coaxial cable, or *coax* as it is commonly referred, has been around for a long time. Coax found success in both TV transmission as well as in network implementations. Coax is constructed with a copper core at the center, which carries the signal, plastic insulation, braided metal shielding, and an outer plastic covering. Coaxial cable is constructed in order to add resistance to *attenuation* (the loss of signal strength as it travels over distance), *crosstalk* (the degradation of a signal caused by signals from other cables running close to it), and EMI (electromagnetic interference). Figure 2.1 shows the construction of coaxial cabling.

Figure 2.1 Coaxial cabling.

Networks use two types of coaxial cabling: thin coaxial and thick coaxial. Both thick and thin cable have fallen out of favor but, because they may still be used in some network environments, they are included on the Network+ exam.

Thin coax

Thin coax is much more likely to be seen than thick coax in today's networks but it isn't common, either. Thin coax is only .25 inches in diameter, making it fairly easy to install. Unfortunately, one of the disadvantages of all thin coax types are that they are prone to cable breaks, which increase the difficulty when installing and troubleshooting coaxial-based networks.

There are several types of thin coax cable, each of which has a specific use. Table 2.1 summarizes the categories of thin coax.

Table 2.1 Thin Coax Categories	
Cable	**Type**
RG-58 /U	Solid copper core
RG-58 A/U	Stranded wire core
RG-58 C/U	Military specification
RG-59	Often used for cable TV and cable modems
RG-62	Used for ARCnet specifications

RG-58 and RG-62—The Same but Different

ARCnet is an older, obsolete, networking standard. However, the appearance of RG-62 cable is basically the same as RG-58 cable, so be sure you are using the correct cable.

Thick coax

The chances that you will encounter a network using thick coaxial cable today are slim indeed. Still, in the remote chance that you might see thick cable, it is included in the Network+ objectives. Thick coax, RG-8, is considerably more robust and harder to damage than its thinner counterpart. The construction of thick coax makes it more resistant to attenuation, crosstalk, and EMI and therefore able to transmit data over longer distances. Because of this, thick coax found popularity as a network backbone. However, the faster fiber-optic media has all but taken over in this role.

Thick coax is far more difficult to connect and install than thin coax. Thick coax requires a *vampire tap*, a special connector that pierces the thick cable to make a connection to the copper core, and a drop cable to connect a LAN device. This combination is bulky and expensive.

Twisted-pair cabling

Twisted-pair cabling has been around a very long time. It was originally created for voice transmissions and has been widely used for telephone communication. Today, in addition to telephone communication, twisted pair is the most widely used media for networking.

The popularity of twisted pair can be attributed to the fact that it is lighter, more flexible, and easier to install than coaxial or fiber-optic cable. It is also cheaper than other media alternatives and can achieve greater speeds than its coaxial competition. These factors make twisted pair the ideal solution for most network environments.

There are two types of twisted-pair cabling: *unshielded twisted pair (UTP)* and *shielded twisted pair (STP)*. UTP is significantly more commonplace than STP and is used for most networks. Shielded twisted pair is used in environments where greater resistance to EMI and attenuation is required. The greater resistance comes at a price, however. The additional shielding, plus the need to ground that shield (which requires special connectors), can significantly add to the cost of a cable installation of STP.

STP provides the extra shielding by using an insulating material that is wrapped around the wires within the cable. This extra protection increases the distances that data signals can travel over STP but also increases the cost of the cabling. Figure 2.2 shows STP and UTP cabling.

STP

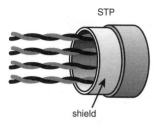

shield

UTP

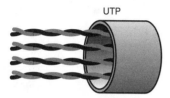

Figure 2.2   STP and UTP cabling. (Reproduced with permission from Computer Desktop Encyclopedia © 1981-2001; The Computer Language Co. Inc., **www.computerlanguage.com**.)

There are several categories of twisted-pair cabling, with the early categories most commonly associated with voice transmissions. There are five main categories specified by the Electronics Industries Association/Telecommunications Industries Association (EIA/TIA). The details of each of these categories are listed in Table 2.2.

Table 2.2 UTP Cable Categories		
Category	**Cable Type**	**Application**
1	UTP	Analog voice
2	UTP	Digital voice, 1Mbps data
3	UTP, STP	16Mbps data
4	UTP, STP	20Mbps data
5	UTP, STP	100Mbps data
6	UTP, STP	155Mbps data
7	UTP, STP	1000Mbps data

Reproduced with permission from Computer Desktop Encyclopedia © 1981-2001; The Computer Language Co. Inc., (**www.computerlanguage.com**).

Fiber-optic cable

In many ways, fiber-optic media addresses the shortcomings associated with copper-based media. Because fiber-based media use light transmissions instead of electronic pulses, threats such as EMI, crosstalk, and attenuation become a non-issue. Fiber is well suited for the transfer of data, video, and voice transmissions. In addition, fiber-optic is the most secure of all cable media. Anyone trying to access data signals on a fiber line must physically tap into the fiber cable. Given the composition of the cable, this is a particularly difficult task.

Unfortunately, despite the advantages of fiber-based media over copper, it does still not enjoy the popularity of twisted-pair cabling. The difficult installation and maintenance procedures of fiber often require skilled technicians with specialized tools. Furthermore, the cost of a fiber-based solution limits the number of organizations that can afford to implement it. Another sometimes hidden drawback of implementing a fiber solution is the cost of retrofitting existing network equipment. Fiber is incompatible with most electronic network equipment. This means you have to purchase fiber-compatible network hardware.

 Fiber-optic cable, although still more expensive than other types of cable, is well suited for high-speed data communications. It eliminates the problems associated with copper-based media, such as near-end crosstalk, electromagnetic interference (EMI), and signal tampering.

Fiber-optic cable itself is composed of a core glass fiber surrounded by *cladding*. An insulated covering then surrounds both of these within an outer protective sheath. Figure 2.3 shows the composition of a fiber-optic cable.

Two types of fiber-optic cable are available: single and multimode fiber. In multimode fiber, many beams of light travel through the cable bouncing off of the cable walls. This strategy actually weakens the signal, reducing the length and speed the data signal can travel. Single-mode fiber uses a single direct beam of light, thus allowing for greater distances and increased transfer speeds. Some of the common types of fiber-optic cable include the following:

➤ 62.5 micron core/125 micron cladding multimode

➤ 50 micron core/125 micron cladding multimode

➤ 100 micron core/140 micron cladding multimode

➤ 8.3 micron core/125 micron cladding single mode

In the ever-increasing search for bandwidth that will keep pace with the demands of modern applications, fiber-optic cables are sure to play a key role.

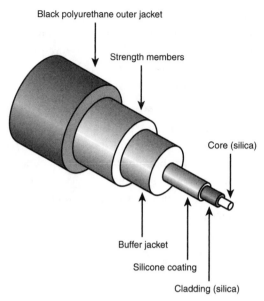

Black polyurethane outer jacket

Strength members

Core (silica)

Buffer jacket

Silicone coating

Cladding (silica)

Figure 2.3   Fiber-optic cable.

Understanding the types of fiber optics available, as well as their advantages and their limitations, is important for real-world application, as well as the Network+ exam.

Wireless media

Wireless media provides the alternative to traditional cable-based media. Although wireless media does not require traditional cabling, it still requires a method to transfer data. Wireless transmissions use three types of media: radio wave, infrared, and microwave.

Radio waves

Three types of radio frequency transmissions can be used to accommodate network transmissions: single-frequency low power, single-frequency high power RF, and something called *spread spectrum*.

Single-frequency low power RF transmissions offer very short transmission distances and are used when the distance the signal is required to travel is short. The exact distance depends on many factors, including atmospheric conditions, but in general, transmissions from 50 to 70 meters are typical. These are short-range transmissions that do not require a direct line-of-sight between the transmitting and receiving device. Low-power RF offers transmissions speeds of 1 to 10Mbps.

Single frequency high power allows data transmissions to travel significantly farther than low frequency transmissions. Single frequency high power is more complicated in terms of installation and configuration, often requiring skilled technicians. High power radio frequencies maintain the same data transfer rates as low power frequency, with transmissions speeds of 1 to 10Mbps.

The third type of radio frequency is *spread spectrum*. Spread spectrum is more secure than the single frequency RF transmissions and less susceptible to interference. Spread spectrum uses frequency hopping and direct sequence modulation. *Frequency hopping* is a technique that switches data between multiple frequencies and *direct sequence modulation* breaks segments into *chips* and sends this data on multiple frequencies.

 One of the concerns of RF transmissions is security. RF transmissions are a security risk because the interception of RF transmissions is a possibility.

Infrared

As the name suggests, wireless *infrared* networking uses infrared beams for data transmissions. Infrared wireless networking requires a direct line-of-sight. There are two types of infrared network transmissions: broadcast and point-to-point. *Broadcast infrared*, although still requiring a line-of-sight between the sending and receiving devices, disperses the light beam to allow for a wider scope. *Point-to-point infrared* is a direct, focused infrared beam requiring more careful configuration than the broadcast method.

Of the wireless technologies available, infrared wireless networking offers faster data transfer rates (from 10 to 16Mbps). The infrared signal can be disrupted by obstructions blocking the infrared signal.

Microwave

Microwave is another wireless media requiring a direct line-of-sight. There are two types of microwave wireless networking available—terrestrial and satellite.

Terrestrial microwave networking is, as the name suggests, earth-bound. Microwave transmissions require transmitters and receivers for point-to-point connection with the devices mounted high to avoid blocking and ensuring a clean line-of-sight. Common installation points include tall buildings or mountains.

Terrestrial microwave transmissions are susceptible to atmospheric interference and are often difficult to install and configure.

NOTE | Terrestrial microwave installations often require licensing approval.

As you might imagine, *satellite wireless microwave* transmissions require a satellite. Satellite microwave still requires a line-of-sight and, due to the distance the signal has to travel, there can be delays in transmissions. These delays, known as *propagation delays*, typically range from .05 to 5 seconds.

The cost of implementing a satellite solution can be particularity high, but satellite microwave allows access to remote areas where other forms of media cannot reach. Rain or heavy fog can cause interference problems for satellite microwave. In addition to atmospheric interference, microwave transmissions are susceptible to signal tampering.

Despite the obvious advantages of wireless data transmissions, there are some definite tradeoffs. First, the data transfer speeds of wireless solutions, particularly in a LAN environment, simply don't keep pace with cabled solutions. Installation and maintenance are far more complicated and costly than cabling. In addition, wireless solutions that require a line-of-sight communication, such as infrared and microwave, are limited in some situations.

In most cases, wireless will not replace traditional network cabling, but will augment the traditional LAN to allow remote access. As the army of mobile users increases, so too will the popularity of wireless networking.

Media connectors

There are a variety of connectors used with the associated network media. Media connectors attach to the transmission media and allow the physical connection into the computing device. For the Network+ exam, it is necessary to identify the connectors associated with the specific media. The following sections identify the connectors and associated media.

BNC connectors

BNC connectors are associated with coaxial media and 10Base2 networks. BNC connectors are not as common as they once were, but still are used on some networks, older network cards, and older hubs. Common BNC connectors include a barrel connector, T-connector, and terminators. Figure 2.4 shows several BNC connectors.

Figure 2.4 BNC connectors.

RJ-45 connectors

RJ-45 connectors are the ones you are most likely going to encounter in your network travels. RJ-45 connectors are used with twisted-pair cabling, the most prevalent network cable in use today. RJ-45 connectors resemble ordinary phone jacks, called RJ-11, but use eight wires instead of the four used with common phone cables. RJ-45 connectors are also larger. Figure 2.5 shows the RJ-45 connectors.

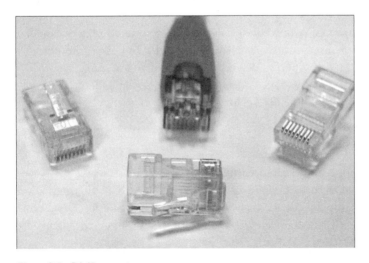

Figure 2.5 RJ-45 connectors.

AUI connectors

The Attachment Unit Interface (AUI) connectors are a 15-pin D-shell connector often seen on hubs, switches, and 10Base5 implementations. Given the rarity of 10Base5 networks, it is unlikely that you will see AUI on 10Base5, but you might get an exam question on it just the same. Figure 2.6 shows an example of the AUI connectors.

Figure 2.6 AUI connector on a network router.

For the Network+ exam, you are expected to identify the connectors discussed in this chapter by their appearance.

Fiber connectors

There are a variety of connectors associated with fiber cabling and several ways of connecting these connectors. These include bayonet, snap-lock, and push-pull connectors. Figure 2.7 shows the various fiber connectors.

As with the other connectors discussed in this section, be prepared to identify fiber connectors by their appearance and by how they are physically connected.

Fiber-Optic Connectors

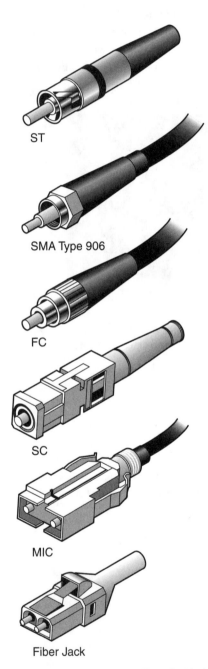

All fiber-optic connectors use ferrules to hold the ends of the fiber and keep them properly aligned.

The ST connector uses a half-twist bayonet type of lock, while SMA and FC use threaded connections.

The SC uses a push-pull connector similar to common audio and video plugs and sockets.

The MIC is the standard FDDI connector.

The Fiber Jack connector attaches two fibers in a snap lock connector similar in size and ease of use to an RJ-45 connector.

ST

SMA Type 906

FC

SC

MIC

Fiber Jack

Figure 2.7 Fiber connectors. (Reproduced with permission from Computer Desktop Encyclopedia © 1981-2001; The Computer Language Co. Inc., **www.computerlanguage.com**.)

IEEE 802.3 standards

The IEEE 802.3 standards define a range of networking systems that are based on the original Ethernet standard. The variations include speed, physical topology, and implementation considerations. The following sections describe these standards.

10Base2

The IEEE 10Base2 standard specifies data transmission speeds of 10Mbps and a total segment length of 185 meters using RG-58 coaxial cable. The 10Base2 standard specifies a physical bus topology and uses BNC connectors with 50-ohm terminators at each end of the cable. One of the physical ends of each segment must be grounded.

10Base2 networks allow a maximum of five segments with only three of those segments populated. Each of the three populated segments can have a maximum of 30 nodes attached. 10Base2 requires that there is a minimum of .5 meters between nodes. For the network to function properly, the segment must be complete. With this in mind, the addition or removal of systems may make the network unusable.

 The coax cable used in 10Base2 networks is prone to cable breaks. A break anywhere in the cable will make the entire network inaccessible.

10Base5

Like 10Base2, 10Base5 has a maximum transfer speed of 10Mbps and specifies a physical bus topology. Although not implemented in modern networks, 10Base5 was well suited for a network backbone as it allowed for a maximum distance of 500 meters with high resistance to EMI and crosstalk. The maximum number of devices that can be attached per 500 meter segment is 100. Like 10Base2, the total number of populated segments is three. Each segment must have at least one ground.

10Base5 is more difficult to install than 10Base2 requiring transceivers and special *vampire taps* that pierce the cable to make a connection. When installing a 10Base5 network, the distance between vampire taps can be no less than 2.5 meters. The maximum allowed distance between the tap to the networked device is 5 meters.

Coaxial and the 5-4-3 Rule

When working with Ethernet networks that use coaxial media, the 5-4-3 rule applies. The rule specifies that the network is limited to a total of five cable segments. These five segments can be connected using no more than four repeaters, and only three segments on the network can be populated.

10BaseT

The 10BaseT standard is another 10Mbps standard using twisted-pair cabling. 10BaseT networks have a maximum segment length of 100 meters, up to a total of five segments per network.

10BaseT networks use a star topology with a point-to-point connection between the computer and the hub or switch. 10BaseT can use different categories of UTP cabling, including 3, 4, and 5. Table 2.3 summarizes the characteristics of 10Mbps networks.

Table 2.3	10Mbps Network Comparison			
Standard	**Cable Type**	**Segment Length**	**Connector**	**Topology**
10Base2	Thin coaxial	185 meters	BNC	Physical bus
10Base5	Thick coaxial	500 Meters	Vampire taps	Physical bus
10BaseT	Category 3, 4, 5 twisted pair	100 meters	RJ-45	Physical star

Ensure that you understand the information provided in Table 2.3; there will certainly be questions on the exam that come directly from this information.

UTP and the 5-4 Rule

As with coaxial implementations, there are rules governing UTP networks. UTP Ethernet networks use the 5-4-3 rule, but in a slightly modified form. As with coaxial, a total of five segments can be used on the network and these five segments can be connected using four repeaters, but all five segments can be populated.

Fast Ethernet

Many of the applications used on modern networks demand more bandwidth than what's provided by the 10Mbps network standards. To address this need for faster networks, the IEEE has developed the IEEE 802.3u specifications, of which there are three variations:

➤ 100BaseTX

➤ 100BaseT4

➤ 100BaseFX

100BaseTX

100BaseTX is the most widely implemented of the Fast Ethernet standards. 100BaseTX uses two pairs of wire in Category 5 UTP cabling and can also use STP cable when a more resistant cable is required. 100BaseTX uses 100Mbps transmission and a total segment length of 100 meters.

100BaseT4

The advantage to 100BaseT4 is its ability to use older categories of UTP cable to perform 100Mbps transfer. In environments already wired with Category 3 or 4 cable, 100BaseT4 can be used instead of replacing the existing cable.

100BaseT4 uses all four pairs of wire of Category 3, 4, and 5 twisted pair and, as such, is prevented from using full-duplex transmissions. The other characteristics of standard 100BaseTX are in effect with 100BaseT4.

100BaseFX

The IEEE 100BaseFX standard specifies 100Mbps transmissions speeds over fiber-optic cable. 100BaseFX can use both multimode and single mode fiber. It has a maximum segment length of 412 meters when used over multimode fiber and 10,000 meters when used over single mode fiber. Table 2.4 summarizes the characteristics of Fast Ethernet.

Table 2.4	Fast Ethernet			
Standard	**Cable Type**	**Segment Length**	**Connector**	**Topology**
100BaseTX	Category 5 UTP	100 meters	RJ-45	Physical star
100BaseT4	Category 3, 4, 5 UTP	100 meters	RJ-45	Physical star
100BaseFX	Multimode/single-mode fiber-optic cable	412/multimode fiber-optic 10,000/single-mode fiber-optic	SC, ST, MIC	Physical star

Gigabit Ethernet

The quest for faster networks speeds has now brought us to the 1Gbps range. Gigabit Ethernet networking is achieved using both copper-based media as well as fiber, with fiber being the most versatile. The two IEEE standards that specify Gigabit transfer are 802.3z and 802.3ab.

802.3z

Three distinct standards are specified under the 802.3z standard; they are referred to collectively as 1000X. The three standards are 1000BaseLX, 1000BaseSX, and 1000BaseCX. 1000BaseLX and 1000BaseSX use long wavelength laser and short wavelength laser respectively. Both 1000BaseSX and 1000BaseLX can be supported over two types of multimode fiber, 62.5 and 50 micron-diameter fibers. Only long wave lasers support the use of single mode fiber.

The 1000BaseCX standard specifies Gigabit Ethernet over STP cabling. Segment length of 1000BaseCX is extremely limited, reaching a maximum of 25 meters. 1000BaseCX is not widely implemented.

802.3ab

The 802.3ab standard specifies Gigabit Ethernet transfer over Category 5 UTP cable. To achieve the 1000Mbps speeds, each of the four pairs of wires in a twisted-pair cable can transmit 250Mbps. Table 2.5 summarizes the characteristics of the Gigabit standards.

Table 2.5	Gigabit Ethernet		
Standard	**Cable Type**	**Segment Length**	**Connector**
1000BaseLX	Multimode/ single-mode fiber	550/multimode 5000/single-mode	Fiber connectors
1000BaseSX	Multimode fiber	550 meters using 50 Micron multimode fiber	Fiber connectors
1000BaseCX	STP twisted pair	25 meters	9-pin shielded connector, 8-pin fiber channel type 2 connector
1000BaseT	Category 5 UTP	100 meters	RJ-45

Ensure that you understand the information provided in Table 2.5; there will be questions on the exam that are derived from this information.

Review and test yourself

The following sections provide you with the opportunity to review what you learned in this chapter and to test yourself.

The facts

For the exam, don't forget these key concepts:

➤ 10Base2, sometimes called Thinnet or Thin Ethernet, is the 802.3 specification for a network that uses thin coaxial cable (that is, RG-58 cable).

➤ 10Base2 specifies a maximum speed of 10Mbps and uses BNC barrel and BNC T-connectors to connect the cable and computers. At the physical ends of each cable segment, a 50-ohm terminator absorbs the signal, thus preventing signal reflection.

➤ Thinnet cable is prone to breaks, and a break anywhere in the cable renders the entire network segment unusable.

➤ The 10Base2 standard specifies a limit of 185 meters per segment (that is, approximately 600 feet).

➤ In a 10Base2 network, only 30 networked devices can be attached to a single segment. A maximum of three segments can have network devices.

➤ 10BaseT networks use UTP cable and RJ-45 connectors to transfer data at up to 10Mbps.

➤ 10Base5 networks use thick coaxial cable (RG-8 cable), also known as Thicknet or Thick Ethernet, and devices attach to it by using external transceivers and AUI ports.

➤ 10Base5 uses baseband transmission, has a maximum transfer rate of 10Mbps, and has a cable distance of 500 meters per segment.

➤ 100BaseTX networks use RJ-45 connectors and use Category 5 STP or UTP cable.

➤ 100BaseT4 networks use Category 3, 4, and 5 cable with RJ-45 connectors.

➤ 100BaseFX uses fiber-optic cable and often uses SC, ST, or MIC fiber connectors.

➤ 1000BaseSX and 1000BaseTX offer 1000Mbps transfer speed using fiber-optic cable.

➤ 1000BaseCX offers 1000Mbps transfer speed over copper cable. Distances are restricted to 25 meters.

➤ Attachment unit interface (AUI) ports are network interface ports that are often associated with thick coax (that is, 10Base5) networks. The AUI port is a 15-pin socket to which a transceiver is connected.

➤ SC and ST connectors are associated with fiber cabling. ST connectors offer a twist type attachment, whereas SCs have a push-on connector.

➤ RJ-45 connectors are used with UTP cabling.

Key terms

➤ Media

➤ Bandwidth

➤ Baseband/broadband

➤ Duplexing

➤ Thin coax/Thick coax/Twisted pair/Fiber-optic cable

➤ 10BaseT/10Base2/10Base5/100BaseTX/100BaseFX/Gigabit Ethernet

➤ D-Shell/RJ/BNC/AUI/Fiber connectors

➤ Crosstalk

➤ Attenuation

➤ EMI

Practice exam

Question 1

> You are troubleshooting a network using 1000BaseCX cable and suspect that
> the maximum length has been exceeded. What is the maximum length of
> 1000BaseCX cable?
>
> ○ A. 1000 meters
>
> ○ B. 100 meters
>
> ○ C. 25 meters
>
> ○ D. 10,000 meters

The correct answer is C. The 802.3ab standard specifies Gigabit Ethernet
transfer over Category 5 UTP cable, including 1000BaseCX. It uses STP
twisted-pair cable and has a 25-meter length restriction.

Question 2

> As system administrator you find yourself working on a legacy 10Base2 network.
> Which of the following technologies would you be working with? (Choose three.)
>
> ❑ A. UTP
>
> ❑ B. RG-58
>
> ❑ C. BNC connectors
>
> ❑ D. Terminators
>
> ❑ E. RJ-45 connectors

The correct answers are B, C, and D. 10Base2 networks use thin coax (RG-
58) media, BNC connectors, and a terminator at each end of the bus to
dampen the signal reflection. Answers A and E are incorrect as they are used
by other network standards such as 10BaseT and 100BaseTX.

Question 3

> If you are working on a network and using vampire taps, which of the following cable types are you working with and what is the speed of your network?
>
> ○ A. Thin coax at 100Mbps
>
> ○ B. Thin coax at 10Mbps
>
> ○ C. Thick coax at 100Mbps
>
> ○ D. Thick coax at 10Mbps

The correct answer is D. Vampire taps are used with thick coax in 10Base5 networks. 10Base5 networks have a maximum transmission speed of 10Mbps. Answer A and B are incorrect, as thin coax does not use vampire taps and does not transmit at 100Mbps speeds. Answer C is incorrect as thick coax does not transmit at speeds of 100Mbps.

Question 4

> Which of following connectors are commonly used with fiber cabling?
>
> ○ A. RJ-45
>
> ○ B. BNC
>
> ○ C. SC
>
> ○ D. RJ-11

The correct answer is C. SC connectors are used with fiber-optic cable. RJ-45 connectors are used with UTP cable, BNC is used for thin coax cable, and RJ-11 is used for regular phone connectors.

Question 5

> Which of the following definitions describe the loss of signal strength as a signal travels through a particular media?
>
> ○ A. Attenuation
>
> ○ B. Crosstalk
>
> ○ C. EMI
>
> ○ D. Chatter

The correct answer is A. The term used to describe the loss of signal strength for media is attenuation. Crosstalk refers to the interference between two cables, EMI is electromagnetic interference and chatter is not a valid media interference concern.

Question 6

You install a new 10Mbps network card into an existing system and configure it for full-duplex communication. What is the maximum throughput of the card?

○ A. 10Mbps

○ B. 20Mbps

○ C. 100Mbps

○ D. 200Mbps

The correct answer is B. Full-duplex communication allows for two-way communication between devices, doubling the transmission speeds. In this case, the 10Mbps network card will transmit at 20Mbps.

Question 7

In a 100BaseT network environment, what is the maximum distance between the device and the networking equipment, assuming that no repeaters are used?

○ A. 1000 meters

○ B. 100 meters

○ C. 500 meters

○ D. 185 meters

The correct answer is B. 100BaseT networks use UTP cabling, which has a maximum cable length of 100 meters. Answer A is incorrect. This distance could only be achieved with UTP cabling by using repeaters. Answer C specifies the maximum cable length for 10Base5 networks; and answer D specifies the maximum cable length for 10Base2 networks.

Question 8

> You are troubleshooting a problem in which a user is experiencing periodic problems connecting to the network. Upon investigation you find that the cable connecting the user's PC to the switch is close to a fluorescent light fitting. What condition is most likely causing the problem?
>
> ○ A. Crosstalk
>
> ○ B. EMI
>
> ○ C. Attenuation
>
> ○ D. Faulty cable

The correct answer is B. EMI is a type of interference that is often seen when cables run too closely to electrical devices. Answer A is incorrect; crosstalk describes the interference whereby two cables interfere with each other. Attenuation identifies the loss of signal strength. Answer D is incorrect also. It may be that a faulty cable is causing the problem however the question asks for the most likely cause and because the cable is running near the fluorescent lights, the problem is more likely associated with EMI.

Question 9

> Which connector is represented in the following picture?
>
>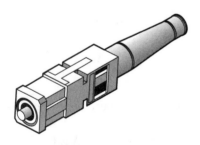
>
> (Reproduced with permission from Computer Desktop Encyclopedia © 1981–2001; The Computer Language Co. Inc., **www.computerlanguage.com**.)
>
> ○ A. ST connector
>
> ○ B. SC connector
>
> ○ C. BNC connector
>
> ○ D. SCSI-2 connector

The correct answer is B. SC is represented in the figure and is used with fiber cable. None of the other answers are applicable.

Question 10

Which of the following fiber connectors uses a twist-type connection method?

○ A. ST

○ B. SC

○ C. BNC

○ D. SA

The correct answer is A. ST fiber connectors use a twist-type connection method. Answer B is incorrect as SC connectors use a push-type connection method. The other choices are not valid fiber connectors.

Want to know more?

Bird, Drew and Harwood, Mike. *Network+ Training Guide*, Que Publishing, 2002.

Sheldon, Thomas. *McGraw-Hill's Encyclopedia of Networking and Telecommunications*. McGraw-Hill Professional Publishing, 2001.

Tulloch, Mitch. *Microsoft Encyclopedia of Networking* (with CD-ROM). Microsoft Press, 2000.

Networking Devices

Objectives

1.6 Identify the purpose, features, and functions of the following network components:

- ✓ Hubs
- ✓ Switches
- ✓ Bridges
- ✓ Routers
- ✓ Gateways
- ✓ CSU/DSU
- ✓ Network Interface Cards (NICs)
- ✓ ISDN adapters
- ✓ System area network cards
- ✓ Wireless access points
- ✓ Modems

2.1 Given an example, identify a MAC address.

What you need to know

- ✓ Describe how hubs and switches work
- ✓ Explain how hubs and switches can be connected to create larger networks
- ✓ Describe how bridges, routers, and gateways work
- ✓ Describe how routing protocols are used for dynamic routing
- ✓ Explain the purpose of other networking components such as Channel Service Unit/Digital Service Unit (CSU/DSU) and gateways
- ✓ Describe the purpose and function of network cards
- ✓ Describe how to identify a MAC address

Introduction

All but the most basic of networks require devices to provide connectivity and functionality. Understanding how these networking devices operate and identifying the functions they perform are essential skills for any network administrator and requirements for a Network+ candidate.

This chapter introduces commonly used networking devices and, although it is true that you are not likely to encounter all of the devices mentioned in this chapter on the exam, you can be assured of working with at least some of them.

Hubs

At the bottom of the networking food chain, so to speak, are hubs. Hubs are used in networks that use twisted-pair cabling to connect devices. Hubs can also be joined together to create larger networks. *Hubs* are simple devices that direct data packets to all devices connected to the hub, regardless of whether the data package is destined for the device. This makes them inefficient devices and can create a performance bottleneck on busy networks.

In their most basic form, a hub does nothing except provide a pathway for the electrical signals to travel along. Such a device is called a *passive* hub. Far more common nowadays is an *active* hub, which as well as providing a path for the data signals, regenerates the signal before it forwards it to all of the connected devices. A hub does not perform any processing on the data that it forwards, nor does it perform any error checking.

Hubs come in a variety of shapes and sizes. Small hubs with five or eight connection ports are commonly referred to as *workgroup hubs*. Others can accommodate larger numbers of devices (normally up to 32). These are referred to as *high-density devices*. Because hubs don't perform any processing, they do little except enable communication between connected devices. For today's high-demand network applications, something with a little more intelligence is required. That's where switches come in.

MSAU

In a Token Ring network, a Multistation Access Unit (MSAU) is used in place of the hub that is used on an Ethernet network. The MSAU performs the token circulation inside the device, giving the network a physical star appearance. Each MSAU has a Ring In (RI) port on the device, which is connected to the Ring Out (RO) port on another MSAU. The last MSAU in the ring is then connected to the first, to complete the ring. Because Token Ring networks are few and far between nowadays, it is far more likely that you will find yourself working with Ethernet hubs and switches.

 Even though MSAU and Token Ring networks are not common, you can expect a few questions on them on the exam.

Switches

Like hubs, *switches* are the connectivity points of an Ethernet network. Devices connect to switches via twisted-pair cabling, one cable for each device. The difference between hubs and switches is in how the devices deal with the data that they receive. Whereas a hub forwards the data it receives to all of the ports on the device, a switch forwards it only to the port that connects to the destination device. It does this by *learning* the MAC address of the devices attached to it, and then by matching the destination MAC address in the data it receives. Figure 3.1 shows how a switch works.

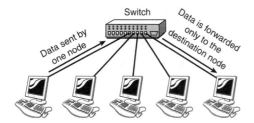

Figure 3.1   How a switch works.

By forwarding data only to the connection that should receive it, the switch can improve network performance in two ways. First, by creating a direct path between two devices and controlling their communication, it can greatly reduce the number of collisions on the network. As you might recall, collisions occur on Ethernet networks when two devices attempt to transmit at exactly the same time. In addition, the lack of collisions allows switches to communicate with devices in full-duplex mode. In a full-duplex configuration, devices can send and receive data from the switch at the same time. Contrast this with half-duplex communication, in which communication can occur in only one direction at a time. Full-duplex transmission speeds are double a standard, half-duplex, connection. So, a 10Mbps connection becomes 20Mbps and a 100Mbps connection becomes 200Mbps.

The net result of these measures is that switches can offer significant performance improvements over hub-based networks, particularly when network use is high.

Irrespective of whether a connection is at full or half duplex, the method of switching dictates how the switch deals with the data it receives. The following is a brief explanation of each method:

➤ **Cut-through**—In a cut-through switching environment, the packet begins to be forwarded as soon as it is received. This method is very fast, but creates the possibility of errors being propagated through the network, as there is no error checking.

➤ **Store-and-forward**—Unlike cut-through, in a store-and-forward switching environment, the entire packet is received and error checked before being forwarded. The upside of this method is that errors are not propagated through the network. The downside is that the error checking process takes a relatively long time, and store-and-forward switching is considerably slower as a result.

➤ **FragmentFree**—To take advantage of the error checking of store-and-forward switching, but still offer performance levels nearing that of cut-through switching, FragmentFree switching can be used. In a FragmentFree-switching environment, enough of the packet is read so that the switch can determine whether the packet has been involved in a collision. As soon as the collision status has been determined, the packet is forwarded.

Hub and switch cabling

In addition to acting as a connection point for network devices, hubs and switches can also be connected to create larger networks. This connection can be achieved through standard ports with a special cable, or by using special ports with a standard cable.

The ports on a hub to which computer systems are attached are called *Medium Dependent Interface-Crossed (MDI-X)*. The crossed designation is derived from the fact that two of the wires within the connection are crossed, so that the send signal wire on one device becomes the receive signal of the other. Because the ports are crossed internally, a standard or *straight-through* cable can be used to connect devices.

Another type of port, called a *Medium Dependent Interface (MDI)* port, is often included on a hub or switch to facilitate the connection of two switches or hubs. Because the hubs or switches are designed to see each other as simply an extension of the network, there is no need for the signal to be crossed. If a hub or switch does not have an MDI port, hubs or switches can be connected by using a *crossover* cable between two MDI-X ports. The crossover cable serves to uncross the internal crossing. You can see diagrams of the cable pinouts for both a straight-through and crossover cable in Figures 3.2 and 3.3, respectively.

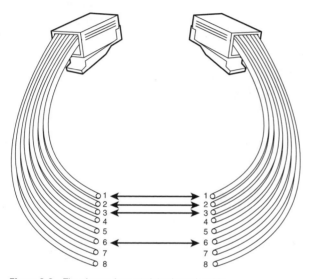

Figure 3.2 The pinouts for a straight-through cable.

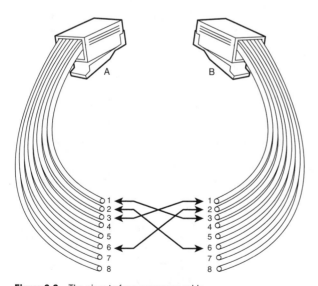

Figure 3.3 The pinouts for a crossover cable.

Bridges

Bridges are used to divide larger networks into smaller sections. They do this by sitting between two physical network segments and managing the flow of data between the two. By looking at the MAC address of the devices connected to each segment, bridges can elect to forward the data (if they believe that the destination address is on another interface), or block it from crossing (if they can verify that it is on the interface from which it came). Figure 3.4 shows how a bridge can be used to segregate a network.

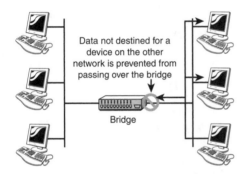

Figure 3.4 How a bridge is used to segregate networks.

When bridges were introduced, the MAC addresses of the devices on the connected networks had to be entered manually, a time-consuming process that had plenty of opportunity for error. Nowadays, almost all bridges can build a list of the MAC addresses on an interface by watching the traffic on the network. Such devices are called *learning bridges* because of this functionality.

Bridge placement and bridging loops

There are two issues that you must consider when using bridges. The first is the bridge placement, and the other is the elimination of bridging loops:

➤ **Placement**—Bridges should be positioned in the network using the 80/20 rule. This rule dictates that 80% of the data should be local, and that the other 20% should be destined for devices on the other side of the bridge.

➤ **Bridging loops**—Bridging loops can occur when more than one bridge is implemented on the network. In this scenario, the bridges can confuse each other by leading one another to believe that a device is located on a certain segment when it is not. To combat the bridging loop problem, the IEEE 802.1d Spanning Tree protocol allows bridge interfaces to be assigned a value that is then used to control the bridge-learning process.

Types of bridges

Three types of bridges are used in networks:

➤ **Transparent bridge**—Derives its name from the fact that the devices on the network are unaware of its existence. A transparent bridge does nothing except block or forward data based on the MAC address.

➤ **Source route bridge**—Used in Token Ring networks. The source route bridge derives its name from the fact that the entire path that the packet is to take through the network is embedded within the packet.

➤ **Translational bridge**—Used to convert one networking data format to another, for example from Token Ring to Ethernet and vice versa.

Today, bridges are slowly but surely falling out of favor. Ethernet switches offer similar functionality; they can provide logical divisions, or segments, in the network. In fact, switches are sometimes referred to as multiport bridges because of the way they operate.

Routers

Routers are used to create larger networks by joining two network segments. A router can be a dedicated hardware device or a computer system with more than one network interface and the appropriate routing software. All modern network operating systems include the functionality to act as a router.

A router derives its name from the fact that it can route data it receives from one network onto another. When a router receives a packet of data, it reads the header of the packet to determine the destination address. Once it has determined the address, it looks in its routing table to determine whether it knows how to reach the destination and, if it does, it forwards the packet to the next hop on the route. The next hop may be the final destination or it may be another router. Figure 3.5 shows, in basic terms, how a router works.

As you can see from this example, routing tables play a very important role in the routing process. They are the means by which the router makes its decisions. For this reason, a routing table needs to be two things. It must be up to date, and it must be complete. There are two ways that the router can get the information for the routing table—through static routing or dynamic routing.

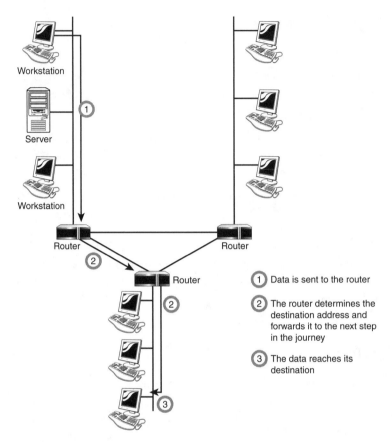

Figure 3.5 How a router works.

Static routing

In environments that use *static routing*, routes and route information are entered into the routing tables manually. Not only can this be a time-consuming task, but errors are more common. Additionally, when there is a change in the layout, or topology, of the network, statically configured routers must be manually updated with the changes. Again, this is a time-consuming and potentially error-laden task. For these reasons, static routing is suited to only the smallest environments with perhaps just one or two routers. A far more practical solution, particularly in larger environments, is to use dynamic routing.

Dynamic routing

In a *dynamic routing* environment, routers use special routing protocols to communicate. The purpose of these protocols is simple; they allow routers to pass on information about themselves to other routers so that other routers can build routing tables. There are two types of routing protocols used—the older distance vector protocols and the newer link state protocols.

Distance vector routing

The two most commonly used distance vector routing protocols are both called Routing Information Protocol (RIP). One version is used on networks running TCP/IP, the other, sometimes referred to as IPX RIP, is designed for use on networks running the IPX/SPX protocol.

RIP works on the basis of *hop counts*. A hop is defined as one step on the journey to the data's destination. Each router that the data has to cross to reach its destination constitutes a hop. The maximum number of hops that RIP can accommodate is 15. That is to say that in a network that uses RIP, all routers must be within 15 hops of each other to communicate. Any hop count that is in excess of 15 is considered unreachable.

Distance vector routing protocols operate by having each router send updates about all the other routers it knows about to the routers directly connected to it. These updates are used by the routers to compile their routing tables. The updates are sent out automatically every 30 or 60 seconds. The actual interval depends on the routing protocol being used. Apart from the periodic updates, routers can also be configured to send a *triggered update* if a change in the network topology is detected. The process by which routers learn of a change in the network topology is known as *convergence*.

Although distance vector protocols are able to maintain routing tables, they have three problems. The first is that the periodic update system can make the update process very slow. The second problem is that the periodic updates can create large amounts of network traffic, much of the time unnecessarily as the topology of the network should rarely change. The last, and perhaps more significant problem, is that because the routers only know about the next hop in the journey, incorrect information can be propagated between routers creating routing loops.

Two strategies are used to combat this last problem. One, *split horizon*, works by preventing the router from advertising a route back to the other router from which it was learned. The other, *poison reverse* (also called split horizon with poison reverse), dictates that the route *is* advertised back on the interface from which it was learned, but that it has a metric of 16. Recall that a metric of 16 is considered an unreachable destination.

Link state routing

Link state routing works quite differently from distance vector-based routing. Rather than each router telling each other connected router about the routes it is aware of, routers in a link state environment send out special packets, called *link state advertisements (LSA)*, which contain information only about that router. These LSAs are forwarded to all of the routers on the network, which enables them to build a map of the entire network. The advertisements are sent when the router is first brought onto the network and when a change in the topology is detected.

Of the two (distance vector and link state), distance vector routing is better suited to small networks and link state routing to larger ones. Link state protocols do not suffer from the constant updates and limited hop count, and they are also quicker to correct themselves (to converge) when the network topology changes.

On TCP/IP networks, the most commonly used link state routing protocol is the Open Shortest Path First (OSPF). On IPX networks, the NetWare Link State Protocol (NLSP) is used. Table 3.1 summarizes the distance vector and link state protocols used with each network protocol.

It is necessary to know which distance vector and link state routing protocols are associated with which network protocols.

Table 3.1 Routing Protocols		
Network Protocol	Distance Vector	Link State
TCP/IP	RIP	OSPF
IPX/SPX	RIP*	NLSP

IPX RIP

Sometimes, to distinguish between the versions of RIP for IP and IPX, the version for IPX is referred to as IPX RIP.

Gateways

Any device that translates one data format to another is called a *gateway*. Some examples of gateways include a router that translates data from one network protocol to another, a bridge that converts between two networking systems, and a software application that converts between two dissimilar formats. The key point about a gateway is that only the data format is translated, not the data itself. In many cases, the gateway functionality is incorporated into another device.

Gateways and Default Gateways

Don't confuse a gateway with the term *default gateway*, which is discussed in Chapter 6, "WAN Technologies, Remote Access, and Security Protocols." The term default gateway refers to a router to which all network transmissions not destined for the local network are sent.

CSU/DSU

A Channel Service Unit/Digital Service Unit (CSU/DSU), sometimes called Data Service Unit, is a device that converts the digital signal format used on LANs into one used on WANs. Such translation is necessary because the networking technologies used on WANs are different from those used on LANs.

The CSU/DSU sits between the LAN and the access point provided by the telecommunications company. Many router manufacturers are now incorporating CSU/DSU functionality into their products.

Wireless access points

Wireless Access Points (WAPs) are devices that provide connectivity between wireless LAN devices and in most cases a wired network. Wireless access points are distinguishable by their antennae, which are normally directional. Wireless access points are commonly used in 802.11b wireless Ethernet networks. Wireless access points can convert the signal from a radio wave into that used on the LANs.

Modems

A modem, short for modulator/demodulator, is a device that converts the digital signals generated by a computer into analog signals that can travel over conventional phone lines. The modem at the receiving end converts the signal back into a format the computer can understand. Modems can be used as a means to connect to an ISP, or as a mechanism for dialing up to a LAN.

Modems can be internal add-in expansion cards, external devices that connect to the serial or USB port of a system, PCMCIA cards designed for use in laptops, or proprietary devices designed for use on other devices such as portables and handhelds.

The configuration of a modem depends on whether it is an internal or external device. For internal devices, the modem must be configured with an interrupt request (IRQ) and a memory I/O address. It is common practice, when installing an internal modem, to disable the built-in serial interfaces and assign the modem the resources of one of those (typically COM2). Table 3.2 shows the resources associated with serial (COM) port assignments.

Table 3.2 Common Serial (COM) Port Resource Assignments			
Port ID	IRQ	I/O Address	Associated Serial I/F Number
COM1	4	03F8	1
COM2	3	02F8	2
COM3	4	03E8	1
COM4	3	02E8	2

For external modems, you need not concern yourself directly with these port assignments, as the modem connects to the serial port and so uses the resources assigned to it. This is a much more straightforward approach and one favored by those who work with modems on a regular basis. For PCMCIA and USB modems, the plug-and-play nature of these devices makes them simple to configure, and no manual resource assignment is required. Once the modem is installed and recognized by the system, drivers must be configured to enable use of the device.

Two factors directly affect the speed of the modem connection—the speed of the modem itself and the speed of the Universal Asynchronous Receiver/Transmitter (UART) chip in the computer that is connected to the modem. The UART chip controls the serial communication of a computer, and although modern systems have UART chips that can accommodate far greater speeds than the modem is capable of, older systems should be checked to make sure the UART chip is of sufficient speed to support the modem speed. The UART chip installed in the system can normally be determined by looking at the documentation that comes with the system. Table 3.3 shows the maximum speed of the commonly used UART chip types.

Table 3.3 UART Chip Speeds	
UART Chip	Speed (Kbps)
8250	9600
16450	9600
16550	115,200
16650	430,800
16750	921,600
16950	921,600

 If you have installed an internal modem and are experiencing problems with other devices such as a mouse, there might be a resource conflict between the mouse and the modem.

Network cards

Network cards, also called Network Interface Cards, are devices that allow computers to connect to the network.

When specifying or installing a NIC, you must consider the following issues:

➤ **System bus compatibility**—If the network interface you are installing is an internal device, bus compatibility must be verified. The most common bus system in use is the Peripheral Component Interconnect (PCI) bus, but some older systems may still use Industry Standard Architecture (ISA) expansion cards.

➤ **System resources**—Network cards, like other devices, need IRQ and memory I/O addresses. If the network card does not operate correctly after installation, there might be a device conflict.

➤ **Media compatibility**—Nowadays, the assumption is that networks use twisted-pair cabling, so if you need a card for coaxial or fiber-optic connections you must specify this. Wireless network cards are also available.

More so even than the assumption that you are using twisted-pair cabling is that the networking system being used is Ethernet. If you require a card for another networking system such as Token Ring, this must be specified when you order.

 When working on a Token Ring network, you have to ensure that all network cards are set to transmit at the same speeds. NICs on an Ethernet network can operate at different speeds.

To install or configure a network interface you will need drivers of the device, and may need to configure it, although many devices are now plug and play. Most network cards are now software configured. Many of these software configuration utilities also include testing capabilities. The drivers and software configuration utilities supplied with the cards are often not the latest available and so it is best practice to log onto the Internet and download the latest drivers and associated software.

ISDN adapters

Integrated Services Digital Networking (ISDN) is a remote access and WAN technology that can be used in place of a Plain Old Telephone System (POTS) dial-up link if it is available. The availability of ISDN depends on whether your local telecommunications service provider offers the service, the quality of the line to your premises, and your proximity to the provider's location. ISDN offers greater speeds than a modem and can also pick up and drop the line considerably faster.

If ISDN is available and you do elect to use it, a special device called an *ISDN terminal adapter* is needed to connect to the line. ISDN terminal adapters can be add-in expansion cards, external devices that connect to the serial port of the system, or specialized interfaces built into routers or other networking equipment. The ISDN terminal adapter is necessary because, although it uses digital signals, the signals are formatted differently from those used on a LAN. In addition, ISDN can create multiple communication channels on a single line.

More information on ISDN is provided in Chapter 6.

System area network cards

System area network cards are interfaces installed for the purpose of connecting computer systems in a cluster. *Clustering* is a principle by which server systems are configured, and operate, as a single unit. In addition to providing increased processing and storage capabilities, it is also possible to configure servers to be fault-tolerant in either a compensatory or fail-over capacity.

In order for the systems in a cluster to communicate, network interfaces are installed that allow them to communicate directly without the need to use standard network links. These cards are normally high-performance units that utilize either twisted-pair or fiber-optic cabling. If there are only two systems in the cluster, a special cable can connect the two systems directly. If there are more than two, a hub is used to facilitate the connection.

Some clustering configurations allow a standard network link to be used as the communications path. This approach is not recommended, because excessive network traffic or a failure in an intermediary network device will cause network communication to fail and thus make the cluster think that the other system has failed.

MAC addresses

A *MAC address* is a unique 6-byte address that is burned into each network interface. The number must be unique as the MAC address is the basis by which almost all network communication takes place. No matter which networking protocol is being used, the MAC address is still the means by which the network interface is identified on the network. Notice that I say network interface. That's very important, as a system that has more than one network card in it will have more than one MAC address.

MAC addresses are expressed in six hexadecimal values. In some instances the six values are separated by colons (:), in others, hyphens (-) are used, and in still others, a space is simply inserted between the values. In any case, because the six values are hexadecimal, they can only be numbers (0-9) and the letters A through F. So, a valid MAC address might be 00-D0-56-F2-B5-12 or 00-26-DD-14-C4-EE. There is a way of finding out whether a MAC address exists through the IEEE, which is responsible for managing MAC address assignment. The IEEE has a system in place that lets you identify the manufacturer of the network interface by looking at the MAC address.

For example, in the MAC address 00-80-C8-E3-4C-BD, the 00-80-C8 portion identifies the manufacturer and the E3-4C-BD portion is assigned by the manufacturer to make the address unique. The IEEE is the body that assigns manufacturers their IDs, called Organizationally Unique Identifiers, and the manufacturer then assigns the second half, called the Universal LAN MAC address. From the IEEE's perspective, leaving the actual assignment of addresses to the manufacturers significantly reduces the administrative overhead for the IEEE.

As discussed, MAC addresses are expressed in hexadecimal format. For that reason they can only use the numbers 0-9 and the letters A-F. There are only six bytes, so a MAC address should be six groups of two characters. Any other number of characters or any answer that contains a letter other than those described can be immediately discounted as an answer.

The method by which you can discover the MAC address of the network interfaces in your equipment depends on which operating system is being used. Table 3.4 shows you how to obtain the MAC address on some of the more common platforms.

Be prepared to identify the commands used to view a MAC address as shown in Table 3.4. You may be asked to identify these commands on the Network+ exam.

Table 3.4 Commands to Obtain MAC Addresses	
Platform	Method
Windows 95/98/Me	Run the **winipcfg** utility.
Windows NT/2000	Run **ipconfig /all** from a command prompt.
Linux/Some Unix	Run the **ifconfig -a** command.
Novell NetWare	Run the **config** command.
Cisco Router	Run the **sh int <*interface name*>** command.

As you work with network interfaces more and more, you may start to become familiar with which ID is associated with which manufacturer. Although this is a skill that may astound your friends and impress your colleagues, it won't help you with the Network+ exam. Just knowing what does, and doesn't, represent a valid MAC address will be sufficient on the exam.

Review and test yourself

The following sections provide you with the opportunity to review what you learned in this chapter and to test yourself.

The facts

➤ Both hubs and switches are used in Ethernet networks. Token Ring networks, which are few and far between, use special devices called multistation access units (MSAUs) to create the network.

➤ The function of a hub is to take data from one of the connected devices and forward it to all the other ports on the hub.

➤ Most hubs are considered *active* because they regenerate a signal before forwarding it to all the ports on the device. In order to do this, the hub needs a power supply.

➤ Rather than forwarding data to all the connected ports, a switch forwards data only to the port on which the destination system is connected.

➤ Switches make forwarding decisions based on the Media Access Control (MAC) addresses of the devices connected to them to determine the correct port.

➤ In cut-through switching, the switch begins to forward the packet as soon as it is received.

➤ In a store-and-forward configuration, the switch waits to receive the entire packet before beginning to forward it.

➤ FragmentFree switching works by reading only the part of the packet that enables it to identify fragments of a transmission.

➤ Hubs and switches have two types of ports: Medium Dependent Interface (MDI) and Medium Dependent Interface-Crossed (MDI-X).

➤ A straight-through cable is used to connect systems to the switch or hub using the MDI-X ports.

➤ In a crossover cable, wires 1 and 3 and wires 2 and 6 are crossed.

➤ Both hubs and switches come in managed and unmanaged versions. A managed device has an interface through which it can be configured to perform certain special functions.

➤ Bridges are used to divide up networks and thus reduce the amount of traffic on each network.

➤ Unlike bridges and switches, which use the hardware-configured MAC address to determine the destination of the data, routers use the software-configured network address to make decisions.

➤ With distance-vector routing protocols, each router communicates all the routes it knows about to all other routers to which it is directly attached.

➤ RIP is a distance routing protocol for both TCP and IPX.

➤ Link state protocols communicate with all other devices on the network to build complete maps of the network. They generate less network traffic than distance vector routing protocols but require more powerful network hardware.

➤ Open Shortest Path First (OSPF) and NetWare Link State Protocol (NLSP) are the most commonly used link state routing protocols used on IP and IPX networks respectively.

➤ The term *gateway* is applied to any device, system, or software application that can perform the function of translating data from one format to another.

➤ A CSU/DSU acts as a translator between the LAN data format and the WAN data format.

➤ Wireless network devices gain access to the network via Wireless Access Points.

➤ Modems translate digital signals from a computer into analog signals that can travel across conventional phone lines.

Key terms

➤ Hub

➤ Bridge

➤ Gateway

➤ Network Interface Cards

➤ ISDN adapters

➤ Switch

➤ Router

➤ CSU/DSU

➤ System area network cards

➤ Wireless Access Points (WAPs)

➤ Modems

➤ MAC addresses

➤ Distance vector

➤ Link state

➤ Dynamic routing

➤ Static routing

➤ NLSP

➤ OSPF

➤ RIP

➤ Convergence

➤ Bridging loops

Practice exam

Question 1

Users are complaining that the performance of the network is not satisfactory. It takes a long time to pull files from the server and, under heavy loads, workstations can become disconnected from the server. The network is heavily used and a new video conferencing application is about to be installed. The network is a 100BaseT system created with Ethernet hubs. Which of the following devices are you most likely to install to alleviate the performance problems?

○ A. Switch

○ B. Router

○ C. Bridge

○ D. Gateway

The correct answer is A. Replacing Ethernet hubs with switches can yield significant performance improvements. Of the devices listed, they are also the only one that can be substituted for hubs. Answer B, router, is incorrect as a router is used to separate networks, not as a connectivity point for workstations. A bridge could be used to segregate the network and so improve performance, but a switch is a more obvious choice in this example. Therefore, answer C is incorrect. Answer D, gateway, is incorrect. A gateway is a device, system, or application that translates data from one format to another.

Question 2

Which of the following devices forwards data packets to all connected ports?

○ A. Router

○ B. Switch

○ C. Bridge

○ D. Hub

The correct answer is D. Hubs are inefficient devices that send data packets to all connected devices. Many of today's networks are upgrading to switches that pass data packets to the specific destination device. This method significantly increases network performance.

Question 3

> Of the following routing methods, which is likely to take the most amount of administration time in the long term?
>
> ○ A. Static
>
> ○ B. Link state
>
> ○ C. Distance vector
>
> ○ D. Dynamic

The correct answer is A. Static routing will take more time to administer in the long term, as any changes to the network routing table must be entered manually. Answers B and C are incorrect. Distance vector and link state are both dynamic routing methods. Answer D is also incorrect. Dynamic routing might take more time to configure initially, but in the long term it will require less administration time. It can adapt to changes in the network layout automatically.

Question 4

> Your manager asks you to look into some upgrades for your network. The current network is a 10Base2 system and you have been experiencing numerous hard-to-track-down cable problems. As a result, you have decided to upgrade to a 10BaseT system. On the networking vendor's price list are both active and passive hubs. The passive hubs are considerably cheaper than the active ones and you are tempted to opt for them so that you come in under budget. A colleague advises you against the purchase of passive hubs. What is the primary difference between an active and a passive hub?
>
> ○ A. Passive hubs do not offer any management capabilities.
>
> ○ B. Passive hubs cannot be used in full-duplex mode.
>
> ○ C. Passive hubs do not regenerate the data signal.
>
> ○ D. Passive hubs forward data to all ports on the hub, not just the one for which they are intended.

The correct answer is C. An active hub regenerates the data signal before forwarding it. Answer A is incorrect. The management capabilities of a hub have nothing to do with the active/passive aspect of the device. Answer B is incorrect. Hubs are not able to operate in full-duplex mode. Only network switches are able to perform this function in this context. Answer D describes the function of a switch, not a hub.

Question 5

Which of the following statements best describes a gateway?

○ A. It is a device that allows data to be routed from one network to another.

○ B. It is a term used to refer to any device that resides at the entrance of a network.

○ C. It is a device, system, or application that translates data from one format to another.

○ D. It is a network device that can forward or block data based on the MAC address embedded within the packet.

The correct answer is C. A gateway can be a device, system, or application that translates data from one format to another. Answers B and D are more likely to describe a router than a gateway. Answer D describes a bridge. A bridge is a device that is used to segregate a network. It makes forwarding or blocking decisions based on the MAC address embedded within the packet.

Question 6

You have a thin coaxial-based Ethernet network and are experiencing performance problems on the network. By using a network performance-monitoring tool, you determine that there are a large number of collisions on the network. In an effort to reduce the collisions you decide to install a network bridge. What kind of bridge are you most likely to implement?

○ A. Collision bridge

○ B. Transparent bridge

○ C. Visible bridge

○ D   Translational bridge

The correct answer is B. A transparent bridge can be used to segment a network, which reduces the amount of collisions and the overall network traffic. It is called transparent because the other devices on the network do not need to be aware of the device and will in fact operate as if it wasn't there. Answer D is incorrect as a translational bridge is used in environments where it is necessary to translate from one data format to another. Such a conversion is not necessary in this scenario. Answers A and C are invalid. There is no such thing as a collision bridge or a visible bridge.

Question 7

> Which of the following represents a valid MAC address?
>
> ○ A. **00-D0-56-F2-B5-12**
> ○ B. **00-63-T6-4H-7U-78**
> ○ C. **00-62-DE-6F-D2**
> ○ D. **000-622-DE5-75E-EA6**

The correct answer is A. A MAC address is a 6-byte address which is expressed in hexadecimal format. Answer B contains the letters T and U, which are not valid. Hexadecimal format uses only numbers and the letters A through F. For this reason, answer B is incorrect. Answer C is only five bytes and so is incorrect. Answer D is incorrect because a byte in hexadecimal is expressed in two characters and the answer uses three.

Question 8

> Which of the following devices passes data based on the MAC address?
>
> ○ A. Hub
> ○ B. Switch
> ○ C. MSAU
> ○ D. Router

The correct answer is B. When determining the destination for a data packet, the switch learns the MAC address of all devices attached to it and then matches the destination MAC address in the data it receives. None of the other devices pass data based solely on the MAC address.

Question 9

> What is the speed of the 16550 UART chip?
>
> ○ A. 921,600
> ○ B. 430,800
> ○ C. 115,200
> ○ D. 9600

The correct answer is C. 115,200 is the speed of the 16550 UART chip. Answer A is incorrect as 921,600 is the speed of the 16750 and 16950 UART chips. Answer B is incorrect as 430,800 is the speed of the 16650 UART chip and 9600 is the speed of the 8250 UART chip.

Question 10

Which of the following devices would you find only on a Token Ring network?

○ A. Hub

○ B. Switch

○ C. MSAU

○ D. Router

The correct answer is C. A Multistation Access Unit (MSAU) is used as the connectivity point on a Token Ring network. Answers A and B are incorrect. Switches and hubs are associated with Ethernet networks. Answer D is incorrect. Routers can be found on both Token Ring and Ethernet networks.

Want to know more?

Sheldon, Thomas. *McGraw-Hill's Encyclopedia of Networking and Telecommunications*. McGraw-Hill Professional Publishing, 2001.

Tulloch, Mitch. *Microsoft Encyclopedia of Networking* (with CD-ROM). Microsoft Press, 2000.

OSI Model and Network Protocols

Objectives

2.2 Identify the seven layers of the OSI model and their functions.

2.3 Differentiate among the following protocols in terms of routing, addressing schemes, interoperability, and naming conventions:

✓ TCP/IP

✓ IPX/SPX

✓ AppleTalk

✓ NetBEUI

2.4 Identify the OSI layers at which various network components, including the following, operate:

✓ Hubs

✓ Switches

✓ Bridges

✓ Routers

✓ Network interface cards (NICs)

What you need to know

✓ Identify the seven layers of the OSI model.

✓ Identify the function of each of the layers in the OSI model.

✓ Identify the layer at which networking devices function.

✓ Identify the various protocols used with networks.

✓ Understand the characteristics of the commonly used protocols.

Introduction

One of the most important networking concepts to understand is the *Open Systems Interconnect (OSI)* reference model. This conceptual model, created by the *International Organization for Standardization (ISO)* in 1978 and revised in 1984, describes a network architecture that allows data to be passed between computer systems.

This chapter takes a detailed look at the OSI model and describes how it relates to real-world networking. It also examines how common network devices relate to the OSI model.

OSI seven layer model

As shown in Figure 4.1, the OSI reference model is built, bottom to top, in the following order: physical, data-link, network, transport, session, presentation, and application. The physical layer is classified as layer 1 and the top layer of the model, the application layer, as layer 7.

 On the Network+ exam, you may either see an OSI layer referenced by its name, such as data-link, or by its layer number. For instance, you might find that a router is referred to as a layer 3 device.

| 7 - Application |
| 6 - Presentation |
| 5 - Session |
| 4 - Transport |
| 3 - Network |
| 2 - Data-link |
| 1 - Physical |

Figure 4.1 The OSI seven layer model.

Each layer of the OSI model has a specific function. The following sections describe the function of each layer, starting with the physical layer and working up the model.

Physical layer (Layer 1)

The physical layer of the OSI model identifies the physical characteristics of the network, including the following specifications:

➤ **Hardware**—The type of media used on the network such as type of cable, type of connector, type of NIC used, and pinout format for cables.

➤ **Topology**—The physical layer identifies the topology to be used in the network. Common topologies include ring, mesh, star, and bus.

In addition to these, the physical layer also defines the voltage used on a given media and the frequency at which the signals that carry the data move from one state to another. These characteristics dictate the speed and bandwidth of a given media as well as the maximum distance over which a certain media type can be used.

Data-link layer (Layer 2)

The data-link layer is responsible for getting data to the physical layer so that it can be transmitted over the network. The data-link layer is also responsible for error detection, error correction, and hardware addressing.

The data-link layer has two distinct sublayers—the *Media Access Control* (*MAC*) sublayer and the *Logical Link Control* (*LLC*) sublayer.

➤ **MAC layer**—The MAC address is defined at this layer. The MAC address is the physical or hardware address burned into each NIC. The MAC sublayer also controls access to network media.

➤ **LLC**—The LLC layer is responsible for the error and flow-control mechanisms of the data-link layer. The LLC layer is specified in the 802.2 standard.

Network layer (Layer 3)

The primary responsibility of the network layer is *routing*—providing mechanisms by which data can be passed from one network system to another. It does not specify how the data is passed, but rather provides the mechanisms to do so. Functionality at the network layer is provided through protocols, which are software components.

Protocols at the network layer are also responsible for *route selection*, which refers to determining the best path for the data to take throughout the network. In contrast to the data-link layer, which uses MAC addresses to communicate on the LAN, network protocols use software configured addresses and special routing protocols to communicate on the network.

When working with networks, there are two ways in which routes can be configured: *statically* or *dynamically*. In a static routing environment, routes are added manually to the routing tables. In a dynamic routing environment, routing protocols such as *Routing Information Protocol (RIP)* and *Open Shortest Path First (OSPF)* are used. These protocols communicate routing information between networked devices on the network.

Transport layer (Layer 4)

The basic function of the transport layer is to provide mechanisms to transport data between network devices. Primarily it does this in three ways:

➤ **Error checking**—Protocols at the transport layer ensure that data is sent or received correctly.

➤ **Service addressing**—Protocols such as TCP/IP support many network services. These services are identified by ports. The transport layer makes sure that data is passed to the right service.

➤ **Segmentation**—To traverse the network, blocks of data need to be broken into chunks which are of a manageable size for the lower layers to handle. This process, called *segmentation*, is the responsibility of the transport layer.

Protocols at the transport layer

Protocols that operate at the transport layer can either be connectionless (such as the *User Datagram Protocol [UDP]* and the *Internetwork Packet Exchange Protocol [IPX]*), or connection-oriented, examples of which include the *Transmission Control Protocol (TCP)* and the *Sequenced Packet Exchange Protocol (SPX)*. For a further discussion of these protocols, and of the difference between connection-oriented and connectionless protocols, refer to the information on network protocols later in this chapter.

Flow control

The transport layer is also responsible for *data flow control*, which refers to the way in which the receiving device can accept data transmissions. There are two common methods of flow control used, *buffering* and *windowing*:

➤ **Buffering**—When buffering flow control is used, data is temporarily stored and waits for the destination device to become available. Buffering can cause a problem if the sending device transmits data much faster than the receiving device is able to manage it.

➤ **Windowing**—In a windowing environment, data is sent in groups of segments that require only one acknowledgment. The size of the window (that is, how many segments fit into one acknowledgment) is defined at the time the session between the two devices is established. As you can imagine, the need to have only one acknowledgment for every, say, five segments can greatly reduce overhead.

Session layer (Layer 5)

The session layer is responsible for managing and controlling the synchronization of data between applications on two devices. It does this by establishing, maintaining, and breaking sessions. Whereas the transport layer is responsible for setting up and maintaining the connection between the two devices, the session layer performs the same function on behalf of the application.

Presentation layer (Layer 6)

The presentation layer's basic function is to convert the data intended for or received from the application layer into another format. Such conversion is necessary because of the way in which data is formatted so it can be transported across the network. This conversion is not necessarily readable by applications. Some common data formats handled by the presentation layer include the following:

➤ **Graphics files**—JPEG, TIFF, GIF, and so on are graphics file formats that require the data be formatted in a certain way.

➤ **Text and data**—The presentation layer can translate data into different formats such as American Standard Code for Information Interchange (ASCII) and the Extended Binary Code Decimal Interchange Code (EBCDIC).

➤ **Sound/video**—MPEGs, QuickTime video, and MIDI files all have their own data formats to and from which data must be converted.

Another very important function of the presentation layer is *encryption*, which is the scrambling of data so that it can't be read by anyone other than the intended recipient. Given the basic role of the presentation layer—that of data-format translator—it is the obvious place for encryption and decryption to take place.

Application layer (Layer 7)

In simple terms, the function of the application layer is to take requests and data from the users and pass them to the lower layers of the OSI model. Incoming information is passed to the application layer, which then displays the information to the users. Some of the most basic application-layer services include file and print capabilities.

The most common misconception about the application layer is that it represents applications that are used on a system such as a word processor or a spreadsheet. Instead, the application layer defines the processes that allow applications to use network services. For example, if an application needs to open a file from a network drive, the functionality is provided by components that reside at the application layer. However, just to confuse things, some applications, such as e-mail clients and Web browsers, do in fact reside at the application layer.

OSI model summary

In summary, Table 4.1 lists the seven layers of the OSI model and describes some of the most significant points of each layer.

Table 4.1	OSI Model Summary
OSI Layer	**Major Functions**
Physical (Layer 1)	Defines the physical structure of the network and the topology.
Data-link (Layer 2)	Provides error detection and correction. Uses two distinct sublayers: the media access control (MAC) and logical link control (LLC) layers. Identifies the method by which media is accessed. Defines hardware addressing through the MAC sublayer.
Network (Layer 3)	Handles the discovery of destination systems and addressing. Provides the mechanism by which data can be passed from one network system to another.
Transport (Layer 4)	Provides connection services between the sending and receiving devices and ensures reliable data delivery. Manages flow-control through buffering or windowing. Provides segmentation, error checking, and service identification.
Session (Layer 5)	Synchronizes the data exchange between applications on separate devices.
Presentation (Layer 6)	Translates data from the format used by applications into one that can be transmitted across the network. Handles encryption and decryption of data. Provides compression and decompression functionality. Formats data from the application layer into a format that can be sent over the network.
Application (Layer 7)	Provides access to the network for applications.

Identifying the OSI layers at which various network components operate

When you have an understanding of the OSI model, it is possible to relate network connectivity devices discussed in Chapter 3, "Networking Devices," to the appropriate layer of the OSI model. Knowing at which OSI level a device operates allows you to better understand how it functions on the network. Table 4.2 identifies various network devices and maps them to the OSI model.

 For the Network+ exam, you are expected to be able to identify at which layer of the OSI model certain network devices operate.

Table 4.2   Mapping Network Devices to the OSI Model

Device	OSI Layer
Hub	Physical (Layer 1)
Switch	Data-link (Layer 2)
Bridge	Data-link (Layer 2)
Router	Network (Layer 3)
NIC	Data-link (Layer 2)

Differentiating among protocols

You might find yourself working with a number of protocols in today's networked environments. The primary function of these protocols is to facilitate communication between network devices. This section reviews the characteristics of the most widely used protocols.

Connectionless and connection-oriented protocols

Before getting into the characteristics of the various network protocols and protocol suites, it's important to first identify the difference between connection-oriented and connectionless protocols.

In a *connection-oriented* communication, there is guaranteed delivery of the data. Any packet that is not received by the destination system is resent by the sending device. Communication between the sending and receiving devices continues until the transmission has been verified. Because of this, connection-oriented protocols have a higher overhead and place greater demands on bandwidth.

Connection-oriented protocols such as TCP (Transmission Control Protocol) are able to accommodate lost or dropped packets by asking the sending device to retransmit them. Connection-oriented protocols also assume that a lack of acknowledgment is sufficient reason to resend.

In contrast to connection-oriented communication, *connectionless* protocols offer only a *best-effort* delivery mechanism. Basically, the information is sent—there is no confirmation that the data has been received. If there is an error in the transmission, there is no mechanism to resend the data. Connectionless communication requires far less overhead than connection-oriented communication.

As you work through the various protocols, keep an eye out for the protocols that are connectionless and those that are connection-oriented.

The TCP/IP protocol suite

Quite often, TCP/IP is referred to as a network protocol, although that's not entirely accurate. TCP/IP is actually a *protocol suite* comprised of several separate protocols, each of which has its own purpose and function. Combined, they all provide the TCP/IP functionality. The following list contains some of the more well-known protocols found within the TCP/IP protocol suite:

➤ Address Resolution Protocol (ARP)

➤ File Transfer Protocol (FTP)

➤ Internet Control Message Protocol (ICMP)

➤ Internet Protocol (IP)

➤ Reverse Address Resolution Protocol (RARP)

➤ Simple Mail Transfer Protocol (SMTP)

➤ Transmission Control Protocol (TCP)

This is just an introduction to the protocols found within the TCP/IP protocol suite. Chapter 5, "TCP/IP (Transmission Control Protocol/Internet Protocol)," as well as objectives 2.5 through 2.10, discuss TCP/IP in much more detail.

TCP/IP standards

One of the strengths of the TCP/IP protocol suite is that it is not owned by any one party and is not licensed. This is in contrast to protocols such as AppleTalk and IPX/SPX, which are owned by Apple and Novell, respectively. Because of its non-proprietary nature, TCP/IP has an *open development model* with its standards published in documents known as *Requests for Comments (RFCs)*. RFCs are maintained by the *Internet Engineering Task Force (IETF)*. You can find RFCs pertaining to TCP/IP on their Web site at www.ietf.org.

TCP/IP addressing

Anyone who has worked with TCP/IP knows that TCP/IP addressing can be a complex topic. This section provides an overview of TCP/IP addressing to compare how other protocols handle addressing. However, Chapter 5 provides a detailed look at the TCP/IP protocol including addressing.

TCP/IP addresses are comprised of four sets of 8 bits referred to as *octets*. These are expressed in numbers and separated by periods. An example of a TCP/IP address is 192.168.3.2.

A single TCP/IP address represents both the IP address of an individual system, and the network to which the system is attached. Determining which part of the IP address belongs to the network and which belongs to the node is the responsibility of the *subnet mask*. If part of the address refers to the network, it is assigned a binary value of 1 within the subnet mask. If it is the node address, it's assigned a binary value of 0 within the subnet mask.

For example, if you had a subnet mask of 255.255.0.0, the first two octets refer to the network and the second refer to the node address. So using the previous IP address as an example, the 192.168 portion of the address represents the network ID, and the 3.2 portion of the address represents the node ID. Table 4.3 shows default subnet masks and addressing examples.

You can expect to have to identify the parts of an IP address for the exam.

Table 4.3 Determining Network and Node Addresses

Subnet Mask	IP Address	Network Address	Node Address
255.0.0.0	192.168.10.100	192	168.10.100
255.255.0.0	192.168.10.100	192.168	10.100
255.255.255.0	192.168.10.100	192.168.10	100

As mentioned, more information is provided in Chapter 5 on TCP/IP addressing.

TCP/IP interoperability
Of all the protocols used on today's networks, TCP/IP is by far the most versatile and interoperable. All of the popular operating systems today not only support TCP/IP but the vast majority use it as the default protocol. This means that in any network environment, you can have Linux, Windows, and NetWare servers and clients all communicating using TCP/IP.

TCP/IP naming
Systems on a TCP/IP network can be accessed from the network either by their IP address or by a hostname. Hostnames are the names assigned to the system to make them easier to remember. For instance the secretary's computer may have the address of 192.168.4.23 but you can access it using its hostname of *secretary1* or whatever name you assign it.

The name-resolution process from IP address to hostname is often performed dynamically through a *Domain Name Server (DNS)*. It can also be done statically using a Hosts file on the workstation system. More information on name resolution is provided in Chapter 5.

TCP/IP routing
TCP/IP is a fully routable protocol, making it a natural choice for large networks and those that span multiple locations. As mentioned, TCP/IP is a protocol suite; there are two protocols within TCP/IP that provide the routing functionality—the *Routing Information Protocol (RIP)* and the *Open Shortest Path First (OSPF)*.

Internetwork packet exchange/sequenced packet exchange
Like TCP/IP, IPX/SPX is not a single protocol but rather a protocol suite. IPX/SPX was created by Novell for use on Novell networks. When Novell had a larger presence in the network arena, so too did the IPX/SPX protocol

suite. Today the popularity of IPX/SPX has yielded to TCP/IP although it is still used in some network environments, enough at least to include it in the CompTIA exam objectives. TCP/IP's suitability for large multisite networks and its general acceptance has now even led Novell to adopt TCP/IP as the protocol of choice. Table 4.4 shows some of the protocols that comprise the IPX/SPX suite and their functions.

Table 4.4 IPX/SPX Protocols and Their Functions		
Protocol	**Function**	**Related OSI Layer(s)**
Internetwork Packet Exchange (IPX)	A connectionless transport protocol that is primarily responsible for logical network addressing, route selections, and connection services.	Network, Transport
NetWare Link State Protocol (NLSP)	NLSP uses a link-state route discovery method to build routing tables.	Network
NetWare Core Protocol (NCP)	NCP is a connection-oriented protocol that provides the connection between clients and services.	Application, Presentation, Session
Routing Information Protocol (RIP)	Similar to the routing protocol used with TCP/IP, RIP is responsible for the routing of packets on an IPX/SPX network.	Network
Service Advertising Protocol (SAP)	SAP allows systems providing services to the network, such as file and print services, to announce their services and addresses to the network.	Application, Presentation, Session
Sequenced Packet Exchange (SPX)	SPX is a connection-based protocol used when guaranteed message delivery is required on the network.	Transport

IPX addressing

An example of an IPX address is 0BAD33CE:0003FE7C06EC. The 0BAD33CE portion represents the IPX address for the network segment; 0003FE7C06EC is the MAC address of the node, which is used for the second part of the address. In addition to this format, IPX addresses can also be written with each group of four hexadecimal characters separated by colons—for example, 0000:0007:003C:7F53:04CF. In some cases, any leading 0s on the network address portion are dropped. For example, 00000007 can be expressed simply as 7. The address would then be 7:003C:7F53:04CF.

Because IPX addresses are expressed in hexadecimal, they can only contain the letters A through F and the numbers 0 through 9. There can be a maximum of eight characters in the segment portion and 12 characters in the MAC address portion. You should be prepared to identify how IPX addressing works for the Network+ exam.

IPX interoperability

As you might expect, the IPX/SPX protocol suite is fully supported by Novell NetWare but it can also be used in a Microsoft Windows environment. Microsoft includes its own version of the IPX/SPX protocol, NWLink, which provides this interoperability. Using the NWLink protocol and the Microsoft Client for NetWare, Windows systems can connect to a NetWare server using IPX/SPX.

Because of the prevalence of TCP/IP, interoperability with the IPX/SPX protocol has become less important. Even on the later versions of NetWare, TCP/IP is used as the default protocol. As far as Linux is concerned, there is a way to use the IPX/SPX protocol on a Linux system, but TCP/IP is the protocol of choice there too.

IPX/SPX naming

Unlike TCP/IP, naming also is not an issue with IPX/SPX because servers are normally the only parts of a network that are assigned addresses. These addresses are names of up to 47 characters (in current versions of NetWare). Workstations do not need such addresses and instead just use IPX addresses.

AppleTalk

AppleTalk is a protocol associated with Apple networks. The AppleTalk protocol is an established protocol having been introduced in the early 1980s, and continued development toward the end of the 1980s enabled it to become a viable internetworking protocol.

Like the IPX/SPX and TCP/IP protocol suites, the AppleTalk protocol suite is comprised of several protocols. Table 4.5 lists the protocols within the AppleTalk protocol suite and their functions.

Table 4.5 AppleTalk Protocols and Their Functions		
Protocol	**Function**	**OSI Layer**
AppleShare	AppleShare provides application layer services, including file and print sharing.	Application (Layer 7)
AppleTalk Address Resolution Protocol (AARP)	AARP is used to map AppleTalk addresses to Ethernet and Token Ring physical addresses.	Data-link (Layer 2)
AppleTalk Data Stream Protocol (ADSP)	ADSP is a session layer protocol used to establish connections between network devices. It also functions at the transport layer and manages flow control.	Session (Layer 5)
AppleTalk Filing Protocol (AFP)	The AFP protocol manages file sharing for the network.	Session (Layer 5)
AppleTalk Session Protocol (ASP)	Similar to the ADSP protocol, ASP works at the session layer of the OSI model and establishes and releases connections between networked devices.	Session (Layer 5)
AppleTalk Transaction Protocol (ATP)	ATP establishes a connectionless session between networked systems. ATP functions at the transport layer.	Transport (Layer 4)
EtherTalk Link Access Protocol (ELAP)	ELAP is a variation of the AppleTalk protocol that is compatible with the Ethernet protocol.	Physical (Layer 1)
Name Binding Protocol (NBP)	The NBP protocol is used to map computer hostnames to network layer addresses.	Network/Transport (Layers 3 and 4)
Printer Access Protocol (PAP)	PAP is a session layer protocol used to provide printing services on an AppleTalk network.	Session (Layer 5)
Routing Table Maintenance Protocol (RTMP)	RTMP is the protocol on AppleTalk networks that maintains the routing tables for the network.	Transport (Layer 4)
TokenTalk Link Access Protocol (TLAP)	TLAP is a variation on the AppleTalk protocol that is compatible with the Token Ring protocol.	Physical (Layer 1)
Zone Information Protocol (ZIP)	ZIP is used to divide network devices into logical groups called *zones*.	Session (Layer 5)

Be prepared to identify the protocols found within the AppleTalk protocols suite for the Network+ exam.

AppleTalk addressing

Like the other protocols discussed, the AppleTalk protocol uses a two-part addressing scheme, a node and a network section. The node portion of the address is assigned automatically when the system is first brought up onto the network. It is a randomly generated number and then broadcast to the entire network. If a duplicate node address is assigned, another will be assigned and rebroadcast to the network. The network portion of the address is assigned by the network administrator.

The actual AppleTalk address is 24 bits long with 16 bits used for the network address and 8 for the node address.

When working with AppleTalk networks, you are likely going to work with *zones*. Zones are a method used to divide the network into logical areas to simplify administration.

AppleTalk interoperability

AppleTalk was designed for the purpose of being used on Apple networks and, as such, is not natively supported by most of the other major operating systems. Because of this, today, other protocols such as TCP/IP are a more common choice, even for Apple-based networks. In fact, Macintosh systems themselves support the use of TCP/IP. AppleTalk can be configured to work with other platforms but, given the proliferation of TCP/IP, this is not widely done.

AppleTalk routing

The earliest implementations of AppleTalk were not routable, but later versions were. Routing functionality for AppleTalk is provided by the RTMP protocol. RTMP provides similar functionality to the RIP protocol used with IPX/SPX and TCP/IP networks.

AppleTalk naming

AppleTalk networks use logical hostnames, making systems readily recognizable on the network. The network address-to-hostname resolution is handled by the NBP protocol in the AppleTalk protocol suite. It performs a similar function to that provided by DNS on a TCP/IP network.

NetBEUI protocol

NetBEUI was once a popular protocol for smaller networks. It is fast and easy to configure but has one significant drawback in that it is not routable. This one fact limits NetBEUI to a single network segment, far too restrictive for the majority of today's networking environments.

NetBEUI addressing

In terms of addressing, NetBEUI is perhaps the simplest of all the protocols discussed here. Because of this, it is still used on small simple networks such as those found in a small business or a home. Computers on a NetBEUI network are identified by NetBIOS names. The NetBIOS can be no longer than 15 characters and must be unique to the network. Using the 15 characters, you can assign the computers descriptive names such as *workstation*, *student1*, or *secretary2*.

Interoperability with NetBEUI

The discussion on interoperability with NetBEUI is a short one; it is used on Windows platforms exclusively.

Protocol summary

To help you in your exam preparations, the most pertinent information from this section is listed in Table 4.6.

Table 4.6 Comparison of the Various Protocols Discussed in This Chapter			
Protocol	**Overview**	**Routable**	**Addressing**
TCP/IP	Used by default with Unix, Linux, NetWare, Windows, and Macintosh systems. The most interoperable of all protocols.	Yes	Uses four sets of 8 bits referred to as *octets*. The first part of the address refers to the network and the second part to the node.
IPX/SPX	Used to be the default protocol for NetWare, but now TCP/IP is preferred. Still supported by NetWare, Windows, and Linux. Simplest addressing scheme of routable protocols discussed here.	Yes	Uses the MAC address to identify the node, and an eight-character hexadecimal address to identify the network.

(continued)

Table 4.6 Comparison of the Various Protocols Discussed in This Chapter *(continued)*			
Protocol	**Overview**	**Routable**	**Addressing**
AppleTalk	Used by Macintosh, with some support on other platforms.	Yes	Uses a two-part addressing scheme. The first is a randomly generated number for the node address and the second an administrator assigned number for the network address.
NetBEUI	Used by Windows.	No	Uses NetBIOS names to identify systems on the network.

Review and test yourself

The following sections provide you with the opportunity to review what you learned in this chapter and to test yourself.

The facts

➤ The application layer provides access to the network for applications and certain user functions. Displays incoming information and prepares outgoing information for network access.

➤ The presentation layer converts data from the application layer into a format that can be sent over the network. Converts data from the session layer into a format that can be understood by the application layer. Handles encryption and decryption of data. Provides compression and decompression functionality.

➤ The session layer synchronizes the data exchange between applications on separate devices. Handles error detection and notification to the peer layer on the other device.

➤ The transport layer establishes, maintains, and breaks connections between two devices. Determines the ordering and priorities of data. Performs error checking and verification and handles retransmissions, if necessary.

➤ The network layer provides mechanisms for the routing of data between devices across single or multiple network segments. Handles the discovery of destination systems and addressing.

➤ The data-link layer has two distinct sublayers: LLC and MAC. It performs error detection and handling for the transmitted signals and defines the method by which the medium is accessed. Finally, it defines hardware addressing through the MAC sublayer.

➤ The physical layer defines the physical structure of the network. It defines voltage/signal rates and the physical connection methods as well as the physical topology.

➤ Application protocols map to the application, presentation, and session layers of the OSI model. These include AFT, FTP, TFTP, NCP, and SNMP.

➤ Transport protocols map to the transport layer of the OSI model and are responsible for the transporting of data across the network. These include ATP, NetBEUI, SPX, TCP, and UDP.

➤ The NetBEUI protocol uses names as addresses.

➤ Network protocols are responsible for providing the addressing and routing information. These include IP, IPX, and DDP.

➤ RIP is responsible for the routing of packets on an IPX/SPX network.

Key terms

➤ OSI

➤ Physical layer

➤ Data-link layer

➤ Network layer

➤ Transport layer

➤ Session layer

➤ Presentation layer

➤ Application layer

➤ LLC

➤ MAC

➤ Static routing

➤ Dynamic routing

➤ TCP

➤ UDP

➤ SPX

➤ Connectionless protocols

➤ Connection-oriented protocols

➤ NetBEUI

➤ AppleTalk

➤ Protocol suite

➤ Application protocol

➤ Transport protocol

➤ Network protocol

➤ Packet

➤ ATP

➤ FTP

➤ SNMP

➤ SMTP

➤ TCP

➤ UDP

➤ SPX

➤ IPX

➤ IP

➤ TCP/IP addressing

➤ Routing protocols

➤ OSPF

➤ RIP

Practice exam

Question 1

> Which of the following protocols provide network routing functionality? (Choose two.)
>
> ❑ A. NBP
> ❑ B. RIP
> ❑ C. RTMP
> ❑ D. NCP

The correct answers are B and C. RIP is a distance-vector routing protocol used on TCP/IP and IPX/SPX networks. RTMP is a routing protocol used on AppleTalk networks. Answer A, NBP, is incorrect. The NBP protocol is used to map computer hostnames to network layer addresses on AppleTalk networks. Answer D is incorrect—NCP is a part of the IPX/SPX protocol suite that makes network services available to clients.

Question 2

> Which of the following protocols uses the MAC address as part of the addressing scheme?
>
> ○ A. IPX/SPX
> ○ B. TCP/IP
> ○ C. AppleTalk
> ○ D. NetBEUI

The correct answer is A. IPX/SPX uses the MAC address to identify the node and network addresses. TCP/IP, answer B, uses a four octet address to identify the node and network. AppleTalk uses a 24-bit address, part of which is randomly generated, part of which is manually assigned. NetBEUI uses alphanumeric names to refer to devices.

Question 3

> At which OSI layer does a hub operate?
>
> ○ A. Network
>
> ○ B. Physical
>
> ○ C. Data-link
>
> ○ D. Session

The correct answer is B. A hub operates at the physical layer of the OSI model. An example of a network layer device is a router. An example of a data-link layer device is a NIC. Session layer components are normally software, not hardware.

Question 4

> Which of the following are sublayers of the data-link layer? (Choose two.)
>
> ❏ A. MAC
>
> ❏ B. LCL
>
> ❏ C. Session
>
> ❏ D. LLC

The correct answers are A and D. The data-link layer is broken into two distinct sublayers, the Media Access Control (MAC) and the Logical Link Control (LLC). LCL is not a valid term, and session is another of the OSI model layers.

Question 5

> Which of the following protocols uses names as network addresses?
>
> ○ A. NetBEUI
>
> ○ B. TCP/IP
>
> ○ C. IPX/SPX
>
> ○ D. AppleTalk

The correct answer is A. NetBEUI uses names as network addresses. All of the other network protocols listed use numbered addressing schemes at the network layer to identify systems.

Question 6

> Which of the following characteristics best describe the SPX protocol? (Choose two.)
>
> ❑ A. Provides a connectionless communication between network devices.
> ❑ B. Provides connection-oriented communication between network devices.
> ❑ C. Functions at the network layer of the OSI model.
> ❑ D. Functions at the transport layer of the OSI model.

The correct answers are B and D. SPX is a connection-oriented protocol that operates at the transport layer of the OSI model. The other answers are incorrect.

Question 7

> Which of the following OSI layers is responsible for establishing connections between two devices?
>
> ○ A. Network
> ○ B. Transport
> ○ C. Session
> ○ D. Data-link

The correct answer is B. The transport layer is responsible for establishing a connection between networked devices. None of the other answers are correct.

Question 8

> Which of the following protocol suites uses ZIP?
>
> ○ A. TCP/IP
> ○ B. IPX/SPX
> ○ C. NetBEUI
> ○ D. AppleTalk

The correct answer is D. The Zone Information Protocol (ZIP) is used to divide AppleTalk network devices into logical groups called *zones*. None of the other protocol suites listed use ZIP.

Question 9

Which of the following protocols offer guaranteed delivery? (Choose two.)

☐ A. SPX

☐ B. IPX

☐ C. IP

☐ D. TCP

The correct answers are A and D. Both SPX and TCP are connection-oriented protocols, which guarantee delivery of data. IPX is a connectionless transport protocol, and IP is a network layer protocol that's responsible for tasks such as addressing and route discovery.

Question 10

At which OSI layer does a switch operate?

○ A. Layer 1

○ B. Layer 2

○ C. Layer 3

○ D. Layer 4

The correct answer is B. A switch uses the MAC addresses of connected devices to make its forwarding decisions. Therefore, it is referred to as a data-link, or Layer 2, network device. None of the other answers are correct.

Want to know more?

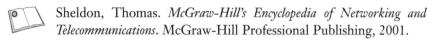

Sheldon, Thomas. *McGraw-Hill's Encyclopedia of Networking and Telecommunications*. McGraw-Hill Professional Publishing, 2001.

Tulloch, Mitch. *Microsoft Encyclopedia of Networking* (with CD-ROM). Microsoft Press, 2000.

TCP/IP (Transmission Control Protocol/Internet Protocol)

Objectives

2.5 Define the purpose, function, and/or use of the following protocols within TCP/IP: Internet Protocol, Transmission Control Protocol, User Datagram Protocol, File Transfer Protocol, Trivial File Transfer Protocol, Simple Message Transfer Protocol, Hypertext Transfer Protocol, Hypertext Transfer Protocol Secure, Post Office Protocol/Internet Message Access Protocol, Telnet, Internet Control Message Protocol, Address Resolution Protocol, and Network Time Protocol.

2.6 Define the function of TCP/UDP ports and identify well-known ports.

2.7 Identify the purposes of the following network services: Dynamic Host Configuration Protocol/BOOT Protocol, Domain Name Service, Network Address Translation/Internet Connection Sharing, Windows Internet Name Service, and Simple Network Management Protocol.

2.8 Identify IP addresses (IPv4, IPv6) and their default subnet masks.

2.9 Identify the purposes of subnetting and default gateways.

2.10 Identify the differences between public and private networks.

What you need to know

✓ Identify the function of protocols within the TCP/IP protocol suite.

✓ Identify the ports associated with common network services.

✓ Understand the function of various network services.

✓ Understand IPv4 and IPv6 addressing.

✓ Identify the purposes of subnetting and default gateways.

✓ Identify the differences between public and private networks.

Introduction

Without question, the TCP/IP protocol suite is the most dominant protocol used on networks today. As such, it is a focus on the Network+ exam. To pass the exam, you will definitely need to understand the material presented in this chapter.

This chapter deals with the individual protocols within the protocol suite. The chapter looks at the function of the individual protocols and their purposes. It starts by discussing the IP of TCP/IP.

Internet Protocol (IP)

The IP protocol is a network layer protocol and is responsible for transporting data between network devices. IP is a connectionless protocol, meaning that data delivery is not guaranteed; it takes the best-effort approach.

Another function of IP is *addressing*. IP addressing is a complex subject and warrants its own section. A more detailed discussion of addressing is covered in the "IP Addressing" section, later in this chapter.

Transmission Control Protocol (TCP)

TCP functions at the transport layer of the OSI model and is a connection-oriented protocol that uses IP as its network protocol. Being connection-oriented means that TCP requires a session to be established between two hosts before communication can take place. TCP provides reliability to IP communications. Specifically, TCP adds features such as flow control, sequencing, and error detection and correction. For this reason, higher-level applications that need guaranteed delivery use TCP rather than its light-weight and connectionless brethren, the User Datagram Protocol (UDP).

User Datagram Protocol (UDP)

UDP operates at the transport layer of the OSI model and performs functions similar to that of TCP, with one notable difference; UDP is a connectionless protocol and does not guarantee data delivery. Both TCP and UDP use IP as its transport protocol.

Because UDP does not need to guarantee data delivery it is much more efficient than TCP, so for applications that don't need the added features of TCP, UDP is much more economical in terms of bandwidth and processing effort. A good example of UDP is an online radio station that sends data but does not confirm data delivery.

File Transfer Protocol (FTP)

The FTP protocol is an application layer protocol that provides a method for uploading and downloading files from a remote system running FTP server software. FTP uses the TCP transport protocol to guarantee the delivery of data packets.

FTP has some security capabilities, namely, it has mechanisms in place that can be used to authenticate users. However, rather than create a user account for every user, you can configure FTP server software to accept anonymous logons. When you do this, the username is anonymous, and the password is normally the user's email address. Most FTP servers that offer files to the general public operate in this way.

FTP is popular for distributing files over the Internet but is also used within organizations that need to frequently exchange large files with other people or organizations that find it impractical to use regular email.

FTP Security Concerns

One potential issue with FTP is that usernames and passwords are communicated between client and host in clear text. This is a potential security concern.

FTP is platform independent, meaning that all of the common network operating systems offer FTP server capabilities. In addition, all commonly used client operating systems offer FTP client functionality. Alternatively, third-party utilities such as SmartFTP and CuteFTP are often used.

There are several commands that can be used with FTP; you are expected to understand these commands for the Network+ exam. Table 5.1 lists the commands that are used with the FTP protocol.

Table 5.1	FTP Commands
Command	**Purpose**
ls	Lists the files in the current directory.
cd	Changes the working directory on the remote host.
lcd	Changes the working directory on the local host.
put	Uploads a single file to the remote host.
get	Downloads a single file from the remote host.
mput	Uploads multiple files to the remote host.
mget	Downloads multiple files from the remote host.
binary	Switches transfers into binary mode.
ascii	Switches transfers into ASCII mode (the default).

Trivial File Transfer Protocol (TFTP)

A variation on FTP is TFTP, which is also a file transfer mechanism. FTP and TFTP are both application layer protocols; however, TFTP does not have the security capability or the level of functionality that FTP has. TFTP uses only UDP as a transport protocol, making it a *connectionless* protocol. As such, it has a lower overhead than FTP.

 The big difference between TFTP and FTP is that TFTP is a connectionless protocol, using only the UDP transport protocol.

Another feature that TFTP does not offer is directory navigation. In FTP, commands can be executed to navigate around and manage the file system; TFTP offers no such capability. TFTP requires that you request not only exactly what you want, but also the particular location you want.

Simple Mail Transfer Protocol (SMTP)

The SMTP protocol is associated with email and defines how mail messages are sent between hosts. SMTP is a connection-oriented protocol; it uses TCP connections to guarantee error-free delivery of messages. SMTP is not overly sophisticated and requires that the destination host always be available. For this reason, mail systems spool incoming mail so that users can read it at a later time. How the user then reads the mail depends on how the client accesses the SMTP server. SMTP is an application layer protocol.

Hypertext Transfer Protocol (HTTP)

HTTP uses UDP as a transport protocol, making HTTP a connectionless protocol. HTTP functions at the application layer of the OSI model. In practical uses, HTTP is the protocol that allows text, graphics, multimedia, and other material to be downloaded from an HTTP server. HTTP defines which actions can be requested by clients and how servers should answer those requests.

HTTP uses a uniform resource locator (URL) to determine which page should be downloaded from the remote server. The URL contains the type of request (for example, `http://`), the name of the server being contacted (for example, `www.novell.com`), and optionally the page being requested (for example, `/support`). The result is the syntax that Internet-savvy people are familiar with: `http://www.novell.com/support`.

Hypertext Transfer Protocol Secure (HTTPS)

Normal HTTP requests are sent in clear text and for some Internet transactions such as online banking or e-commerce, this poses a significant security problem. The solution for such applications is to use the HTTPS protocol. HTTPS uses a system known as *Secure Sockets Layer (SSL)*, which encrypts the information that is sent between the client and the host. An example of an HTTPS URL address is `https://www.banking.com`.

Like HTTP, HTTPS uses the UDP transport protocol and operates at the application layer of the OSI model.

Post Office Protocol (POP) and Internet Message Access Protocol (IMAP)

Both POP and IMAP are mechanisms for downloading, or pulling, email from a server. They are necessary because, although the mail is transported around the network via SMTP, users cannot always read it immediately so it must be stored in a central location. From this location, it must then be downloaded, which is what POP and IMAP allow you to do.

One of the problems with POP is that the password used to access a mailbox is transmitted across the network in clear text. That means if someone wanted to, he could determine your POP password with relative ease. This is an area in which IMAP offers an advantage over POP. It uses a more sophisticated authentication system, which makes it harder for someone to determine a password.

Telnet

Telnet uses TCP for transport. Telnet functions at the application layer of the OSI model. The function of Telnet is to establish sessions on a remote host, and then allow commands to be executed on that remote host. Telnet is widely used to access Unix and Linux systems as well as to administer some managed networking equipment such as switches or routers.

One of the problems with Telnet is that it is not secure. As a result, remote session functionality is now almost always achieved by using alternatives such as Secure Shell (SSH).

Internet Control Message Protocol (ICMP)

ICMP is a protocol that works with IP to provide error checking and reporting functionality. In effect, ICMP is a tool that IP uses in its quest to provide best-effort delivery. ICMP functions at the network layer of the OSI model.

ICMP can be used for a number of functions. Its most common is probably the widely used and incredibly useful ping utility. ping sends a stream of ICMP echo requests to a remote host. If the host is able to respond, it does so by sending echo reply messages back to the sending host. In that one simple process, ICMP enables the verification of the protocol suite configuration of both the sending and receiving nodes and any intermediate networking devices.

Address Resolution Protocol (ARP)

The basic function of the ARP protocol is to resolve IP addresses to Media Access Control (MAC) addresses. When a system attempts to contact another host, IP first determines whether the other host is on the same network it is on, by looking at the IP address. If IP determines that the destination is on the local network, it consults the ARP cache to determine whether it has a corresponding entry.

The function of ARP is to resolve IP addresses to MAC addresses or layer 2 addresses.

If there is not an entry for the host in the ARP cache, IP sends a broadcast on the local network, asking the host with the target IP address to send back its MAC address. The communication is sent as a broadcast because without the target system's MAC address, the source system is unable to communicate directly with the target system.

Network Time Protocol (NTP)

NTP uses the TCP transport protocol and is the protocol that facilitates the communication of time information between systems. The idea is that one system configured as a time provider transmits time information to other systems that can be both the time receivers and the time providers to other systems.

TCP/IP protocol suite summary

The details of each of the protocols discussed in the preceding sections are summarized in Table 5.2. You can use this table for review before you take the Network+ exam.

Table 5.2 TCP/IP Protocol Suite Summary

Protocol	Full Name	Description	OSI Layer
IP	Internet Protocol	Connectionless protocol used for moving data around a network.	Network
TCP	Transmission Control Protocol	Connection-oriented protocol that offers flow control, sequencing, and retransmission of dropped packets.	Transport
UDP	User Datagram Protocol	Connectionless alternative to TCP that is used for applications that do not require the functions offered by TCP.	Transport
FTP	File Transfer Protocol	Protocol for uploading and downloading files to and from a remote host; also accommodates basic file-management tasks.	Application
TFTP	Trivial File Transfer Protocol	File transfer protocol that does not have the security or error-checking capabilities of FTP; uses UDP as a transport protocol and is therefore connectionless.	Application
SMTP	Simple Mail Transfer Protocol	Mechanism for transporting email across networks.	Application
HTTP	Hypertext Transfer Protocol	Protocol for retrieving files from a Web server.	Application
HTTPS	Hypertext Transfer Protocol Secure	Secure protocol for retrieving files from a Web server.	Application
POP/IMAP	Post Office Protocol/Internet Message Access Protocol	Used for retrieving email from a server on which the mail is stored.	Application
Telnet	Telnet	Allows sessions to be opened on a remote host.	Application
ICMP	Internet Control Message Protocol	Used for error reporting, flow control, and route testing.	Network
ARP	Address Resolution Protocol	Resolves IP addresses to MAC addresses, to enable communication between devices.	Network
NTP	Network Time Protocol	Used to communicate time synchronization information between devices.	Application

TCP/UDP port functions

Each TCP/IP protocol or application has a port associated with it. When a communication is received, the target port number is checked to determine which protocol or service it is destined for. The request is then forwarded to that protocol or service. Take, for example, HTTP, whose assigned port number is 80. When a Web browser forms a request for a Web page, the request is sent to port 80 on the target system. When the target system receives the request, it examines the port number and when it sees that the port is 80, it forwards the request to the Web server application.

TCP/IP has 65,535 ports available with 0 to 1023 being labeled as the well-known ports. Although a detailed understanding of the 65,535 ports is not necessary for the Network+ exam, it is important to understand the function of some of some of the well-known ports, as administration often requires you to specify port assignments when working with applications and configuring services. Table 5.3 shows some of the most common port assignments.

For the Network+ exam, you should concentrate on the information provided in this table, and you should be able to answer any port-related questions you might receive.

Table 5.3   TCP/IP Port Assignments and Delivery Service

Protocol	Port Assignment	TCP/UDP Service
FTP	21	TCP
SSH	22	TCP
Telnet	23	TCP
SMTP	25	TCP
DNS	53	UDP
TFTP	69	UDP
HTTP	80	TCP/UDP
POP3	110	TCP
NNTP	119	TCP
NTP	123	TCP
IMAP4	143	TCP
SNMP	161	UDP
HTTPS	443	TCP

The term *well-known ports* identifies the ports ranging from **0** to **1023**. When CompTIA states "identify the well-known ports," this is what it is referring to.

Network services

Network services provide the ability to manage and administer TCP/IP-based networks. Today, it is quite likely that a network of any size will use a number of network services, making them an important component of network administration. The following sections discuss each of the network services covered on the CompTIA exam.

For the Network+ exam, be prepared to identify the function of the network services discussed in this chapter.

Dynamic Host Configuration Protocol (DHCP) and Boot Protocol (BOOTP)

The basic function of the DHCP service is to automatically assign IP addresses to client systems. To do this, ranges of IP addresses, known as *scopes*, are defined on a system that is running a DHCP server application. When another system configured as a DHCP client is initialized, it asks the server for an address. If all things are as they should be, the server assigns an address to the client for a predetermined amount of time, which is known as the *lease*, from the scope.

A DHCP server can typically be configured to assign more than just IP addresses; they are often used to assign the subnet mask, the default gateway, Domain Name Service (DNS) and Windows Internet Name Service (WINS) information.

Using DHCP means that administrators do not have to manually configure each client system with a TCP/IP address. This removes the common problems associated with statically assigned addresses such as human error. The potential problem of assigning duplicate IP addresses is also eliminated. DHCP also removes the need to reconfigure systems if they move from one subnet to another, or if you decide to make a wholesale change of the IP addressing structure.

Concerns for using DHCP are few; however, DHCP is a broadcast system that generates network traffic, albeit a very small amount. In a practical scenario, the negative effects in terms of network bandwidth are minimal. After the initial configuration, though, DHCP is about as maintenance free as a service can get, with only occasional monitoring normally required.

DHCP—Dependent and Independent

DHCP is a protocol-dependent service, and it is not platform dependent. This means you can use, for example, a Linux DHCP server for a network with Windows clients or a Novell DHCP server with Linux clients.

BOOTP (BOOT Protocol) is essentially an early version of DHCP and was originally created so that diskless workstations could obtain the TCP/IP information needed to connect to the network. Such a system was necessary because diskless workstations had no way of storing the information.

Like DHCP, BOOTP is a broadcast-based system. Therefore, routers must be configured to forward BOOTP broadcasts. Today, it is far more likely that DHCP, rather than BOOTP, is used.

Domain Name Service (DNS)

The function of the DNS service is to resolve hostnames, such as www.microsoft.com, to IP addresses. Such a resolution system makes it possible for people to remember the names of, and refer to frequently used hosts, using the easy-to-remember hostnames rather than the hard-to-remember IP addresses.

Like other TCP/IP-based services, DNS is a platform-independent protocol. Therefore, it can be used on Linux, UNIX, Windows, NetWare, and almost every other platform.

On networks where there is no DNS server, it is possible to resolve hostnames to IP address using the *HOSTS* file. The HOSTS file is a text file, found on almost all PC operating systems, in which you can place hostname-to-IP-address resolution information. When HOSTS files are used, it's up to the administrator to manually make changes to the file if needed.

 On the Network+ exam, you might be asked to identify the purpose and function of a DNS HOSTS file and a DNS server.

Network Address Translation (NAT) and Internet Connection Sharing (ICS)

NAT and ICS are two strategies that allow networks to access the Internet through a single connection. Having a single access point for the network enables an organization to have Internet access with a single IP address.

NAT

The basic principle of NAT is that many computers can "hide" behind a single registered IP address, or a group of registered IP addresses. Using NAT means that, in its most basic implementation, only one registered IP address is needed on the external interface of the system that is acting as the gateway between the internal and external networks.

A system performing the NAT service funnels the requests that are given to it to the Internet. For instance, a client requests a Web site, and the request goes through the NAT server to the Internet. To the remote system, the request looks like it is originating from a single address, the NAT server, and not the individual client systems. The system that is performing the NAT function keeps track of who asked for what and makes sure that when the data is returned it is directed to the correct system.

Servers that provide NAT functionality do so in different ways. For example, it is possible to statically map a single internal IP address to an external one, so that outgoing requests are always tagged with the same IP address. Alternatively, if you have a group of public IP addresses, you can have the NAT system assign addresses to devices on a first-come, first-serve basis. Either way, the basic function of NAT is the same.

ICS

Although ICS is discussed separately from NAT, it is nothing more than an implementation of NAT on Windows platforms. More specifically, Windows Me, Windows XP, and Windows 2000 include the ICS feature, which makes it simple for users to create shared Internet connections.

Because ICS was intended as a simple mechanism for a small office network or a home network to share a single Internet connection, configuration is simple. However, simplicity is also the potential downfall of ICS. ICS provides no security, and the system providing the shared connection is not secure against outside attacks. For that reason, ICS should be used only when there are no other facilities available, or in conjunction with a firewall application.

Simple Network Management Protocol (SNMP)

SNMP is a management protocol that allows network devices to communicate information about their state to a central system. It also allows the central system to pass configuration parameters to the devices.

In an SNMP configuration, a system known as a *manager* acts as the central communication point for all the SNMP-enabled devices on the network. On each device that is to be managed and monitored via SNMP, software called an *SNMP agent* is set up and configured with the IP address of the manager. Depending on the configuration, the SNMP manager is then able to communicate with and retrieve information from the devices running the SNMP agent software. In addition, the agent is able to communicate the occurrence of certain events to the SNMP manager as they happen. These messages are known as *traps*.

An important part of SNMP is an *SNMP management system*, which is a computer running a special piece of software called a *Network Management System (NMS)*. These software applications can be free, or they can cost thousands of dollars. The difference between the free applications and those that cost a great deal of money normally boils down to functionality and support. All NMS systems, regardless of cost, offer the same basic functionality. Today, most NMS applications use graphical maps of the network to locate a device and then query it. The queries are built into the application and are triggered by a point and click. You can actually issue SNMP requests from a command-line utility, but with so many tools available, it is simply not necessary.

An SNMP agent can be any device that is capable of running a small software component that facilitates communication with an SNMP manager. SNMP agent functionality is supported by almost any device that is designed to be connected to a network.

Windows Internet Name Service (WINS)

On Windows networks, a system called WINS enables Network Basic Input/Output System (NetBIOS) names to be resolved to IP addresses. NetBIOS name resolution is necessary on Windows networks so that systems can locate and access each other by using the NetBIOS computer name rather than the IP address. It's a lot easier for a person to remember a computer called *secretary* than to remember its IP address, 192.168.2.34. The NetBIOS name needs to be resolved to an IP address and subsequently to a MAC address (by ARP).

NetBIOS name resolution can be performed three ways on a network. The simplest way is to use a WINS server on the network that will automatically perform the NetBIOS name resolution. If a WINS server is not available, the NetBIOS name resolution can be performed statically using a LMHOSTS file. Using a LMHOSTS file requires that you manually configure at least one text file with the entries. As you can imagine, this can be a time-consuming process, particularly if the systems on the network change frequently. The third method, and the default, is that systems will resolve NetBIOS names using broadcasts. There are two problems with this approach. First, the broadcasts create additional network traffic and second, the broadcasts cannot traverse routers unless the router is configured to do so. This means that resolutions between network segments are not possible.

TCP/IP service summary

Table 5.4 helps you quickly identify the purpose and function of each of the TCP/IP services covered in the previous sections.

Table 5.4 Summary of TCP/IP Services	
Service	**Purpose/Function**
DHCP/BOOTP	Automatically assigns IP addressing information
DNS	Resolves hostnames to IP addresses
NAT/ICS	Translates private network addresses into public network addresses
SNMP	Provides network management facilities on TCP/IP-based networks
WINS	Resolves NetBIOS names to IP addresses

Identifying IP addresses (IPv4, IPv6) and their default subnet masks

IP addressing is one of the most challenging aspects of TCP/IP and one that can leave even the most seasoned network administrators scratching their heads. Fortunately, the Network+ exam requires only a fundamental knowledge of IP addressing.

The following sections look at how IP addressing works for both IPv4 and the newest version of the IP, IPv6.

IP addressing

To communicate on a network using the TCP/IP protocol, each system has to be assigned a unique address. The address defines both the number of the network to which the device is attached and the address of the node on that network. In other words, the IP address provides two pieces of information. It's a bit like a street name and a house number of a person's home address.

Each device on a logical network segment must have the same network address as all the other devices on the segment. All the devices on that network segment must then have different node addresses.

So, how does the system know which part of the address is the network part and which is the node part? That is the function of a *subnet mask*. On its own, an IP address is no good to the system because it is simply a set of four numbers. The subnet mask is used in concert with the IP address to determine which portion of the IP address refers to the network address and which refers to the node address.

IPv4

An IPv4 address is composed of four sets of 8 bits each (that is, four octets). The result is that IP addresses are 32 bits in length. Each bit in the octet is assigned a decimal value. The leftmost bit has a value of 128, followed by 64, 32, 16, 8, 4, 2, and 1, left to right.

Each bit in the octet can be either a 1 or a 0. If the value is 1, it is counted as its decimal value, and if it is 0, it is ignored. If all the bits are 0, the value of the octet is 0. If all the bits in the octet are 1, the value is 255, which is 128+64+32+16+8+4+2+1.

By using the set of 8 bits and manipulating the 1s and 0s, you can obtain any value between 0 and 255 for each octet.

Table 5.5 shows some examples of decimal-to-binary value conversions.

Table 5.5 Decimal-to-Binary Value Conversions		
Decimal Value	**Binary Value**	**Decimal Calculation**
10	00001010	8+2=10
192	11000000	128+64=192
205	11001101	128+64+8+4+1=205
223	11011111	128+64+16+8+4+2+1=223

IP address classes

IP addresses are grouped into logical divisions called *classes*. In the IPv4 address space, there are five address classes (A through E), although only three (A, B, C) are used for assigning addresses to clients. Class D is reserved for multicast addressing, and Class E is reserved for future development.

Of the three classes available for address assignments, each uses a fixed-length subnet mask to define the separation between the network and the node address. A Class A address uses only the first octet to represent the network portion, a Class B address uses two octets, and a Class C address uses the first three octets. The upshot of this system is that Class A has a small number of network addresses but a very large number of possible host addresses. Class B has a larger number of networks but a smaller number of hosts, and Class C has an even larger number of networks, and an even smaller number of hosts. The exact numbers are provided in Table 5.6.

Table 5.6 IPv4 Address Classes and the Number of Available Network/Host Addresses				
Address Class	Range	Number of Networks	Number of Hosts per Network	Binary Value of First Octet
A	1-126	126	16,777,214	0xxxxxxx
B	128-191	16384	65,532	10xxxxxx
C	192-223	2,097,152	254	110xxxxx
D	224-247	NA	NA	1110xxxx
E	248-255	NA	NA	1111xxxx

Notice in Table 5.6 that the network number 127 is not included in any of the ranges. The 127 network ID is reserved for the local loopback. The local loopback is a function of the protocol suite used in the troubleshooting process.

For the Network+ exam, you should be prepared to identify into which class a given address falls. You should also be prepared to identify the loopback address.

Subnet mask assignment

Like an IP address, a *subnet mask* is a 32-bit address expressed in dotted-decimal format. Unlike an IP address, though, a subnet mask performs just one function: It defines which parts of the IP address refer to the network address and which refer to the node address. Each of the classes of IP address used for address assignment has a standard subnet mask associated with it. The default subnet masks are listed in Table 5.7.

Table 5.7	Default Subnet Masks Associated with IP Address Classes
Address Class	**Default Subnet Mask**
A	255.0.0.0
B	255.255.0.0
C	255.255.255.0

IPv6 addressing

Although IPv4 has served us well for a number of years, it is finally starting to reach its end. The main problem with IPv4 is simply that the demand for IP addresses outweighs what IPv4 is able to provide. That is where IPv6 comes in.

By far, the most significant aspect of IPv6 is its addressing capability. The address range of IPv4 is nearly depleted, and it is widely acknowledged that we are at just the beginning of the digital era. Therefore, we need an addressing scheme that offers more addresses than can possibly be used in the foreseeable future. IPv6 delivers exactly that. Whereas IPv4 uses a 32-bit address, IPv6 uses a 128-bit address that yields a staggering 340,282,366,920,938,463,463,374,607,431,768,211,456 possible addresses!

IPv6 addresses are expressed in a different format from those used in IPv4. An IPv6 address is composed of eight octet pairs expressed in hexadecimal, separated by colons. The following is an example of an IPv6 address:

```
42DE:7E55:63F2:21AA:CBD4:D773:CC21:554F
```

 Be ready to identify both a valid IPv4 and IPv6 address for the Network+ exam.

Identifying the purposes of subnetting and default gateways

Now that you have looked at how IP addresses are used, you can learn the process of subnetting. *Subnetting* is a process by which the node portions of an IP address are used to create more networks than you would have if you used the default subnet mask.

To illustrate subnetting, let's use an example. Suppose that you have been assigned the Class B address 150.150.0.0. Using this address and the default subnet mask, you could have a single network (150.150) and use the rest of the address as node addresses. This would give you a large number of possible node addresses, which in reality is probably not very useful. So, what you can do is "borrow" bits from the node portion of the address to use as network addresses. This would reduce the number of nodes per network, but chances are, you would still have more than enough.

There are two main reasons for subnetting. First, it allows you to utilize IP address ranges more effectively. Second, it provides increased security and manageability to IP networking by providing a mechanism to create multiple networks rather than having just one.

Default gateways

Default gateways are the means by which a device can access hosts on other networks for which it does not have a route. Most workstation configurations actually default to just using default gateways rather than having any static routes configured.

When a system wants to communicate with another device, it first determines whether the host is on the local network or a remote network. If the host is on a remote network, the system looks in the routing table to determine whether it has an entry for the network that the remote host is on. If it does, it uses that route. If it does not, the data is sent to the default gateway.

In essence, the default gateway is simply the path out of the network for a given device.

 If a system is not configured with any static routes or a default gateway, it is limited to operating on its own network segment.

Identifying the differences between public and private networks

IP addressing involves many considerations, not least important of which are public and private networks. A *public network* is a network to which anyone can connect. The best, and perhaps only pure, example of such a network is the Internet. A *private network* is any network to which access is restricted. A corporate network and a school network are examples of private networks.

The Internet Assigned Numbers Authority (IANA) is responsible for assigning IP addresses to public networks.

The main difference between public and private networks, apart from the fact that access to a private network is tightly controlled and access to a public network is not, is that the addressing of devices on a public network must be considered carefully, whereas addressing on a private network has a little more latitude.

As already discussed, in order for hosts on a network to communicate by using TCP/IP, they must have unique addresses. This number defines the logical network each host belongs to and the host's address on that network. On a private network with, say, three logical networks and 100 nodes on each network, addressing is not a particularly complex task. On a network on the scale of the Internet, however, addressing is very complex.

Between them, these organizations ensure that there are no IP address space conflicts and that the assignment of addresses is carefully managed.

If you are connecting a system to the Internet, you need to get a valid registered IP address from one of these organizations. Alternatively, you can obtain an address from your ISP (Internet Service Provider). Because of the nature of their business, ISPs have large blocks of IP addresses that they can then use to assign to their clients. If you need a registered IP address, getting one from an ISP will almost certainly be a simpler process than going through a regional numbers authority. In fact, most people get their addresses from ISPs. Some ISPs' plans actually include blocks of registered IP addresses, working on the principle that businesses are going to want some kind of permanent presence on the Internet. Of course, if you discontinue your service with the ISP, you will no longer be able to use the IP address they provided.

Private address ranges

To provide flexibility in addressing and to prevent an incorrectly configured network from polluting the Internet, certain address ranges are set aside for private use. These address ranges are called *private ranges* because they are designated for use only on private networks. These addresses are special because Internet routers are configured to ignore any packets they see that use these addresses. This means that if a network "leaks" onto the Internet, it won't make it any farther than the first router it encounters.

Three ranges are defined in RFC 1918; one each from Classes A, B, and C. You can use whichever range you want, although the Class A and Class B address ranges offer more addressing options than does Class C. The address ranges are defined in Table 5.8.

Table 5.8	Private Address Ranges	
Class Mask	**Address Range**	**Default Subnet**
A	10.0.0.0–10.255.255.255	255.0.0.0
B	172.16.0.0–172.31.255.255	255.255.0.0
C	192.168.0.0–192.168.255.255	255.255.255.0

Review and test yourself

The following sections provide you with the opportunity to review what you learned in this chapter and to test yourself.

The facts

For the exam, don't forget these important concepts:

➤ DHCP/BOOTP automatically assigns IP addressing information.

➤ DNS resolves hostnames to IP addresses.

➤ NAT/ICS translates private network addresses into public ones.

➤ WINS resolves NetBIOS names to IP addresses.

➤ SNMP provides network-management facilities on TCP/IP-based networks.

➤ A Class A address uses only the first octet to represent the network portion, a Class B address uses two octets, and a Class C address uses three octets.

➤ Class A addresses span from 1 to 126 with a default subnet mask of 255.0.0.0.

➤ Class B addresses span from 128 to 191 with a default subnet mask of 255.255.0.0.

➤ Class C addresses span from 192 to 223 with a default subnet mask of 255.255.255.0.

➤ The 127 network ID is reserved for the local loopback.

➤ A valid IPv6 address is 42DE:7E55:63F2:21AA:CBD4:D773:CC21:554F.

➤ A public network is a network to which anyone can connect, such as the Internet.

➤ A private network is any network to which access is restricted. Reserved IP addresses are 10.0.0.0, 172.16.0.0, and 192.168.0.0.

Practice exam

Question 1

What is the function of ARP?
- ○ A. It resolves IP addresses to MAC addresses.
- ○ B. It resolves NetBIOS names to IP addresses.
- ○ C. It resolves WINS addresses to DNS addresses.
- ○ D. It resolves hostnames to IP addresses.

The correct answer is A. The function of ARP is to resolve IP addresses to MAC addresses. Answer B is incorrect; the responsibility for resolving NetBIOS names to IP addresses is a function of WINS. Answer C is invalid. Resolving hostnames to IP addresses is a function of DNS, thus, answer D is incorrect.

Question 2

As the network administrator you decide to block port **80**. Which of the following services will be unavailable for network users?
- ○ A. DNS
- ○ B. POP3
- ○ C. FTP
- ○ D. HTTP

The correct answer is D. This is correct because the HTTP service uses port 80, so blocking port 80 will prevent users from using the HTTP service. Answer A is incorrect as DNS uses port 53; answer B is also incorrect, as POP3 uses port 110, and finally FTP (answer C) is incorrect as it uses port 21.

Question 3

Which of the following addresses is a Class B address?
- ○ A. 129.16.12.200
- ○ B. 126.15.16.122
- ○ C. 211.244.212.5
- ○ D. 193.17.101.27

The correct answer is A. Class B addresses fall into the range 128 to 191. Therefore, answer A is the only one of the addresses listed that falls into that range. Answer B is a Class A address, and answers C and D are both Class C IP addresses.

Question 4

You are the administrator of a small organization. All the workstations used in the office are Windows-based systems, and the server is a Windows 2000 Server system. Presently, the only Internet access is from a single PC that uses a modem, but your manager has asked you to get cable Internet access and share the connection with all the other workstations on the network. Which of the following services might you use to accomplish this?

○ A. SNMP
○ B. ICS
○ C. DNS
○ D. WINS

Answer B is correct, as ICS allows a single Internet connection to be shared among multiple computers. None of the other services mentioned are used to share an Internet connection.

Question 5

Which of the following port ranges is described as "well known"?

○ A. 0 to 1023
○ B. 1024 to 49151
○ C. 49152 to 65535
○ D 65535 to 78446

Answer A is correct, as well-known ports are defined in the range 0 to 1023. None of the other answers are referred to as the well-known ports.

Question 6

> You are called into troubleshoot a problem whereby two workstations on a network are unable to resolve hostnames to IP address. The network does not use a DNS server. What can you do to correct the problem?
>
> ○ A. Edit the LMHOSTS file on the server.
>
> ○ B. Edit the LMHOSTS file on the workstations.
>
> ○ C. Edit the HOSTS file on the server.
>
> ○ D. Edit the HOSTS file on the workstations.

Answer D is correct as the HOSTS file on workstations can be used to resolve hostnames to the IP address when a DNS server is not used in a network. Answers A and B are incorrect as LMHOSTS is a text file used to manually configure NetBIOS to IP resolution. Answer C is incorrect as the HOSTS file resides on the workstations.

Question 7

> You have been tasked with temporarily disabling Telnet access for external users. Which is the best way to accomplish this?
>
> ○ A. Block port 53 on the corporate firewall.
>
> ○ B. Block port 23 on the corporate firewall.
>
> ○ C. Uninstall the Telnet service.
>
> ○ D. Configure ICS to ignore client-initiated Telnet requests.

The correct answer is B. By blocking port 23, you can disable the Telnet service. Answer A is incorrect as port 53 is used by DNS. Uninstalling the Telnet service (answer C) is not a practical solution and D is an invalid answer.

Question 8

> Which of the following layer 4 protocols is used to provide connectionless service?
>
> ○ A. UDP
>
> ○ B. TCP
>
> ○ C. IP
>
> ○ D. FTP

Answer A is correct; UDP provides connectionless service and operates at layer 4 or the transport layer of the OSI model. TCP also operates at layer 4 but provides connection-oriented service. None of the other options function at the transport layer.

Question 9

Which of the following protocols provides the security for HTTPS?

○ A. HTTP

○ B. SSL

○ C. Telnet

○ D. TCP

Answer B is correct as the secure socket layer protocol is used to provide security for HTTPS. None of the other answers are valid.

Question 10

Which of the following best describes the function of the default gateway?

○ A. Provides the route for destinations outside of the local subnet.

○ B. Allows a single Internet connection to be used by several users.

○ C. Identifies the local subnet and formulates a routing table.

○ D. Used to communicate in a multiple-platform environment.

The correct answer is A. The default gateway allows systems on one local subnet to access those on another. None of the other descriptions define the function of a default gateway.

Want to know more?

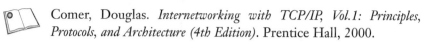 Comer, Douglas. *Internetworking with TCP/IP, Vol.1: Principles, Protocols, and Architecture (4th Edition)*. Prentice Hall, 2000.

Sheldon, Thomas. *McGraw-Hill's Encyclopedia of Networking and Telecommunications*. McGraw-Hill Professional Publishing, 2001.

Tulloch, Mitch. *Microsoft Encyclopedia of Networking* (with CD-ROM). Microsoft Press, 2000.

6

WAN Technologies, Remote Access, and Security Protocols

. . . .

Objectives

2.11 Identify the basic characteristics (for example, speed, capacity, and media) of the following WAN technologies:

- ✓ Packet switching versus circuit switching
- ✓ Integrated Services Digital Network (ISDN)
- ✓ Fiber Distributed Data Interface (FDDI)
- ✓ Asynchronous Transfer Mode (ATM)
- ✓ Frame relay
- ✓ Synchronous Optical Networking/Synchronous Digital Hierarchy (SONET/SDH)
- ✓ T1/E1
- ✓ T3/E3
- ✓ OC-*x*

2.12 Define the functions of the following remote access protocols and services:

- ✓ Remote Access Service (RAS)
- ✓ Point-to-Point Protocol (PPP)
- ✓ Point-to-Point Tunneling Protocol (PPTP)
- ✓ Independent Computing Architecture (ICA)

2.13 Identify the following security protocols and describe their purposes and functions:

✓ Internet Protocol Security (IPSec)

✓ Layer 2 Tunneling Protocol (L2TP)

✓ Secure Sockets Layer (SSL)

✓ Kerberos

3.7 Given a remote connectivity scenario Internet Protocol (IP), Internetwork Packet Exchange (IPX), dial-up, Point-to-Point Protocol over Ethernet (PPoE), authentication, and physical connectivity, configure the connection.

What you need to know

✓ Identify the various characteristics of WAN technologies.

✓ Identify the functions and characteristics of various remote access protocols.

✓ Identify the functions and characteristics of various security protocols.

✓ Identify the technologies needed to establish remote connectivity.

Introduction

There are many technologies used to create today's Wide Area Networks (WANs). Each of these technologies has advantages and disadvantages, making some of them well suited for certain environments and completely impractical in others. Each of the technologies varies in terms of media, speed, availability, and cost. This chapter examines each of these WAN technologies and the protocols that are used with them.

WAN technologies

Many of today's network environments are not restricted to a single location or LAN. Instead, many of these networks span great distances, becoming Wide Area Networks (WANs). When they do, hardware and software are needed to connect these networks. This section reviews the characteristics of various WAN technologies, starting with the oldest of them all, modems.

Dial-up modem connections

Those new to IT are far more likely to see a modem used to access the Internet than they are to see a modem used to create a WAN. However, a WAN created over a standard modem is all that is needed in some network environments—particularly those where budget constraints dictate the technologies used.

 Modem WAN links are inexpensive and easy to implement compared to other WAN connectivity methods.

Those that have worked with modems are well aware that the biggest drawback of the modem connection is the speed. The connection is generally limited to a 56Kbps transfer rate—far too slow for many business applications. In reality, actual speeds are even slow, with the FCC limiting speeds to 53Kbps in most areas.

Having said that, in parts of the world where local calls are free (such as North America), modem links can provide an inexpensive WAN solution where there would otherwise be no WAN connectivity at all.

All that is needed to create the modem WAN link is a phone line and a modem at each end of the link. You also need software to enable, support, and configure the link, but all modern network operating systems include this functionality, so this is not a problem.

Integrated Services Digital Network (ISDN)

ISDN has long been an alternative to the slower modem WAN connections but at a higher cost. ISDN allows the transmission of voice and data over the same physical connection.

ISDN connections are considerably faster than regular modem connections. To access ISDN, a special phone line is required, and this line is usually paid for through a monthly subscription. You can expect these monthly costs to be significantly higher than those for a dial-up modem account.

To establish an ISDN connection, you dial the number for the end of the connection, much as you do with a conventional phone call or modem dial-up connection. A conversation between the sending and receiving devices is then established. The connection is dropped when one end disconnects or hangs up. The line pickup of ISDN is very fast, allowing a connection to be established, or brought up, much more quickly than a conventional phone line.

ISDN has two defined interface standards—Basic Rate Interface (BRI) and Primary Rate Interface (PRI).

BRI

BRI ISDN uses three separate channels, two bearer (B) channels of 64Kbps each and a delta (D) channel of 16Kbps. The B channels carry the voice or data, and the D channel is used for signaling.

The two B channels can be used independently as 64Kbps carriers or they can be combined to provide 128Kbps transfer speeds.

 BRI ISDN channels can be used separately using 64Kbps transfer or combined to provide 128Kbps transfer rates.

PRI

PRI is a form of ISDN that is generally carried over a T1 line and can provide transmission rates of up to 1.544Mbps. PRI is composed of 23 B channels, each providing 64Kbps for data/voice capacity, and one 64Kbps D channel, which is used for signaling. Table 6.1 compares BRI and PRI ISDN.

ISDN is considered a *leased line* because access to ISDN is leased from a service provider.

Table 6.1 BRI and PRI ISDN Comparison		
Characteristic	**PRI**	**BRI**
Speed	1.544Mbps	128Kbps
Channels	23B+D	2B+D
Transmission carrier	T1	PSTN

Be ready to answer questions about the characteristics of both BRI and PRI for the Network+ exam.

T-carrier lines

T-carrier lines are high-speed lines that can be leased from telephone companies. T-carrier lines can support both voice and data transmissions and are often used to create point-to-point private networks. Four types of T-carrier lines are available:

➤ **T1**—T1 lines offer transmission speeds of 1.544Mbps, and they can create point-to-point dedicated digital communication paths. T1 lines have commonly been used for connecting LANs.

➤ **T2**—T2 leased lines offers transmission speeds of 6.312Mbps. They accomplish this by using 96 64Kbps B channels.

➤ **T3**—T3 lines offer transmission speeds of up to 44.736Mbps, using 672 64Kbps B channels.

➤ **T4**—T4 lines offer impressive transmission speeds of up to 274.176Mbps by using 4,032 64Kbps B channels.

Of these T-carrier lines, the ones commonly associated with networks and the ones most likely to appear on the Network+ exam are the T1 and T3 lines.

Ensure you know the speeds of the various T-carriers for the Network+ exam.

Fiber Distributed Data Interface (FDDI)

FDDI is an American National Standards Institute (ANSI) topology standard that uses fiber-optic cable and token-passing media access.

FDDI is implemented using both multimode and single-mode fiber cable and can reach transmissions speeds of up to 100Mbps at distances of over two kilometers. FDDI combines the strengths of Token Ring, the speed of Fast Ethernet, and the security of fiber-optic cable. Such advantages make FDDI a strong candidate for creating network backbones and connecting private LANs to create MANs and WANs.

 The Copper Distributed Data Interface (CDDI) standard defines FDDI over copper cable rather than fiber-optic cable. However, the limitations of copper cable—such as increased EMI risk and attenuation—are in effect.

Unlike the regular 802.5 network standard, FDDI uses a dual-ring configuration. The first, or primary, ring is used to transfer the data around the network, and the secondary ring is used for redundancy and fault tolerance; the secondary ring waits to take over if the primary ring fails. If the primary ring fails, the secondary ring kicks in automatically, with no disruption to network users.

 Even though the second ring sits dormant, you can connect network devices to both rings. Network devices that attach to both rings are referred to as *Class A stations*, or dual attached stations (DASs). Network devices that connect to a single ring are called *Class B stations*, or single attached stations (SASs).

FDDI has a few significant advantages, some of which stem directly from the fact that it uses fiber-optic cable as its transmission media. These include a resistance to EMI, the security offered by fiber, and the longer distances available with fiber cable. In addition to the advantages provided by the fiber-optic cable, FDDI itself has a few strong points, including:

➤ **Fault-tolerant design**—By using a dual-ring configuration, FDDI provides some fault tolerance. If one cable fails, the other can be used to transmit the data throughout the network.

➤ **Speed due to the use of multiple tokens**—Unlike the IEEE 802.5 standard, FDDI uses multiple tokens, which increase the overall network speed.

➤ **Beaconing**—FDDI uses beaconing as a built-in error-detection method, making finding faults, such as cable breaks, a lot easier.

Like every technology, there are always a few caveats:

➤ **High cost**—The costs associated with FDDI and the devices and cable needed to implement an FDDI solution are very costly; too costly for many small organizations.

➤ **Implementation difficulty**—FDDI setup and management can be very complex, requiring trained professionals with significant experience to manage and maintain the cable and infrastructure.

Asynchronous Transfer Mode (ATM)

ATM is a packet-switching technology that provides transfer speeds ranging from 1.544Mbps to 622Mbps. It is well suited for a variety of data types, such as voice, data, and video. Using fixed-length packets, or *cells*, that are 53 bytes long, ATM can operate much more efficiently than variable-length-packet packet-switching technologies such as frame relay. Having a fixed-length packet allows ATM to be concerned only with the header information of each packet. It does not need to read every bit of a packet to determine the beginning and end of the packet. ATM's fixed cell length also makes it easily adaptable to other technologies as they develop. Each cell has 48 bytes available for data, with five bytes reserved for the ATM header.

ATM is a circuit-based network technology because it uses a virtual circuit to connect two networked devices. Two types of circuits are used in an ATM network:

➤ **Switched virtual circuits (SVCs)**—SVCs are set up only for the duration of a conversation or data transmission. An SVC is a temporary connection that is dropped when the transmission is complete.

➤ **Permanent virtual circuits (PVCs)**—PVCs are permanently established virtual circuits between two devices.

ATM is compatible with the most widely used and implemented networking media types available today, including single-mode and multimode fiber, coaxial cable, unshielded twisted pair, and shielded twisted pair. Although it can be used over various media, the limitations of some of the media types make them impractical choices. ATM can also operate over other media, including FDDI, T1, T3, SONET, OC-3, and Fiber Channel.

X.25

One of the older WAN technologies is X.25. X.25 is a packet-switching technology. Today, X.25 is not as widely implemented as it once was. X.25's veteran status is both its greatest advantage and its greatest disadvantage. On the upside, X.25 is a global standard that can be found in many places. On the downside, its maximum transfer speed is 56Kbps, which when compared to other technologies in the mid-1970s was fast but almost unusable for most applications on today's networks.

Because X.25 is a packet-switching technology, it uses different routes to get the best possible connection between the sending and receiving device at a given time. As conditions on the network change, such as increased network traffic, so do the routes that the packets take. Consequently, each packet is likely to take a different route to reach its destination during a single communication session. The devices that make it possible to use X.25 service are called *packet assemblers/disassemblers* (PADs). A PAD is required at each end of the X.25 connection.

Frame relay

Frame relay was designed to provide standards for transmitting data packets in high-speed bursts over digital networks, using a public data network service. Frame relay is a packet-switching technology that uses variable-length packets. Essentially, frame relay is a streamlined version of X.25. It uses smaller packet sizes and fewer error-checking mechanisms than X.25, and consequently it has less overhead than X.25.

A frame relay connection is built by using PVCs that establish end-to-end circuits. This means that frame relay is not dependent on the best-route method of X.25. Frame relay offers speeds starting at 56Kbps and can be implemented on T1, T3, and ISDN lines.

SONET/OC-*x* levels

Bell Communications Research developed SONET, a fiber-optic WAN technology that delivers voice, data, and video at speeds in multiples of 51.84Mbps. Bell's main goals in creating SONET were to create a standardized access method for all carriers and to unify different standards around the world. SONET is capable of transmission speeds between 51.84Mbps and 2.488Gbps

One of Bell's biggest accomplishments with SONET was to create a new system that defined data rates in terms of Optical Carrier (OC) levels, as shown in Table 6.2.

Table 6.2 OC Levels and Transmission Rates	
OC Level	**Transmission Rate**
OC-1	51.84Mbps
OC-3	155.52Mbps
OC-12	622.08Mbps
OC-24	1.244Gbps
OC-48	2.488Gbps
OC-192	9.953Gbps

 Synchronous Digital Hierarchy (SDH) is the European counterpart to SONET.

Remote access protocols and services

Today, there are many ways to establish remote access into networks. Some of these include such things as Virtual Private Networks (VPNs) or plain old modem dial-up access. Regardless of the technique used for remote access or the speed at which access is achieved, certain technologies need to be in place in order for the magic to happen. These technologies include the protocols to allow the access to the server and to secure the data transfer after the connection is established. Also necessary are methods of access control that make sure only authorized users are using the remote access features.

All the major operating systems include built-in support for remote access. They provide both the access methods and security protocols necessary to secure the connection and data transfers.

Remote Access Service (RAS)

RAS is a remote access solution included with Windows Server products. RAS is a feature-rich, easy-to-configure, and easy-to-use method of configuring remote access.

 In Windows 2000, Microsoft renamed the RAS service Routing and Remote Access Service (RRAS). The basic RAS functionality, however, is the same as in previous versions of Windows.

Any system that supports the appropriate dial-in protocols, such as PPP, can connect to a RAS server. Most commonly, the clients are Windows systems that use the dial-up networking feature; but any operating system that supports dial-up client software will work. Connection to a RAS server can be made over a standard phone line, using a modem, over a network, or via an ISDN connection.

RAS supports remote connectivity from all the major client operating systems available today, including the following:

➤ Windows for Workgroups–based clients

➤ LAN Manager–based clients

➤ Windows 95–based clients

➤ Windows NT Workstation–based clients

➤ Windows NT Server–based clients

➤ Windows 2000 Professional–based clients

➤ Windows XP Home based clients

➤ Windows XP Professional based clients

➤ Unix-based\Linux clients

➤ Macintosh-based clients

➤ OS/2-based clients

Although the system is called RAS, the underlying technologies that enable the RAS process are dial-up protocols such as Serial Line Internet Protocol (SLIP) and Point-to-Point Protocol (PPP).

SLIP

SLIP was designed to allow data to be transmitted via Transmission Control Protocol/Internet Protocol (TCP/IP) over serial connections in a Unix environment. SLIP did an excellent job, but time proved to be its enemy. SLIP was developed in an atmosphere in which security was not an overriding concern; consequently, SLIP does not support encryption or authentication. It transmits all the data used to establish a connection (username and password) in clear text, which is, of course, dangerous in today's insecure world.

 Clear text simply means that the information is sent unencrypted, and anyone can intercept with a packet capture program and read the data with his or her favorite word processor.

In addition to its inadequate security, SLIP also does not provide error checking or packet addressing, so it can be used only in serial communications. It supports only TCP/IP, and login is accomplished through a terminal window.

Many operating systems still provide at least minimal SLIP support for backward capability to older environments, but SLIP has been replaced by a newer and more secure alternative: PPP. SLIP is still used by some government agencies and large corporations in Unix remote access applications, so you might come across it from time to time.

PPP

PPP is the standard remote access protocol in use today. PPP is actually a family of protocols that work together to provide connection services.

Because PPP is an industry standard, it offers interoperability between different software vendors in various remote access implementations. PPP provides a number of security enhancements compared to regular SLIP, the most important being the encryption of usernames and passwords during the authentication process. PPP allows remote clients and servers to negotiate data encryption methods and authentication methods and support new technologies. PPP even gives administrators the ability to choose which particular local area network (LAN) protocol to use over a remote link. A Windows 2000 administrator can choose among NetBIOS Extended User Interface (NetBEUI), NWLink (Internetwork Packet Exchange/Sequenced Packet Exchange [IPX/SPX]), AppleTalk, or TCP/IP.

PPP can use a variety of LAN protocols to establish a remote link.

During the establishment of a PPP connection between the remote system and the server, the remote server needs to authenticate the remote user and does so by using the PPP authentication protocols. PPP accommodates a number of authentication protocols and it's possible on many systems to configure more than one authentication protocol. The protocol used in the authentication process depends on the security configurations established between the remote user and the server. The following are some of the common authentication protocols used by PPP:

➤ **Challenge Handshake Authentication Protocol (CHAP)**—CHAP is an authentication system that uses the MD5 encryption scheme to secure authentication responses. CHAP is a commonly used protocol, and as the name suggests, anyone trying to connect is challenged for authentication information. When the correct information is supplied, the systems "shake hands," and the connection is established.

➤ **Microsoft Challenge Handshake Authentication Protocol (MS-CHAP)**—MS-CHAP, based on CHAP, was developed to authenticate remote Windows-based workstations. There are two versions of MS-CHAP; the main difference between the two is that MS-CHAP version 2 offers mutual authentication. This means that both the client and the server must prove their identities in the authentication process. Doing so ensures that the client is connecting to the expected server.

➤ **Password Authentication Protocol (PAP)**—PAP is the least secure of the authentication methods because it uses unencrypted passwords. PAP is often not the first choice of protocols used; rather, it is used when more sophisticated types of authentication fail between a server and a workstation.

➤ **Extensible Authentication Protocol (EAP)**—EAP is an extension made to standard PPP. EAP has additional support for a variety of authentication schemes. It is often used with VPNs to add security against brute-force or dictionary attacks.

➤ **Shiva Password Authentication Protocol (SPAP)**—SPAP is an encrypting authentication protocol used by Shiva remote access servers. SPAP offers a higher level of security than other authentication protocols such as PAP, but it is not as secure as CHAP.

 Macintosh users can dial in to a Windows 2000 server by using PPP over AppleTalk Control Protocol (ATCP). ATCP is installed when the AppleTalk protocol is installed, or it can be installed separately.

 If you are working on a network that uses SLIP and run into connectivity problems, try using PPP, as it is more flexible and secure.

PPTP

The function of the Point-to-Point Tunneling Protocol (PPTP) is to create a secure transmission *tunnel* between two points on a network. The tunneling functionality that PPTP provides forms the basis for creating multiprotocol Virtual Private Networks (VPNs), which allow users to access remote networks through a secure connection. PPTP works in conjunction with PPP and as such uses PPP authentication methods including PAP, CHAP, and MS-CHAP.

PPTP uses tunneling to provide secure data transmissions over a public network. In many cases, PPTP is used to create a VPN across the Internet.

To establish a PPTP session between a client and server, a TCP connection known as a *PPTP control connection* is required to create and maintain the communication tunnel. The PPTP control connection exists between the IP address of the PPTP client and the IP address of the PPTP server, using TCP port 1723. It is the function of the PPTP control connection to pass the PPTP control and management messages used to maintain the PPTP communication tunnel between the remote system and the server. Once the PPTP connection is made, it provides a secure channel, or tunnel, using the original PPP connection between the devices.

Independent Computing Architecture (ICA)

The Citrix ICA protocol allows client systems to access and run applications on a server, using the resources of the server, with only the user interface, keystrokes, and mouse movement being transferred between the client and server computers. In effect, although you are working at a remote computer, the system functions as if you were physically sitting at the server itself. Such technology is often referred to as *thin client* because only a very small piece of software is needed on the client system.

Because ICA requires only minimal traffic back and forth between the client and the server, the connection is not bandwidth intensive, thus allowing clients to simultaneously use ICA. In addition, processing is performed on the server rather than on the client workstation. This enables client systems to use applications they would not normally be able to run. For example, using ICA, it would be possible for a user on a 486 computer with only 16MB of RAM to run the latest Office suite or a complex graphics system. Doing so would be impossible using only the resources of the client system.

ICA is platform independent. It provides client software for all the major operating systems, including Windows, Macintosh, and Linux, and it even supports handheld devices.

Security protocols

Any discussion of remote access is sure to include security, and for a good reason: Remote access opens your network to remote users. Although you'd like to think that only authorized users would try to connect from remote locations, the reality is that an equal number of illegitimate users will probably attempt to connect. Because many of the methods used to establish remote access are over public networks, securing the data you send and the points at which you connect is an important consideration. A significant element of this security is encryption.

Encryption is the process of encoding data so that it can be securely sent over remote connections. As well as encrypting the data itself, the usernames and passwords used to gain access to the remote network are also typically encrypted. In practical terms, *encryption* is the process of encoding data using a mathematical algorithm that makes it difficult for unauthorized users to read the data if they are able to intercept it. The algorithm used in the encryption is actually a mathematical value known as a *key*. The key is required in order to read the encrypted data. Encryption techniques use public and private keys; public keys can be shared and private keys cannot.

IP Security (IPSec)

IPSec was created by the Internet Engineering Task Force (IETF) and can be used on both IPv4 and IPv6 networks. It is designed to encrypt data during communication between two computers. The function of IPSec is to ensure that data on a network cannot be viewed, accessed, or modified by those who should not have access to it. IPSec provides security for both internal and external networks. It might seem that protection on an internal network is less necessary than on an external network; however, much of the data you send across networks has little or no protection, allowing unwanted eyes to access it.

IPSec provides three key security services:

➤ **Data verification**—It verifies that the data received is from the intended source.

➤ **Protection from data tampering**—It ensures that the data has not been tampered with and changed between the sending and receiving devices.

➤ **Private transactions**—It ensures that the data sent between the sending and receiving devices is unreadable by any other devices.

IPSec operates at the network layer of the Open Systems Interconnect (OSI) model and provides security for protocols that operate at higher layers of the OSI model. Thus, by using IPSec, you can secure practically all TCP/IP-related communications.

Layer 2 Forwarding (L2F)

L2F is a proprietary protocol and technology that was developed by Cisco Systems. It allows tunneling to be utilized as a connection method over insecure networks. L2F is still around today; it has been folded into new implementations of tunneling protocols, and it is included in the new and improved L2TP.

Layer 2 Tunneling Protocol (L2TP)

The *Layer 2 Tunneling Protocol (L2TP)* is a combination of PPTP and Cisco's L2F technology. L2TP utilizes tunneling to deliver data. It authenticates the client in a two-phase process: It first authenticates the computer and then the user. By authenticating the computer, it prevents the data from being intercepted, changed, and returned to the user in what is known as a *man-in-the-middle attack*. L2TP assures both parties that the data they are receiving is the data sent by the originator.

L2TP operates at the data-link layer, making it protocol independent. This means that an L2TP connection can support protocols such as IPX and AppleTalk.

L2TP and PPTP are both tunneling protocols, so you might be wondering which you should use. Here is a quick list of some of the advantages of each, starting with PPTP:

➤ PPTP has been around the longest; it offers more interoperability than L2TP.

➤ PPTP is easier to configure than L2TP because L2TP requires digital certificates.

➤ PPTP has less overhead than L2TP.

The following are some of the advantages of L2TP:

➤ L2TP offers greater security than PPTP.

➤ L2TP supports common public key infrastructure technology.

➤ L2TP provides support for header compression.

Secure Sockets Layer (SSL)

SSL is a security protocol that is used on the Internet. Originally developed by Netscape for use with its Navigator browser, SSL uses public key encryption to establish secure connections over the Internet. SSL provides three key services:

➤ **Server authentication**—SSL allows a user to confirm a server's identity. For example, you can use this ability when you are purchasing something online with a credit card but first want to verify the server's identity.

➤ **Client authentication**—SSL allows a server to confirm a user's identity. This functionality is often used when a server is sending sensitive information—such as banking information or sensitive documents—to a client system and wants to verify the client's identity.

➤ **Encrypted connections**—It is possible to configure SSL to require all information sent between a client and a server to be encrypted by the sending software and decrypted by the receiving software. Doing this establishes private and secure communication between two devices. In addition, SSL has a mechanism to determine whether the data sent has been tampered with or altered in transit.

You can see SSL security on the Web when you access a secure universal resource locator (URL). Secure Web sites begin with `https://` instead of the `http://`. Hypertext Transfer Protocol over SSL (HTTPS) connections require a browser with built-in security features to establish a secure connection.

Kerberos

Sending clear-text unencrypted passwords over a network is never a good idea. The Kerberos network authentication protocol is designed to ensure that the authentication data sent across networks is encrypted and not easily accessed by unwanted users. Its purpose is to provide authentication for client/server applications.

 Kerberos is the default authentication method for Windows 2000 and Windows XP computers and cannot be used with prior Microsoft operating systems.

With Kerberos, the client must prove its identity to the server, and the server must also prove its identity to the client. In this way, the function of Kerberos is to provide a method to verify the identity of a computer system over an insecure network connection.

The security tokens used in Kerberos are known as *tickets*.

SSH

Because Unix- and Linux-based systems are prominent in modern network environments, network administrators face huge security interoperability concerns. Windows-based clients often use Telnet to remotely access Unix/Linux servers. Unfortunately, Telnet is a very insecure remote access method; it sends the entire session including passwords and login information in clear text.

Secure Shell (SSH) provides a secure multiplatform replacement for Telnet. SSH allows users to connect to a remote server, and it encrypts the entire session. SSH has become an IETF standard, and development for SSH now includes a number of operating systems besides Linux and Unix. Using SSH, Windows 9x/NT/2000 as well as Macintosh systems can securely access remote servers.

Configuring remote connectivity

The capability to remotely access networks has become an important part of the modern IT infrastructure. All organizations, from the smallest business to the largest corporation, are taking advantage of the potential that remote network access provides. Therefore, today's network administrators are as likely to be responsible for managing remote network access as they are for LAN access. Configuring and managing remote access requires knowledge of the protocols and procedures involved in establishing a remote connection.

The following sections explore some of the common considerations in configuring a remote connection, including a discussion of physical connections, protocols (which facilitate the connection), software (which establishes the connection), the dial-up connection method, and security issues.

Physical connections

There are many ways to connect to a remote network. Some, such as the plain old telephone system (POTS), offer a direct connection between you and the remote host. Others, such as cable and Digital Subscriber Lines (DSL), allow you to connect, but the connection occurs over a public network (the Internet), which can bring additional considerations such as authentication and security problems. The methods that can be used to establish a remote connection are discussed in detail in Chapter 8, "Fault Tolerance, Disaster Recovery, VLANs, and NAS." For that reason, only a brief recap is included in this list:

➤ **Public switched telephone network (PSTN)**—The PSTN offers by far the most popular method of remote connectivity. A modem and a POTS line allow for inexpensive and reliable, if not fast, remote access.

➤ **Integrated Services Digital Network (ISDN)**—ISDN is a dial-up technology that works much like the PSTN, but instead of using analog signals to carry the data, ISDN uses digital signals. This makes it faster than the PSTN.

➤ **Cable**—In an effort to take advantage of the increasing demand for high-speed Internet access, cable TV providers now offer broadband Internet access over the same connection that is used to carry cable TV signals.

➤ **DSL**—DSL services are the telecom companies' broadband offering. *x*DSL (that is, the family of DSL services) comes in many varieties, and as with cable, you need a special modem in order to use it.

➤ **Satellite**—Perhaps the least popular of the connection methods discussed here, satellite provides wireless Internet access, although in some scenarios a PSTN connection is also required for upstream access. Of the technologies discussed in this section, satellite is the least suitable for remote access.

Protocols

When you have decided on the physical aspect of the connection, the next consideration is the protocols that allow you to make a connection to the remote server.

To facilitate a connection between a remote system and a remote access server, common protocols must be used between the systems. Two types of protocols are required to establish a remote connection. You first need to have the protocols that communicate at the data-link layer, including the following:

➤ **Point-to-Point Protocol (PPP)**—PPP is actually a family of protocols that work together to provide connection services. PPP allows remote clients and servers to negotiate authentication between devices. PPP can employ a variety of encryption methods to secure transmissions.

➤ **Serial Line Internet Protocol (SLIP)**—SLIP is an older connection protocol than PPP, and it was originally designed to allow data to be transmitted via Transmission Control Protocol/Internet Protocol

(TCP/IP) over serial connections in a Unix environment. Unfortunately, SLIP does not support encryption or authentication and therefore has largely fallen out of favor. If you have users that employ SLIP to connect from remote systems, you should move them to PPP connections as soon as possible.

➤ **Point-to-Point Protocol over Ethernet (PPPoE)**—PPPoE is a method of using PPP connections over Ethernet. Using PPPoE and a broadband connection such as xDSL or cable Internet access, it is possible for individual users to have authenticated access to high-speed data networks, which provides an efficient way to create a separate connection to a remote server for each user. This strategy allows Internet access and billing on a per-user basis rather than a per-site basis. Users accessing PPPoE connections require the same information as required with standard dial-up phone accounts, including a username and password combination. As with a dial-up PPP service, an Internet service provider (ISP) will most likely automatically assign configuration information such as the IP address, subnet mask, default gateway, and DNS server information.

After a data link has established the connection between the devices, other network-layer and transport-layer protocols are required to facilitate signal transmission. Examples of these protocols include the following:

➤ **TCP/IP**—TCP/IP is the most widely used protocol today, and it is the protocol that is most commonly used to configure remote connectivity. As with access for systems on a LAN, remote access requires unique TCP/IP addressing. The most common way for remote clients to get IP information from the remote server is through automatic assignment from a DHCP server. However, it is possible to manually assign IP addresses from a static pool of addresses that have been assigned to the remote access server by the network administrator.

➤ **Internetwork Packet Exchange/Sequenced Packet Exchange (IPX/SPX)**—Like TCP/IP, IPX/SPX is a fully routable protocol, and it can therefore be used for connecting to a remote system. However, just as TCP/IP is replacing IPX/SPX on LANs, it is also replacing IPX/SPX on remote access links.

Generally speaking, TCP/IP is the protocol suite to use for remote access. However, popular remote access solutions such as Microsoft Remote Access Service (RAS) can accommodate connections established using IPX/SPX, so you should be aware of the fact that IPX/SPX can be used.

Software

With the physical connection and the protocols in place, you are almost ready to establish a connection. You just need some software to make the magic happen.

To establish a remote connection, the remote system typically requires software that initiates contact to the remote server. This software can take many forms: In some Windows client systems, for example, a remote connection can be configured by using dial-up networking.

In addition to the client-side software that initiates the remote connection, server-side software that is responsible for answering the request is required. The server responding to the remote access requests is referred to as the *remote access server*. On Windows server platforms, the network service responsible for handling remote client connections is the Remote Access Service.

 Many remote access products are available; however, Windows RAS is the most likely of these products to appear on the Network+ exam.

Dial-up access

As noted previously, dial-up is one of the most popular methods of gaining remote access to a LAN. There was a time when dial-up referred to using a modem on a POTS line, but today the term is applied generally to any connection that must be manually established to a remote system. For example, the establishment of a virtual private network (VPN) connection to a remote system over a cable Internet connection is considered a dial-up connection.

The specifics of configuring dial-up access to a remote server depend on the client system being used. Linux, Macintosh, and the various Windows client systems all have different methods and means of connecting to a remote server via a dial-up connection. Instead of individually documenting the procedures for configuring each of the respective client systems, the following list identifies the configuration information and hardware required by all client systems to access a remote server using a dial-up connection:

➤ **Hardware**—To access the remote server, the client system has to have the correct hardware installed to make the connection. Most dial-up remote connections require a modem on the client and a modem on the server system.

➤ **Phone number, hostname, or IP address**—To connect to a remote access server over a dial-up connection, you need to have the phone number of the remote server, the IP address, or the hostname.

➤ **Transmission protocols**—You need to choose the compatible protocol used by the remote server—NetBIOS Extended User Interface (NetBEUI), TCP/IP, or IPX/SPX. If the server is using TCP/IP, you might need to configure the IP configuration information manually, or this information might be assigned through a remote DHCP server.

➤ **Security**—On the client system, you might need to establish security information so it can be authenticated by the server. The security information includes a username-and-password combination that will be verified by the remote server, as well as data-encryption options.

➤ **Client connection options**—On the client side, you can configure connection options such as redialing or disconnecting after a certain amount of time.

It would be nice if every time you dialed in to a remote server, it answered, and you were authenticated to the network. Although this happens most of the time, there are times when you just can't connect. If you are unable to establish the remote connection through dial-up, consider the following:

➤ **Verify that the remote access server is operational**—You might be trying to log on to a remote server that is down. This might require a call to the remote network administrator to confirm.

➤ **Verify that you have correct authentication information**—To access the remote access server, you need a valid user account for the remote network and permissions to access the server.

➤ **Confirm that you are calling the correct number or trying to connect to the correct server**—Frequently, the cause of a problem can be traced to something simple. In the case of remote connectivity, this can often be using the wrong phone number or IP address for the remote server.

➤ **Verify local settings**—In order to connect to the remote server, the client system needs to be correctly configured to access the server. These configuration settings include protocol information and compatible security settings.

Review and test yourself

The following sections provide you with the opportunity to review what you learned in this chapter and to test yourself.

The facts

For the exam, don't forget these important concepts:

➤ BRI ISDN uses two B channels of 64Kbps each.

➤ PRI ISDN uses 23 B channels offering 1.5Mbps transfer rates.

➤ T1 lines offer transmission speeds of 1.544Mbps but are more costly than an ISDN solution.

➤ T3 lines offer transmission speeds of 44.736Mbps.

➤ T-carrier lines are used to create point-to-point network connections for private networks.

➤ FDDI uses a dual-ring configuration for fault tolerance.

➤ FDDI uses a token-passing media-access method.

➤ ATM offers transmissions speeds of 1.544Mbps to 622Mbps.

➤ X-25 is restricted to transmission rates of 56Kbps.

➤ SONET can transfer speeds of 51.8Mbps to 2.4Gbps.

➤ When a connection is made to the RAS server, the client is authenticated and the system that is dialing in becomes a part of the network.

➤ RAS supports remote connectivity from all the major client operating systems.

➤ Although the system is called RAS, the underlying technologies that enable the RAS process are dial-up protocols such as PPP and SLIP.

➤ SLIP also does not provide error checking or packet addressing, so it can be used only in serial communications.

➤ PPP provides a number of security enhancements compared to SLIP, the most important being the encryption of usernames and passwords during the authentication process.

➤ Windows 2000 clients natively support SLIP and PPP.

➤ The ICA protocol allows client systems to access and run applications on a server, using the resources of the server, with only the user interface, keystrokes, and mouse movement being transferred between the client and server computers.

➤ IPSec is designed to encrypt data during communication between two computers.

➤ IPSec operates at the network layer of the OSI model and provides security for protocols that operate at higher layers of the OSI model.

➤ L2F allows tunneling to be utilized as a connection method over insecure networks.

➤ L2TP operates at the data-link layer, making it protocol independent.

➤ SSL is a security protocol that is used on the Internet.

➤ Secure Web sites begin with `https://` instead of the `http://`. Hypertext Transfer Protocol over SSL (HTTPS) connections require a browser to establish a secure connection.

➤ Secure SSL connections for Web pages are made through port `443` by default.

➤ Kerberos provides a method to verify the identity of a computer system over an insecure network connection.

➤ The security tokens used in Kerberos are known as *tickets*.

Key terms

➤ PSTN

➤ Modem

➤ ISDN

➤ BRI

➤ PRI

➤ T-carrier

➤ T1/E1

➤ T3/E3

➤ FDDI

➤ ATM

- X.25
- Frame relay
- SONET/OC-*x*
- RAS
- SLIP
- PPP
- CHAP
- MS-CHAP
- PAP
- EAP
- SPAP
- PPTP
- ICA
- Security protocol
- Encryption
- IPSec
- L2F
- L2TP
- SSL
- Kerberos
- SSH
- VPN
- Tickets

Practice exam

Question 1

> Which of the following dial-up protocols can use multiple LAN protocols over a link?
>
> ○ A. PPP
>
> ○ B. SLIP
>
> ○ C. IPX/SPX
>
> ○ D. UDP/TCP

The correct answer is A. The PPP protocol can use multiple LAN protocols such as IPX/SPX, TCP/IP, or NetBEUI.

Question 2

> Which of the following protocols is used with HTTPS?
>
> ○ A. SSH
>
> ○ B. SSL
>
> ○ C. Proxy
>
> ○ D. IPSec

The correct answer is B. HTTPS uses SSL to create secure connections over the Internet. Answer A is incorrect as SSH provides a secure multiplatform replacement for Telnet. Answer C is not valid, and IPSec is designed to encrypt data during communication between two computers.

Question 3

> What is the total bandwidth available when combining all BRI ISDN communication channels?
>
> ○ A. 128Kbps
>
> ○ B. 64Kbps
>
> ○ C. 96Kbps
>
> ○ D. 1,544Kbps

The correct answer is A. BRI ISDN uses two 64Kbps channels which, when combined, offer 128Mbps transfer speeds. None of the other options are valid.

Question 4

As a remote user you need to access your company's private network through the Internet. Which of the following protocols can you use to establish a secure connection?

- ○ A. IPX/SPX
- ○ B. TCP/IP
- ○ C. PPP
- ○ D. PPTP

The correct answer is D. PPTP is used to establish a secure transmission tunnel over an insecure public network such as the Internet. The other protocols mentioned do not provide secure transmissions over a public network.

Question 5

Which of the following is an advantage of ISDN over PSTN?

- ○ A. ISDN is more reliable.
- ○ B. ISDN is cheaper.
- ○ C. ISDN is faster.
- ○ D. ISDN uses fixed-length packets called cells.

The correct answer is C. One clear advantage that ISDN has over the PSTN is its speed. ISDN can combine 64Kbps channels for faster transmission speeds than the PSTN can provide. ISDN is no more or less reliable than the PSTN. ISDN is more expensive than the PSTN. Answer D describes ATM, not ISDN, thus it is not a valid answer.

Question 6

Which of the following technologies requires dial-up access?

- ○ A. FDDI
- ○ B. ISDN
- ○ C. Packet switching
- ○ D. ATM

The correct answer is B. ISDN require dial-up connections to establish communication sessions. The other answers are not valid.

Question 7

> Your company wants to create a secure link between two networks over the Internet. Which of the following protocols would you use to do this?
>
> ○ A. PPP
>
> ○ B. VPN
>
> ○ C. PPTP
>
> ○ D. SLIP

The correct answer is C. To establish the VPN connection between the two networks, you should use PPTP. PPP is a protocol used on dial-up links. A VPN is a type of network, not a protocol. SLIP is not a secure dial-up protocol.

Question 8

> Which of the following protocols is used in thin-client computing?
>
> ○ A. ICA
>
> ○ B. PPP
>
> ○ C. PPTP
>
> ○ D. RAS

The correct answer is A. The ICA protocol is used in thin-client networking, where only screen, keyboard, and mouse inputs are sent across the line. PPP is a dial-up protocol used over serial links. PPTP is a technology used in VPNs, and RAS is a remote access service.

Question 9

> Which of the following URLs is using SSL?
>
> ○ A. **http:ssl//www.comptia.org**
>
> ○ B. **http://www.comptia.org**
>
> ○ C. **httpssl://www.comptia.org**
>
> ○ D. **https://www.comptia.org**

The correct answer is D. You can identify when SSL is used by the s in the URL (in this case https://www.comptia.org). Answer B is a valid HTTP URL, but it is not secure. None of the other answers are correct.

Question 10

In a remote access scenario, what function does PPP serve?

○ A. It is a secure technology that allows information to be securely down-loaded from a Web site.

○ B. It is a dial-up protocol used over serial links.

○ C. It is a technology that allows a secure tunnel to be created through a public network.

○ D. It provides a public key/private key exchange mechanism.

The correct answer is B. PPP is a protocol that allows for dial-up connections over serial links. Answer A describes SSL; answer C describes a VPN, and answer D describes PKI.

Want to know more?

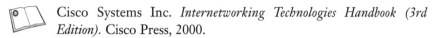 Cisco Systems Inc. *Internetworking Technologies Handbook (3rd Edition)*. Cisco Press, 2000.

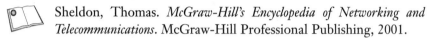 Sheldon, Thomas. *McGraw-Hill's Encyclopedia of Networking and Telecommunications*. McGraw-Hill Professional Publishing, 2001.

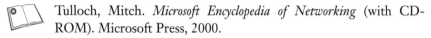 Tulloch, Mitch. *Microsoft Encyclopedia of Networking* (with CD-ROM). Microsoft Press, 2000.

Network Operating Systems and Clients

Objectives

3.1 Identify the basic capabilities (that is, client support, interoperability, authentication, file and print services, application support, and security) of the following server operating systems:

✓ Unix/Linux

✓ NetWare

✓ Windows

✓ Macintosh

3.2 Identify the basic capabilities of client workstations (that is, client connectivity, local security mechanisms, and authentication).

3.11 Given a network configuration, select the appropriate NIC and network configuration settings (DHCP, DNS, WINS, protocols, NetBIOS/hostname, and so on).

4.4 Given specific parameters, configure a client to connect to the following servers:

✓ Unix/Linux

✓ NetWare

✓ Windows

✓ Macintosh

What you need to know

✓ Identify the main features and characteristics of network operating systems.

✓ Identify the main features and characteristics of client operating systems.

✓ Configure network settings.

✓ Configure client systems to access network and server resources.

Introduction

Network operating systems represent some of the most powerful and complex software available today. As a network administrator, it is your responsibility to maintain and manage these operating systems and ensure they consistently provide the network services they were designed to. Even though the Network+ exam does not require that you be an expert in the operating systems discussed in this chapter, a basic knowledge of each is required.

In addition to working with network operating systems, network administrators are also called upon to manage the other side of the OS equation, *client operating systems*. This chapter outlines the characteristics of the client operating systems that are most commonly used today and discusses how these are used with the network operating systems.

The information described in this chapter is not intended to provide a complete tutorial in any of the operating systems discussed. Rather, this chapter provides an overview of each operating system, highlighting the areas you can expect to know for the Network+ exam.

Network operating systems

Early network operating systems provided just the basics in terms of network services, such as file and printer sharing. Today's network operating systems offer a far broader range of network services; some of these services are used in almost every network environment and others are used in only a few.

Despite the complexity of operating systems, the basic function and purpose of a network operating system is straightforward: to provide services to the network. Network operating systems provide several services to the client systems on the network. The following are some of the most common of these services:

➤ Authentication services

➤ File and print services

➤ Web server services

➤ Firewall and proxy services

➤ Dynamic Host Configuration Protocol (DHCP) and Domain Name System (DNS) services

These are just a few of a large number of services that a network operating system can provide. When you take the time to list all the aspects of network operating systems, you gain an appreciation for their complexity and the many functions they are designed to perform.

The following sections discuss the major operating systems currently in use and how each of them deals with basic services such as authentication and file and print services.

Windows NT 4

Windows NT 4 is the network operating system that was introduced following the Windows NT 3.51 operating system. Because Windows NT 3.51 is not found in many organizations today and is not on the Network+ exam, this chapter does not discuss it. You will, however, know if you are working on a Windows NT 3.51 server because the graphics might look unfamiliar. Windows NT 3.51 uses the graphical interface of Windows 3.x, whereas Windows NT 4 and later versions have the look of the Windows 95/98/Me type of desktop.

Two versions of Windows NT 4 are available: *Windows NT Workstation* and *Windows NT Server*. The former is designed for desktop use, and the latter is for servers. Windows NT Workstation is a scaled-down version of Windows NT Server. It is based on the same code as Windows NT Server, and the two versions share a similar look and similar features. Unlike Windows 95 client systems, which accommodate games and older DOS-based programs, Windows NT Workstation was built for reliability and security.

Although Windows NT 4 has been superseded by *Windows 2000* and *Windows XP,* many servers are still operating with Windows NT 4. Microsoft is providing less and less support for Windows NT now because it hopes that organizations will make the switch to the new generation of Windows products. Still, Windows NT continues to function adequately for many organizations, making the likelihood that you will encounter Windows NT very great.

Domains and workgroups

One of the key considerations for anyone installing or working with Windows NT 4 is whether to use a workgroup or domain model. *Domains* and *workgroups* are logical groups of computers that are created for the purposes of administration and resource access. A Windows NT 4 system can be configured as either a member of a workgroup or a member of a domain.

Workgroups are used in small networks of usually no more than 10 computers. In a workgroup scenario, a dedicated, or centralized, network server is nonexistent, and each system in the workgroup can offer services to and use services from other systems in the workgroup. Security in a workgroup model is handled by each system; that is, each computer has its own list of users who can access the system. There is no centralized database of user accounts, which results in a situation that can lead to a variety of administrative headaches. For example, changing user passwords and making sure that they are changed on each system in the workgroup can be an administrative nightmare. Also, when a new user joins the company, an account must be created on every system to which the user needs access.

Domains are very different from workgroups. In a Windows environment, a *domain model* is a network model that uses a centralized approach to resource management, meaning that computers within the domain can access data and network services from a central location. A Windows NT server that is configured in the domain model can be set up to perform three roles on the network:

> **Primary domain controller (PDC)**—The PDC is the main server and is responsible for the majority of server-related tasks on the network, including authentication and managing the network user account information. A Windows NT domain can have only a single PDC, and every effort should be made to ensure that it is running at all times. Without a PDC, certain administrative tasks, such as adding users, cannot be completed. If the PDC is the only Windows NT server system on the network, its role is even more important because without it, users are unable to log on.

> **Backup domain controller (BDC)**—As a company grows, its reliance on a single server can create a problem. A single server represents a single point of failure and in many cases, cannot handle the workload for an entire network. That is where a BDC comes in. The BDC holds a second copy of the information that is stored on the PDC, including the database of user accounts and other important network information. Having duplicate information provides a level of fault tolerance for the network and a second server to help with the network load. If the PDC goes offline for any reason, the BDC holds the information necessary to authenticate users and keeps the network functioning. Depending on the size of the network, there might be several BDCs on a single network. If the PDC on a network fails, a BDC can be promoted to a PDC through a simple process. After the problem with the PDC has been corrected and the PDC has been brought back online, the BDC's role can be reversed again. Whereas a domain can have only a single PDC, many BDCs can be used.

> **Member server**—The member server does not take part in domain authentication and does not hold a copy of the user account database. Member servers provide file, print, and application services.

Windows NT 4 authentication

Windows NT is a secure operating system in that users have to provide a user ID and password in order to gain access to the system. When a user logs on, the information is compared with a database of user information that is maintained on the server. If the user ID and password are valid, restrictions such as logon times and workstation restrictions are compared. If there are no restrictions in force, a token is generated by the system and passed back to the authentication system, which then allows the user access.

The token created for the user contains information such as the user's ID (which is expressed as a number called a *security identifier [SID]* rather than the user's name) and any group memberships that the user holds. Each time a user attempts to access a protected resource, the token is compared against the access control list for that resource. If you add a user to a group after the user has logged on, the user must log off and log back on again in order for the change to take effect.

Windows NT 4 file and print services

As with other operating systems, file and print services are at the core of the services offered by Windows NT 4. Any folder on any drive on the server can be made available to clients through a process called *sharing*. Sharing involves designating a certain folder to be available to clients and then setting up the parameters that govern how it is shared. These parameters can include a share name (which can be different from the folder name), the number of users who are able to connect to the share, and the security of the folder.

The security capabilities of the folder depend on which file system the disk that holds the folder is using. Folders on a *File Allocation Table (FAT)* partition can be secured at the share point only, and the rights assigned at that point are in effect from that point in the directory structure down. FAT volumes do not offer any file-level security, which is why in environments where more security is required, *New Technology File System (NTFS)* is used. With folders on NTFS partitions, it is possible to combine or choose the share-level permissions with additional NTFS permissions, which can then be assigned to each file or directory.

Print services are provided in much the same way. Any printer that is defined on the server system can be shared with users.

Windows NT 4 application support

Windows NT 4 has been around for a number of years, and it is largely responsible for putting a dent in the vast market share that other operating systems, such as Novell NetWare, have enjoyed. Its proliferation has led to the development of a huge number of third-party applications, covering every need from the most basic to the most complex. If you have a Windows NT 4 server and are looking for a certain type of application, you are likely to have a great deal of choice.

Nearly every application that an organization could want is provided with Windows NT 4, including DHCP and DNS server programs, a Web server application, a backup utility, performance-monitoring and system-management utilities, and even (perhaps inappropriately for a server system) a selection of games. Windows NT 4 also includes various products for integration with other operating systems, so it is one of the most comprehensive single-package network operating system offerings available.

Windows NT 4 security

The Windows server platforms, like the other network operating systems, provide a range of security options for securing the resources on a network. The following are some of the security areas commonly used on Windows-based servers. Note that this list is far from being comprehensive of the security features in Windows NT 4 servers. To provide such a list could take an entire book. Instead, the list provides the highlights, to help you answer the security-related questions on the Network+ exam.

➤ **Object-based security**—Object-based security refers to the ability to establish access control over specific devices and resources on the server. To be able to access a resource such as a printer, users must have permissions to access it. Permissions to devices, resources, or files on the network can be granted to an individual user, or they can be assigned to entire groups of users.

➤ **User authentication**—To access a Windows-based network and the resources on the network, a user needs a logon username and password. Windows uses a feature known as *single sign-on*, which allows a user to log on to the network domain once and authenticate to any computer in the domain.

 Watch the Cap Locks. To log on to a Windows NT 4 system, a valid username and password are required. The password is case sensitive, but the username is not.

➤ **File and directory security**—Windows server systems can use NTFS. NTFS has many advantages over the FAT file system found in Windows desktop systems. NTFS allows file-level security, meaning that individual files, such as spreadsheets or documents, can require access permissions.

Although Windows NT 4 was a major product in the IT landscape for a number of years, Microsoft has built on the success of Windows NT by introducing a new and updated version, Windows 2000, which is discussed in the following section.

Windows NT 4 and Windows 2000 file system security

Both Windows NT 4 and Windows 2000 use the New Technology File System (NTFS) to provide file system security. Rights can be assigned to users, groups, and some special entities, which include the "everyone" assignment. Table 7.1 describes the basic file permissions that can be used with NTFS on Windows NT 4 and Windows 2000.

 NOTE Windows 2000 is discussed in detail in the next section. The information on file permission has been presented here as it applies to both Windows NT 4 and Windows 2000.

Table 7.1 File Permissions with NTFS on Windows NT 4 and Windows 2000	
Right	**Description**
Full Control	Provides all rights
Modify	Allows files to be modified
Read & Execute	Allows files to be read and executed (that is, run)
List Folder Contents	Allows the files in a folder to be listed
Read	Allows a file to be read
Write	Allows a file to be written to

An added complexity to file system security on Windows platforms is that the shares created to allow users to access folders across the network can also be assigned a set of permissions. Although these permissions are quite basic (Full Control, Change, Read and No Access), they must be considered because they can be combined with NTFS permissions. The rule when this situation occurs is that the most restrictive permissions assignment applies. For example, if a user connects through a share with Read permission and then tries to access a file to which she has the NTFS Full Control right, the actual permissions would be Read. The most restrictive right (in this case, Read) overrides the other permissions assignment.

 ALERT On the Network+ exam, you might be asked to identify valid and invalid file permissions for certain platforms.

Windows 2000

Windows 2000 was the follow-up to Windows NT 4, and quickly established itself as a reliable and robust operating system. Windows 2000 is built on the success of its predecessor and offers many improvements and advancements. In many ways, Windows 2000 functions in the same way as Windows NT 4. In others, it functions very differently.

The biggest difference between the two operating systems is the addition of *Active Directory*—a directory services system that provides improved user account management capabilities—in Windows 2000. Many tasks have been streamlined in Windows 2000, and additional wizards are available to assist with administrative tasks.

Three versions of Windows 2000 are available for server platforms: Windows 2000 Server, Advanced Server, and Datacenter Server. There are some subtle and not-so-subtle differences between these respective offerings, such as processor support and cost. Windows 2000 is also available as a workstation operating system: Windows 2000 Professional. Like Windows NT Workstation is to Windows NT Server, Windows 2000 Professional has the majority of features, capabilities, and strengths of Windows 2000 Server products but omits the server-type network services and capabilities.

Windows 2000 Active Directory and domains

Many administrators have found user management in Windows NT awkward, especially in large organizations. In the past, NetWare had the preferred method of account management for large numbers of user accounts. For this reason, Microsoft introduced its new approach to user and account management in Windows 2000 platforms—Active Directory. Active Directory is a cornerstone concept for Windows 2000 because it significantly affects the layout and makeup of a Windows 2000–based network.

Active Directory allows network objects such as users and groups to be placed into logical areas of a database. This database can then be distributed among various servers, all of which participate in the Active Directory structure. Because all the network object information is placed in a single database, albeit a distributed one, it can be used by any network application or subsystem, eliminating the need for duplicate information.

Active Directory obviates the old Windows NT PDC and BDC network layout. Instead, servers on a Windows 2000 network can either be domain controllers or member servers. Domain controllers are servers that have Active Directory installed and configured on them. Domain controllers store user account information and provide network authentication. Unlike a Windows NT domain, which can have only a single PDC, a Windows 2000 domain can have several domain controllers, with each one having a read/write copy of the Active Directory database. For fault-tolerant reasons, this is a good strategy to employ.

 Active Directory is a complex subject, and the information presented here is only intended as a brief overview. For the Network+ exam this is all that is needed, but for the real world you will need to do more studying. For further information on Active Directory, refer to Microsoft's Web site (**www.microsoft.com**).

Member servers are not involved in the authentication of network users and do not take part in the Active Directory replication process. Member servers are commonly employed as file and print servers, or with additional software, as database servers, firewalls, or servers for other important network services.

Windows 2000 authentication

The Windows authentication process allows users logging on to the network to access all network resources to which they have permissions. This means it is necessary to log on only once to access all the resources on the network. In Windows 2000, two processes are required for a successful logon:

> **Interactive logon**—This logon is used to confirm the identity of the person logging on to the domain or local system.

> **Network authentication**—This logon is used to verify the user's identification for access to network resources.

A few industry-supported types of authentication are used in Windows 2000. The type of authentication used depends on what is being accessed. Table 7.2 lists some of the various authentication methods.

Table 7.2 Authentication Methods	
Authentication Method	**Description**
Kerberos version 5	Kerberos is an authentication mode that is used for interactive logon and the default method of network authentication for services.
NTLM	NTLM is used for authentication in a mixed-mode network configuration. *Mixed-mode network* is a Microsoft term that describes a network that uses a combination of Windows NT and Windows 2000 systems. If a network exclusively uses one or the other, NTLM authentication is not required. An example of NTLM authentication is a Windows NT workstation authenticating to a Windows 2000 Server system.
Secure Sockets Layer/Transport Layer Security (SSL/TLS)	SSL/TLS is an authentication method that is used when a user is attempting to access a secure Web server.

Windows 2000 file and print services

Like Windows NT, Windows 2000 provides file and print services. Similarly to Windows NT, Windows 2000 uses shares to make areas of the disk available to clients. And as in Windows NT, in Windows 2000 these shares can be secured by file permissions if they are resident on NTFS partitions. In addition to these features, which are common in Windows NT, Windows 2000 also includes some new features, such as the following:

> **Disk quotas**—The amount of disk space available to a user can be restricted and managed through disk quotas. This is a useful element of control over disk usage.

> **Encrypting File System (EFS)**—EFS allows files to be encrypted while on the disk, preventing unauthorized access. The main advantage of EFS is that it keeps the files encrypted even if the user or organization loses physical control of the drives, such as with a laptop computer.

> **Distributed File System (DFS)**—DFS allows multiple directories on distributed servers to be represented through a single share point, simplifying access for users and administration.

Another difference between Windows NT and Windows 2000 has to do with the file systems they support. Windows 2000 supports the FAT, FAT32, and NTFS file systems, whereas Windows NT 4 offers only FAT and NTFS.

In addition to its support for FAT32, Windows 2000 introduces a newer version of NTFS, which provides more options and capabilities, including support for Active Directory and increased security options. Remember that Active Directory and other security-related features are available only on NTFS partitions. To convert from FAT or FAT32 to NTFS in Windows 2000, you use the same command, convert.exe, at a command prompt as you do in Windows NT 4. This command has the same considerations in both operating systems in that it cannot be converted back again.

 NOTE It is recommended that, whenever possible, you format a drive as NTFS when you are creating partitions rather than convert from FAT to NTFS at a later date. Drives originally formatted with NTFS have less fragmentation and better performance than those converted from FAT.

All these features combine to make Windows 2000 a very solid choice as a file and print server.

Windows 2000 application support

Of all the network operating systems discussed in this chapter, Windows 2000 has perhaps the best overall level of support by third-party applications.

Why is Windows so well supported? If you were a software developer, wouldn't you rather develop a program for the most popular operating system than for one of the others? The answer is probably yes, and this is perhaps the largest factor that influences application development for Windows. A lesser factor is that the programming tools for Windows are easy-to-use, graphical tools created by Microsoft. Therefore, Windows is an easy platform for which to develop applications.

In addition to having superb third-party application support, Windows 2000 Server comes with a complete set of tools and services that satisfy almost every need a company could have from a network operating system. These applications include DNS and DHCP server services, performance-monitoring tools, and Web server applications.

Windows 2000 security

Windows 2000 brings with it a full range of security features that make for a very strong operating system. Authentication security is provided through *Kerberos version 5*, files system security and encryption are provided through NTFS permissions and EFS, and network communication can be protected by IPSec. These features are combined with the underlying features introduced in Windows NT 4.

Novell NetWare

Once the network operating system of choice for all but a few networks, NetWare's popularity has declined somewhat. However, *NetWare* is still widely used in many large organizations. The latest version of NetWare, version 6, has garnered a number of awards and continues to prove that Novell can produce a world-leading network operating system.

The information this chapter provides on Novell NetWare is intended to apply to NetWare 5 and 6. If you find yourself working on an older version of NetWare, you might find that some of the commands and utilities are different from those discussed here.

NDS (Novell Directory Services)

One of the features that really put NetWare on the networking map was Novell Directory Services (NDS), now called Novell e-Directory. Like Microsoft's Active Directory, NDS (which has been around since 1994) is a *directory services system* that allows network objects to be stored in a database. This database can then be divided and distributed among different servers on the network. These processes are known as *partitioning* (the dividing up) and *replication* (the distribution among servers on the network). Although introduced as NDS with NetWare 4.x, Novell has now renamed the product *e-Directory* and has made it platform independent.

 Although a detailed understanding of NDS is not required for the Network+ exam, working with a NetWare server will most certainly require a thorough knowledge of NDS.

Like the other network operating systems, NetWare is a full-featured operating system that offers all the functions required by an organization, including file and print services, DNS and DHCP servers, and FTP and Web servers. NetWare also supports a wide range of third-party hardware and software.

NetWare authentication

As with all the other network operating systems discussed in this chapter, NetWare authentication is performed by using a username and password combination. As well as supplying this information, users also need to tell client software which NDS tree to authenticate to and the location of the user object in the NDS tree.

After a user has been validated, an assortment of restrictions is verified, including allowed logon times and station restrictions, which prevent users from logging on from certain workstations. Information about the user account and what the user can and can't access is stored in the NDS. For this reason, a copy of the NDS must be available in order for the user to be able to log on. Also, each time a user attempts to access a resource, her authentication status is checked in the NDS to make sure she is who she says she is and that she is allowed to access the resource.

NetWare file and print services

As mentioned earlier in this chapter, NetWare has long been regarded as the king of file and print services, and indeed, for many years, it was *the* operating system of choice for this purpose. Although that might no longer be the case, many people in the IT industry still see NetWare as primarily a file and print server platform.

Of all the network operating systems discussed in this chapter, NetWare has by far the most comprehensive (and complex) file system security structure. In addition to allowing an administrator to assign a comprehensive set of rights to users and groups, NetWare provides file permission inheritance systems, as well as the ability to block the inherited rights if needed. All this adds up to a sophisticated file system security method that can take some getting used to.

In addition to file permission rights, files can also be assigned a range of attributes. These attributes work the same as file attributes in DOS and Windows, except that the Windows file permissions are limited to attributes such as read-only and hidden, whereas the NetWare file attributes include such possibilities as rename inhibit and copy inhibit.

Printing with NetWare can be implemented in a variety of ways. Traditionally, printers were defined on the server, and print queues were associated with those printers. In NetWare 6, a feature called *Novell Distributed Print Services* allows a more dynamic printing environment to be created, with increased functionality. NetWare 6 also includes a new feature called *iPrint*, which allows users to see graphical maps of the network and point and click to access network devices.

To access a printer on NetWare, clients capture the output that would normally be directed to a local printer port and send it to the network printer. In early versions of NetWare, this was a process performed by using a command-line utility, called `capture`. Nowadays, the process has been hidden behind the graphical interface of the client software and is largely unnoticed.

NetWare application support

Although application support will always be a topic of much debate, the reality is that third-party application support for NetWare is not nearly at the same level as it is for the Windows server platforms. In terms of third-party application support, NetWare would even have a hard time competing against Linux. However, many applications are available for NetWare, and you are likely to have a choice of applications for any given purpose.

 On a NetWare server, console utilities and drivers are implemented through pieces of software called NetWare Loadable Modules (NLMs). Most NLMs can be loaded and unloaded as needed.

Even though third-party support might be lacking, the applications included with the NetWare package leave little to be desired. Included in NetWare are a DHCP server, a DNS server, a Web server application (and two of them in NetWare 6), and a range of other services. Pretty much any application that is needed in a modern networking environment is available in the network operating system.

NetWare security

Like the other network operating systems, NetWare has many security features to help secure the server and the network. The key areas of NetWare security include the following:

➤ **Resource access**—Resource access in NetWare is controlled, as is everything else related to security, through directory services. For a user to gain access to a network resource—whether it be a file, directory, printer, server, or gateway—the appropriate permissions must be applied through the directory. Permissions can be granted to the user, to a group to which the user belongs, or to an NDS container object in which the user resides. Rights to objects can be inherited or gained from other user IDs through a process called *security equivalence*.

➤ **User authentication**—As with the other network operating systems, accessing a NetWare server and network resources requires a username and password combination. To log on to a NetWare server, the context of the user must also be specified and, in some instances, the name of the NDS tree must also be provided. *Context* is a term used to refer to the user IDs location in the NDS tree. Without the correct context, the security subsystem is unable to identify the correct user ID and does not grant access to the server. Because the context can be complex and because the tree name is generally not used except at the point of login, it's common practice to configure users' workstations to default to a certain tree and context. This way, a user needs to provide only a username and password.

To gain access to a NetWare server, four pieces of information are normally required: a username, a password, a directory context, and the name of the tree to which the user wants to log in. In addition, you can specify a server name, although this is not required.

➤ **File and directory security**—NetWare provides a very comprehensive file and directory permissions system, which allows rights to be assigned to users, groups, and other NDS objects. Rights are inheritable, which means that rights assigned at one directory level flow down through the directory structure until they reach the end of the directory tree, unless they are countered by an inherited rights mask or by an explicit trustee assignment. A similar process is used to manage and assign rights within the NDS directory tree, although the actual set of rights that can be assigned is different.

Like the Windows console, the NetWare console can and should be locked for security purposes. You can lock the NetWare console by using a utility called scrsaver, which you run from the server command line.

With the proliferation of Microsoft Windows server platforms, you might not actually get to work with a NetWare server. But if you do, you'll find that there is good reason why NetWare was king of the network operating system hill for so long.

File system security on NetWare is the most sophisticated of any of the popular network operating systems. In addition to a full set of file permissions, NetWare also accommodates file permission inheritance, as well as filters to cancel out that inheritance. For those who are unfamiliar with the various features of NetWare file system security, it can seem a bit bewildering. When you are used to it, though, you realize that it allows an extremely high level of control over files and directories.

 The term *inheritance* is used to describe the process of rights flowing down the directory tree. For example, rights are assigned at the top of the directory structure, and unless they are blocked at a lower level, they flow to the bottom of the structure. All common network operating systems employ file inheritance in one way or another.

At the core of NetWare file system security are the basic permissions. These permissions can be assigned to individual files or, where appropriate, directories (that is, folders). The file system rights available on a NetWare server are listed in Table 7.3.

Table 7.3   File Permissions on a NetWare Server

Right	Description
Supervisor	Supervisory—implies all rights
Read	Allows the file to be read
Write	Allows the file to be written to
Create	Allows new files to be created
Erase	Allows files to be deleted
Modify	Allows the attributes of the file to be changed
Filescan	Allows the file to be viewed
Access Control	Allows the file permissions to be manipulated

Linux

Providing a summary of Linux in a few paragraphs is a difficult task. Unlike other operating systems, each of which has only a single variation, Linux has many distributions, each offering a slightly different approach. Some of the most common Linux distributions include RedHat, SuSE, Debian, and Caldera. In light of the many versions of Linux, if a command or an approach is listed in this section and is not available in the version of Linux you are using, you can look for an equivalent command or approach in your version, and you will very likely find one.

Linux authentication

People who are used to working on a Windows-based system will no doubt discover that administration on a Linux system is very different. For instance, authentication information such as a list of users is kept in a text file. This file, /etc/passwd, controls who can and cannot log on to the system.

For a user to log on to the system, a valid username and password combination must be supplied. Both of these pieces of information are case-sensitive.

Linux file and print services

Although it is not the most obvious choice for a file and print server platform, Linux can perform the role of a file and print server admirably. In a base configuration, the volumes on a Linux server are not available to network clients. To make them available, one of two file sharing services is commonly used:

➤ **NFS**—NFS is the original file-sharing system used with Linux. NFS makes it possible for areas of the hard disk on a Linux system to be shared with other clients on the network. Once the share has been established from the client side, the fact that the drive is on another system is transparent to the user.

➤ **Samba**—Samba provides Server Message Block functionality so that areas of the Linux server disks can be made available to Windows clients. In much the same way as on Windows servers, Samba facilitates the sharing of folders that can then be accessed by Windows client computers. Samba also makes it possible for Linux printer resources to be shared with Windows clients.

As with Windows NT/2000 and NetWare, Linux has a file system permission structure that makes it possible to restrict access to files or directories. In Linux, each file or directory can be assigned a very basic set of file rights that dictates the actions that can be performed on the file. The basic rights are Read, Write, and Execute. The rights can be expressed in an alphabetic format (that is, RWX) or a numeric format (777). The rights to a file can be derived from the file ownership, from a group object, or from an "everyone" designator, which covers all users who are authenticated on the server. The Linux file permission structure might not be as sophisticated as those found in other network operating systems, but it is still more than sufficient in many environments.

Printing on a Linux system occurs through a service called the *Line Printer daemon*. The Line Printer functionality can be accessed by any user on the network who is properly authorized and connected. In later versions of Linux, some distributions have started to provide a more enhanced printing system called the *Common Unix Printing System* (*CUPS*). Many people, however, still prefer to use the traditional Line Printer system because of its simplicity and efficiency.

Linux application support

If you can think of an application that you might need, chances are that it is available for Linux in some form. As well as highly sophisticated commercial applications produced by large software companies, you can find software for the Linux platform that is written by an equally enthusiastic army of small software development companies and individuals. This means that application support for Linux is on par with if not greater than that in other network operating systems, such as NetWare, even if it has not yet reached the levels achieved by Windows server platforms.

In a sense, all applications created for Linux are third-party applications in that Linux itself is only an operating system kernel. The applications that run on this kernel provide Linux with its functionality.

On the assumption that a network server will have a number of requirements, it is common practice for the Linux kernel to be bundled with various applications and provided to customers as a package, which, as discussed earlier, is called a *distribution*.

One respect in which Linux certainly has the edge over the other operating systems is that many Linux applications are free. Developed in the same spirit as Linux itself, and in many cases governed by the same licensing types, these free applications can seriously reduce the cost of maintaining a network server. Although it can be said that there are also free server-type applications for Windows and NetWare, there are certainly not as many of them as there are for Linux. (Note that we are referring to server applications, not applications targeted at workstation or end-user applications.)

Linux security

Considerable effort has been put into making Linux a very secure network operating system, and those efforts are evident. When it is configured correctly, Linux is a very secure operating system, and therefore it is often used as a company's firewall server. The following are a few highlights of Linux security:

➤ **Resource access**—As in the other network operating systems, access to resources on a Linux network is controlled through permissions. Access control lists identifying which systems and who can access what resources are held in text files such as hosts.deny and hosts.allow. Permissions for network resources and services can be assigned to an individual user or to a group of users.

> **User authentication**—To access the local system resources or any network resources, user authentication, in the form of a username and a password, is required. The user account information is kept in a text file known as the /etc/passwd file in the Linux system.

 To log on to a Linux server, the user must supply a valid username and password. Both of these values are case-sensitive.

> **File and directory security**—The default file system used by Linux is the EXT2 file system. Like NTFS, which is used with Windows servers, EXT2 allows administrators to assign permissions to individual files and folders. These permissions are used to control who is allowed access to specific data on the server. A secure server should have permissions set on the important data in the system.

As Linux continues to grow in popularity, it will become an increasingly common sight in server rooms of organizations of all sizes. As a network administrator, you should prepare yourself for *when* you encounter a Linux system—not *if.*

Of the platforms discussed in this chapter, Unix and Linux have the most simplistic approach to file system security, although for most environments, this approach is more than sufficient. File permissions can be assigned to either the creator of a file or directory, a group, or the entity "everyone," which includes any authenticated user.

Unix and Linux have only three rights that can be assigned. These rights are listed in Table 7.4.

Table 7.4   File Permissions on Unix/Linux

Right	Description
Read	Allows files to be listed, opened, and read
Write	Allows files to be created, written to, or modified
Execute	Allows files to be executed (that is, run)

The file permissions are listed to the right of the file. There first value specifies whether the file is a file (-) or a directory (d). The next three values specify the file rights for the user, the next three for the group, and the next three for the "everyone" assignment.

Operating system interoperability

Rather than use the same network operating system on all servers, modern networks often work in multivendor environments, meaning that you might encounter more than one of the major network operating systems functioning on the same network. In such a scenario, you might, for example, have a NetWare server that handles authentication as well as file and print services, a Windows 2000 server that hosts the corporate e-mail system, and two Linux systems—one acting as a server and the other providing firewall services. It is possible to use a single operating system for all these tasks, but in some situations a more flexible approach is required.

To facilitate such environments, network operating system manufacturers build in features and services that allow their operating systems to coexist on networks with other vendors' operating systems. In some cases, the manufacturers appear to do so grudgingly, but in the IT environment of the 21st century, it would be a bold move indeed not to provide such services.

The following sections take a brief look at how well some of the major network operating systems "play" with each other.

Using Windows with NetWare

A typical combination in many environments is the use of Windows and NetWare servers. Unfortunately for NetWare, some of these situations are part of a migration to a completely Windows-based environment. In other environments, organizations leverage the power of NDS (or e-Directory) and NetWare for file and print services and use a Windows server product for application hosting. Because it realizes that there will be such environments, Microsoft supplies a range of tools, including the following, to help in the communication between Windows server products and NetWare:

➤ **Client Services for NetWare (CSNW)**—CSNW is designed to allow Windows client systems to access file and print services on a NetWare server. CSNW is installed on a client system and allows only that client to connect to the NetWare server.

➤ **Gateway Services for NetWare (GSNW)**—GSNW is used to allow systems in a Windows domain to access resources on a NetWare server. GSNW is installed on the server and allows all permitted Windows clients to connect to the NetWare server through it.

➤ **File and Print Services for NetWare (FPNW)**—FPNW is used for NetWare clients to access file and print services from a Windows server system. Basically, it makes a Windows Server system look like a NetWare server or a reasonable facsimile thereof.

Be sure to understand the functions of CSNW and GSNW for the Network+ exam. You should also understand where they are installed.

Using Windows and Linux servers

In today's environments, Linux and Windows servers are commonly used together, and therefore, clients and the servers themselves must be able to communicate. One of the programs used to increase interoperability between Linux and Windows is *Samba*. Samba is a software package for Linux that allows Linux workstations to share resources with Windows workstations in a Windows-based network. Samba is available free of charge and is commonly installed by default during a Linux installation. Connection to a Samba server requires the use of the Microsoft network client, which is installed by default with most Windows client operating systems.

You might be asked to identify the function and purpose of Samba for the Network+ exam.

Using NetWare and Linux servers

NetWare and Linux servers are fully interoperable and are often found together in network environments. For instance, a NetWare file and print server might coexist with a Linux firewall and proxy server. In addition, it is possible, by using *e-Directory*, to integrate the management of Linux servers into the directory services system in order to streamline administration.

To make these scenarios possible, Linux supports both IPX/SPX, which is required for NetWare 3.x and 4.x, and TCP/IP, which is used in the later NetWare versions. However, many of the Linux distributions do not natively support IPX/SPX. If you use one of those distributions, you need to download extra software and perform additional configuration.

Operating system client support

Because many client systems—including Linux, Windows, and Macintosh systems—are used in today's networks, network operating systems need to support each of these client systems. Of the three client systems mentioned, Microsoft Windows is by far the most popular. However, in recent years, other platforms have experienced a surge in popularity.

Windows server client support

Windows-based servers support all the client software that is used on networks today. Many types of client software, including Windows 95, Windows 98, and Windows Me, Windows NT Workstation, Windows XP Professional, Windows 2000 Professional, Windows 3.x, and editions of Windows NT Server, are natively supported by Windows servers and can be integrated with relative ease. To connect to a Windows server, *Client for Microsoft Networks* needs to be installed on the client systems.

Unix systems are fully interoperable with Windows servers, via a special add-on pack called *Windows Services for Unix*. This add-on pack provides compatibility with the Unix NFS and a variety of Unix utilities. Macintosh, on the other hand, requires the Services for Macintosh product, which allows Macintosh clients to use TCP/IP and access shared files, directories, and printers on a Windows 2000 server.

NetWare server client support

As a major player in the network operating system world, NetWare provides support for a variety of clients. When connecting Windows systems in a NetWare environment, you need to consider the following:

➤ To connect a Windows NT/2000 workstation to a NetWare 3.x or 4.x network, you need the *NWLink* protocol and you need CSNW installed. NetWare 5.x does not specifically require the NWLink protocol, but it does require client software to access the NetWare server. Alternatively, you can use the Novell-supplied client software, which, in fact, offers more functionality than the CSNW product.

➤ Connecting a Windows server system to a NetWare server to act as a gateway requires NWLink and GSNW.

➤ To connect Windows desktop systems to a NetWare 3.x or 4.x network, IPX/SPX (or Microsoft's own version of it, NWLink) is required on the workstation, as is CSNW or the Novell client software. NetWare 5.x does not specifically require IPX/SPX, and NetWare 6 does not necessarily require client-side software.

Linux server client support

Because the operating system running on a Linux workstation is the same as that running on the server, client support is both integrated and seamless. Linux client systems can access all the resources offered by a Linux server with ease. The most common resources are file sharing, which is normally facilitated through NFS, and printing, which is made available through the Line Printer daemon.

As discussed earlier in this chapter, Windows clients are able to access resources on a Linux server through the Samba product. Macintosh clients can also use the Samba functionality.

Client operating systems

Whereas a network operating system works behind the scenes, providing the services that make the network function, the workstation operating systems act as the window to the network. For that reason, network administrators must be aware of the operating systems that grace the front end of the network.

As stated previously, Microsoft's Windows products dominate the desktop operating systems market. The other operating systems discussed in this chapter hold single-figure percentages of the market share. However, these other systems are readily available, and their numbers are growing.

Windows 95, Windows 98, and Windows Me

Perhaps the most widely used client operating systems are the Windows-based clients—Windows 95, Windows 98, and Windows Me. These clients are used in network environments of all sizes, ranging from small office and home office environments to large corporations. Their popularity can be attributed to the familiar, easy-to-navigate graphical interfaces, compatibility with most of the current popular applications, and their low cost, at least in comparison to other Windows products, such as Windows NT Workstation and Windows 2000 Professional.

Application support for Windows 95, Windows 98, and Windows Me

Windows 95, Windows 98, and Windows Me systems support all but a few of the major applications used today. They were designed to be used with office productivity tools such as spreadsheets and word processors. In addition, they support a range of entertainment applications. Of all the operating systems in use today, they have the greatest commercial software support.

Local security mechanisms for Windows 95, Windows 98, and Windows Me

If there is one failing in Windows 95-, Windows 98-, and Windows Me-based clients, it is their local security. Windows clients have no file system security, which means that the files you save on your system can be accessed by anyone who uses your computer. There are third-party products designed to either hide folders and files or password-protect them, but as with all third-party products, they cost extra.

Windows 95, Windows 98, and Windows Me clients also do not provide a mechanism to prevent tampering with systems and application settings. Perhaps even more significantly, anyone can use a Windows 95, Windows 98, and Windows Me system without providing a username and password.

The lack of a local security mechanism makes Windows 95, Windows 98, and Windows Me clients an unsuitable operating system for many network environments and for particular categories of users on a network. If local security is required, an operating system such as Windows NT or 2000 should be used.

Authentication for Windows 95, Windows 98, and Windows Me

Windows 95, Windows 98, and Windows Me clients require a username-and-password combination in order for users to log on to the network and access network resources. The system is then authenticated by the server that is being used. Authentication is a function of the server operating system rather than the local workstation.

Windows NT Workstation, Windows 2000 Professional, and Windows XP Professional

Windows NT Workstation, Windows 2000, and Windows XP Professional were introduced to provide robust, secure, high-performance alternatives to Microsoft's other workstation operating systems, such as Windows 95, Windows 98, and Windows Me. Since the introduction of Windows NT Workstation as a business-oriented operating system, Microsoft has succeeded it with two other versions: Windows 2000 Professional and its latest offering, Windows XP Professional.

Built on the same basic building blocks as Windows NT Server, these products are popular in corporate environments where local workstation security is as important as the security of the server. Windows NT Workstation, Windows 2000, and Windows XP Professional use the same authentication mechanisms as their corresponding server products, and they support NTFS for file system security.

Application support for Windows NT Workstation, Windows 2000 Professional, and Windows XP Professional

Application support for Windows NT Workstation, Windows 2000, and Windows XP Professional Workstation is very high, although certain applications are simply not supported. All the operating systems discussed in this chapter have the ability to support DOS applications and 16-bit and 32-bit Windows applications, as well as some other platforms. In general, this compatibility works flawlessly, although certain applications can cause problems. One such problem is that any application that interfaces directly with hardware won't work. This is because Windows NT Workstation, Windows 2000, and Windows XP Professional have a special set of drivers that intercept calls made to the hardware. Only applications that understand the function of these drivers and know how to interface with them can be used on these systems.

Client connectivity for Windows NT Workstation, Windows 2000 Professional, and Windows XP Professional

Windows NT Workstation, Windows 2000, and Windows XP Professional are intended to be suitable clients for any of the common network operating systems. To connect to NetWare servers, Microsoft provides CSNW, although Novell offers client software that has more functionality. To connect to a Linux server running Samba, no additional software is required.

Local security mechanisms for Windows NT Workstation, Windows 2000 Professional, and Windows XP Professional

Windows NT Workstation, Windows 2000, and Windows XP Professional share the same security subsystem as their server counterparts and use the same security mechanisms. User accounts can be defined locally on the workstation, or the system can be made a member of a domain, in which case user accounts from the central user account database can be used to log on to the workstation and therefore the domain as well.

Authentication for Windows NT Workstation, Windows 2000 Professional, and Windows XP Professional

Two pieces of information are required to log on to a Windows NT/2000 system: a username and a password. Of the two, the username is not case-sensitive, but the password is. If the workstation has also been made a member of the domain, an additional dialog box allows you to specify whether you want to log on as an account from the local workstation or as a user account from the domain.

Linux

Although Linux has not experienced the same success as a workstation operating system as it has at the server level, it is increasingly being looked to as an alternative to the other offerings. Many Linux distributions actually include a "workstation" option that can be selected during the installation process. Instead of installing server-type applications (proxy server, Web server, and so on), the installation focuses on workstation-type applications and utilities.

Applications for Linux

One of the myths that has traditionally surrounded Linux is the lack of applications that have been written for it. In the early stages of Linux, this might have been true, but it is certainly no longer the case. The range and quality of applications and utilities available for Linux is truly impressive.

As the popularity of Linux has increased, so has the number of software companies developing Linux-friendly applications. One of the most high profile of these companies is Corel, which has developed a WordPerfect Office suite for Linux. Commercially available software for Linux is licensed in the same way as the software for other operating systems: You need a license to install the product, and you do not receive the source code for the program.

In addition to commercially available software, there is also a larger amount of "free" Linux software. For every commercially available Linux software package, there is an equivalent that is available free of charge. A good example of free software is StarOffice, which is an office suite from Sun Microsystems that includes a spreadsheet, word processor, and all the productivity tools required by desktop users. Free Linux software does not end there. You can get firewall software, proxy software, and backup software— just about any software you need to use Linux as a server or desktop solution.

Client connectivity for Linux

In either a server or client configuration, Linux supports many networking protocols, giving it the capability to operate as a client in many network environments. The latest versions of Linux include support for TCP/IP, IPX/SPX, and other protocols. This allows Linux clients to interoperate with common network operating systems, although you might need to install client software on either the client or the server to facilitate connectivity.

In NetWare 6, native file access makes it possible for Linux clients to access NetWare server resources without additional software.

Local security mechanisms for Linux

Linux is an inherently secure operating system, although the system administrator might need to have a detailed understanding of the operating system to make it completely bulletproof. For local security measures, a username and password combination is required to log on to the system, providing the basis of user verification. In the past, username and password information was stored in a plain-text format, which constitutes a security risk. Today, it is far more common to use the password shadowing technique discussed earlier in this chapter, in the section "Linux User Management Basics."

For file system security, the EXT2 file system, and others, can be used to secure the files that are held on a system.

Note that unlike Windows systems, where there are differences in the security measures and mechanisms from version to version, a Linux system used as a workstation and a Linux system used as a server utilize the same underlying operating system. Therefore, the information provided earlier about security on Linux servers is equally applicable to Linux clients.

Authentication for Linux

Linux authentication is based on a username and password combination. Without a valid user ID, it is very difficult to access a local system. Of important note is that on a Linux system, there is a root account that can be authenticated on any system. The root account is comparable to the Administrator account on Windows networks. On a Linux system, both the username and password are case-sensitive.

Macintosh

Since its introduction, Macintosh has supplied network connectivity features including hardware as well as protocols to facilitate communications. Early systems included a networking interface called a LocalTalk adapter. Networking functionality was also built into the operating system, using AppleTalk as the protocol suite.

Although today's Macintosh computers might look very different from those early systems, their networking legacy remains intact. A Macintosh makes a great client for all the common network operating systems. However, depending on the type and version of network operating system and Mac OS being used, additional software might be required at either the server end or the client end.

Application support for Macintosh

There is no shortage of software for Macintosh computers. In fact, many of the programs Windows users have come to know and love were first written for the Macintosh and, according to Macintosh users, worked better on Macintosh than they do on Windows. Some areas of particular software strength for Macintosh computers include graphical and desktop publishing applications and educational programs.

In addition, Macintosh systems can use Windows applications by using a process called *emulation*. This allows Windows-based programs to run on Macintosh, but there are performance losses, and in some cases, the programs won't run at all.

Client connectivity for Macintosh

Macintosh computers make suitable clients for most network operating systems, but in some cases, there is a need for additional software. For example, to connect to a NetWare server, special client software is required. NetWare now includes native file access that can allow Macintosh clients to access a NetWare file system without additional software. For Windows NT/2000 servers, a product called Services for Macintosh can be installed; this product makes selected shares and printers available to Macintosh clients.

Selecting a NIC and network configuration settings

Part of the role of the network administrator is to install and configure network interface cards (NICs) in client and server systems. Today, this is a fairly simple process, although you need to consider many factors. Let's start with perhaps the most basic of considerations—how to choose a NIC.

Choosing a NIC

The choice of what NIC to use depends on certain criteria, including the following:

➤ **Bus compatibility**—Some older systems have only Industry Standard Architecture (ISA) slots, but most modern systems have either Peripheral Component Interconnect (PCI) slots or both PCI and ISA slots. Either way, you should verify that there is an expansion slot of the correct type available.

> ➤ **Type of network**—As mentioned in the discussion on NICs in Chapter 3, "Networking Devices," unless you are using a networking system other than Ethernet, you should not need to specify another type of NIC.

> ➤ **Media compatibility**—As mentioned in Chapter 3, NICs can come with one, two, or even three types of network connectors.

Besides these criteria, which dictate to a certain extent which NICs you can use, the choice then depends on manufacturer, cost, and requirements. The NIC might come preinstalled in the system or, as in an increasing number of cases, the NIC might be built on to the system board. In either of these situations, you do not have to install a NIC.

Connecting the PC to the network

With the NIC installed and functioning, the next step is to connect the PC to the network. This can be simple or complicated, depending on the type of network you are using. The following are some of the factors you should consider when connecting a new system to an existing network:

> ➤ **Connecting to a coaxial network**—The biggest consideration when connecting to a coaxial network is that it might be necessary to break the coaxial segment to insert a British Naval Connector (BNC) T-connector to physically connect the PC. Unfortunately, breaking a coaxial cable segment prevents any device connected to it from working. This means if you are adding a computer to a coaxial segment and you need to add a length of cable and a connector, you need to either arrange with network users for a few minutes when the network will be unavailable or add the cable and connector before or after working hours. The good news is that you can leave spare BNC T-connectors in the coaxial cable segment as a just-in-case precaution. Doing so can mean that you can add a system to the coaxial segment without affecting users other than the one whose system you are connecting.

> ➤ **Connecting to a twisted-pair network**—Twisted pair is the easiest of all the network types to connect to. All you need to connect is a cable (referred to as a *patch cable*) that connects the system to a hub or switch. In environments that use a structured cable system, the cable can be connected to a wall jack or a jack in a floor box. In a less structured environment, the cable can be run directly between the system and the hub or switch. One item worthy of note is that if you are using a Token Ring network, you must configure the NIC to work at the correct speed. Twisted-pair Ethernet networks can accommodate different speeds, if the networking hardware supports a speed higher than the base 10Mbps.

Token Ring networks do not offer this function; all devices on the ring must operate at the same speed (4Mbps or 16Mbps). Connecting a system to the network with a NIC configured for the wrong speed prevents the system from communicating on the network, and it might even cause problems with other devices on the segment.

After the physical connection to the network has been established, you need to consider which other parameters need to be set. In the case of twisted-pair Ethernet networks, these parameters can include the following:

➤ **Speed of the network**—Unlike coaxial networks that operate at 10Mbps, twisted-pair networks can run at speeds of 10Mbps, 100Mbps, or even 1Gbps. Most NICs are able to automatically sense the speed of the network to which they are connected, although it is normally possible to configure the speed manually.

➤ **Duplex settings**—One of the advantages of Ethernet switches is that they allow you to use full-duplex links between the switch and the client computer. Full-duplex links allow the system and the switch to "talk" in both directions at the same time. Most modern NICs are able to automatically detect whether a full-duplex link is available and then use it. If you are using a switched network and have NICs that are able to support full-duplex links, you should make sure that this feature is being utilized.

Testing and troubleshooting the NIC

With the NIC installed and the PC connected to the network, the next step is to test whether the NIC is functioning correctly and whether the link to the network is established.

With today's plug-and-play environment and software configurable NICs that have a range of autodetection features, testing whether the NIC is operating should be a matter of routine. You might not even have to test the NIC specifically, but just configure the NIC through the operating system and connect to the network. If all is working correctly, you should be able to connect, and by doing so prove that everything is working as it should be.

However, there is always a possibility that the installation of the NIC might have some problems. Understanding how to fix such problems is an important network administration skill.

Before considering troubleshooting the NIC at a protocol level, you should ensure that the NIC is installed and operating correctly.

Depending on the results of the tests, you might need to further troubleshoot the installation of the NIC. If you are using a manufacturer-supplied testing utility, and it reports that it can't find the NIC, you might have the wrong utility for the NIC, or the NIC might not be working at all. Manufacturer-supplied testing utilities do not need separate driver software, so if the testing utility can't find the NIC, you can eliminate the drivers as the cause of the problem.

Configuring the NIC settings

When you have confirmed that the NIC is operating correctly, you can configure the software settings for the NIC. The settings and configuration information you need depend on the protocol you are using.

Choosing protocols

Choosing the correct protocol is an important consideration when configuring a network or adding systems to an existing network. The client and the server must use the same protocol in order for communication to take place. This section provides a brief summary of the commonly used protocols. For a complete description of the various protocols, refer to Chapter 4, "OSI Model and Network Protocols."

➤ **TCP/IP**—By far the most prevalent of network protocol suites, TCP/IP is available for almost every computing platform and has widespread industry support. The majority of LANs now use TCP/IP as the default protocol. Configuring TCP/IP connectivity requires the use of an IP address, a subnet mask, a default gateway, and possibly Domain Name Service (DNS) server information and Windows Internet Naming System (WINS) information.

➤ **IPX/SPX**—Novell invented and implemented IPX/SPX when it introduced NetWare in the 1980s. At that time, TCP/IP was for the most part an academic/military/government protocol, and Novell realized the need for a robust, routable protocol. IPX/SPX is one of the main reasons that Novell owned the networking market through the 1980s and most of the 1990s. IPX/SPX was also easy to install and configure. Today, TCP/IP has largely displaced IPX. One of the advantages of IPX is that workstation configuration is very simple. Generally speaking, the only item that might need to be configured is the frame type, which determines the format in which data is grouped into the frames that are placed on the network. Older versions of NetWare use a frame type called 802.3, whereas newer versions use a frame type called 802.2. Fortunately, most client software is able to detect the frame type automatically.

➤ **NWLink**—When Microsoft began working on adding support for inter-operability with NetWare, it opted to develop its own fully compatible version of Novell's proprietary IPX/SPX. This development was necessary because earlier versions of NetWare did not support authentication over TCP/IP.

On the Network+ exam, be careful when determining whether connectivity to a NetWare server is required from a Microsoft client. NWLink is the required protocol because Microsoft does not directly support IPX/SPX. Watch for this same situation in reverse as well: NetWare uses IPX/SPX to communicate with a Windows NT Server running NWLink.

➤ **NetBEUI**—Microsoft chose IBM's NetBEUI as the protocol for its first networking implementation in the mid-1980s. One of the reasons Microsoft chose to base its early networking efforts on NetBEUI was the protocol's simplicity and speed. Microsoft wanted to offer a very simple, easy workgroup configuration. Name services and addressing are both handled automatically with NetBEUI. There are no configuration issues, other than setting up the NIC and installing NetBEUI as the protocol. Because of NetBEUI's simplicity, administrators sometimes use it to troubleshoot hard-to-find communication problems between two machines. The simplicity of NetBEUI also created problems for Microsoft as the 1980s progressed. NetBEUI is a non-routable protocol, and as networks began to interconnect, Microsoft found its clients stranded within the confines of small LANs.

As mentioned earlier, TCP/IP is by far the most common of the networking protocols in use today. For that reason, the next section takes a more in-depth look at configuring client systems to use TCP/IP.

Configuring client systems for TCP/IP

Configuring a client system for TCP/IP can be a relatively complex task, or it can be simple. Any complexity involved is related to the possible need to configure TCP/IP manually. The simplicity is related to the fact that TCP/IP configuration can occur automatically via DHCP. DHCP is covered later in this chapter; this section looks at some of the basic information required to make a system function on a network, using TCP/IP. At the very least, a system needs an IP address and a subnet mask. The default gateway, DNS server, and WINS server are all optional, but network functionality is limited without them. Brief explanations of the IP related settings used to connect to a TCP/IP network follow:

➤ **IP address**—Each system must be assigned a unique IP address so it can communicate on the network.

➤ **Subnet mask**—The subnet mask allows the system to determine which portion of the IP address represents the network address and which portion represents the node address.

➤ **Default gateway**—The default gateway allows the system to communicate with systems on a remote network, without the need for explicit routes to be defined.

➤ **DNS server addresses**—DNS servers allow dynamic hostname resolution to be performed. It is common practice to have two DNS server addresses defined so that if one server becomes unavailable, the other can be used.

➤ **WINS server addresses**—A WINS server enables Network Basic Input/Output System (NetBIOS) names to be resolved to IP addresses. As with DNS servers, it is common practice to enter two WINS server addresses, to provide a degree of fault tolerance.

 At the very minimum, an IP address and a subnet mask are required to connect to a TCP/IP network. With just this minimum configuration, connectivity is limited to the local segment, and DNS and WINS resolution are not be possible.

Exactly how this information is entered on the client depends on the operating system being configured. In any case, the parameters required need to be entered into the respective dialog boxes carefully. In the case of Windows Me, the DNS Configuration and WINS Configuration tabs must be used to input the DNS and WINS information. In Windows 2000, the DNS server fields are on the same screen as the main IP address.

Other systems, such as Macintosh and Linux, use different utilities to allow TCP/IP configuration information to be entered.

Configuring DNS server information

DNS is used on TCP/IP networks for name resolution. It resolves fully qualified domain names (FQDNs) to IP addresses. For example, DNS resolves the address www.comptia.org to its IP address, 216.119.103.72.

Regardless of the operating systems used, at least one DNS server must be accessible by a client system in order for dynamic name resolution to take place. Clients on the TCP/IP network must be configured with the IP address of the DNS server.

Configuring WINS server information

WINS converts NetBIOS names to IP addresses. NetBIOS names are the friendly names by which people refer to the computers on the network (for example, sales1, Maryscomp, secretary).

Many client operating systems are WINS enabled, which means they can be configured to use WINS servers. WINS-enabled clients use the WINS server to resolve NetBIOS names to IP addresses, allowing communication across subnets and reducing broadcast traffic. The following is a partial list of the client systems that can use WINS:

➤ Windows 2000 Server/Professional

➤ Windows NT Workstation/Server

➤ Windows 95/98/Me

➤ Windows for Workgroups

➤ OS/2

➤ Unix/Linux (requires Samba)

Each of the WINS-enabled client systems needs to be configured to use WINS. To do so, the IP address of the WINS server is required.

Using DHCP (Dynamic Host Control Protocol)

Now that you've learned how TCP/IP configuration information is entered manually, it's time to kick back a little and look at how you can handle this configuration with a single click—thanks to DHCP. As mentioned previously, DHCP is used to simplify the assignment of IP configuration information on a TCP/IP network. DHCP allows you to dynamically assign IP addressing information to client systems on the network, reducing possible human error and administrative overhead. DHCP is not restricted to a single platform; it is a generic technology that is supported by all the major operating systems.

When DHCP is used on a network, the client systems must be configured to use DHCP. Each of the client operating systems has some method of configuring the system to receive IP information from the DHCP server. Configuring a client to use DHCP is often as simple as clicking a check box or selecting a radio button.

When client systems are configured to use DHCP, they can receive more than just the IP address. They can also be assigned any of the other TCP/IP information, such as the default gateway, subnet mask, and any DNS or WINS servers. In addition, some DHCP server platforms support a range of other information.

When the networking configuration is complete, the system should be able to function on the network. However, to connect to a server system and use its resources, the system needs client software, which is discussed in the following section.

Configuring clients to access servers

Many clients can be used on modern networks, and a network administrator must be prepared to manage and support client connectivity in a multiplatform network environment. Learning how to connect the various clients to the major network operating systems used today is a hands-on task. To prepare you for the inevitable, the following sections provide an overview of the various client operating systems and what is required to connect them to common network operating systems.

Configuring Microsoft Windows clients

The most widely used of all client platforms is Microsoft Windows. Configuring Microsoft Windows clients for server connectivity depends on which version of Windows you are using and to what server you want to connect. Versions of Windows, such as 98 and Me, require that client software be installed in order to connect to a Windows Server platform. Products such as Windows 2000 Professional assume that a connection to a server will be forthcoming and therefore install the client software automatically.

Client software for Microsoft networks on Windows 95/98/Me

The Client for Microsoft Networks can be installed on a Windows 95/98/Me system to facilitate connection to a Windows Server platform such as Windows NT 4 Server or Windows 2000 Server. The client is included on the workstation operating system distribution CD and is installed through the Network dialog box, which can be accessed through the Network Control Panel or a variety of other methods.

No information is needed to install the client software, but to configure it, you must open the Client for Microsoft Networks Properties, check the Log on to Windows NT Domain box, and specify the domain name.

After you change these settings, you need to set the primary network logon to the type of client you are using—in this case the Client for Microsoft Networks.

Active Directory Client Software

Some client platforms, including Windows 95 and 98, require an additional client in order to take advantage of Microsoft's Active Directory system. Active Directory client software can be found in the **Clients** folder on the Windows 2000 Server CD. All Windows 2000 products have Active Directory enabled natively.

Client software for Microsoft networks on a Windows NT/2000 system

Because networking functionality is built in to Windows NT/2000, you do not need to add extra client software. However, you must still configure the domain to which the system is supposed to authenticate. Before you can "join" a domain, you must first create an account for the system, or the computer must be joined to the domain with a user account that is able to create a computer account automatically.

Novell client software

Novell produces a full range of client software for Windows platforms. The client software is supplied when you buy a copy of NetWare, or it can be downloaded free of charge from the Novell download Web site, at `http://download.novell.com`. There are different versions of the client for Windows 95/98/Me, NT/2000, and XP.

Installing the Novell client software is much like installing any other application. After the client software is installed, the system normally needs to be rebooted. When the system boots back up again, the Novell client appears automatically. On systems that require local login, such as Windows NT Workstation and Windows 2000 Professional, the Novell client replaces the Microsoft authentication dialog box but still offers the capability to log on to the local system.

To connect to a Novell network, certain criteria need to be supplied to the client software, including the following:

➤ **Username**—This is the name of the user ID that is being used to authenticate.

➤ **Password**—The password is not case-sensitive.

> **Tree**—This is the name of the Novell Directory Services (NDS) tree to which you want to connect.

> **Context**—This is the name of the NDS container in which the user object you are trying to log in as resides. This parameter is optional, but if it is not supplied, the username must be typed in, along with the full path to the user's container.

> **Server**—This field is optional. Specifying a server causes the client to connect to a specific server. If none is specified, the nearest server that is able to authenticate the user into NDS is used.

To log on to NDS, you must specify at least a username, a context, and a tree name. It is possible to combine the username and context into a single entry, although it is not common to do so.

For the Tree, Context, and Server fields, navigation boxes to the right of each field allow you to browse the network for suitable resources.

When the Novell Login dialog box first opens on a system, it is displayed in a simplified format, with just the Username and Password fields. You must click the Advanced button to display the screen.

If you prefer not to use the Novell software, you can use the client Microsoft supplies that can be used with NetWare networks. Like any other network service, this client is added through the Network applet in the Control Panel or through the properties of a network connection in Windows 2000. The basic functionality of the Novell-supplied client and the Microsoft-supplied client is the same, but in terms of advanced features, the Novell Client exceeds the Microsoft offering, by providing support for features such as ZENWorks, Novell's client system management software, and Novell Distributed Printing Services (NDPS).

Unix/Linux client software

Unix/Linux systems are actually hybrid systems in that such a system can act as either a client or a server or both. In the Unix/Linux world, every machine is called a *host*, and a host can perform as either a client or a server or both.

Unix and Linux utilize the *Network File System* (*NFS*) protocol to provide file-sharing capabilities between computers. NFS, like TCP/IP, is actually a suite of protocols, and many people refer to NFS as an *application*. The most widely used version of NFS is version 2, which is based on RFC 1094. Version 3, which is documented in RFC 1813, exists but has not been widely implemented at the present time. You can find more information on NFS at the Sun Microsystems Web site, www.sun.com.

NFS is a popular system for sharing files between Linux and Unix systems; however, it does little to allow Windows-based clients to access the same shares (although NFS software is available for Windows). To get around this limitation, Windows clients use the *Samba (SMB) service*. Samba allows Windows-based clients to access resources such as files and printers on a Linux server. The smbd daemon provides the Samba service to the network.

Review and test yourself

The following sections provide you with the opportunity to review what you learned in this chapter and to test yourself.

The facts

For the exam, don't forget these important concepts:

➤ The Client for Microsoft Networks can be installed on a Windows 95/98/Me system to facilitate connection to a Windows Server platform such as Windows NT 4 Server or Windows 2000 Server.

➤ To log onto a Netware server you may need a username, password, tree, and context.

➤ Unix and Linux utilize the Network File System (NFS) protocol to provide file-sharing capabilities between computers.

➤ The following list summarizes the file permissions on a Windows 2000 server:

Right	Description
Full Control	Provides all rights
Modify	Allows files to be modified
Read & Execute	Allows files to be read and executed (that is, run)
List Folder Contents	Allows the files in a folder to be listed
Read	Allows a file to be read
Write	Allows a file to be written to

➤ Valid file permissions on a Unix/Linux system include read, write, and execute.

➤ When a user cannot access files that other users can, verify that the correct permissions are set.

➤ Three common authentication methods include Kerberos, NTLM, and SSL/TLS.

➤ To convert from FAT partitions to NTFS partitions, the convert command is used.

➤ Valid permissions for NetWare systems include Supervisor, Read, Write, Create, Erase, Modify, Filescan, and Access Control.

➤ The usernames and passwords are case-sensitive when logging on to a Linux system.

➤ CSNW allows Windows-based clients to access file and print services on a NetWare server.

➤ GSNW allows systems in a Windows domain to access resources on a NetWare server.

➤ Samba allows Linux workstations to share resources with Windows workstations.

Key Terms

➤ Authentication

➤ File and print services

➤ Web server services

➤ Novell NetWare

➤ Unix

➤ Linux

➤ Macintosh

➤ Workgroup

➤ Domain

➤ PDC

➤ BDC

➤ tracert

➤ ipconfig

➤ `ping`

➤ Active Directory

➤ FAT

➤ FAT32

➤ NTFS

➤ NDS

➤ `config`

➤ `inetcfg`

➤ `ipxping`

➤ NLMs

➤ Multitasking

➤ `ifconfig`

➤ `traceroute`

➤ NFS

➤ Samba

➤ CSNW

➤ GSNW

➤ FPNW

Practice Exam

Question 1

> You have been instructed to install a Novell NetWare server onto your network. All the other servers are Windows NT 4 systems. You want Windows 98 clients to be able to access both the Windows NT systems and the NetWare server. Which of the following strategies could you adopt? (Choose the two best answers.)
>
> ❑ A. Install the Novell NetWare client for Windows 98 on each workstation.
>
> ❑ B. Install Gateway Services for NetWare on the server.
>
> ❑ C. Install Gateway Services for NetWare on the clients.
>
> ❑ D. Install the Microsoft Network Client, and select NetWare during the installation.

The correct answers are A and B. To facilitate connection to a NetWare server from Windows clients, you can install the Novell client on each workstation or install Gateway Services for NetWare on the server. In addition, Microsoft supplies a client for NetWare that can be used. GSNW is a server-based service and would not be installed on the client. Answer D is not valid.

Question 2

> Which of the following security systems are associated with Windows 2000? (Choose the two best answers.)
>
> ❑ A. NTLM
>
> ❑ B. Shadow passwords
>
> ❑ C. The Bindery
>
> ❑ D. Kerberos

The correct answers are A and D. NTLM and Kerberos are security systems that are available on Windows 2000 systems. Shadow passwords are associated with Linux. The Bindery is associated with NetWare versions up to 4.

Question 3

> Which of the following services can be installed on a Windows NT 4 server to
> enable Windows clients to access the resources on a NetWare server?
>
> ○ A. IPSec
> ○ B. NDS
> ○ C. CSNW
> ○ D. GSNW

The correct answer is D. GSNW can be installed on the server to allow
Windows clients to access a NetWare server. IPSec is a security protocol and
does not provide access to a NetWare server. NDS is the directory services
system that is provided on NetWare. CSNW is installed on the client to
allow it to connect to a NetWare server.

Question 4

> What is the maximum number of PDCs allowed in a Windows NT domain?
>
> ○ A. 1
> ○ B. 10
> ○ C. 256
> ○ D. Unlimited

The correct answer is A. Only one PDC can be used on a Windows NT 4
network. Numerous BDCs can be used to provide functionality in case of a
PDC failure. The other answers are invalid.

Question 5

> Which of the following services would you install on a Windows 2000 system
> to enable Macintosh clients to use the resources on the server?
>
> ○ A. Services for Macintosh
> ○ B. MacGW
> ○ C. GSNW
> ○ D. MacGate

The correct answer is A. Services for Macintosh needs to be loaded on a
Windows server to allow Macintosh clients to access file and print services in
a Windows environment. None of the other answers are valid.

Question 6

Which of the following services is required to make the file and print resources of a Linux server available to Windows clients?

○ A. Squid

○ B. GSFL

○ C. FP4Linux

○ D. Samba

The correct answer is D. Samba is used to provide Windows clients with file and print services from a Linux server. None of the other options are valid.

Question 7

When configuring a client to connect to a TCP/IP network, which of the following must be included to gain network connectivity? (Choose two.)

❏ A. WINS information

❏ B. Subnet mask

❏ C. DNS information

❏ D. IP address

❏ E. Default gateway

The correct answers are B and D. To log on to a TCP/IP network, you need both the subnet mask and the IP address. Without entering the DNS and WINS configurations, these services will be unavailable but you would still be able to log on to the network. Without the gateway configured, the client system would be restricted to the local segment.

Question 8

Which of the following services would you install on a Windows 2000 system to enable Macintosh clients to use the resources on the server?

○ A. Services for Macintosh

○ B. MacGW

○ C. GSNW

○ D. MacGate

The correct answer is A. Services for Macintosh needs to be loaded on a Windows server to allow Macintosh clients to access file and print services in a Windows environment.

Question 9

> Which of the following allows individual files on a Windows 2000 system to be secured against unauthorized access or viewing? (Choose two.)
>
> ❏ A. EFS
> ❏ B. HPFS
> ❏ C. WINS
> ❏ D. NTFS

The correct answers are A and D. Both EFS and NTFS are mechanisms that are used to secure individual files or folders from unauthorized viewing or access. HPFS is the High Performance File System used with the OS/2 operating system. WINS resolves NetBIOS names to the IP address.

Question 10

> Which of the following two terms are applied to the division and distribution of an NDS e-Directory tree?
>
> ❏ A. RAID 0
> ❏ B. Partitioning
> ❏ C. Replication
> ❏ D. Synchronization
> ❏ E. Capture

The correct answers are B and C. Partitioning and replication are terms used to describe the division and distribution of an NDS e-Directory tree. All other answers are invalid.

Want to know more?

Minasi, Mark, Christa Anderson, Brian M. Smith, and Doug Toombs. *Mastering Windows 2000 Server (4th Edition)*. Sybex, 2002.

Gaskin, James E. *Mastering NetWare 6*. Sybex, 2002.

Pogue David. *Mac OS X: The Missing Manual*. O'Reilly & Associates, 2001.

Negus, Christopher. *Red Hat Linux 7.3 Bible*. John Wiley & Sons, 2002.

Fault Tolerance, Disaster Recovery, VLANs, and NAS

Objectives

3.5 Identify the purpose and characteristics of fault tolerance.

3.6 Identify the purpose and characteristics of disaster recovery.

3.3 Identify the main characteristics of VLANs.

3.4 Identify the main characteristics of NAS.

What you need to know

✓ Understand the importance of data redundancy.

✓ Explain how the various RAID levels function.

✓ Understand the difference between fault tolerance and disaster recovery.

✓ Understand the various backup strategies.

✓ Identify tape rotation strategies.

✓ Understand the function of NAS devices.

✓ Understand the function of VLANs.

Introduction

As far as network administration goes, there is nothing more important than *fault tolerance* and *disaster recovery*. First and foremost, it is the responsibility of the network administrator to safeguard the data held on the servers and to ensure that when requested, this data is ready to go.

Because both fault tolerance and disaster recovery are such an important part of network administration, they are well represented in the CompTIA Network+ exam. In that light, this chapter is important both in terms of real-world application as well as the exam itself.

In addition to fault tolerance and disaster recovery, this chapter also identifies the function of *Virtual LANs* and *Network Attached Storage (NAS)* devices.

Fault tolerance

As far as computers are concerned, *fault tolerance* refers to the capability of the computer system or network to provide continued data availability in the event of hardware failure. Every component within a server from CPU fan to power supply has a chance of failure. Some components such as processors rarely fail, whereas hard disk failures are well documented.

Almost every component has fault-tolerant measures. These measures typically require redundant hardware components that can easily or automatically take over when there is a hardware failure.

Of all the components inside computer systems, the one that requires the most redundancy are the hard disks. Not only are hard disk failures more common than any other component but they also maintain the data, without which there would be little need for a network.

Hard Disks Are Half the Problem

In fact, according to recent research, hard disks are responsible for one of every two server hardware failures. This is an interesting statistic to think about.

Disk-level fault tolerance

Making the decision to have *hard disk fault tolerance* on the server is the first step; the second is deciding which fault-tolerant strategy to use. Hard disk fault tolerance is implemented according to different *RAID* levels. Each RAID level offers differing amounts of data protection and performance.

The RAID level appropriate for a given situation depends on the importance placed on the data, the difficulty of replacing that data, and the associated costs of a respective RAID implementation. Often times, the cost of data loss and replacement outweigh the costs associated with implementing a strong RAID fault-tolerant solution.

RAID 0: stripe set without parity

Although it's given RAID status, *RAID 0* does not actually provide any fault tolerance; in fact using RAID 0 may even be less fault tolerant than storing all of your data on a single hard disk.

RAID 0 combines unused disk space on two or more hard drives into a single logical volume with data being written to equally sized stripes across all of the disks. By using multiple disks, reads and writes are performed simultaneously across all drives. This means that disk access is faster, making the performance of RAID 0 better than other RAID solutions and significantly better than a single hard disk. The downside of RAID 0 is that if any disk in the array fails, the data is lost and must be restored from backup.

Because of its lack of fault tolerance, RAID 0 is rarely implemented. Figure 8.1 shows an example of RAID 0 striping across three hard disks.

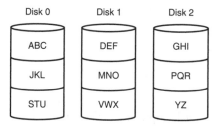

Figure 8.1   RAID 0 striping without parity.

RAID 1

One of the more common RAID implementations is *RAID 1*. RAID 1 requires two hard disks and uses *disk mirroring* to provide fault tolerance. When information is written to the hard disk, it is automatically and simultaneously written to the second hard disk. Both of the hard disks in the mirrored configuration use the same hard disk controller; the partitions used on the hard disk need to be approximately the same size to establish the mirror. In the mirrored configuration, if the primary disk were to fail, the second mirrored disk would contain all of the required information and there would be little disruption to data availability. In some configurations it is even possible for the server to continue operating in the case of the primary disk failure.

There are some key advantages to a RAID 1 solution. First, it is cheap, as only two hard disks are required to provide fault tolerance. Second, no additional software is required for establishing RAID 1 as modern network operating systems have built-in support for it. RAID levels using striping are often incapable of including a boot or system partition in fault-tolerant solutions. Finally, RAID 1 offers load balancing over multiple disks, which increases read performance over that of a single disk.

Because of its advantages RAID 1 is well suited as an entry-level RAID solution but it has a few significant shortcomings that exclude its use in many environments. It has limited storage capacity—two 100GB hard drives only provide 100GB of storage space. Organizations with large data storage needs may exceed a mirrored solutions capacity in very short order. RAID 1 also has a single point of failure, the hard disk controller. If it were to fail, the data would be inaccessible on either drive. RAID 1 has a high overhead in terms of disk space; for every megabyte used, another is needed in the mirror. Figure 8.2 shows an example of RAID 1 disk mirroring.

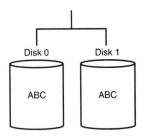

Figure 8.2   RAID 1 disk mirroring.

An extension of RAID 1 is *disk duplexing*. Disk duplexing is the same as mirroring with the exception of one key detail: It places the hard disks on separate hard disk controllers, eliminating the single point of failure.

 Be aware of the differences between disk duplexing and mirroring for the exam.

RAID 5

RAID 5, also known as *disk striping with parity*, uses *distributed parity* to write information across all disks in the array. Unlike the striping used in RAID 0, RAID 5 includes parity information in the striping, which provides fault tolerance. This parity information is used to re-create the data in the event of a failure. RAID 5 requires a minimum of three disks with the equivalent of a single disk being used for the parity information. This means that if you have three 40GB hard disks, you have 80GB of storage space with the other 40GB used for parity. To increase storage space in a RAID 5 array, you need only add another disk to the array. Depending on the sophistication of the RAID setup you are using, the RAID controller will be able to incorporate the new drive into the array automatically, or you will need to rebuild the array and restore the data from backup.

There are many factors that have made RAID 5 a very popular fault-tolerant design. RAID 5 can continue to function in the event of a single drive failure. If a hard disk were to fail in the array, the parity would re-create the missing data and continue to function with the remaining drives. By writing to multiple drives simultaneously, the read performance of RAID 5 is improved over a single disk.

There are only a few drawbacks for the RAID 5 solution. These are as follows:

➤ The costs of implementing RAID 5 are initially higher than other fault-tolerant measures requiring a minimum of three hard disks. Given the costs of hard disks today, this is a minor concern.

➤ RAID 5 suffers from poor write performance because the parity has to be calculated and then written across several disks. The performance lag is minimal and won't have a noticeable difference on the network.

➤ When a new disk is placed in a failed RAID 5 array, there is a regeneration time when the data is being rebuilt on the new drive. This process requires extensive resources from the server.

Figure 8.3 shows an example of RAID 5 striping with parity.

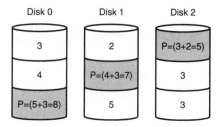

Figure 8.3 RAID 5 striping with parity.

RAID 10

Sometimes RAID levels are combined to take advantage of the best of each. One such strategy is *RAID 10*, which combines RAID levels 1 and 0. In this configuration four disks are required. As you might expect, the configuration consists of a *mirrored stripe set*. To some extent, RAID 10 takes advantage of the performance capability of a stripe set while offering the fault tolerance of a mirrored solution. As well as having the benefits of each though, RAID 10 also inherits the shortcomings of each strategy. In this case, the high overhead and the decreased write performance are the disadvantages. Figure 8.4 shows an example of a RAID 10 configuration. Table 8.1 provides a summary of the various RAID levels.

 RAID levels 2, 3, and 4 are omitted from this discussion as they are infrequently used and will rarely if at all be seen in modern network environments.

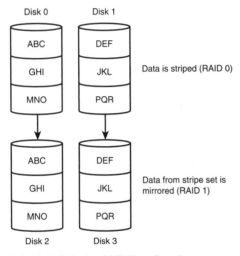

Figure 8.4 Disks in a RAID 10 configuration.

Table 8.1	Summary of RAID Levels			
RAID Level	**Description**	**Advantages**	**Disadvantages**	**Required Disks**
RAID 0	Disk striping	Increased read and write performance. RAID 0 can be implemented with only two disks.	Does not offer any fault tolerance.	Two or more
RAID 1	Disk mirroring	Provides fault tolerance. Can also be used with separate disk controllers, reducing the single point of failure (called *disk duplexing*).	RAID 1 has a 50% overhead and suffers from poor write performance.	Two

(continued)

Table 8.1	Summary of RAID Levels *(continued)*			
RAID Level	Description	Advantages	Disadvantages	Required Disks
RAID 5	Disk striping with distributed parity	Can recover from a single disk failure; increased read performance over a single disk. Disks can be added to the array to increase storage capacity.	May slow down network during regeneration time and may suffer from poor write performance.	Minimum of three
RAID 10	Striping with mirrored volumes	Increased performance with striping; offers mirrored fault tolerance.	High overhead as with mirroring.	Four

Server fault tolerance

In addition to providing fault tolerance for individual hardware components, some organizations go the extra mile to include the entire server in the fault-tolerant design. When it comes to server fault tolerance, two key strategies are commonly employed: stand-by servers and server clustering.

Stand-by servers

Stand-by servers are a fault-tolerant measure where there is a second server configured identically to the first one. The second server may be stored remotely or locally and set up in a *failover configuration*. In a failover configuration, the secondary server is connected to the primary and ready to take over the server functions at a heartbeat's notice. If the secondary server detects that the primary has failed, it will automatically cut in. Network users will not notice the transition as there will be little or no disruption in data availability.

The primary server communicates with the secondary server by issuing special notification notices referred to as *heartbeats*. If the secondary server stops receiving the heartbeat messages, it assume that the primary has died and so assumes the *primary server configuration*. Figure 8.5 shows an example of a failover server solution.

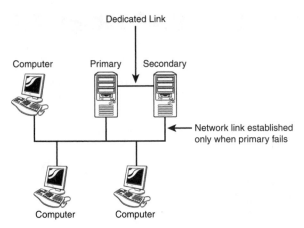

Figure 8.5 Failover server solution.

Server clustering

Those companies wanting maximum data availability that have the funds to pay for it may choose to use *server clustering*. As the name suggests, server clustering involves grouping servers together for the purposes of fault tolerance and load balancing. In this configuration, other servers in the cluster can compensate for the failure of a single server. The failed server will have no impact on the network and the end users will have no idea that a server has failed.

The clear advantage of server clusters is that they offer the highest level of fault tolerance and data availability. The disadvantages are equally clear-cost. The cost of buying a single server can be a huge investment for many organizations; having to buy duplicate servers is far too costly. Figure 8.6 shows servers in a cluster configuration.

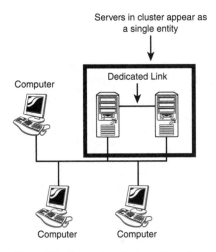

Figure 8.6 Servers in a cluster configuration.

Using uninterruptible power supplies

No discussion of fault tolerance can be complete without a look at power-related issues and the mechanisms used to combat them. When you're designing a fault-tolerant system, your planning should definitely include UPSs (Uninterruptible Power Supplies). A *UPS* serves many functions and is a major part of server consideration and implementation.

On a basic level, a UPS is a box that holds a battery and a built-in charging circuit. During times of good power, the battery is recharged; when the UPS is needed, it's ready to provide power to the server. Most often, the UPS is required to provide enough power to give the administrator time to shut down the server in an orderly fashion, preventing any potential data loss from a dirty shutdown.

Why use a UPS?

Organizations of all shapes and sizes need UPSs as part of their fault-tolerance strategies. A UPS is as important as any other fault-tolerance measure. Three key reasons make a UPS necessary:

➤ **Data availability**—The goal of any fault-tolerance measure is data availability. A UPS ensures access to the server in the event of a power failure—or at least as long as it takes to save a file.

➤ **Protection from data loss**—Fluctuations in power or a sudden power down can damage the data on the server system. In addition, many servers take full advantage of caching, and a sudden loss of power could cause the loss of all information held in cache.

➤ **Protection from hardware damage**—Constant power fluctuations or sudden power downs can damage hardware components within a computer. Damaged hardware can lead to reduced data availability while the hardware is being repaired.

Power threats

In addition to keeping a server functioning long enough to safely shut it down, a UPS also safeguards a server from inconsistent power. This inconsistent power can take many forms. A UPS protects a system from the following power-related threats:

➤ **Blackout**—A total failure of the power supplied to the server.

➤ **Spike**—A spike is a very short (usually less than a second) but very intense increase in voltage. Spikes can do irreparable damage to any kind of equipment, especially computers.

➤ **Surge**—Compared to a spike, a surge is a considerably longer (sometimes many seconds) but usually less intense increase in power. Surges can also damage your computer equipment.

➤ **Sag**—A sag is a short-term voltage drop (the opposite of a spike). This type of voltage drop can cause a server to reboot.

➤ **Brownout**—A brownout is a drop in power supply that usually lasts more than a few minutes.

Many of these power-related threats can occur without your knowledge; if you don't have a UPS, you cannot prepare for them. For a few hundred dollars, it is worth buying a UPS, if for no other reason than to sleep better at night.

Disaster recovery

Even the most fault-tolerant networks will fail, which is an unfortunate fact. When those costly and carefully implemented fault-tolerant strategies do fail, you are left with *disaster recovery*.

Disaster recovery can take on many forms. In addition to real disaster, fire, flood, theft, and the like, many other potential business disruptions can fall under the banner of disaster recovery. For example, the failure of the electrical supply to your city block may interrupt the business function. Such an event, although not a disaster per se, may invoke the disaster recovery methods.

The cornerstone of every disaster recovery strategy is the preservation and recoverability of data. When talking about preservations and recoverability, we are talking about backups. When we are talking about backups, we are likely talking about tape backups. Implementing a regular backup schedule can save you a lot of grief when fault tolerance fails or when you need to recover a file that has been accidentally deleted. When it comes time to design a backup schedule, there are three key types of backups that are used—full, differential, and incremental.

Full backup

The preferred method of backup is the *full backup* method, which copies all files and directories from the hard disk to the backup media. There are a few reasons why doing a full backup is not always possible. First among them is likely the time involved in performing a full backup.

A full backup is the fastest way to restore of all the methods discussed here, because only one tape, or set of tapes, is required for a full restore.

Depending on the amount of data to be backed up, full backups can take an extremely long time and use extensive system resources. Depending on the configuration of the backup hardware, this can slow down the network considerably. In addition, some environments have more data than can fit on a single tape. This makes staking a full backup awkward, as someone needs to be there to change the tapes.

The main advantage of full backups is that a single tape or tape set holds all of the data you need backed up. In the event of a failure, a single tape may be all that is needed to get all data and system information back. The upshot of all this is that any disruption to the network is greatly reduced.

Unfortunately, its strength can also be its weakness. A single tape holding an organization's data can be a security risk. If the tape were to fall into the wrong hands, all of the data can be restored on another computer. Using passwords on tape backups and using a secure offsite and onsite location can minimize the security risk.

Differential backup

For those companies that just don't quite have enough time to complete a full backup, there is the *differential backup*. Differential backups are faster than a full backup as they backup only the data that has changed since the last full backup. This means if you do a full backup on a Saturday and a differential backup on the following Wednesday, only the data that has changed since Saturday is backed up. Restoring the differential backup will require the last full backup and the latest differential backup.

Differential backups know what files have changed since the last full backup by using a setting known as the *archive bit*. The archive bit flags files that have changed or been created and identifies them as ones that need to be backed up. Full backups do not concern themselves with the archive bit as all files are backed up regardless of date. A full backup however will clear the archive bit after data has been backed up to avoid future confusion. Differential backups take notice of the archive bit and use it to determine which files have changed. The differential backup does not reset the archive bit information.

If you experience trouble with any type of backup, you should clean the tape drive and then try the backup again.

Incremental backup

Some companies have a very finite amount of time they can allocate to back-up procedures. Such organizations are likely to use *incremental backups* in their backup strategy. Incremental backups save only the files that have changed since the last full or incremental backup. Like differential backups, incremental backups use the archive bit to determine the files that have changed since the last full or incremental backup. Unlike differentials however, incremental backups clear the archive bit so files that have not changed are not backed up.

Full and incremental backups clear the archive bit after files have been backed up.

The faster backup times of incremental backups comes at a price—the amount of time required to restore. Recovering from a failure with incremental backups requires numerous tapes—all the incremental tapes and the most recent full backup. For example, if you had a full backup from Sunday and an incremental for Monday, Tuesday, and Wednesday, you would need four tapes to restore the data. Keep in mind: Each tape in the rotation is an additional step in the restore process and an additional failure point. One damaged incremental tape and you will be unable to restore the data. Table 8.2 summarizes the various backup strategies.

Table 8.2 Backup Strategies				
Backup Type	**Advantages**	**Disadvantages**	**Data Backed Up**	**Archive Bit**
Full	Backs up all data on a single tape or tape set. Restoring data requires the least amount of tapes.	Depending on the amount of data, full backups can take a long time.	All files and directories are backed up.	Does not use the archive bit but resets it after data has been backed up.
Differential	Faster backups than a full.	Uses more tapes than a full backup. Restore process takes longer than a full backup.	All files and directories that have changed since the last full or differential backup.	Uses the archive bit to determine the files that have changed but does not reset the archive bit.

(continued)

Table 8.2	Backup Strategies (continued)			
Backup Type	Advantages	Disadvantages	Data Backed Up	Archive Bit
Incremental	Faster backup times.	Requires multiple disks; restoring data takes more time than the other backup methods.	The files and directories that have changed since the last full or incremental backup.	Uses the archive bit to determine the files that have changed and resets the archive bit.

Tape rotations

After you have decided on the backup type you will use, you are ready to choose a *backup rotation*. There are several backup rotation strategies in use, some good, some bad, and some really bad. The most common and perhaps the best rotation strategy is the Grandfather, Father, Son rotation (GFS).

The *GFS* backup rotation is the most widely used and for good reason. A typical GFS rotation requires 12 tapes: four tapes for daily backups (son), five tapes for weekly backups (father) and three tapes for monthly backups (grandfather).

Using this rotation schedule it is possible to recover data from days, weeks, or months previous. Some network administrators choose to add tapes to the monthly rotation to be able to retrieve data even further back, sometimes up to a year. In most organizations however, data that is a week old is out of date, let alone six months or a year.

Backup best practices

There are many details that go into making a backup strategy a success. The following list contains issues to consider as part of your backup plan.

> ➤ **Offsite storage**—Consider having backup tapes stored offsite so that in the event a disaster in a building a current set of tapes is still available offsite. The offsite tapes should be as current as any onsite and should be secure.

> ➤ **Label tapes**—The goal is to restore the data as quickly as possible and trying to find the tape you need can be difficult if not marked. Further it can prevent you from recording over a tape you need.

> ➤ **New tapes**—Like old cassette tapes, the tape cartridges used for the backups wear out over time. One strategy used to prevent this from becoming a problem is to introduce new tapes periodically into the rotation schedule.

➤ **Verify backups**—Never assume the backup was successful. Seasoned administrators know that checking backup logs and performing periodic test restores are parts of the backup process.

➤ **Cleaning**—From time to time it is necessary to clean the tape drive. If the inside gets dirty, backups may fail.

 A backup strategy must include offsite storage to account for theft, fire, flood, or other disasters.

Network Attached Storage (NAS)

As the storage needs of organizations of all sizes increase, new technologies must be developed to accommodate those needs. One strategy for increased storage needs is NAS. Essentially, *NAS* is a specialized file server.

NAS is a box that typically has no mouse, keyboard, or monitor, and that has a very streamlined operating system. Several hard disks and perhaps a tape drive hold the network files. Additional hard drives can be added to the NAS to increase storage capacity. Clients typically access a NAS over an Ethernet connection; each NAS box is seen as a node on the network and requires an IP address.

Because NAS systems are not attached to a server, they must be able to communicate on the network by using an application protocol designed for file access. Most commonly, the *Network File System* (*NFS*) or *Server Message Block* (*SMB*) protocols are supported by NAS devices for this purpose.

 For the Network+ exam, you should be prepared to identify the file system access protocols (sometimes referred to as *application protocols*) that are commonly supported by NAS devices.

Because NAS is dedicated to data storage, it's a more costly solution than providing data storage from an existing server. However, the advantages of NAS over the traditional file server are compelling. First, NAS can provide higher data availability; as a dedicated device, the NAS is less likely than a traditional file server to be brought down or to crash, disabling file access. Second, a NAS system is more secure and less susceptible to security attacks than a traditional file server. Third, and somewhat subjectively, a NAS system offers easy administration.

Virtual LANs

VLANs provide a means to segment a network, which can significantly increase the performance capability of the network and remove potential performance bottlenecks. A VLAN is a group of computers that are connected and act as if they are on their own network segments, even though they might not be. For instance, suppose you work in a three-story building in which the advertising employees are spread over all three floors. A VLAN can let all the advertising personnel use the network resources as if they were connected on the same segment. This virtual segment can be isolated from other network segments. In effect, it would appear to the advertising group that they were on a network by themselves.

VLANs allow you to create multiple broadcast domains on a single switch. In essence, this is the same as creating separate networks for each VLAN.

VLANs offer some clear advantages. Being able to create logical segmentation of a network gives administrators flexibility beyond the restrictions of the physical network design and cable infrastructure. VLANs allow for easier administration because the network can be divided into well-organized sections. Further, you can increase security by isolating certain network segments from others. For instance, you can segment the marketing personnel from finance or the administrators from the students. VLANs can ease the burden on overworked routers and reduce broadcast storms. Table 8.3 summarizes the benefits of VLANs.

802.1q is the Institute of Electrical and Electronics Engineers (IEEE) specification developed to ensure interoperability of VLAN technologies from the various vendors.

Table 8.3 Benefits of VLANs	
Advantages	**Description**
Increased security	By creating logical (virtual) boundaries, network segments can be isolated.
Increased performance	By reducing broadcast traffic throughout the network, VLANs free up bandwidth.
Organization	Network users and resources that are linked and communicate frequently can be grouped together in a VLAN.
Simplified administration	With a VLAN the network administrator's job is easier when moving users between LAN segments, recabling, addressing new stations, and reconfiguring hubs and routers.

VLAN membership

You can use several methods to determine VLAN membership or how devices are assigned to a specific VLAN. The following sections describe the common methods of determining how VLAN membership is assigned.

Protocol-based VLANs

With *protocol-based VLAN* membership, computers are assigned to VLANs by using the protocol that is in use and the Layer 3 address. For example, this method allows an Internetwork Packet Exchange (IPX) network or a particular Internet Protocol (IP) subnet to have its own VLAN.

It is important to note that although VLAN membership may be based on Layer 3 information, this has nothing to do with routing or routing functions. The IP numbers are used only to determine the membership in a particular VLAN—not to determine routing.

Port-based VLANs

Port-based VLANs require that specific ports on a network switch be assigned to a VLAN. For example, ports 1 through 8 may be assigned to marketing, ports 9 through 18 may be assigned to sales, and so on. Using this method, a switch determines VLAN membership by taking note of the port used by a particular packet.

MAC address–based VLANs

As you may have guessed, the *Media Access Control (MAC)* address type of VLAN assigns membership according to the MAC address of the workstation. To do this, the switch must keep track of the MAC addresses that belong to each VLAN. The advantage of this method is that a workstation computer can be moved anywhere in an office without needing to be reconfigured; because the MAC address does not change, the workstation remains a member of a particular VLAN. Table 8.4 provides examples of MAC address–based VLANs.

Table 8.4 MAC Address–Based VLANs		
MAC Address	VLAN	Description
44-45-53-54-00-00	1	Sales
44-45-53-54-13-12	2	Marketing
44-45-53-54-D3-01	3	Administration
44-45-53-54-F5-17	1	Sales

Although the acceptance and implementation of VLANs has been slow, the ability to logically segment a LAN provides a new level of administrative flexibility, organization, and security.

Review and test yourself

The following sections provide you with the opportunity to review what you learned in this chapter and to test yourself.

The facts

For the exam, don't forget these important concepts:

➤ RAID 0 uses disk striping over two or more disks but offers no fault tolerance.

➤ RAID 1 uses two disks in a mirrored configuration.

➤ Disk duplexing is a RAID 1 implementation using separate hard disk controllers.

➤ RAID 5 is disk striping with parity, requiring three disk minimum.

➤ With a full backup, all data is backed up and data can be restored from a single tape set. Full backups do not use the archive bit but clear it after files have been copied to tape.

➤ With incremental backups all data changed since the last full or incremental is backed up. The restore procedure requires several tapes: the latest full backup and all incremental tapes since the last full backup. Incremental uses the archive bit and clears it after a file is saved to disk.

➤ With a differential backup, all data changed since the last full backup is backed up. The restore procedure requires the latest full backup tape and the latest differential backup tape. Differential uses the archive bit to determine which files need to be backed up, but does not clear it.

➤ You should use an offsite tape rotation scheme to store current copies of backups in a secure offsite location. A commonly used rotation is the Grandfather, Father, Son (GFS) rotation.

➤ You should periodically introduce new tapes into the tape rotation and destroy the old tapes.

➤ There are two key strategies commonly employed for server fault tolerance: stand-by servers and server clustering.

➤ VLANs are used to segment networks.

➤ NAS devices use the SMB and NFS application protocols.

Key terms

➤ RAID

➤ Disk mirroring

➤ Disk duplexing

➤ Disk striping

➤ Full backup

➤ Incremental backup

➤ Differential backup

➤ VLANs

➤ NAS

Practice exam

Question 1

> During your lunch break you rummage around the company's storage closet and discover two 20GB SCSI hard disks and an additional hard disk controller. You decide to use the equipment to provide a fault-tolerant solution in one of your company's existing servers. Which of the following fault-tolerant RAID levels could you implement? (Choose two answers.)
>
> ❑ A. RAID 0
> ❑ B. RAID 1
> ❑ C. Disk duplexing
> ❑ D. RAID 5

The correct answers are B and C. Using the equipment that you found, it would be possible to implement RAID 0 as there are two hard disks. You could also implement disk duplexing, as there was an additional hard disk controller. Answer A is incorrect as RAID 0 is not a fault-tolerant RAID level. Answer D is incorrect because RAID 5 requires a minimum of three disks.

Question 2

> Which two types of tape backup methods clear the archive bit after the backup has been completed?
>
> ❑ A. Full
> ❑ B. Differential
> ❑ C. Incremental
> ❑ D. GFS

The correct answers are A and C. The archive bit is reset after a full backup and an incremental backup. Answer B is incorrect as the differential backup does not reset the archive bit and answer D is wrong because GFS is a rotation strategy, not a backup method.

Question 3

You come into work on Thursday morning to find that the server has failed and you need to restore the data from backup. You had finished a full backup on Sunday and incremental backups on Monday, Tuesday, and Wednesday. How many tapes are required to restore the backup?

○ A. 4

○ B. 2

○ C. 3

○ D. 5

The correct answer is A. Incremental backups save all files and directories that have changed since the last full or incremental backup. To restore, you need the latest full backup and all incremental tapes. In this case, you need four tapes to complete the restore process.

Question 4

Having previously found two 20GB SCSI drives in a storage closet, you decide to return to the closet and look for some more. This time, you find five 15GB hard disks. If you were to implement a RAID 5 solution using all five disks, how much storage space would you have for the actual data?

○ A. 75GB

○ B. 60GB

○ C. 30GB

○ D. 45GB

The correct answer is B. RAID 5 uses distributed parity. The parity information is spread across all disks and requires the equivalent space of a single hard disk. In this example, there are five 15GB disks, giving a total of 75GB of storage. 15GB is required for the parity information, leaving 60GB for saving actual data.

Question 5

Which of the following RAID levels offers the greatest read and write performance?

- ○ A. RAID 0
- ○ B. RAID 1
- ○ C. Disk duplexing
- ○ D. RAID 5
- ○ E. RAID 10

The correct answer is A. Although not a fault-tolerant RAID level, RAID 0 offers the best performance of any RAID level. Other RAID levels do offer some performance improvements over a single disk; their fault-tolerant considerations inhibit the write operations.

Question 6

Which file system access protocols are commonly supported by a NAS device?

- ❑ A. FAT
- ❑ B. NFS
- ❑ C. SMB
- ❑ D. NTFS

The correct answers are B and C. NAS devices typically support NFS and SMB file system access protocols. NTFS and FAT are file systems, not file system access protocols.

Question 7

As part of your network administrative responsibilities, you have completed your monthly backups. As part of backup best practices, where should the tapes be stored?

- ○ A. In a secure location in the server room.
- ○ B. In a secure onsite location in the building.
- ○ C. In an offsite location.
- ○ D. In a secure offsite location.

The correct answer is D. Although not always done, it is a best practice to store tape backups in a secure offsite location in case of fire or theft. Answer A is incorrect because if the server room is damaged by fire or flood, the tapes and the data on the server can be compromised by the same disaster. Similarly, answer B is incorrect because storing the backups onsite does not eliminate the threat of a single disaster destroying the data on the server and tapes. Answer C is incorrect for security reasons. The offsite tapes must be secured.

Question 8

As network administrator you have been tasked with designing a disaster recovery plan for your network. Which of the following might you include in a disaster recovery plan?

- ○ A. RAID 5
- ○ B. Offsite tape backup
- ○ C. Mirrored hard disks
- ○ D. UPS

The correct answer is B. Offsite tape storage is part of a disaster recovery plan. The other answers listed are considered fault tolerance measures as they are implemented to ensure data availability.

Question 9

Which of the following power-related problems is associated with a short-term voltage drop?

- ○ A. Surge
- ○ B. Brownout
- ○ C. Sag
- ○ D. Spike

The correct answer is C. A sag is a short-term voltage drop. A brownout is also a voltage drop, but it lasts longer than a sag. A surge is an increase in power that lasts a few seconds. A spike is a power increase that lasts a few milliseconds.

Question 10

As a network administrator, you have been asked to implement a RAID solution that offers high performance. Fault tolerance is not a concern. Which RAID level are you likely to use?

○ A. RAID 0

○ B. RAID 1

○ C. RAID 2

○ D. RAID 5

○ E. RAID 10

The correct answer is A. RAID 0 offers the highest level of performance but does not offer any fault tolerance. If the performance of RAID 0 is required and so is fault tolerance, RAID 10 is a better choice. RAID 1 offers fault tolerance but no increase in performance.

Want to know more?

 Toigo, Jon William and Margaret Romano Toigo (Illustrator). *Disaster Recovery Planning: Strategies for Protecting Critical Information Assets* (2nd Edition). Prentice Hall PTR, 1999.

 Sheldon, Thomas. *McGraw-Hill's Encyclopedia of Networking and Telecommunications*. McGraw-Hill Professional Publishing, 2001.

 Tulloch, Mitch. *Microsoft Encyclopedia of Networking* (with CD-ROM). Microsoft Press, 2000.

Network Security

Objectives

3.8 Identify the purpose, benefits, and characteristics of using a firewall.

3.9 Identify the purpose, benefits, and characteristics of using a proxy server.

3.10 Given a scenario, predict the impact of a particular security implementation on network functionality (for example, blocking port numbers and encryption).

What you need to know

✓ Understand the function of a firewall in a networked environment.

✓ Understand the function of a proxy server in a networked environment.

✓ Identify the effects of port blocking.

✓ Identify encryption methods.

✓ Understand how to create a secure password policy.

Introduction

Two important elements of a network security picture are the use of proxy servers and firewall systems. A firewall system acts as a protective layer to network access by controlling the traffic that passes between the interfaces on the system. Proxy servers allow you to centralize access to the Internet and therefore provide a way to control and monitor network access.

This chapter looks at the role firewalls and proxy servers play in a networked environment and how port blocking and other security measures, such as password policies and encryption, fit together to form a secure network.

Firewalls

In today's network environments, for both home and corporate environments, firewalls are being used to protect systems from external as well as internal threats.

Essentially, a firewall is a system or group of systems that controls the flow of traffic between two networks. The most common use of a firewall is to protect a private network from a public network such as the Internet. However, firewalls are also increasingly being used as a means to separate a sensitive area of a private network from less-sensitive areas.

At its most basic, a *firewall* is a device (it could be a computer system or a dedicated hardware device) that has more than one network interface and manages the flow of network traffic between those interfaces. How it manages the flow and what it does with certain types of traffic depends on its configuration. Figure 9.1 shows the most basic firewall configuration.

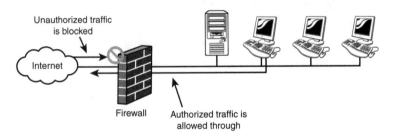

Figure 9.1 A basic firewall implementation.

Strictly speaking, a firewall performs no action on the packets it receives besides the basic functions just described. However, in a real-world implementation, a firewall is likely to offer other functionality, such as *Network*

Address Translation (NAT) and proxy server services. Without NAT, any host on the internal network that needs to send or receive data through the firewall needs a registered IP address. Although there are such environments, most people have to settle for using a private address range on the internal network and therefore rely on the firewall system to translate the outgoing request into an acceptable public network address.

Although the fundamental purpose of a firewall is to protect one network from another, you need to configure the firewall to allow some traffic through. If you don't need to allow traffic to pass through a firewall, you can dispense with it entirely and completely separate your network from others.

A firewall can employ a variety of methods to ensure security. A firewall can use just one of these methods, or it can combine different methods to produce the most appropriate and robust configuration. The following sections discuss the various firewall methods that are commonly used: packet-filtering firewalls, circuit-level firewalls, and application gateway firewalls.

Packet-filtering firewalls

Of the firewall methods discussed in this chapter, *packet filtering* is the most commonly implemented. Packet filtering allows the firewall to examine each packet that passes through it and determine what to do with it, based on the configuration. A packet-filtering firewall deals with packets at the data-link and network layers of the *Open Systems Interconnect (OSI)* model. The following are some of the criteria by which packet filtering can be implemented:

> ▶ **IP address**—By using the IP address as a parameter, the firewall can allow or deny traffic, based on the source or destination IP address. For example, you can configure the firewall so that only certain hosts on the internal network are able to access hosts on the Internet. Alternatively, you can configure it so that only certain hosts on the Internet are able to gain access to a system on the internal network.

> ▶ **Port number**—As discussed in Chapter 5, "TCP/IP (Transmission Control Protocol/Internet Protocol)," the TCP/IP suite uses port numbers to identify which service a certain packet is destined for. By configuring the firewall to allow certain types of traffic, you can control the flow. You might, for example, open port 80 on the firewall to allow Hypertext Transfer Protocol (HTTP) requests from users on the Internet to reach the corporate Web server. You might also, depending on the application, open the HTTP Secure (HTTPS) port, port 443, to allow access to a secure Web server application.

➤ **Protocol ID**—Because each packet transmitted with IP has a protocol identifier in it, a firewall can read this value and then determine what kind of packet it is. If you are filtering based on protocol ID, you specify which protocols you will and will not allow to pass through the firewall.

➤ **MAC address**—This is perhaps the least used of the packet-filtering methods discussed, but it is possible to configure a firewall to use the hardware-configured MAC address as the determining factor in whether access to the network is granted. This is not a particularly flexible method, and it is therefore suitable only in environments in which you can closely control who uses which MAC address. The Internet is not such an environment.

Circuit-level firewalls

Circuit-level firewalls are similar in operation to packet-filtering firewalls, but they operate at the transport layer of the OSI model. The biggest difference between a packet-filtering firewall and a circuit-level firewall is that a circuit-level firewall validates TCP and UDP sessions before opening a connection, or circuit, through the firewall. When the session is established, the firewall maintains a table of valid connections and lets data pass through when session information matches an entry in the table. The table entry is removed and the circuit is closed when the session is terminated.

Application gateway firewalls

The *application gateway firewall* is the most functional of all the firewall types. As its name suggests, the application gateway firewall functionality is implemented through an application. Application gateway firewall systems can implement sophisticated rules and closely control traffic that passes through. Features of these firewalls can include user authentication systems and the ability to control which systems an outside user can access on the internal network.

 The three firewall methods described in this chapter are often combined into a single firewall application. Packet filtering is the basic firewall function. Circuit-level functionality provides NAT, and an application gateway firewall provides proxy functionality. This is a good point to remember for the Network+ exam.

Firewalls have become common in businesses of all sizes. As the Internet becomes an ever more hostile place, firewalls and the individuals who understand them are likely to become an essential part of the IT landscape.

Proxy servers

Proxy servers provide what is now a common feature of any modern network Internet access. A proxy server acts as an intermediary between a user on the internal network and a service on the external network (normally the Internet). The proxy server takes requests from a user and then performs those requests on behalf of the user. To the external system, the request looks as if it originated from the proxy server, not from the user on the internal network. Figure 9.2 shows how a proxy server fits into a network configuration.

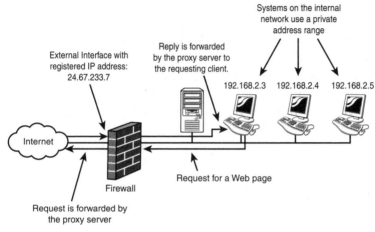

Systems on the internal network use a private address range

External Interface with registered IP address: 24.67.233.7

Reply is forwarded by the proxy server to the requesting client.

192.168.2.3   192.168.2.4   192.168.2.5

Internet

Firewall

Request for a Web page

Request is forwarded by the proxy server

Figure 9.2   A proxy server in a typical network configuration.

A proxy server enables a network to appear to external networks as a single IP address—that of the external network interface of the proxy server.

There are a couple of reasons to implement a proxy server:

➤ **To perform NAT functions**—A proxy server can process and execute commands on behalf of clients that have *private* IP addresses. This enables an organization with only one registered IP address to provide Internet access to a large number of computers.

➤ **To allow Internet access to be controlled**—Having a centralized point of access allows for a great deal of control over the use of the Internet. By using the functionality of a proxy server application or by using an add-on feature, proxy servers can filter requests made by clients and either allow or disallow them. You can, for example, implement *uniform resource locator* (*URL*) filtering, which allows or denies users access to certain sites. More sophisticated products can also perform tests on retrieved material, to see if it fits acceptable criteria. Such measures are intended to prevent users from accessing inappropriate Internet Web pages. As an "after the event" feature, proxy server applications also normally provide logging capabilities so that Internet usage can be monitored.

 The function of a proxy server should not be confused with the function of a firewall, even though some applications integrate the functionality of both. In basic terms, a proxy server is a centralized point of access to the Internet. It also, generally, provides caching capabilities.

Although the most common function of a proxy server is to provide access to the Web for internal clients, that is not its only function. A proxy server, by definition, can be used as an intermediary for anything, not just HTTP requests. Other services can be supported by a proxy server, depending on the proxy server application being used and its configuration. For example, you might configure a proxy server to service HTTP requests (TCP port 80), Post Office Protocol 3 (POP3) email retrieval (TCP port 110), Simple Mail Transfer Protocol (SMTP) mail sending (TCP port 25), and HTTPS requests (TCP port 443). With an understanding of what a proxy server is designed to do, you can look at one additional feature built into proxy server functionality, *caching*.

Caching proxy servers

An additional feature offered by many proxy server applications is caching; such a server is known as a *caching proxy server*. Caching allows the proxy server to store pages that it retrieves as files on disk. Consequently, if the same pages are requested again, they can be provided more quickly than if the proxy server had to continue going back to the Web server from which the pages were originally retrieved. This approach has two benefits:

 Proxy servers are sometimes referred to as *HTTP proxies* or *HTTP proxy servers*. In reality, most proxy servers provide proxy services for multiple protocols, not just HTTP.

➤ **Significantly improves performance**—Performance is improved particularly in environments such as a school, where there is a great likelihood that more than one user might retrieve the same page.

➤ **Reduces demands on Internet connections**—Because there are fewer requests to the Internet when a caching proxy server is in use, there is a reduced demand on the Internet connection. In some cases, this results in a general speed improvement. In extreme cases, it might even be possible to adopt a less expensive Internet connectivity method because of the lower level of demand.

As with any technology, with caching proxy servers there are issues to be considered. Sometimes a sizable amount of hard disk space is required to store the cached pages. With the declining cost of hard disk space in recent years, this is not likely to be much of a problem, but it still needs to be considered.

Another factor is that it's possible for pages held in the cache to become stale. As a result, a user might retrieve a page and believe it is the latest version when in fact it has since changed but the new page has not been updated in the proxy server cache. To prevent this problem, caching proxy servers can implement measures such as aging of cached information so that it is removed from the cache after a certain amount of time. Some proxy applications can also make sure that the page stored in the cache is the same as the page currently available on the Internet. If the page in the cache is the same as the one on the Internet, it is served to the client from the cache. If the page is not the same, the newer page is retrieved, cached, and supplied to the client.

More advanced features of caching proxy servers are *Internet Cache Protocol* (*ICP*) and *Caching Array Routing Protocol* (*CARP*). Using these protocols, a proxy server can ask another proxy server if it has a user-requested page in its cache. If it does, the page is retrieved from the other proxy server, stored in cache, and then supplied to the client. Such an arrangement can be used only in environments where there are multiple proxy servers. The increasing availability of broadband and high-speed Internet access is making such environments increasingly rare.

Using a proxy server

Before clients can use a proxy server, it is necessary to configure the client applications to use it, and in some cases, additional client software is needed. In the case of Web browsers, it is necessary to manually tell the application that it needs to use a proxy server. Figure 9.3 shows the configuration screen in Microsoft Internet Explorer that allows the configuration of proxy parameters.

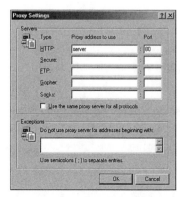

Figure 9.3   The Proxy Settings configuration screen in Internet Explorer.

Other applications besides Web browsers might need to use the proxy server functionality. In some cases, you might need to actually load client software. In essence, this client software modifies elements of the TCP/IP software on the system, to either make it aware of or allow it to cope with the existence of a proxy server.

By now, you might have realized that both firewalls and proxy servers play an important part in the network infrastructure. For that reason, many applications are now available that combine the functionality of both roles. These *firewalling proxy servers* provide a convenient means for an organization to control and secure the access of its network, and at the same time provide the benefits of Internet access to users.

Understanding how security affects a network

Implementing security measures has an effect on the network. How much of an effect it has depends on which security measures are implemented and the habits of the network users. CompTIA specifies two examples of network security measures (blocking ports and encryption) and asks that you determine what effect the implementation of those measures will have on the network. The following sections help you prepare for this part of the exam.

Blocking port numbers

Port blocking is one of the most widely used security methods on networks. Port blocking is associated with firewalls and proxy servers, although in fact it can be implemented on any system that provides a means to manage network data flow, according to data type.

Essentially, when you block a port, you disable the ability for traffic to pass through that port. Port blocking is typically implemented to prevent users on a public network from accessing systems on a private network, although it is equally possible to block internal users from external services by using the same procedure.

Depending on the type of firewall system in use on a network, you might find that all the ports are disabled (blocked) and that the ones you need traffic to flow through must be opened. The benefit of this strategy is that it forces the administrator to choose the ports that should be unblocked rather than specify those that need to be blocked. This ensures that you allow only those services that are absolutely necessary into the network.

What ports remain open largely depends on the needs of the organization. For example, the ports associated with the services listed in Table 9.1 are commonly left open.

Table 9.1 Commonly Opened Port Numbers and Their Associated Uses		
Port Number	Protocol	Purpose
80	HTTP	Web browsing
443	HTTPS	Secure Web transactions
21	FTP	File transfers
25	SMTP	Email sending
110	POP3	Email retrieval
53	DNS	Hostname resolution

These are, of course, only a few of the services you might need on a network, and allowing other services on a network is as easy as opening the port. Keep in mind that the more ports that are open, the more vulnerable you become to outside attacks. You should never open a port on a firewall unless you are absolutely sure that you need to.

Port blocking and network users

Before you implement port blocking, you should have a very good idea of what the port is used for. Although it is true that blocking unused ports does not have any impact on internal network users, if the wrong port is blocked, you can suffer many headaches.

For example, a network administrator was given the task of reducing the amount of spam emails received by his company. He decided to block port 25. He succeeded in blocking the spam email, but in the process, he also prevented users from sending email.

Encryption

Encryption is the process of encoding data so that, without the appropriate unlocking code, the encrypted data can't be read. Encryption is increasingly being used as a means of protecting data from unauthorized users. If you have ever used a secure Web site, you have used encryption.

On private networks, encryption is generally not a very big issue. Modern network operating systems often implement encryption so that passwords are not transmitted openly throughout the network. On the other hand, normal network transmissions are not usually encrypted, although they can be if the need arises. A far more common use for encryption is for data that is sent across a public network such as the Internet. In this case, the administrator has little or no control over the path the data takes to get to its destination. During data transmission, there is plenty of opportunity for someone to take the data from the network and then read the contents of the packets. This process is often referred to as *packet sniffing*.

By sniffing packets from the network and reading their contents, unauthorized users can gain access to private information. But packet sniffing is not possible with encrypted data. Without the necessary code to decrypt the data, the sniffer is able to see only jumbled code. There is a chance that the sniffer might be able to work out what the code is, but the stronger the form of encryption used, the harder it is for the sniffer to work out the code. Therefore, the stronger the encryption method that is used, the better protected the data is.

A number of encryption methods are commonly used. The following sections explain some of the most popular ones, which include:

➤ IP Security (IPSec)

➤ Data Encryption Standard (DES)

➤ Triple DES (3DES)

➤ Pretty Good Privacy (PGP)

IPSec

IPSec is a set of protocols developed by the Internet Engineering Task Force to establish secure transmission of data packets between computer systems. IPSec is commonly used for transmitting data across public networks, where privacy and security are an ever-present concern. Therefore, IPSec is often used to create virtual private networks (VPNs), among other things.

IPSec works at the network layer of the OSI model. Therefore, all applications and services that use IP for the transport of data can use IPSec security. In comparison, security mechanisms such as *Secure Sockets Layer* (*SSL*), operate above the network layer and provide security only for applications that can use SSL, such as Web browsers.

DES

DES was originally developed by IBM in the mid-1970s, and it became a standard in 1977. DES encrypts and decrypts data in 64-bit chunks, using a 64-bit key.

For a time, DES was a proven and trusted encryption method. However, over time, attacks against DES encryption methods were successful, and data security was compromised. Quite simply, as faster and less expensive computer systems became available, 56-bit key encryption became inadequate.

Interestingly, DES cracking contests in the late 1990s highlighted DES weaknesses. One system, which was developed for $250,000 and code-named the *DES Cracker*, shattered DES encryption in less than three days. Today's systems reduce both the cost and time necessary to crack DES encryption.

However, some companies still use the DES encryption method. But for organizations whose data is more sensitive, something stronger is needed.

3DES

Often referred to as "triple DES," *3DES* is an improvement on the DES encryption standard and is much more widely used due to the increased difficulty involved in cracking 3DES encryption. Although 3DES is based on the DES standard, it is a much stronger version, and it is able to provide significantly more security for data than traditional DES.

3DES gets its name from the fact that it performs encryption the same way as regular DES, but it does it three times. Regular DES uses a 64-bit key encryption method, whereas 3DES uses three 64-bit keys, for an overall key length of 192 bits.

PGP

Intended mainly as a mechanism to encrypt email transmission, *PGP* is a *public-key encryption method* created by Phil Zimmerman. PGP can be downloaded and used by anyone who wants to add a degree of security to email messages. A detailed discussion of PGP falls outside the scope of the Network+ objectives. For more information and PGP downloads, refer to the Web site at http://www.pgpi.org/.

Auditing

Auditing is an important part of system security. It provides a means to track events that occur on a system. Auditing increases accountability on a network by making it possible to isolate events to certain users. For instance, it is possible to log failed logon attempts that might indicate that someone is trying to gain access to the network by guessing a username or password.

A network administrator might need to audit many events on a system. Some of these events include failed/successful logons, audit printer access, file and directory access, and remote access. Reviewing the log files generated by auditing allows an administrator to better gauge the potential threats to the network.

Authentication, passwords, and password policies

Although there are many methods of authentication, none have attained the level of popularity of username and password combinations. The reason is that, apart from the fact that usernames and passwords do not require any additional equipment, which practically every other method of authentication does, the username and password process is familiar to users, easy to implement, and relatively secure. In the future, other authentication methods, such as *biometrics* (for example, fingerprint recognition and retinal scans), might overtake usernames and passwords in popularity, but if they ever do, that day is some time away.

Before reading about some of the specific considerations for working with usernames and passwords, you should perhaps consider a simple question. Why do we need usernames and passwords in the first place? The obvious answer, of course, is that they provide a mechanism for users to prove that they are entitled to access the network or a specific resource. But there is another reason: accountability. If users must prove their identity, they are made accountable for their actions. This is particularly relevant in environments in which the auditing of system events is performed because it allows events to be attributed to certain users, based on their usernames. Without some form of authentication—be it usernames and passwords or something else—users cannot be held accountable for their actions.

Passwords are a relatively simple form of authentication in that only a string of characters can be used. However, how the string of characters is used and which policies you can put in place to govern them make usernames and passwords an excellent form of authentication.

Password policies

All popular network operating systems include password policy systems that allow the network administrator to control how passwords are used on the system. The exact capabilities vary between network operating systems. However, generally they allow the following:

➤ **Minimum length of password**—Shorter passwords are easier to guess than longer ones. Setting a minimum password length does not prevent a user from creating a longer password than the minimum, although each network operating system has a limit on how long a password can be.

➤ **Password expiration**—Also known as the *maximum password age*, password expiration defines how long the user can use the same password before having to change it. A general practice is that a password is changed every month or every 30 days. In high-security environments, you might want to make this value shorter, but you should generally not make it any longer. Having passwords expire periodically is an important feature because it means that if a password is compromised, the unauthorized user will not have access indefinitely.

➤ **Prevention of password reuse**—Although a system might be able to cause a password to expire and prompt the user to change it, many users are tempted to simply use the same password again. A process by which the system remembers the last, say, 10 passwords is most secure because it forces the user to create completely new passwords.

➤ **Prevention of easy-to-guess passwords**—Some systems have the capability to evaluate the password provided by a user to determine whether it meets a required level of complexity. This prevents users from having passwords such as *password* or *12345678*.

 On the Network+ exam, you will need to identify an effective password policy. For example, a robust password policy would include forcing users to change their passwords on a regular basis.

Password strength

No matter how good a company's password policy, it is only as effective as the passwords that are created within it. A password that is hard to guess, or *strong*, is more likely to protect the data on a system than one that is easy to guess, or *weak*.

To understand the difference between a strong password and a weak one, consider this: A password of six characters that uses only numbers and letters and is not case-sensitive has 10,314,424,798,490,535,546,171,949,056 possible combinations. That might seem like a lot, but to a password-cracking program, it's really not much security. A password that uses eight case-sensitive characters, with letters, numbers, and special characters has so many possible combinations that a standard calculator is not able display the actual number.

There has always been debate over how long a password should be. It should be sufficiently long that it is hard to break but sufficiently short that the user is able to easily remember it (and type it). In a normal working environment, passwords of eight characters are sufficient. Certainly, they should be no fewer than six characters. In environments where security is a concern, passwords should be 10 characters or more.

Users should be encouraged to use a password that is considered strong. A strong password has at least eight characters; has a combination of letters, numbers, and special characters; uses mixed case; and does not form a proper word. Examples might include *3Ecc5T0b* and *e1oXPn3r*. Such passwords might be secure, but users are likely to have problems remembering them. For that reason, a strategy that is popular is to use a combination of letters and numbers to form phrases or long words. Examples include *d1eTc0La* and *tAb1eT0p*. These passwords might not be quite as secure as the preceding examples, but they are still very strong and a whole lot better than the name of the user's household pet.

Passwords—The Last Word

One last password-related topic is worth mentioning. A password is effective only if just the intended users have it. As soon as a password is passed to someone else, its effectiveness as an authentication mechanism is diminished. As a tool for accountability, the password is almost useless. Passwords are a means of accessing a system and the data on it. Passwords that are known by anyone other than the intended user(s) might as well not be set at all.

Review and test yourself

The following sections provide with you the opportunity to review what you learned in this chapter and to test yourself.

The facts

For the exam, don't forget these important concepts:

➤ Common password policies typically include a minimum length of password, password expiration, prevention of password reuse, and prevention of easy-to-guess passwords.

➤ A password that uses eight case-sensitive characters, with letters, numbers, and special characters often makes a strong password policy.

➤ A firewall is a system or group of systems that controls the flow of traffic between two networks.

➤ A firewall often provides such services as NAT, proxy, and packet filtering.

➤ TCP/IP protocol suite uses port numbers to identify which service a certain packet is destined for. By configuring the firewall to allow certain types of traffic, you can control the flow.

➤ A proxy server acts as an intermediary between a user on the internal network and a service on the external network such as the Internet.

➤ A proxy server enables a network to appear to external networks as a single IP address—that of the external network interface of the proxy server.

➤ A proxy server allows Internet access to be controlled; having a centralized point of access allows for a great deal of control over the use of the Internet.

➤ Port blocking is one of the most widely used security methods on networks. Port blocking is associated with firewalls and proxy servers, although in fact it can be implemented on any system that provides a means to manage network data flow, according to data type.

Key terms

➤ Authentication

➤ Password policy

➤ Firewalls

➤ Packet filtering

➤ Port number

➤ MAC address

➤ Circuit-level firewall

➤ Application gateway firewall

➤ Personal firewalls

➤ Proxy server

➤ NAT

➤ Caching proxy server

➤ Encryption

➤ IPSec

➤ DES

➤ 3DES

Practice exam

Question 1

> After noticing that there have been several attempts to access your network from the Internet, you decide to block port 53. Which of the following services is associated with port 53?
>
> ○ A. WINS
>
> ○ B. DNS
>
> ○ C. SMTP
>
> ○ D. POP3

The correct answer is B. DNS uses port 53. None of the other services use port 53.

Question 2

> When defining a password policy for an organization, which of the following would you consider setting? (Choose the three best answers.)
>
> ❑ A. Minimum password length
>
> ❑ B. Password expiration period
>
> ❑ C. Prevention of password reuse
>
> ❑ D. Maximum password length

The correct answers are A, B, and C. When creating a password policy, you should set a minimum password length, parameters limiting the reuse of old passwords, and a password expiration period. You may even want to set a maximum password length.

Question 3

> What is the basic reason for implementing a firewall?
>
> ○ A. It reduces the costs associated with Internet access.
>
> ○ B. It provides NAT functionality.
>
> ○ C. It provides a mechanism to protect one network from another.
>
> ○ D. It allows Internet access to be centralized.

The correct answer is C. Implementing a firewall allows you to have protection between networks, typically from the Internet to a private network. All the other answers describe functions offered by a proxy server. Note that some firewall systems do offer NAT functionality, but NAT is not a firewall feature; it is an added benefit of these systems.

Question 4

Which of the following are benefits of using a proxy server? (Choose the three best answers.)

- ❑ A. It allows costs associated with Internet access to be reduced.
- ❑ B. It provides a central point of Internet access.
- ❑ C. It allows Internet access to be controlled.
- ❑ D. It allows hostnames to be resolved to IP addresses.

The correct answers are A, B, and C. A proxy server allows the costs associated with Internet access to be reduced, provides a central point of Internet access, and allows Internet access to be controlled. Answer D describes the function of a DNS server.

Question 5

While on vacation, another system administrator decides to use the firewall to filter out all ports between 50 and 100. Which of the following services will now be unavailable to network users?

- ❑ A. HTTP
- ❑ B. HTTPS
- ❑ C. POP3
- ❑ D. DNS

The correct answers are A and D. HTTP uses port 80 and DNS uses port 53; both of these services would be affected by the filtering. HTTPS uses port 443 and POP3 uses port 110; therefore, these services would be unaffected.

Question 6

You are the network administrator for a large company. You have recently been tasked with supplying Internet access to all network users. Which of the following could you do to accomplish this?

- O A. Implement a firewall
- O B. Implement a proxy server
- O C. Enable port 80 on all workstations
- O D. Disable port 80 on all workstations

The correct answer is B. A proxy server allows a central point through which all network users can access the Internet. A firewall typically does not provide this functionality. Enabling or disabling port 80 on the workstations is not a valid answer.

Question 7

Which of the following is the strongest password?

- O A. password
- O B. WE300GO
- O C. l00Ka1ivE
- O D. lovethemusic

The correct answer is C. Strong passwords include a combination of letters and numbers and upper- and lowercase letters. In this question Answer C is by far the strongest password. Answer A is not a strong password because it is a standard word, contains no numbers, and is all in lowercase. Answer B mixes letters and numbers, and it is not a recognized word, so it is a strong password, although it is not as strong as Answer C. Answer D is too easy to guess and contains no numbers.

Question 8

As system administrator you have been asked to prevent users from using Web-based email during work. Which of the following might you do to accomplish this?

- O A. Set a password policy on the Web-based email
- O B. Block port 53
- O C. Block port 80
- O D. Configure the proxy server to filter out Web-based email requests

The correct answer is C. Blocking port 80 would prevent users from accessing Web-based email; it would however also block Web access altogether. Setting a password policy would have little effect. Blocking port 53 is a DNS port and would not prevent Web-based email. A proxy server is not used to filter Web-based email.

Question 9

You suspect that an employee in the company has been logging on to the system from a remote connection and attempting to look through files to which he should not have access. Which mechanism could you use to discover the identity of the person trying to dial in?

- ○ A. Auditing
- ○ B. File permissions
- ○ C. Password policy
- ○ D. Block port 221

The correct answer is A. To determine the user ID of a person trying to log on, you would implement auditing. File permissions, password policies, and blocking ports would not help you to do this.

Question 10

You have installed a proxy server on your network and have configured it to allow all of the hosts on your internal network to access the Internet through it. None of the users on the internal network can access the Internet, although they could before. What is the most likely cause of the problem?

- ○ A. The proxy server is not configured correctly.
- ○ B. The Internet connection is not working.
- ○ C. The Web browser on the client system needs to be reconfigured to use a proxy server.
- ○ D. The HTTP proxy service is not enabled on the system.

The correct answer is C. In order for Web browsers to access the Internet through a Web browser, they must be configured to do so. The Web browsers on client systems must be configured to use the proxy server.

Want to know more?

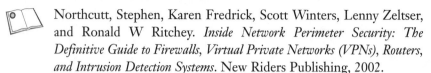 Northcutt, Stephen, Karen Fredrick, Scott Winters, Lenny Zeltser, and Ronald W Ritchey. *Inside Network Perimeter Security: The Definitive Guide to Firewalls, Virtual Private Networks (VPNs), Routers, and Intrusion Detection Systems.* New Riders Publishing, 2002.

Strassberg, Kieth, Gary Rollie, and Richard Gondek. *Firewalls: The Complete Reference.* Osborne McGraw-Hill, 2002.

Sheldon, Thomas. *McGraw-Hill's Encyclopedia of Networking and Telecommunications.* McGraw-Hill Professional Publishing, 2001.

Tulloch, Mitch. *Microsoft Encyclopedia of Networking* (with CD-ROM). Microsoft Press, 2000.

Troubleshooting Connectivity

Objectives

4.1 Given a troubleshooting scenario, select the appropriate TCP/IP utility from among the following:

✓ tracert

✓ ping

✓ arp

✓ netstat

✓ nbtstat

✓ ipconfig/ifconfig

✓ winipcfg

✓ nslookup

4.2 Given a troubleshooting scenario involving a small office/home office network failure (for example, DSL, cable, home satellite, wireless, and POTS), identify the cause of the problem.

4.3 Given a troubleshooting scenario involving a remote connectivity problem (for example, authentication failure, protocol configuration problem, physical connectivity problem), identify the cause of the problem.

4.5 Given a wiring task, select the appropriate tool (for example, wire crimper, media tester, punchdown tool, tone generator, and optical tester).

4.6 Given a network scenario, interpret visual indicators (for example, link lights and collision lights) to determine the nature of the problem.

4.7 Given output from a diagnostic utility (for example, **tracert**, **ping**, or **ipconfig**), identify the utility and interpret the output.

What you need to know

✓ Use various TCP/IP troubleshooting tools including **ping**, **tracert**, **arp**, **netstat**, **nbtstat**, **ipconfig**, **winipcfg**, and **nslookup**.

✓ Identify the cause of a network failure in a small office or home environment.

✓ Identify the procedures in troubleshooting remote connectivity errors.

✓ Use networking tools such as wire crimpers, media testers, punch down tools, and tone generators.

✓ Interpret visual indicators.

Introduction

For anyone working with TCP/IP networks, troubleshooting connectivity is something that is simply going to have to be done. With that it mind, it is important that network administrators familiarize themselves with those tools and the scenarios where they may be used. This chapter identifies the tools that are used in the troubleshooting process and identifies scenarios where these tools may be used.

In addition, the chapter covers the function of various networking tools and troubleshooting a small office environment.

Troubleshooting with diagnostic utilities

Many utilities can be used during troubleshooting. Although the actual utilities available vary from platform to platform, the functionality between platforms is quite similar. The following sections look at some of the more common troubleshooting utilities and the output they produce.

 On the Network+ exam, you will be asked to identify the output from a command, and you should be able to interpret the information provided by the command.

The **tracert** command

The *tracert* command, which is short for *trace route*, does exactly what its name implies—it traces the route between two hosts by using Internet Control Message Protocol (ICMP) echo packets to report back at every step in the journey. The tracert command provides a lot of useful information, including the IP address of every router connection it passes through, and in many cases the name of the router (although this depends on the router's configuration). tracert also reports the length, in milliseconds, of the round trip the packet made from the source location to the router and back. This information can help identify where network bottlenecks or breakdowns may be. The following is an example of a successful tracert command on a Windows 2000 system:

```
C:\>tracert 24.7.70.37
Tracing route to c1-p4.sttlwa1.home.net [24.7.70.37] over a maximum of 30 hops:
  1    30 ms    20 ms    20 ms  24.67.184.1
  2    20 ms    20 ms    30 ms  rd1ht-ge3-0.ok.shawcable.net [24.67.224.7]
```

```
   3    50 ms   30 ms   30 ms   rc1wh-atm0-2-1.vc.shawcable.net [204.209.214.193]
   4    50 ms   30 ms   30 ms   rc2wh-pos15-0.vc.shawcable.net [204.209.214.90]
   5    30 ms   40 ms   30 ms   rc2wt-pos2-0.wa.shawcable.net [66.163.76.37]
   6    30 ms   40 ms   30 ms   c1-pos6-3.sttlwa1.home.net [24.7.70.37]
Trace complete.
```

The `tracert` display on a Windows-based system includes several columns
of information. The first column represents the hop number. The next three
columns indicate the round-trip time, in milliseconds, that a packet takes in
its attempts to reach the destination. The last column is the hostname and
the IP address of the responding device.

Of course, not all `tracert` commands are successful. The following is the output from a `tracert` command that doesn't manage to get to the remote host:

```
C:\>tracert comptia.org

Tracing route to comptia.org [216.119.103.72]
over a maximum of 30 hops:
   1    27 ms   28 ms   14 ms   24.67.179.1
   2    55 ms   13 ms   14 ms   rd1ht-ge3-0.ok.shawcable.net [24.67.224.7]
   3    27 ms   27 ms   28 ms   rc1wh-atm0-2-1.shawcable.net
➡ [204.209.214.19]
   4    28 ms   41 ms   27 ms   rc1wt-pos2-0.wa.shawcable.net [66.163.76.65]
   5    28 ms   41 ms   27 ms   rc2wt-pos1-0.wa.shawcable.net [66.163.68.2]
   6    41 ms   55 ms   41 ms   c1-pos6-3.sttlwa1.home.net [24.7.70.37]
   7    54 ms   42 ms   27 ms   home-gw.st6wa.ip.att.net [192.205.32.249]
   8     *       *       *      Request timed out.
   9     *       *       *      Request timed out.
  10     *       *       *      Request timed out.
  11     *       *       *      Request timed out.
  12     *       *       *      Request timed out.
  13     *       *       *      Request timed out.
  14     *       *       *      Request timed out.
  15     *       *       *      Request timed out.
```

In this example, the `tracert` only gets to the seventh hop, at which point it
fails; this failure indicates that the problem lies on the far side of the device
in step 7 or on the near side of the device in step 8. In other words, the device
at step 7 is functioning but might not be able to make the next hop. The
cause of the problem could be a range of things, such as an error in the routing table or a faulty connection. Alternatively, the seventh device might be
operating 100%, but Device 8 might not be functioning at all. In any case,
you can isolate the problem to just one or two devices.

The CompTIA objectives refer to the **tracert** utility by name. However, the trace route
functionality has different names on other platforms. The output is much the same
across all platforms.

The `tracert` command can also help you isolate a heavily congested network. In the following example, the trace route packets fail in the midst of
the `tracert` but subsequently are able to continue. This behavior can be an
indicator of network congestion:

```
C:\>tracert comptia.org

Tracing route to comptia.org [216.119.103.72]over a maximum of 30 hops:
  1    96 ms    96 ms    55 ms  24.67.179.1
  2    14 ms    13 ms    28 ms  rd1ht-ge3-0.ok.shawcable.net [24.67.224.7]
  3    28 ms    27 ms    41 ms  rc1wh-atm0-2-1.shawcable.net
➥[204.209.214.19]
  4    28 ms    41 ms    27 ms  rc1wt-pos2-0.wa.shawcable.net [66.163.76.65]
  5    41 ms    27 ms    27 ms  rc2wt-pos1-0.wa.shawcable.net [66.163.68.2]
  6    55 ms    41 ms    27 ms  c1-pos6-3.sttlwa1.home.net [24.7.70.37]
  7    54 ms    42 ms    27 ms  home-gw.st6wa.ip.att.net [192.205.32.249]
  8    55 ms    41 ms    28 ms  gbr3-p40.st6wa.ip.att.net [12.123.44.130]
  9     *         *         *    Request timed out.
 10     *         *         *    Request timed out.
 11     *         *         *    Request timed out.
 12     *         *         *    Request timed out.
 13    69 ms    68 ms    69 ms  gbr2-p20.sd2ca.ip.att.net [12.122.11.254]
 14    55 ms    68 ms    69 ms  gbr1-p60.sd2ca.ip.att.net [12.122.1.109]
 15    82 ms    69 ms    82 ms  gbr1-p30.phmaz.ip.att.net [12.122.2.142]
 16    68 ms    69 ms    82 ms  gar2-p360.phmaz.ip.att.net [12.123.142.45]
 17   110 ms    96 ms    96 ms  12.125.99.70
 18   124 ms    96 ms    96 ms  light.crystaltech.com [216.119.107.1]
 19    82 ms    96 ms    96 ms  216.119.103.72
Trace complete.
```

Generally speaking, `tracert` allows you to identify the location of a problem
in the connectivity between two devices. After you have determined this
location, you might need to use a utility such as `ping` to continue troubleshooting. In many cases, as in the examples provided in this chapter, the
routers might be on a network such as the Internet and therefore not within
your control. In that case, there is little you can do except inform your ISP
of the problem.

ping

Most network administrators are very familiar with the *ping* utility and are
likely to use it on an almost daily basis. The basic function of the `ping` command is to test the connectivity between the two devices on a network. All the
command is designed to do is determine whether the two computers can see
each other and to notify you of how long the round trip takes to complete.

Although `ping` is most often used on its own, there are a number of switches that can be used to assist in the troubleshooting process. Table 10.1 shows
some of the commonly used switches with `ping` on a Windows system.

Table 10.1 ping Command Switches	
Option	**Description**
ping -t	Pings a device on the network until stopped
ping -a	Resolves addresses to hostnames
ping -n count	Specifies the number of echo requests to send
ping -r count	Records route for count hops
ping -s count	Timestamp for count hops
ping -w timeout	Timeout in milliseconds to wait for each reply

Ping works by sending ICMP echo request messages to another device on the network. If the other device on the network hears the ping request, it automatically responds with an ICMP echo reply. By default the ping command on a Windows-based system sends four data packets; however, using the -t switch, a continuous stream of ping requests can be sent.

Ping is perhaps the most widely used of all network tools; it is primarily used to verify connectivity between two network devices. On a good day, the results from the ping command will be successful, and the sending device will receive a reply from the remote device. Not all ping results are that successful, and to be able to effectively use ping, you must be able to interpret the results of a failed ping command.

The Destination Host Unreachable message

The *Destination Host Unreachable* error message means that a route to the destination computer system cannot be found. To remedy this problem, you might need to examine the routing information on the local host to confirm that the local host is correctly configured, or you might need to make sure the default gateway information is correct. The following is an example of a ping failure that gives the Destination host unreachable message:

```
Pinging 24.67.54.233 with 32 bytes of data:
Destination host unreachable.
Destination host unreachable.
Destination host unreachable.
Destination host unreachable.
Ping statistics for 24.67.54.233:
    Packets: Sent = 4, Received = 0, Lost = 4 (100% loss),
Approximate round trip times in milli-seconds:
    Minimum = 0ms, Maximum =  0ms, Average =  0ms
```

The Request Timed Out message

The *Request Timed Out* error message is very common when you use the ping command. Essentially, this error message indicates that your host did not receive the ping message within the designated time period. This is typically an indicator that the destination device is not connected to the network, is powered off, or is not configured correctly. It could also mean that some intermediate device is not operating correctly. In some rare cases, it can also indicate that there is so much congestion on the network that timely delivery of the ping message could not be completed. It might also mean that the ping is being sent to an invalid IP address or that the system is not on the same network as the remote host, and an intermediary device is not configured correctly. In any of these cases, the failed ping should initiate a troubleshooting process that may involve other tools, manual inspection, and possibly reconfiguration. The following example shows the output from a ping to an invalid IP address:

```
C:\>ping 169.76.54.3
Pinging 169.76.54.3 with 32 bytes of data:

Request timed out.
Request timed out.
Request timed out.
Request timed out.

Ping statistics for 169.76.54.3:
    Packets: Sent = 4, Received = 0, Lost = 4 (100%
Approximate round trip times in milli-seconds:
    Minimum = 0ms, Maximum =  0ms, Average =  0ms
```

During the ping request, you might receive some replies from the remote host that are intermixed with Request Timed Out errors. This is often a result of a congested network. An example follows; notice that this example, which was run on a Windows Me system, uses the -t switch to generate continuous pings:

```
C:\>ping -t 24.67.184.65
Pinging 24.67.184.65 with 32 bytes of data:

Reply from 24.67.184.65: bytes=32 time=55ms TTL=127
Reply from 24.67.184.65: bytes=32 time=54ms TTL=127
Reply from 24.67.184.65: bytes=32 time=27ms TTL=127
Request timed out.
Request timed out.
Request timed out.
Reply from 24.67.184.65: bytes=32 time=69ms TTL=127
Reply from 24.67.184.65: bytes=32 time=28ms TTL=127
Reply from 24.67.184.65: bytes=32 time=28ms TTL=127
Reply from 24.67.184.65: bytes=32 time=68ms TTL=127
Reply from 24.67.184.65: bytes=32 time=41ms TTL=127

Ping statistics for 24.67.184.65:
    Packets: Sent = 11, Received = 8, Lost = 3 (27% loss),
Approximate round trip times in milli-seconds:
    Minimum = 27ms, Maximum =  69ms, Average =  33ms
```

In this example, three packets were lost. If this continued on your network, you would need to troubleshoot to find out why packets were being dropped.

The Unknown Host message

The Unknown Host error message is generated when the hostname of the destination computer cannot be resolved. This error usually occurs when you ping an incorrect hostname, as shown in the following example, or try to use ping with a hostname when hostname resolution (via DNS or a HOSTS text file) is not configured:

```
C:\>ping www.comptia.ca
Unknown host www.comptia.ca
```

If the ping fails, you need to verify that the ping is being sent to the correct remote host. If it is, and if name resolution is configured, you have to dig a little more to find the problem. This error might indicate a problem with the name resolution process, and you might need to verify that the DNS or WINS server is available. Other commands, such as nslookup, can help in this process.

The Expired TTL message

The *Time to Live* (*TTL*) is an important consideration in understanding the ping command. The function of the TTL is to prevent circular routing, which occurs when a ping request keeps looping through a series of hosts. The TTL counts each hop along the way toward its destination device. Each time it counts one hop, the hop is subtracted from the TTL. If the TTL reaches 0, the TTL has expired, and you get a message like the following:

```
Reply from 24.67.180.1: TTL expired in transit
```

If the TTL is exceeded with ping, you might have a routing problem on the network. You can modify the TTL for ping on a Windows system by using the ping -i command.

Troubleshooting with ping

Although ping does not completely isolate problems, you can use it to help identify where a problem lies. When troubleshooting with ping, take the following steps:

1. ping the IP address of your local loopback adapter, using the command ping 127.0.0.1. If this command is successful, you know that the TCP/IP protocol suite is installed correctly on your system and functioning. If you are unable to ping the local loopback adapter, TCP/IP might need to be reloaded or reconfigured on the machine you are using.

The Loopback Address

The *loopback adapter* is a special function within the protocol stack that is supplied for troubleshooting purposes. The Class A IP address **127.X.X.X** is reserved for the loopback; although convention dictates that you use **127.0.0.1**, you can use any address in the **127.X.X.X** range, except for the network number itself (**127.0.0.0**) and the broadcast address (**127.255.255.255**). You can also **ping** by using the default hostname for the local system, which is called **localhost** (for example, **ping localhost**).

2. ping the IP address of your local network interface card (NIC). If the ping is successful, you know that your NIC is functioning on the network and has TCP/IP correctly installed. If you are unable to ping the local NIC, TCP/IP might not be bound correctly to the NIC or the NIC drivers might be improperly installed.

3. ping the IP address of another node on your local network. By doing so you can determine whether the computer you are using can see other computers on the network. If you can ping other devices on your local network, you have network connectivity.

If you cannot ping other devices on your local network and you were able to ping your local NIC, you might not be connected to the network correctly, or there might be a cable problem on the computer.

4. After you've confirmed that you have network connectivity for the local network, you can verify connectivity to a remote network by sending a ping to the IP address of the default gateway.

5. If you are able to ping the default gateway, you can verify remote connectivity by sending a ping to the IP address of a system on a remote network.

 On the Network+ exam, you might be asked to relate the correct procedure for using **ping** for a connectivity problem.

Using just the ping command in these steps, you can confirm network connectivity on not just the local network but also on a remote network. The whole process requires as much time as it takes to type in the command and you can do it all from a single location.

If you are an optimistic person, you can perform step 5 first. If that works, all the other steps will also work, saving you the need to test them. If your step 4 trial fails, you can go back to step 1 and start the troubleshooting process from the beginning.

The **ping** examples used in this section show the **ping** command using the IP address of the remote host. It is also possible to **ping** the Domain Name Service (DNS) name of the remote host (for example, **ping www.comptia.org**, **ping server1**); this, of course, can be done only if your network uses a DNS server. On a Windows-based network, you can also **ping** by using the Network Basic Input/Output System (NetBIOS) computer name.

ARP

The *Address Resolution Protocol* (*ARP*) is used to resolve IP addresses to MAC addresses. This is important because on a network, devices find each other using the IP address but communication between devices requires the MAC address.

 For the Network+ exam, remember that the function of the ARP command is to resolve IP addresses to Layer 2 or MAC addresses.

When a computer wants to send data to another computer on the network, it must know the MAC address of the destination system. To discover this information, ARP sends out a discovery packet to obtain the MAC address. When the destination computer is found, it sends its MAC address to the sending computer. The ARP resolved MAC addresses are stored temporarily on a computer system in the ARP cache. Inside this ARP cache is a list of matching MAC and IP addresses. This ARP cache is checked before a discovery packet is sent onto the network to determine if there is an existing entry.

Entries in the ARP cache are periodically flushed so the cache doesn't fill up with unused entries. The following code shows an example of the ARP command with the output from a Windows 2000 system.

```
C:\>arp -a
Interface: 24.67.179.22 on Interface 0x3
  Internet Address      Physical Address      Type
  24.67.179.1           00-00-77-93-d8-3d     dynamic
```

As you might notice in the previous code, the type is listed as dynamic. Entries in the ARP cache can be added statically, manually, or dynamically. Static entries are added manually and do not expire. The dynamic entries are added automatically when the system accesses another on the network.

As with other command-line utilities, there are several switches available for the ARP command. Table 10.2 shows the available switches for Windows-based systems.

Table 10.2 ARP Switches	
Switch	Description
-a or -g	Displays both the IP and MAC addresses and whether they are dynamic or static entries.
inet_addr	Specifies a specific internet address.
-N if_addr	Displays the ARP entries for a specified network interface.
eth_addr	Specifies a MAC address.
if_addr	Specifies an Internet address.
-d	Deletes an entry from the ARP cache.
-s	Adds a static permanent address to the ARP cache.

The netstat command

The netstat command displays the protocol statistics and current TCP/IP connections. Used without any switches, the netstat command shows the active connections for all outbound TCP/IP connections. In addition, several switches are available that change the type of information netstat displays. Table 10.3 shows the various switches available for the netstat utility.

Table 10.3 Netstat Switches	
Switch	Description
-a	Displays the current connections and listening ports.
-e	Displays Ethernet statistics.
-n	Lists addresses and port numbers in numerical form.
-p	Shows connections for the specified protocol.
-r	Shows the routing table.
-s	Lists per-protocol statistics.
interval	Specifies the length of time to wait before redisplaying statistics.

The **netstat** and the **route print** command can be used to show the routing table.

The *netstat utility* is used to show the port activity for both TCP and UDP connections, showing the inbound and outbound connections. When used without switches, the netstat utility has four information headings.

➤ **Proto**—Lists the protocol being used, either UDP or TCP

➤ **Local address**—Specifies the local address and port being used

➤ **Foreign address**—Identifies the destination address and the port being used

➤ **State**—Specifies whether the connection is established

The following shows a sample output from a `netstat` command without using any switches.

```
C:\>netstat
Active Connections
  Proto  Local Address          Foreign Address         State
  TCP    laptop:2848            MEDIASERVICES1:1755     ESTABLISHED
  TCP    laptop:1833            www.dollarhost.com:80   ESTABLISHED
  TCP    laptop:2858            194.70.58.241:80        ESTABLISHED
  TCP    laptop:2860            194.70.58.241:80        ESTABLISHED
  TCP    laptop:2354            www.dollarhost.com:80   ESTABLISHED
  TCP    laptop:2361            www.dollarhost.com:80   ESTABLISHED
  TCP    laptop:1114            www.dollarhost.com:80   ESTABLISHED
  TCP    laptop:1959            www.dollarhost.com:80   ESTABLISHED
  TCP    laptop:1960            www.dollarhost.com:80   ESTABLISHED
  TCP    laptop:1963            www.dollarhost.com:80   ESTABLISHED
  TCP    laptop:2870            localhost:8431          TIME_WAIT
  TCP    laptop:8431            localhost:2862          TIME_WAIT
  TCP    laptop:8431            localhost:2863          TIME_WAIT
  TCP    laptop:8431            localhost:2867          TIME_WAIT
  TCP    laptop:8431            localhost:2872          TIME_WAIT
```

Like any other command-line utility, they are often used with switches. The following sections provide a brief explanation of the switches and a sample output from each.

netstat –e

The `netstat -e` command shows the activity for the NIC and displays the number of packets that have been both sent and received. An example of the `netstat -e` command is shown here:

```
C:\WINDOWS\Desktop>netstat -e
Interface Statistics

                          Received            Sent

Bytes                     17412385            40237510
Unicast packets           79129               85055
Non-unicast packets       693                 254
Discards                  0                   0
Errors                    0                   0
Unknown protocols         306
```

As you can see, the `netstat -e` command shows more than just the packets that have been sent and received.

➤ **Bytes**—The number of bytes that have been sent or received by the NIC since the computer was turned on.

➤ **Unicast packets**—Packets sent and received directly to this interface.

➤ **Non-unicast packets**—Broadcast or multicast packets that were picked up by the NIC.

➤ **Discards**—The number of packets rejected by the NIC, perhaps because they were damaged.

➤ **Errors**—The errors that occurred during either the sending or receiving process. As you would expect, this column should be a low number. If it is not, it could indicate a problem with the NIC.

➤ **Unknown protocols**—The number of packets that were not recognizable by the system.

netstat -a

The `netstat -a` command displays statistics for both TCP and User Datagram Protocol (UDP). Here is an example of the `netstat -a` command:

```
C:\WINDOWS\Desktop>netstat -a

Active Connections

  Proto  Local Address          Foreign Address          State
  TCP    laptop:1027            LAPTOP:0                 LISTENING
  TCP    laptop:1030            LAPTOP:0                 LISTENING
  TCP    laptop:1035            LAPTOP:0                 LISTENING
  TCP    laptop:50000           LAPTOP:0                 LISTENING
  TCP    laptop:5000            LAPTOP:0                 LISTENING
  TCP    laptop:1035            msgr-ns41.msgr.hotmail.com:1863  ESTABLISHED
  TCP    laptop:nbsession       LAPTOP:0                 LISTENING
  TCP    laptop:1027            localhost:50000          ESTABLISHED
  TCP    laptop:50000           localhost:1027           ESTABLISHED
  UDP    laptop:1900            *:*
  UDP    laptop:nbname          *:*
  UDP    laptop:nbdatagram      *:*
  UDP    laptop:1547            *:*
  UDP    laptop:1038            *:*
  UDP    laptop:1828            *:*
  UDP    laptop:3366            *:*
```

As you can see, the output includes four columns, which show the protocol, the local address, the foreign address, and the state of the port. The *TCP* connections show the local and foreign destination address and the current state of the connection. *UDP*, however, is a little different; it does not list a state status because as mentioned throughout this book, UDP is a connectionless protocol and does not establish connections. The following list briefly explains the information provided by the `netstat -a` command:

➤ **Proto**—The protocol used by the connection.

➤ **Local Address**—The IP address of the local computer system and the port number it is using. If the entry in the local address field is an asterisk (*), it indicates that the port has not yet been established.

➤ **Foreign Address**—The IP address of a remote computer system and the associated port. When a port has not been established, as with the UDP connections, `*:*` appears in the column.

➤ **State**—The current state of the TCP connection. Possible states include established, listening, closed, and waiting.

netstat -r

The `netstat -r` command is often used to view the routing table for a system. A system uses a routing table to determine routing information for TCP/IP traffic. The following is an example of the `netstat -r` command from a Windows Me system:

The **netstat -r** command output shows the same information as the output from the **route print** command.

```
C:\WINDOWS\Desktop>netstat -r
Route table

===========================================================================
===========================================================================
Active Routes:
Network Destination        Netmask          Gateway       Interface  Metric
        0.0.0.0          0.0.0.0      24.67.179.1    24.67.179.22       1
   24.67.179.0      255.255.255.0    24.67.179.22    24.67.179.22       1
  24.67.179.22    255.255.255.255      127.0.0.1       127.0.0.1       1
24.255.255.255    255.255.255.255    24.67.179.22    24.67.179.22       1
     127.0.0.0          255.0.0.0      127.0.0.1       127.0.0.1       1
     224.0.0.0          224.0.0.0    24.67.179.22    24.67.179.22       1
255.255.255.255    255.255.255.255    24.67.179.22               2       1
Default Gateway:        24.67.179.1
===========================================================================
Persistent Routes:
  None

Active Connections
```

```
Proto  Local Address          Foreign Address              State
TCP    laptop:1030            n239.audiogalaxy.com:ftp  ESTABLISHED
TCP    laptop:1035            msgr-ns41.msgr.hotmail.com:1863  ESTABLISHED
TCP    laptop:1027            localhost:50000           ESTABLISHED
TCP    laptop:50000           localhost:1027            ESTABLISHED
```

netstat -s

The netstat -s command displays a number of statistics related to the TCP/IP protocol suite. Understanding the purpose of every field in the output is beyond the scope of the Network+ exam, but for your reference, sample output from the netstat -s command is shown here:

```
C:\>netstat -s

IP Statistics

    Packets Received               = 389938
    Received Header Errors         = 0
    Received Address Errors        = 1876
    Datagrams Forwarded            = 498
    Unknown Protocols Received     = 0
    Received Packets Discarded     = 0
    Received Packets Delivered     = 387566
    Output Requests                = 397334
    Routing Discards               = 0
    Discarded Output Packets       = 0
    Output Packet No Route         = 916
    Reassembly Required            = 0
    Reassembly Successful          = 0
    Reassembly Failures            = 0
    Datagrams Successfully Fragmented = 0
    Datagrams Failing Fragmentation   = 0
    Fragments Created              = 0

ICMP Statistics

                            Received    Sent
    Messages                40641       41111
    Errors                  0           0
    Destination Unreachable 223         680
    Time Exceeded           24          0
    Parameter Problems      0           0
    Source Quenches         0           0
    Redirects               0           38
    Echos                   20245       20148
    Echo Replies            20149       20245
    Timestamps              0           0
    Timestamp Replies       0           0
    Address Masks           0           0
    Address Mask Replies    0           0

TCP Statistics

    Active Opens                   = 13538
    Passive Opens                  = 23132
    Failed Connection Attempts     = 9259
```

```
Reset Connections                = 254
Current Connections              = 15
Segments Received                = 330242
Segments Sent                    = 326935
Segments Retransmitted           = 18851

UDP Statistics

Datagrams Received       = 20402
No Ports                 = 20594
Receive Errors           = 0
Datagrams Sent           = 10217
```

nbtstat

The nbtstat utility is used to view protocol statistics and information for NetBIOS over TCP/IP connections. nbtstat is commonly used to troubleshoot NetBIOS name resolution problems. Because nbtstat provides the resolution of NetBIOS names, it's available only on Windows systems.

There are a number of case-sensitive switches available for the nbtstat command. Table 10.4 summarizes these switches.

Table 10.4 nbtstat Switches	
Switch	**Description**
nbtstat -a	(Adapter status) Outputs the NetBIOS name table and MAC addresses of the card for the specified computer.
nbtstat -A (IP address)	(Adapter status) Lists the remote machine's name table given its IP address.
nbtstat -c (cache)	Provides a list of the contents of the NetBIOS name cache.
nbtstat -n (names)	Lists local NetBIOS names.
nbtstat -r (resolved)	Lists names resolved by broadcast or WINS.
nbtstat -R (Reload)	Purges and reloads the remote cache name table.
nbtstat -S (Sessions)	Summarizes the current NetBIOS sessions and their status.
nbtstat -s (sessions)	Lists sessions table converting destination IP addresses to computer NetBIOS names.
nbtstat -RR (ReleaseRefresh)	Sends Name Release packets to WINS, and then starts Refresh.
nbtstat RemoteName	Remote host machine name.
nbtstat IP address	Dotted decimal representation of the IP address.
nbtstat interval	Redisplays selected statistics, pausing interval seconds between each display. Press Ctrl+C to stop redisplaying statistics.

As an example, the following is the output from the `nbtstat -n` command.

```
C:\>nbtstat -n
Lana # 0:
Node IpAddress: [169.254.196.192] Scope Id: []

                NetBIOS Local Name Table

      Name               Type        Status
   ----------------------------------------------
      LAPTOP      <00>  UNIQUE      Registered
      KCS         <00>  GROUP       Registered
      LAPTOP      <03>  UNIQUE      Registered
```

The ipconfig command

The `ipconfig` command is a technician's best friend when it comes to viewing the TCP/IP configuration of a Windows system. At least most Windows-based systems: The `ipconfig` command cannot be used on Windows 95 systems. Used on its own, the `ipconfig` command shows basic information such as the name of the network interface, the IP address, the subnet mask, and the default gateway. Combined with the /all switch, it shows a detailed set of information, as you can see in the following example:

```
C:\>ipconfig /all
Windows 2000 IP Configuration
      Host Name . . . . . . . . . . . . : server
      Primary DNS Suffix . . . . . . . : write
      Node Type . . . . . . . . . . . . : Broadcast
      IP Routing Enabled. . . . . . . . : Yes
      WINS Proxy Enabled. . . . . . . . : No
      DNS Suffix Search List. . . . . . : write
                                          ok.anyotherhost.net
Ethernet adapter Local Area Connection:

Connection-specific DNS Suffix  . : ok.anyotherhost.net
Description . . . . . . . . . . . : D-Link DFE-530TX PCI Fast Ethernet
Physical Address. . . . . . . . . : 00-80-C8-E3-4C-BD
DHCP Enabled. . . . . . . . . . . : Yes
Autoconfiguration Enabled . . . . : Yes
IP Address. . . . . . . . . . . . : 24.67.184.65
Subnet Mask . . . . . . . . . . . : 255.255.254.0
Default Gateway . . . . . . . . . : 24.67.184.1
DHCP Server . . . . . . . . . . . : 24.67.253.195
DNS Servers . . . . . . . . . . . : 24.67.253.195
                                    24.67.253.212
Lease Obtained.. . . . . : Thursday, February 07, 2002 3:42:00 AM
Lease Expires .. . . . . : Saturday, February 09, 2002 3:42:00 AM
```

As you can imagine, you can use the output from an `ipconfig /all` command in a massive range of troubleshooting scenarios. Table 10.5 lists some of the most common troubleshooting symptoms, along with where to look for clues about solving them in the `ipconfig /all` output.

When looking at **ipconfig** information, you should be sure that all information is present and correct. For example, a missing or incorrect default gateway parameter limits communication to the local segment.

Table 10.5 Common Troubleshooting Symptoms That **ipconfig** Can Help Solve	
Symptom	Field to Check in **ipconfig** Output
User is unable to connect to any other system.	Make sure the TCP/IP address and subnet mask are correct. If the network uses DHCP, make sure DHCP is enabled.
User is able to connect to another system on the same subnet but is not able to connect to a remote system.	Make sure the default gateway is correctly configured.
User is unable to browse the Internet.	Make sure the DNS server parameters are configured correctly.
User is unable to browse across remote subnets.	Make sure the WINS server parameters are configured correctly, if applicable.

You should be prepared to identify the output from an **ipconfig** command in relationship to a troubleshooting scenario for the Network+ exam.

Using the /all switch may be far and away the most popular, but there are a few others. These include the switches listed in Table 10.6.

The **ipconfig** and its associated switches are widely used by network administrators and therefore should be expected to make an appearance on the exam.

Table 10.6 **ipconfig** Switches	
Switch	Description
?	Displays the **ipconfig** help screen.
/all	Displays additional IP configuration information.
/release	Releases the IP address of the specified adapter.
/renew	Renews the IP address of a specified adapter.

The **ipconfig /renew** and **ipconfig /release** commands work only when your system is using DHCP.

The **ifconfig** command is similar to the **ipconfig** command but is used to view the IP configuration information on a Linux or OS/2-based system. Whichever platform you are using, the information shown with the IP configuration will include the information you need to determine if there are IP configuration problems on the system.

The **winipcfg** command

On a Windows 95/98/Me system, the `winipcfg` command is used instead of the `ipconfig` command. The difference between the two utilities is that `winipcfg` is a graphical utility.

In basic mode, `winipcfg` shows information including the Media Access Control (MAC) address and IP address of the interface, the subnet mask, and the default gateway. For detailed information, similar to that produced with `ipconfig /all`, a More Info button allows you to switch into a much more detailed screen.

The same troubleshooting scenarios, with the same solutions, apply to `winipcfg` as to `ipconfig`. Table 10.7 lists some solutions to common problems.

Table 10.7 Common Troubleshooting Problems That **ipconfig** Can Help Solve	
Symptom	Field to Check in **ipconfig** Output
User is unable to connect to any other system.	Check that the TCP/IP address and subnet mask are correct. If using DHCP, make sure DHCP is enabled.
User is able to connect to other system on the same subnet, but is not able to connect to a remote system.	Check that the default gateway is correctly configured.
User is unable to browse the Internet.	Make sure the DNS server parameters are configured correctly.
User is unable to browse across remote subnets.	Make sure the WINS server parameters are configured correctly (if applicable).

nslookup

`nslookup` is a utility used to troubleshoot DNS related problems. When `nslookup` is started, it displays the current hostname and the IP address of the locally configured DNS server. You will then see a command prompt, which allows you to specify further queries. The additional commands you can enter are listed in Table 10.8.

Table 10.8 nslookup Switches	
Switch	Description
all	Print options, current server and host
[no]debug	Print debugging information
[no]d2	Print exhaustive debugging information
[no]defname	Append the domain name to each query
[no]recurse	Ask for recursive answer to query
[no]search	Use domain search list
[no]vc	Always use a virtual circuit
domain=NAME	Set default domain name to **NAME**
srchlist=N1[/N2/.../N6]	Set domain to N1 and search list to N1, N2, and so on
root=NAME	Set root server to **NAME**
retry=X	Set number of retries to **X**
timeout=X	Set initial timeout interval to **X** seconds
type=X	Set query type (for example, A, ANY, CNAME, MX, NS, PTR, SOA, or SRV)
querytype=X	Same as type
class=X	Set query class (for example, **IN** (Internet), **ANY**)
[no]msxfr	Use MS fast zone transfer
ixfrver=X	Current version to use in IXFR transfer request
server NAME	Set default server to **NAME**, using current default server
exit	Exit the program

Supporting and troubleshooting the small office and home environment

Today's networks are not restricted to large corporations; rather, they are relied upon in organizations of all sizes and are increasingly being used in the home. As a network administrator you may find yourself troubleshooting in a small office or home environment as often as you will in a corporate office. Although many of the troubleshooting steps are the same for large and small networks, there are some that are unique to the smaller networks.

One of the most common areas for troubleshooting in the small and home network environment is Internet access. Both home users and organizations alike depend on their Internet access and cannot or will not function without it. To effectively troubleshoot Internet access, you must be familiar with the various technologies used. This section discusses the various methods and what is involved in troubleshooting them.

POTS

Perhaps the best place to start when talking about Internet access for smaller networks is with the *Plain Old Telephone System (POTS)*. POTS access refers to using a standard dial-up line, and to connect you will need both a modem and an account with an ISP. The modems are responsible for converting digital signals from the computer system into analog signals that are used on a regular phone line.

When troubleshooting a POTS connection, there are several areas to be aware of. Table 10.9 identifies some of the common problem areas for POTS connections.

Table 10.9 Troubleshooting POTS	
Problem	**Solution**
Unable to dial out	Confirm that there is a physical connection; ensure that the cable has not become unplugged. Verify that there is a dial tone on the line.
Can dial out but unable to make connection	Verify the correct phone number, and username and password combination is being used. Problem may be with the ISP; it may be necessary to call the ISP to verify.
Can get a connection, but connection drops	Verify modem settings are correct. It may be the modem or modem drivers. Verify that you have the latest drivers for the modem and that the modem is working correctly. It may also be necessary to look at the manufacturer's Web site for the modem and look for firmware updates to documents pertaining to your problem. Verify that call waiting is disabled.

Working with a modem

It is possible to test a modem to verify it is working using *AT commands*. AT commands are modem-specific commands that can be used to communicate directly with the modem. Table 10.10 outlines the various AT commands.

Command	Description
Table 10.10	**AT commands**
ATA	Sets the modem to auto-answer
ATH	Hangs up an active connection
ATD	Dials a number
ATZ	Resets the modem
ATI3	Displays the name and model of the modem

One of the more common complaints among those using a standard phone line is the inconsistent speeds obtained by their modems. The fastest modem available today is the 56Kbps modem but rarely if ever does it reach this speed. There are some very good reasons for this problem:

➤ **Poor quality modem**—As far as modems are concerned, the truth is that you get what you pay for. Many modems are shipped with computers now, giving little choice on the modem model. It may however be more beneficial to buy a modem from a reputable manufacturer.

➤ **Modem driver**—If users are complaining of poor performance, verify that the latest drivers are being used. If not, they will have to be downloaded and installed.

➤ **Modem configuration**—To get the highest possible transfer speeds from the modem, it has to be properly configured. Confirm modem settings to get the maximum speed from the modem.

➤ **Phone line**—It may be that the lower speeds of the modem can be directly attributed to the phone line itself. Phone lines can suffer from interference of all sorts, which directly affects the speed that data can be transferred over the phone line.

Cable Internet access

Those of us who have used the traditional phone for Internet access are aware of its biggest shortcoming—speed. POTS may be the cheapest way to get on the Web, but it is very slow. For those who need or want something a little faster there are a few alternatives; one of the more popular of these is *cable Internet access*. Businesses and home users alike have embraced the speeds that cable access provides.

Cable Internet requires a cable modem, which is supplied by the ISP. The modem connects to the computers network card using UTP cable and RJ-45 connectors. The cable modem connects to the wall socket using coaxial cable. When troubleshooting cable Internet errors there are a few key areas to consider.

➤ **Physical connectivity**—A cable modem must be physically connected to the computer's network card, and the modem itself. If one end of the cable becomes unplugged or loose, the Internet connection won't work. In addition, if the cable itself is faulty, it won't work. In either case, the modem's LEDs may flash, warning you of the problem.

➤ **Confirm network card settings**—It may be necessary to confirm that the network card within the computer works and to test the card and, if appropriate, obtain the latest drivers.

➤ **Verify network card configuration**—After verifying that the card is working within the system, the next step is to confirm that the card has been assigned the correct IP configuration. Most ISPs assign the network configuration through DHCP. To test whether the correct IP information has been assigned, you can use the ipconfig command if using Windows, or ifconfig if using Linux.

➤ **Check LEDs**—The LEDs on the modem provide an indication if there is a problem with the modem connectivity. The ISP will have information on the light sequences and what they mean.

After exhausting all possible avenues on your end, a call to the Internet Service Provider may be necessary. You never know; the problem may be at their end and all your troubleshooting efforts would be for nothing.

DSL

Although cable may be popular, it is certainly not without its competition and the main competition for cable Internet access is *Digital Subscriber Line* *(DSL)*. Priced about the same as cable, instead of using a dedicated coaxial cable to connect, DSL uses the existing phone line to make the connection. Like the cable modem, the DSL modem connects to the network card using the UTP cable with RJ-45 connectors.

The speeds are comparable for the two types of Internet access making choosing cable or DSL a matter of personal preference or perhaps availability. There are other considerations, though, such as the fact that DSL speed is guaranteed whereas cable is not. It may not be possible to choose one or the other and you might be forced to pick the one that is offered in your area. Not everywhere has access to DSL or cable service.

I refer to DSL technology as DSL because there are so many types of DSL options. They can be divided into two distinct types, asymmetric DSL and symmetric DSL. The difference is whether they can or cannot share the existing phone line. Table 10.11 lists the various asymmetric DSL options available and Table 10.12 lists the symmetric DSL options.

Table 10.11 Asymmetric DSL Varieties	
Type	**Description**
Asymmetric DSL (ADSL)	Perhaps the most common DSL used, ADSL can share an existing phone line for Internet access, because the analog line is split into multiple channels. ADSL has faster downloads and slower uploads.
Rate Adaptive DSL (RADSL)	An improvement on regular DSL, it can modify transmissions speeds based on signal quality.
Very High Bit Rate DSL (VHDSL)	Another asymmetric version of DSL and as such can share an existing phone line.

Table 10.12 Symmetric DSL Varieties	
Type	**Description**
Symmetric DSL (SDSL)	SDSL offers the same download and upload speeds, making it a more practical solution in many business environments. As a symmetric DSL however, it cannot share an existing phone line.
IDSL	IDSL is a little different and cannot use analog phone lines. Of the symmetric DSL flavors, IDSL is the slowest.
High Bit Rate DSL (HDSL)	HDSL, offering similar upload and download speeds, cannot share a phone line.

Troubleshooting DSL

Although DSL is a different technology than cable Internet, many of the troubleshooting procedures overlap. The following list contains the hotspots to watch for when troubleshooting Internet connectivity errors with DSL.

➤ **LEDs**—Perhaps the first thing to verify when troubleshooting DSL is to check the lights on the modem. The LEDs can provide a quick answer to the problem and often can determine whether the problem is at your end or with the ISP. The error codes for the various modems differ, so be sure to check with the modem-specific documentation to see what the lights are trying to tell you.

➤ **Network card**—As with the cable modem, the computer system must have an operational network card installed. If you are unable to connect, verify that the network card is correctly installed and functioning. It may be necessary to reinstall the network card drivers or upgrade older software drivers.

➤ **IP configuration**—One quick test is to see if the computer system is being assigned a valid IP address. If you are not getting a valid IP address, you may need to confirm that the card is set to obtain an IP automatically from a DHCP server. Many ISPs assign addresses automatically; if they do provide automatic assignments, verify that you have correctly entered the IP configuration information. This information would include the IP address as well as gateway and DNS server information.

➤ **Cabling**—There are two places to look to verify cabling. First verify the phone jack (RJ-11) is securely attached to the modem and the wall socket. Second, confirm that the network cable, UTP with RJ-45 connectors, is securely attached to the computer systems network card and the modem.

Wireless

Not everyone has access to cable or DSL Internet. For these people there are other technologies available to get their email. Wireless access is one such strategy. Wireless Internet access requires a direct line-of-sight between the receiving antenna and the residence or small office. This line-of-sight connection can be difficult to configure and the technologies involved with wireless are more costly than cable or DSL.

Wireless broadband Internet access is susceptible to a variety of circumstances that are often difficult and sometimes impossible to troubleshoot. One such factor is interference. Interference is produced by many sources, like your microwave oven, cordless phones, and rabbit-ear TV extension devices. If you notice that your Internet connection fails while warming dinner the fault may lie with the interference from the microwave. Another problem, which may be entirely outside of your control, is competition between your ISP and another wireless Internet provider. It may be that a busy wireless competitor is also operating outdoors and using the resources on the same unlicensed frequencies as yours. Wireless connections may also be influenced by atmospheric conditions, which are again out of your control.

The issues you can confirm at your end relate to the hardware configuration. You should verify that your satellite modem or network card is working.

Home satellite

Another alternative to cable and DSL Internet access is the home satellite. *Home satellite* can be used in locations where the more traditional Internet access types are simply not available. Home satellite systems require a satellite card be installed in the computer system or an external satellite modem can be used and a satellite dish mounted on the residence or office building. As a line-of-sight technology, the dish must have an unobstructed view to the sending device. Typically, coaxial cable is used to connect the satellite dish antenna directly to a computer system or to a satellite modem.

Home satellite systems have faster downloads speeds and lower upload speeds. Unlike cable or DSL, satellite speeds can be affected by atmospheric conditions; the worse the conditions, the worse the connection. The initial setup and configuration of a home satellite system can be very difficult to configure and is often done by trained professionals.

As a network administrator troubleshooting *satellite Internet* access, there are a few areas to confirm.

➤ **IP configuration**—As with the other technologies, you must confirm that you have been given a valid IP address.

➤ **Satellite card**—If the system is using a satellite card, verify that the satellite card installed in the system is functioning correctly. It may be necessary to confirm that there are no conflicts between the satellite card and other devices in the system.

➤ **Manufacturer's software**—Satellite systems come with software that allows you to manage and maintain the connection. It may be necessary to uninstall and reinstall the software if it does not work.

➤ **Cabling**—The satellite dish uses physical cabling to connect to the satellite modem of the PC card. It may be necessary to confirm that this cable is securely attached to both the dish and the internal connection.

➤ **Technical support**—Do not be afraid to call technical support when dealing with satellite Internet access. You can spend a lot of wasted time on a problem that is not on your end.

Table 10.13 provides a comparison of the various Internet technologies.

Table 10.13 Internet Access Technologies

Access Method	Advantages	Disadvantages	Common Usage	Troubleshooting
POTS	Low cost, high availability of service	Limited speeds, 56Kbps maximum Possible busy signals and disconnections Cannot share a phone line	Used for environments where limited Internet access is required	Physical cabling Modem installation or configuration Verify correct username and password when unable to make or sustain a connection
Cable	High connection speeds Always on; no need to keep dialing for access Does not require a phone line	Shared line; the number of users can affect the Internet speeds	Used for home and small businesses with higher Internet use and consistent Internet speeds are less important	Isolate issues using the modem's LEDs Verify physical cabling between modem and network card Confirm valid IP config-uration information has been assigned
DSL	Always connected technology Certain DSLs can share a phone line High-speed connection	Not available in all areas Slower upload speeds with several DSL flavors May not share a phone line if using symmetric DSL	Commonly used for home and small offices with heavy Internet access	Use the LEDs on the modem to help isolate the problem Verify physical cabling, including the standard phone and the UTP cabling Ensure the network card is properly installed and configured Ensure that you have the correct IP infor-mation

(continued)

Table 10.13	Internet Access Technologies *(continued)*			
Access Method	Advantages	Disadvantages	Common Usage	Troubleshooting
Wireless	High-speed connection Always connected to the Internet Can be used when other technologies are not available	More expensive than DSL or cable Requires a direct line-of-sight between sending and receiving devices Atmospheric conditions can affect signal	Commonly used where DSL and cable Internet are unavailable	Verify hardware is configured and working correctly at your end If possible, eliminate local sources of interference
Home Satellite	High-speed Internet access Always connected technology	More costly than other Internet access methods Distances that signal must travel can cause slower response times Signal can be affected by atmospheric conditions	Commonly used where DSL and cable Internet are unavailable	Use manufacturer software to verify connectivity Confirm that you have a valid IP address If using a satellite card, ensure that there aren't any resource conflicts and the card is functioning correctly Verify physical cabling from the outside satellite dish

Troubleshooting remote connectivity errors

Modern networking is increasingly taking advantage of remote access capabilities. Remote connectivity opens up yet another area of troubleshooting for the network administrator. In particular, there are three key areas to focus on when troubleshooting a remote connectivity issue—protocol configuration, authentication, and physical connectivity.

Authentication

The first place to look when troubleshooting remote connectivity errors is without question authentication. Network users are required to have a valid username and password before they can access the network and network resources. One of the most common complaints network administrators hear is that users are unable to log on. In many instances, this logon failure can be directly linked to an incorrect username and/or password.

When troubleshooting remote connectivity errors, ensure that the user is using the correct username and password combination. If you are working with a system that requires case-sensitive usernames and passwords, ensure that the Caps Lock key is off and that the correct case is being used.

If the correct username and password are being used, you may need to verify that the account is still active and valid. Some network administrators put security measures on accounts such as locking them out if the username or password has been incorrectly entered three times in a row. To troubleshoot such situations you will need to know if there are any security policies in place for user accounts.

In rare cases, authentication failure can be traced to a downed authentication server, although such a circumstance is rare.

Protocol configuration

To be able to access network resources remotely, the remote system has to have valid protocol configuration, which is similar to connecting to the network locally. When you receive a call that a remote user is unable to log onto the network, it may be necessary to verify the configuration information.

Many networks assign the protocol information using DHCP, which assigns everything from the IP address, subnet mask, gateway, and DNS information. If you are working with a system not using DHCP, it will be necessary to verify all of these settings on the client system.

When verifying the system's IP configuration, you will need to use the tools mentioned at the beginning of this chapter. If you are troubleshooting over the phone, you will need to instruct the user to use the commands and relay the output information to you. The commands you are going to need the most in this case is the `ipconfig`, `winipcfg`, or `ifconfig`, depending on the platform used. The output from this command will determine if your remote system is configured to access the network.

Physical connectivity

It is often taken for granted or overlooked that the cabling used to connect users is securely attached. In fact, cabling-related issues are the root cause of many connectivity issues. Cabling-related problems include a faulty cable, an incorrect cable being used, and an incorrectly attached cable.

In a troubleshooting scenario, isolating a problem to one of physical connectivity can often be done using the ping and tracert utilities. For example, if a network user complains that she is unable to log on to the network and from the server you are able to ping other computers on the same network, it is an indicator that there may be a problem with the physical connectivity of that computer. In this scenario, it would be necessary to confirm that the affected computer is correctly cabled to the network card, wall socket, and hub.

Using network tools

There are a number of tools a network administrator may be required to use. Some of these tools (such as the tone generator and locator) may be used for troubleshooting media connections, and others (such as wire *crimpers* and *punchdown* tools) are used to create network cables and connections. In either case, for the Network+ exam, you will be expected to identify the function of various networking tools.

Wire crimpers

Wire crimpers are tools that most network administrators will find themselves using at some point. Basically, a wire crimper is a tool that you use to attach media connectors to the ends of cables. For instance, you use one type of wire crimper to attach RJ-45 connectors on unshielded twisted-pair (UTP) cable, and you use a different type of wire crimper to attach *British Naval connectors (BNCs)* to coaxial cabling.

In a sense, you can think of a wire crimper as a pair of special pliers. You insert the cable and connector separately into the crimper, making sure the wires in the cable align with the appropriate connectors. Then, by squeezing the crimper's handles, you force metal connectors through the wires of the cable, making the connection between the wire and the connector.

If you do need to make your own cables instead of buying, it is a good idea to test them before putting them on the network. It only takes a momentary lapse to make a mistake when creating a cable, and you can waste time later trying to isolate a problem in a faulty cable.

Punchdown tools

If you have ever looked in a network closet, you have probably seen a distribution block, more commonly called a patch panel. A *patch panel* is a freestanding or wall-mounted unit with a number of port connections on the front. In a way, it looks like a wall-mounted hub without the light-emitting diodes (LEDs). The patch panel provides a connection point between network equipment such as hubs and switches and the ports to which PCs are connected, which are normally distributed throughout a building.

Behind each of the individual RJ-45 jacks on the patch panel are connectors to which are attached the eight wires from a piece of twisted-pair cable. These wires are commonly attached to the patch panel by using a tool called a *punchdown tool*. To use the punchdown tool, you place a wire in the tip of the tool and push it into the connector at the back of the patch panel. The insulation is stripped, and the wire is firmly embedded into the connector. Because the connector strips the insulation on the wire, it is known rather grandiosely as an insulation displacement connector (IDC).

Using a punchdown tool is much faster than using wire strippers to prepare each individual wire and then twisting the wire around a connection pole or tightening a screw to hold the wire in place. In many environments, cable tasks are left to a specialized cable contractor. In others, the administrator is the one with the task of connecting wires to a punchdown block.

Tone generators (and tone locators)

A *tone generator* is a device that can save a network installer many hours of frustration. Strangely, the tone generator has a partner that goes wherever it goes but is seldom mentioned: the tone locator. You might hear the tone generator and the tone locator referred to as the *fox and hound*.

As you might expect, the purpose of the tone generator is to generate a signal that is transmitted on the wire you are attempting to locate. At the other end, you press the tone locator against individual wires. When it makes contact with the wire that has the signal on it, the locator emits an audible signal or tone.

The tone locator is a useful device, but it does have some drawbacks. First, it often takes two people to operate—one at each end of the cable. Of course, one person could just keep running back and forth; but if the cable is run over great distances, this could be a problem. Second, using the tone generator is a time-consuming process because it must be attached to each cable independently.

Media testers

A *media tester*, also called a cable tester, is used to test whether a cable is working properly. Any tool that facilitates the testing of a cable can be deemed a cable tester. One of the simplest cable-testing devices is a *multimeter*. By using the continuity setting, you can test for shorts in a length of coaxial cable; or, if you know the correct cable pinouts and have needlepoint probes, you can test twisted-pair cable. Various other single-purpose and multipurpose devices allow you to test cables. Some of these devices tell you if the cable is working correctly and, if it's not, give you some idea why it's not.

Because the majority of network cabling is copper-based, most of the tools designed to test cabling are designed for copper-based cabling. However, when you test fiber-optic cable, you need an optical tester.

An *optical cable tester* performs the same basic function as a wire media tester, but on optical media. Unlike wire cables, the most common problem with an optical cable is a break in the cable that prevents the signal from reaching the other end. Due to the extended distances that can be covered with fiber-optic cables, degradation is rarely an issue in a fiber-optic LAN environment.

Ascertaining whether a signal reaches the other end of a fiber-optic cable is a relatively easy task, but when you determine that there is a break, the problem becomes locating the break. That's when you need a tool called an *optical time-domain reflectometer* (*OTDR*). By using an OTDR, you can locate how far along in the cable the break occurs. The connection on the other end of the cable might be the source of the problem, or perhaps there is a break halfway along the cable. Either way, an OTDR can pinpoint the problem.

Unless you work extensively with fiber-optic cable, you're unlikely to have an OTDR or even a fiber-optic cable tester in your toolbox. Specialized cabling contractors will have them, though, so knowing they exist is important.

Hardware loopback connectors

Hardware loopback connectors are simple devices that redirect outgoing transmissions from a system directly back into it. Hardware loopback connectors are used in conjunction with diagnostic software for diagnosing transmission problems. Loopback connectors are available for a number of ports, including RJ-45, serial, and parallel ports.

Specifically, a hardware loopback connector loops the outgoing data signal wires back into the system on the incoming data signal line. In effect, it tricks the system into thinking that the PC is sending and receiving data on the network, when in fact the data being sent is just being rerouted back in.

Note that in some cases, a hardware loopback connector is referred to as an adapter or a plug.

 The hardware loopback adapter checks the electrical signals sent out from the NIC.

Interpreting visual indicators

One of the first and easiest methods to spot signs of trouble on a network or with a network component is to look at the LEDs that appear on most network components. Many of the devices used in modern networks such as hubs, routers, switches, and even NICs have LEDs that let you know what, if anything, is going wrong. The following sections examine some of the common networking devices and what you can learn from their LEDs.

LEDs on networking devices

If you have seen a hub or a switch, you have no doubt noticed the LEDs on the front of the device. Each RJ-45 connector has one or two dedicated LEDs. These LEDs are designed to provide the network administrator with a quick idea of the status of a connection or a potential problem. Table 10.14 provides some examples of link-light indicators functioning on a hub.

Note that the LEDs' sequencing and meanings vary among the different hub manufacturers and therefore may be different than those listed in Table 10.14.

Table 10.14 Link-Light Indicator LEDs for a Network Hub	
LED State	**Meaning**
Solid green	A device is connected to the port, but there is no activity on the device.
Blinking green	There is activity on the port. The connected system is sending or receiving data.
No LED lit	There is no detectable link. Either there's a problem with the connection between the device and the hub (such as an unplugged cable), or the remote system is powered down.
Fast continuous blinking	This often indicates a fault with the connection, which can for extended periods commonly be attributed to a faulty NIC.
Blinking amber	There are collisions on the network. A few orange LEDs flashing intermittently are okay, but continuously blinking amber LEDs indicate a problem.

In addition to link-light indicators, some hubs and switches have port-speed LEDs that, when lit, indicate the speed at which the connected device is functioning. Some also have LEDs that indicate whether the link is operating in full-duplex mode.

 If a connection LED on a hub is not lit, all the physical connections are correct, and the connected system is powered on, you might have a faulty patch cable.

By understanding the function of the lights on networking devices, you can tell at a glance the status of a device and the systems connected to it. You should take the time to familiarize yourself with the specific indicator lights on the network devices you work with and with their various states.

LEDs on NICs and other devices

In addition to hubs and switches, most other networking devices have LEDs that provide a variety of information. Most NICs have at least one LED that indicates whether there is a link between the system and the network into which it is plugged. The link light operates at a physical level; in other words, it should be lit when the PC is on, regardless of whether the networking software is loaded, the network configuration is correct, or the user is logged on to the network. In addition to the link LED, many NICs have additional lights to indicate the speed at which the network connection is established and/or when there is network activity on the link.

LEDs are also included on cable modems and DSL modems, which are increasingly common as people want faster methods to connect to the Internet.

The number of LEDs on a device and their functionality depends on the device. For example, one cable modem has four LEDs: one that indicates that the modem is online, a Send indicator, a Receive indicator, and one labeled Message.

The usefulness of LEDs in troubleshooting scenarios cannot be overstated. LEDs provide an instant, visual indicator about the state of a network link. In some cases, as with collision lights, they can even alert you to problems on the network. Understanding how to interpret information provided by LEDs is important for the real world and for the Network+ exam.

Imagine a scenario in which a user who is working at Workstation A calls and tells you she is unable to access the Internet. The Internet connection could be down, but by connecting to the Internet yourself, you determine that it is working correctly; therefore, it is safe to assume that the problem is at the user's end rather than with the Internet connectivity. Next, you decide to visit the user's workstation to see whether you can ping the Internet router. Before you begin the ping test, you look at the back of the system and see that the link LED on the NIC is not lit. You can be fairly sure at this point that the ping test will not work because without the link light, there is no connectivity between the NIC and the switch.

Now you have narrowed the problem to one of few sources. Either the NIC or the cable is faulty, the switch to which the user is connected is not functioning, or the port on the switch to which the user is connected is faulty.

The easiest way to test whether the cable is the problem is to borrow a known working cable from Workstation B or C and swap it with the cable connecting Workstation A to the hub, switch, or wall port. When you try this, if the link light does not come on, you can deduce that the NIC is faulty. If the light does come on, you can deduce that either the port on the switch or a cable is faulty. The next step is to swap the cable out or try the original cable in another port switch.

 Expect to be asked to identify the purposes of link lights on the Network+ exam. You might be presented with diagrams and asked how you would use LEDs in the troubleshooting process.

Whatever the actual problem, link lights play an important role in the troubleshooting process. They give you an easy method of seeing what steps do and don't work.

Review and test yourself

The following sections provide you with the opportunity to review what you learned in this chapter and to test yourself.

The facts

For the exam, don't forget these important concepts:

➤ Ping is a command-line utility designed to test connectivity between systems on a TCP/IP-based network.

➤ Ping the IP address of your local loopback adapter, using the command ping 127.0.0.1. If this command is successful, you know that the TCP/IP protocol suite is installed correctly on your system and functioning.

➤ If you cannot ping other devices on your local network and you were able to ping your local NIC, you might not be connected to the network correctly, or there might be a cable problem on the computer.

➤ Trace route is a TCP/IP utility that is used to track the path a packet takes to reach a remote host and isolate where network problems may be.

➤ Trace route reports the amount of time it takes to reach each host in the path. It is a useful tool for isolating bottlenecks in a network.

➤ ARP is the part of the TCP/IP suite whose function is to resolve IP addresses to MAC addresses.

➤ ARP operates at the network layer of the Open Systems Interconnect (OSI) model.

➤ Netstat is used to view both inbound and outbound TCP/IP network connections.

➤ The netstat -r command can be used to display the routing table of the system.

➤ nbtstat is used to display protocol and statistical information for NetBIOS over TCP/IP connections.

➤ The ipconfig command shows the IP configuration information for all NICs installed within a system.

➤ The ipconfig/all command is used to display detailed TCP/IP configuration information.

➤ The ipconfig/ renew command is used to refresh the systems DNS information.

➤ When looking for client connectivity problems using ipconfig, ensure the gateway is correctly set.

➤ The ifconfig command is the Linux equivalent of the ipconfig command.

➤ winipcfg is the Windows 95, Windows 98, and Windows Me equivalent of the ipconfig command.

➤ The nslookup command is a TCP/IP diagnostic tool that is used to troubleshoot DNS problems.

➤ DSL is an Internet access method that uses a standard phone line to provide high-speed Internet access.

➤ A DSL modem connects to the system using a standard UTP and RJ-45 connectors.

➤ Visual indicators such as link lights are often the first sign that something is not functioning correctly.

Key terms

➤ tracert

➤ ping

➤ arp

➤ netstat

➤ nbtstat

➤ ipconfig/ifconfig

➤ winipcfg

➤ nslookup

➤ POTS

➤ DSL

➤ Cable

➤ Wireless

Practice exam

Question 1

Which of the following commands would issue the following printout?

```
0 Ethernet adapter :
        IP Address. . . . . . . . . : 169.254.196.192
        Subnet Mask . . . . . . . . : 255.255.0.0
        Default Gateway . . . . . . :
1 Ethernet adapter :
        IP Address. . . . . . . . . : 0.0.0.0
        Subnet Mask . . . . . . . . : 0.0.0.0
        Default Gateway . . . . . . :
```

○ A. **ping**

○ B. **tracert**

○ C. **ipconfig /all**

○ D. **ipconfig**

The correct answer is D. Without using any switches, the ipconfig command shows the IP address, subnet mask, and default gateway for available adapters. Answer A is incorrect: ping is used to test the connectivity between devices and does not produce this output. Answer B is incorrect: tracert displays routing information. Answer C is incorrect; the ipconfig /all command shows much more of the IP configuration information than the output listed in the question.

Question 2

You are working as a network administrator for a small organization. You receive a call from one of the company's remote users complaining that they are unable to log on to the network. You decide that you would like them to try and renew the IP configuration information. Which of the following commands would you ask them to use?

○ A. **nbtstat -renew**

○ B. **nbtstat /renew**

○ C. **ipconfig -renew**

○ D. **ipconfig /renew**

The correct answer is D. In addition to viewing IP configuration information, `ipconfig` allows you to release and renew the IP configuration. The correct syntax for renewing IP configuration is `ipconfig /renew`. Answers A and B are incorrect. The `nbtstat` command cannot be used to renew the IP configuration from a DHCP server.

Question 3

Which of the following `ping` switches is used to perform a continuous `ping`?

○ A. `-c`
○ B. `-t`
○ C. `-o`
○ D. `-w`

The correct answer is B. The `ping` command used with the `-t` switch will send out continuous `ping` requests. This is used when troubleshooting and the default four pings are not enough. Answer A and C are incorrect. These switches are not valid for pinging on a Windows system. Answer D is incorrect. The `-w` switch allows you to specify, in milliseconds, the amount of time the system should wait for a reply from the remote host.

Question 4

Which of the following commands can be used to show the systems routing table?

○ A. **ping -R**
○ B. **nbtstat -r**
○ C. **netstat -r**
○ D. **tracert -R**

The correct answer is C. The `netstat -r` command is commonly used by network administrators to show the system's routing table. The `route print` command can also be used to see the current routing table. Answer A is incorrect; the `ping` command is used to test network connectivity, not view TCP/IP configuration information. Answer B is incorrect; the `nbtstat` command displays NetBIOS over TCP/IP-related information. Answer D is incorrect because the `tracert` command is used to track the path between two devices on the network.

Question 5

You are working to provide telephone support for a local ISP. One of the residential users calls you complaining that they are no longer able to access the Internet. Upon further questioning, you determine that they recently moved the computer within their house. Which of the following connectivity problems might you suspect first?

○ A. Protocol configuration

○ B. DNS settings

○ C. Gateway settings

○ D. Physical cabling

The correct answer is D. It is not unusual to get support calls after users have attempted to move their systems. When hearing that a system has recently been moved, one of the first places to explore is the physical cabling verifying that all cables have been securely and correctly attached. Although it may be necessary to confirm settings, such as protocol information, you will likely start with the cabling moving to settings only after verifying correct cabling.

Question 6

When troubleshooting a network connectivity problem, you are able to **ping** your local loopback, the IP address of your system, and the IP address of another system on your network. However, you cannot **ping** the default gateway. Which of the following is *not* a valid reason for this problem?

○ A. The default gateway is not operational.

○ B. The IP address of the default gateway is not configured correctly.

○ C. Routing is disabled on your workstation.

○ D. There is no default gateway present.

The correct answer is C. The routing functionality of the workstation is irrelevant in this scenario. All the other answers are valid reasons for the problem.

Question 7

Which of the following commands can be used to purge and reload the remote cache name table?

- ○ A. **nbtstat -R**
- ○ B. **nbtstat -n**
- ○ C. **nbtstat -r**
- ○ D. **nbtstat -S**

The correct answer is A. The nbtstat -R command purges and reloads the remote cache name table. The -n switch displays the local name table, -r provides resolution information, and -S shows the NetBIOS session table.

Question 8

Which utility would produce the following output?

```
6  55 ms  27 ms  42 ms  so-1-0-0.XL1.VAN1.NET [152.63.137.130]
7  55 ms  41 ms  28 ms  0.so-7-0-0.TL1.VAN1.NET [152.63.138.74]
8  55 ms  55 ms  55 ms  0.so-2-0-0.TL1.SAC1.NET [152.63.8.1]
9  83 ms  55 ms  55 ms  0.so-7-0-0.XL1.SAC1.NET [152.63.53.249]
10 82 ms  41 ms  55 ms  POS6-0.BR5.SAC1.NET [152.63.52.225]
11 55 ms  68 ms  55 ms  uu-gw.ip.att.net [192.205.32.125]
12 55 ms  68 ms  69 ms  tbr2-p013802.ip.att.net [12.122.11.229]
13 96 ms  69 ms  82 ms  tbr1-p012801.ip.att.net [12.122.11.225]
14 82 ms  82 ms  69 ms  tbr2-p012402.ip.att.net [12.122.11.221]
```

- ○ A. **nbtstat -R**
- ○ B. **netstat -R**
- ○ C. **arp -s**
- ○ D. **tracert**

The correct answer is D. The output is from the Windows 2000 tracert command. All the other utilities listed provide different output.

Question 9

> You are trying to access a workstation located on another LAN. The LANs are connected via a router. You are able to access other computers on your own LAN. Which of the following would best help you isolate where the failure is located?
>
> ○ A. **ping** the far side of the router
>
> ○ B. **ping** the near side of the router
>
> ○ C. **Tracert** to the workstation on the other side of the router
>
> ○ D. **Tracert** to a workstation on your local LAN

The correct answer is C. The `tracert` command is used to trace how far a data packet travels before it cannot go further. By running a `tracert` to a workstation on the other side, you will be able to tell from the output where the transmission failed. Pinging is not as useful in determining where the failure occurred as its output only identifies whether the packet delivery was successful but does not indicate where the failure occurred. Using the `tracert` command on a workstation on the local LAN would not help isolate the problem on the far side of the router.

Question 10

> You are troubleshooting a Windows 2000 system on a network and want to renew the IP information on the system. Assuming the system is using DHCP, which of the following commands would accomplish this?
>
> ○ A. **ifconfig /refresh**
>
> ○ B. **ipconfig /renew**
>
> ○ C. **ipconfig /iprenew**
>
> ○ D. **ipconfig /IPrefresh**

The correct answer is B. The `ipconfig` command with the `/renew` switch will refresh the IP information on that system. Answer A is incorrect as `ifconfig` is not a Windows-based command. Answers C and D are not valid Windows commands.

Want to know more?

Haugdahl, J.Scott. *Network Analysis and Troubleshooting.* Addison-Wesley Publishing, 2000.

Cisco Systems, Inc. *Internetworking Troubleshooting Handbook* (Second Edition). Cisco Press, 2001.

Sheldon, Thomas. *McGraw-Hill's Encyclopedia of Networking and Telecommunications.* McGraw-Hill Professional Publishing, 2001.

Tulloch, Mitch. *Microsoft Encyclopedia of Networking* (with CD-ROM). Microsoft Press, 2000.

Troubleshooting and Supporting the Network

. . . .

Objectives

4.8 Given a scenario, predict the impact of modifying, adding, or removing network services (DHCP, DNS, WINS, and so on) on network resources and users.

4.9 Given a network-problem scenario, select an appropriate course of action based on a general troubleshooting strategy that includes the following steps:

   1. Establish what the symptoms are.

   2. Identify the affected areas.

   3. Establish what has changed.

   4. Select the most probable cause.

   5. Implement a solution.

   6. Test the results.

   7. Recognize the potential effects of the solution.

   8. Document the solution.

4.10 Given a troubleshooting scenario involving a network with a particular physical topology (that is, bus, star/hierarchical, mesh, ring, or wireless) and including a network diagram, identify the network area affected and the cause of the problem.

4.11 Given a network-troubleshooting scenario involving a client connectivity problem (for example, incorrect protocol/client, software/authentication configuration, insufficient rights/permissions), identify the cause of the problem.

4.12 Given a network-troubleshooting scenario involving a wiring/infrastructure problem, identify the cause of the problem (for example, bad media, interference, or network hardware).

What you need to know

✓ Use troubleshooting steps to isolate and correct a problem.

✓ Identify and troubleshoot topology-specific errors.

✓ Use troubleshooting techniques to identify and isolate client connectivity errors.

✓ Use troubleshooting techniques to identify and isolate network wiring/infrastructure problems.

✓ Identify the impact on the network of adding or removing network services.

Introduction

Many duties and responsibilities fall under the umbrella of network administration. Of all these, one of the most practiced is that of troubleshooting. No matter how well a network is designed and any preventative maintenance schedules in place, troubleshooting will always be necessary. Because of this, network administrators have to develop those troubleshooting skills.

This chapter focuses on all areas of troubleshooting including troubleshooting best practices and some of the tools and utilities you'll use to assist in the troubleshooting process.

Troubleshooting steps and procedures

Regardless of the problem, effective network troubleshooting follows some specific troubleshooting steps. These steps provide a framework in which to perform the troubleshooting process and, when followed, can reduce the time it takes to isolate and fix a problem. The following sections discuss the common troubleshooting steps and procedures as identified by the CompTIA Network+ objectives.

Establish the symptoms

The first step in the troubleshooting process is to establish the symptoms of the problem. At this stage of troubleshooting, you are simply concerned with determining what the problem actually is. This is often more difficult than it sounds, but it is essential as you could find yourself trying to get to the bottom of a problem that doesn't exist.

The information you need to determine the cause of the problem comes from two common sources—from a user or users who are affected by the problem and from the computer in the form of error messages or logs. Determining the cause of the problem from system generated logs and error messages can be straightforward or it may require accessing a manufacturer's Web site for more information to discover the exact meaning of the error codes or perhaps even a call to tech support.

Getting accurate information from computer users about the nature of a computer problem can be a difficult task, because it's often difficult for non-technical personnel to convey technical information. However, the information you are able to get from the computer users may often make the difference between a drawn-out troubleshooting process and a quick one. From end users, you are specifically seeking answers to the following questions:

➤ When did the problem occur?

➤ What was the user doing when the problem occurred?

➤ How often does the problem occur?

➤ Has anything been done to try to correct the problem?

➤ Has anything changed on the system recently—new hardware or software, or anything else?

The answers to these questions can provide the greatest clues as to the exact cause of the problem.

Identify the affected area

After you have established what the problem is, you can now set your sights towards identifying the magnitude of the problem. This is important for many reasons. Some problems are small and affect only a single user or a handful of users. Equally, there are those problems that affect the whole network. These problems are typically associated with the network infrastructure. Problems of this nature may include problems such as malfunctioning hubs or switches, or insufficient bandwidth for the network. Such problems can affect several users and are difficult and often costly to troubleshoot.

Identifying the affected area can also help you distinguish the priority of the problem. A problem that is affecting numerous users will typically take precedence over single user problems.

Establish what has changed

When a single computer or a network that has been configured properly and has been functioning sufficiently suddenly fails, it is often a sign that something has changed. For this reason when confronted with a troubleshooting problem, one of your first questions should always be: What has changed?

When looking for changes to the network or a single system, consider the following:

➤ Has new software been added to the system?

➤ Has any hardware been added to the system or network?

➤ Have systems been moved around the network?

➤ Have systems been added to the network?

Such changes to the network or a system can create a range of problems. If you know that these changes have taken place you are better able to isolate the problem. For instance, if you know that a system has been moved to a new location on the network, you are likely going to suspect a cabling related issue if the user is unable to connect to the network.

Select the probable cause

It is not always easy to identify the single cause of a problem, as there can quite easily be several potential solutions. Take, for instance, a condition in which a user is unable to log onto the network. This can be a result of many problems, from an invalid logon, faulty cable, bad network card, or an account that has been locked out. The focus of this stage of the troubleshooting process is to start with the most probable cause of the problem. If several causes seem likely, choose the potential cause that has the easiest solution and work from there.

Using this strategy with the example of a failed network logon, the first probable cause is likely to be verifying that the correct username and password combination is being used. If the correct username and password are being used, you should try the next easiest solution.

Implement a solution

After you have selected the most probable cause, it is finally time to try to correct the problem. The implementation of the solution itself often follows planning guidelines. For instance, if the potential solution requires powering down the server to replace hardware, you will need to plan a time to do this. In addition, you might need to make backups of the system.

In this way, there is often much planning that goes into preparing to implement the solution before it is actually implemented.

The important point to remember when implementing a solution is to only try one fix at a time. Trying too many solutions at once will make it very difficult to determine exactly what corrected the problem and why.

Test the results

It would be nice if the first solution you tried corrected the problem; unfortunately this is not often the case. After implementing a solution it is necessary to verify that the solution indeed addressed the problem. Depending on the problem you were fixing, the testing process can be a difficult and arduous task. It may also be that the solution can only be tested in a live networking environment. The key to this step is to remember that whenever and wherever possible, changes made to the network should be tested and verified to be functional.

Recognize the potential effect of the solution

When working with networks, it is always important to keep an eye on the big picture and determine the effect that changes to one area of the network have on another area. Everything you do can impact the network, including such tasks as adding computers, changing networking hardware, and modifying the server.

Document the solution

One of the most important steps in the troubleshooting process is the documentation. The purpose of the documentation is to provide a quick reference to the solution of the problem should it arise again. Some of the network problems you are sure to encounter will require extensive time and resources to correct, and documentation of the solution will make the process easier the next time around. There are several key pieces of information that have to be entered into the documentation in order for it to be effective. When completing your documentation, include the following:

➤ The solution to the problem

➤ Other solutions that may have been tried but were unsuccessful and why

➤ Who implemented the solution

➤ When the solution was applied

 You are likely to have questions on the Network+ exam that require you to identify the order in which the troubleshooting steps should be performed.

Identify and troubleshoot errors with a particular physical topology

Each of the physical network topologies requires its own troubleshooting strategies and methods. When troubleshooting a network it is important to know which topology is used as it can greatly impact the procedures used to resolve any problems. This section lists each of the respective physical network topologies and some common troubleshooting strategies.

In one form or another, you can expect to be asked questions regarding troubleshooting the different topologies.

Star topology

The most common topology used today is the *star topology*. The star topology uses a central connection point such as a hub in which all devices on the network connect. Each device on the network uses its own length of cable, thus allowing devices to be added or removed from the network without disruption to current network users. When troubleshooting a physical star network, consider the following:

➤ The central device, hubs or switches, provide a single point of failure. When troubleshooting a loss of connectivity for several users, it may be a faulty hub. Try placing the cables in a known working hub to confirm.

➤ Hubs and switches provide *Light Emitting Diodes (LEDs)* that provide information regarding the port status. For instance, by using the LEDs you can determine whether there is a jabbering network card, whether there is a proper connection to the network device, and whether there are too many collisions on the network.

➤ Each device, printer, or computer connects to a central device using its own length of cable. When troubleshooting a connectivity error in a star network, it might be necessary to verify that the cable works. This can be done by swapping the cable with a known working one or using a cable tester.

➤ Ensure that the patch cables and cables have the correct specifications.

Ring topology

Although not as commonly used as it once was, you may find yourself troubleshooting a *ring network*. Most ring networks are *logical rings*, meaning that each computer is logically connected to each other. A *physical ring topology* is a rare find but a *Fiber Distributed Data Interface (FDDI)* would be considered a true physical ring topology. A logical ring topology uses a central connecting device as with a star network called a *Multistation Access unit (MSAU)*. When troubleshooting either a logical or physical ring topology, consider the following:

➤ A physical ring topology use a single length of cable interconnecting all computers and forming a loop. If there is a break in the cable, all systems on the network will be unable to access the network.

➤ The MSAU on a logical ring topology represents a single point of failure. If all devices are unable to access the network, it may be that the MSAU is faulty.

➤ Verify that the cabling and connectors have the correct specifications.

➤ All Network Interface Cards (NICs) on the ring network must operate at the same speed.

➤ When connecting MSAUs in a ring network, ensure that the ring in and ring out configuration is properly set.

Bus network errors

Although the bus topology is rarely implemented anymore, there are enough of them out there for it to be included in the CompTIA Network+ exam objectives. So if you do not encounter a bus network in the real world, you will most certainly be faced with one on the exam.

Troubleshooting a bus network can be a difficult and frustrating task. The following list contains a few hotspots to be aware of when troubleshooting a bus network:

➤ A bus topology must be continuous. A break in the cable at any point will render the entire segment unusable. If the location of the break in the cable is not apparent, you can check each length of cable systematically from one end to the other to identify the location of the break, or you can use a tool such as a time domain reflectometer, which can be used to locate a break in a cable.

➤ The cable used on a bus network has two distinct physical endpoints. Each of these cable ends requires a *terminator*. Terminators are used to absorb electronic signals so that they are not reflected back on the media, compromising data integrity. A failed or missing terminator will render the entire network segment unusable.

➤ The addition, removal, or failure of a device on the network might prevent the entire network from functioning. Also, the coaxial cable used in a bus network can be damaged very easily. Moving cables in order to add or remove devices can cause cable problems. The T connectors used on bus networks do allow devices to be added and removed without necessarily affecting the network, but care must be taken when doing this.

➤ One end of the bus network should be grounded. Intermittent problems or a high occurrence of errors may indicate poor or insufficient grounding.

Mesh network errors

A *mesh topology* offers high redundancy by providing several paths for data to reach its destination. In a true mesh network, each device on the network is connected to every other device, and if one cable fails, there is another to provide an alternative data path. Although a mesh topology is resilient to failure, the number of connections involved can make a mesh network some-what tricky to troubleshoot.

When troubleshooting a mesh network, consider the following points:

➤ A mesh topology interconnects all devices on the network, offering the highest level of redundancy of all the topologies. In a pure mesh environment, all devices are directly connected to all other devices. In a hybrid mesh environment, some devices are connected only to certain others in the topology.

➤ Although a mesh topology can accommodate failed links, mechanisms should still be in place so that failed links are detected and reported.

➤ Design and implementation of a true mesh network can be complex and often requires specialized hardware devices.

Mesh networks are so rare that it's unlikely you will be faced with trou-bleshooting one but, there will likely be questions on the Network+ Exam that focus on mesh networks.

 Most mesh networks are used to connect multiple networks, such as in a WAN scenario, rather than to connect computers in a LAN.

Wireless network errors

Wireless networks do not require physical cable to connect computers; rather, they use wireless media. The benefits of such a configuration are clear: Users have remote access to files and resources without the need for physical con-nections. Wireless networking eliminates cable faults and cable breaks. It does, however, introduce its own considerations: signal interference and security.

When troubleshooting a wireless network, consider the following:

➤ Common media types for wireless networks—including infrared, radio waves, and satellite communication—vary in their resistance to signal interference and security. When troubleshooting a wireless connection, ensure that the signal is not being compromised by environmental factors such as storms.

➤ It is possible to eavesdrop on wireless signals. Therefore, security must be carefully considered.

➤ Wireless communication has limited speed compared to cabled Ethernet networks. When troubleshooting, be aware of the expected network speeds.

➤ Some types of wireless communications require a point-to-point direct line-of-sight connection. If something is blocking this line of sight such as a building, the transmissions may fail.

Identifying and troubleshooting client connectivity problems

Any network administrator is likely to tell you that *client connectivity* errors are one of the most common sources of network-related problems. Client connectivity errors range from plain old user error, to more complex protocol and cabling issues and even administrative mistakes. With so many possibilities, it is no wonder that client connectivity persists as one of the biggest network troubleshooting hotspots. The following sections explore the common sources of client connectivity problems and provide scenarios that network administrators might encounter.

Protocol errors

The client system has to have a protocol assigned or bound to its NIC in order to access resources. You can use specialized tools to verify that a protocol is being used by the system; for example, on Windows NT/2000/XP/Me/98 systems you use the ipconfig command, on older Windows client systems you use the winipcfg command, and on Linux systems you use the ifconfig command.

You need to consider a number of factors related to network protocols when you troubleshoot a network. The following list describes some of the protocol-specific issues you should be aware of when dealing with client protocol configurations:

➤ **Transmission Control Protocol/Internet Protocol (TCP/IP)**—For a system to operate on a TCP/IP-based network, it must have at the very least a unique IP address, the correct subnet mask for the network to which it is connected. For cross-network connectivity, you must also have a default gateway entry. In addition, Domain Name Service (DNS) server addresses may be required.

➤ **Internetwork Packet Exchange/Sequenced Packet Exchange (IPX/SPX)**—Each system on an IPX/SPX network must have a unique address, although the addresses are generated and assigned automatically. Care must be taken to ensure that the correct frame type is being used, although systems are usually able to autodetect the frame type that is in use.

➤ **Network BIOS Extended User Interface (NetBEUI)**—Each system on a network that uses NetBEUI must have a unique name to identify the computer on the network. For name resolution between network segments, a network needs either a Windows Internet Naming System (WINS) server or manual name resolution through an LMHOSTS file.

➤ **AppleTalk**—Each system on an AppleTalk network must have a unique address.

On networks that use TCP/IP, Dynamic Host Configuration Protocol (DHCP) is often used to automatically assign protocol information to clients. When DHCP is not used, protocol information has to be entered manually, and many errors can arise—most commonly duplicate IP addresses.

Once correctly configured, protocol problems are infrequent. Unless settings are manually changed, very little can go wrong.

Authentication

Before users can log on to the system, their identities must be verified. By far the most common type of authentication is the standard username and password combination. When a user account is created, it is good practice for the administrator to set a password. The user should change that password immediately so that the administrator no longer knows it.

Users should be forced to change their logon passwords periodically, although that often creates the problem of users forgetting their passwords. Mechanisms should therefore be in place that allow users to get new passwords quickly.

Most user password problems can be traced to users entering an incorrect password or entering the correct password incorrectly. All common operating systems offer the capability for the administrator to change a user's password, but none offer the capability to determine the user's existing password. Therefore, if a user does forget his or her password, a new one has to be created and issued.

Little can be done about users incorrectly typing passwords, except that you can encourage users to be careful. Note that some operating systems such as

Linux and Windows NT/2000 use case-sensitive passwords. Therefore, if a user is having trouble logging on, he or she should ensure that the Caps Lock key is on or off as appropriate.

 Although it may seem obvious, one of the first places to look when troubleshooting logon difficulty is to verify that the Caps Lock key is off.

Permissions errors

Access to programs and data across the network is controlled by *permissions*. Permissions are responsible for protecting the data on the network and ensuring that only those who should have access to it do.

The first rule of permissions troubleshooting is to remember that permissions do not change. If a user cannot access a file, the first question to the user should always be, "Could you ever access the file?" If the user says "Yes, but now I can't access the file," you should check server change logs or documentation to determine whether any changes have been made in the permissions structure.

If no changes have been made, you should verify that the user is in fact allowed access to that file or directory. In large environments, trying to keep track of who should have access to what can be a tricky business—one that is best left to defined policies and documentation.

The following are some other items you should consider when troubleshooting permissions problems:

➤ On some operating systems, rights and permissions can be inherited from parent directories or other directories that are higher in the directory structure. A change in the permissions assignments at one level may have an effect on a lower level in the directory tree.

➤ File permissions can be gained from objects other than the user's account. Depending on the operating system being used, rights can also be gained from group membership, other network objects, or security equivalence. When you are troubleshooting a permissions problem, be sure that you understand where rights are supposed to originate.

➤ File attributes can override file permissions, and they can prevent actions from being performed on certain files. To the uninitiated, this might seem like a file permissions problem, but in fact it is correct operation. For example, on a NetWare file system, the Rename Inhibit permission prevents changes to the name of a file, even if the user has the Supervisor File System permission.

➤ You need to determine that there is actually a problem. Users sometimes decide to clean up by deleting files they think are no longer used. Permissions may have been set that prevent users from doing this, and rightly so, but the user might identify this as a permissions problem and report it as such. To a lesser extent, the same situation can occur when a user tries to manipulate a file while it is in use by another application or user.

Troubleshooting permissions problems can be both challenging and enjoyable. As with many other IT troubleshooting scenarios, you can effectively solve a majority of permissions problems if you fully understand what you are troubleshooting and the factors that affect the situation.

Physical connectivity errors

Although many of the problems associated with client connectivity can be traced to software-based problems such as configuration, authentication, and permissions issues, *physical connectivity* is often the root of the problem.

When you are troubleshooting physical connectivity errors, the first place to look is at the network cables. Although it is a relatively infrequent occurrence, cables can become loose or disconnected from NICs or from the ports on a hub or switch. Often, this is the result of other cables being plugged in or unplugged, or of activity on the connections around the one that is having the problem. Other cable considerations include exceeded maximum lengths, cable breaks, and improperly terminated or made cables, although these are only exceptional cases.

Physical connectivity errors also involve the devices used to establish the physical client/server connectivity. This can include hubs, switches, MSAUs, NICs, routers, and connectivity hardware. As discussed earlier in this chapter, these devices normally have LEDs that indicate the state of the network and the respective links with devices. Although it is possible to have a problem with a single port on one of the aforementioned devices, it is more likely that the entire unit will malfunction. Thankfully, networking devices are very resilient and normally provide many years of reliable service, with few or no problems.

Troubleshooting physical connectivity errors often requires some trial and error. For example, you might switch a cable to a different port in a hub to test whether the port is at fault or replace a cable or NIC with one that is known to be working to see if it fixes the problem. If you are fortunate enough to have them, you can use instruments and devices that are aimed at reducing the hit-or-miss approach to the troubleshooting process, but they are costly devices and they often come a distant second to the trial-and-error method.

Now that you have had a quick overview of the common client connectivity issues, it is time to test your knowledge with some scenarios.

Troubleshooting wiring- and infrastructure-related problems

You will no doubt find yourself troubleshooting wiring and infrastructure problems less frequently than you'll troubleshoot client connectivity problems—and thankfully so. Wiring- and infrastructure-related problems can be very difficult to trace, and sometimes a very costly solution is needed to remedy the situation. When troubleshooting these problems, a methodical approach is likely to pay off.

Wiring problems are related to the actual cable used in a network. For the purposes of the Network+ exam, infrastructure problems are classified as those related to network devices such as hubs, switches, and routers.

Troubleshooting wiring

Troubleshooting wiring involves knowing what wiring your network uses and where it is being used.

Determining your wiring

All cables used in networking have certain limitations, in terms of both speed and distance. It might be that the network problems are a result of trying to use a cable in an environment or a way for which it was not designed. For example, you might find that a network is connecting two workstations that are 130 meters apart with Category 5 UTP cabling. Category 5 UTP is specified for distances up to 100 meters, so exceeding the maximum cable length can be a potential cause of the problem.

Determining the type of cable used by a network is often as easy as reading the cable. The cable should be stamped with its type—whether it is, for example, UTP Category 5, RG-58, or something else. As you work with the various cable types used to create networks, you'll get to the point where you can easily identify them. However, you should be careful when identifying cable types because some cable types are almost indistinguishable. After you have determined the cable being used, you can compare the characteristics and limitations of that cable against how it is being used on the network.

Where the cable is used

Imagine that you have been called in to track down a problem with a network. After some time, you discover that clients are connected to the network via standard UTP cable run down an elevator shaft. Recall from Chapter 2, "Cabling and Connectors," that UTP has very poor resistance to electromagnetic interference (EMI) and therefore UTP and the electrical equipment associated with elevators react to each other like oil and water. The same can be said of cables that are run close to fluorescent light fittings. Such problems might seem farfetched, but you would be surprised at just how many environments you will work in that have random or erratic problems that users have lived with for a long time and not done anything about.

Part of troubleshooting wiring problems is to identify where the cable runs, to isolate whether the problem is a result of crosstalk or EMI. You need to be aware of problems associated with interference and the distance limitations of the cable being used.

If you find a problem with a network cable, there are various measures you can take to correct the problem. For cables that exceed the maximum distance, you can use a repeater to regenerate the signal, try to reroute the cable over a more economical route, or even replace the type of cable with one that has greater resistance to attenuation. The method you choose often depends on your network's design and your budget.

For cable that is affected by EMI or other interference, you should consider replacing the cable with cable that is more resistant to such interference or rerouting the cable away from the source of the interference. If you do reroute cable, pay attention to the maximum distance, and make sure that as you're solving one problem you don't create another.

Troubleshooting the infrastructure

If you are looking for a challenge, troubleshooting infrastructure problems is for you. It is often not an easy task and usually involves many processes, including baselining and performance monitoring.

Only by using a variety of tools and methods can you identify the infrastructure as the cause of your troubles.

You can experience three types of basic problems when troubleshooting infrastructure problems:

> ➤ **Specific failures**—A device such as a hub or switch can cease to function and cause an entire section of the network to fail. Such problems tend to be quite easy to troubleshoot. If you are armed with the network documentation, it should be fairly simple to pinpoint the source of the problem.

> ➤ **Nonspecific failures**—Sometimes users experience random problems with the network, but there doesn't seem to be any common thread to the problems. Such problems can be hard to isolate because it is often difficult to pin down the exact cause.

> ➤ **General performance problems**—A common sign of a problem with the network infrastructure is poor network performance. Of course, *poor performance* is a vague statement that can be attributed to anything from a misconfigured operating system or application to failed hardware. In the troubleshooting process, all these problems would likely be eliminated as causes before the network's infrastructure would become suspect. You are most likely going to encounter infrastructure problems when you're using new equipment or new applications on older networks. For example, perhaps the 10Mbps hubs and the Category 3 UTP cable just won't work with the newer devices you're using. It is the network administrator's job to be aware of possible infrastructure problems before installing new network components or applications. You can save yourself a lot of legwork by fully exploring the impact that changes to the network will have on the existing infrastructure before you modify the network.

Predicting the impact of modifying, adding, or removing network services

All network services require a certain amount of network resources in order to function. The amount of resources required depends on the exact service being used. Before implementing or removing any service on a network, it is very important to understand the impact that these services can have on the entire network. To provide some idea of the demands various services place on the network, this section outlines some of the most common network services and the impact their addition, modification, or removal might have on the network and clients.

Adding, modifying, or removing DHCP

DHCP automatically assigns TCP/IP addressing to computers when they join the network and automatically renews the addresses before they expire. The advantage of using DHCP is the reduced number of addressing errors, which makes network maintenance much easier. Remember from earlier in this chapter that each computer on a TCP/IP network requires a unique IP address.

One of the biggest benefits of using DHCP is that the reconfiguration of IP addressing can be performed from a central location, with little or no effect on the clients. In fact, you can reconfigure an entire IP addressing system without the users noticing. There is, as always, a cost associated with everything good, and with DHCP, the cost is increased network traffic.

You know what the function of DHCP is and the service it provides to the network, but what impact does the DHCP service have on the network itself? Some network services can consume huge amounts of network bandwidth, but DHCP is not one of them. The traffic generated between the DHCP server and the DHCP client is minimal during normal usage periods.

The bulk of the network traffic generated by DHCP occurs during two phases of the DHCP communication process: when the lease of the IP address is initially granted to the client system and when that lease is renewed. The entire DHCP communication process takes less than a second, but if there are a very large number of client systems, the communication process can slow down the network.

For most network environments, the traffic generated by the DHCP service is negligible. For environments where DHCP traffic is a concern, you can reduce this traffic by increasing the lease duration for the client systems, thereby reducing communication between the DHCP client and the server.

If DHCP functionality is removed from the network (which is unusual), each system needs to be manually configured with IP addressing information.

Adding, modifying, or removing WINS

WINS is used on Microsoft networks to facilitate communications between computers by resolving NetBIOS names to IP addresses. Each time a computer starts, it registers itself with a WINS server by contacting that server over the network. If the system then needs to contact another system, it can contact the WINS server to get the NetBIOS name resolved to an IP address. If you are thinking about not using WINS, you should know that the alternative is for computers to identify themselves and resolve NetBIOS names to IP addresses via broadcasts. Broadcasts are inefficient because all data is transmitted to every device on the network segment. Broadcasts can be a significant problem for large network segments. Also, if a network has more than one segment, you cannot browse to remote segments because broadcasts are not typically forwarded by routers, which will eliminate this method of resolution.

Because WINS actually replaces the broadcast communication on a network, it has a positive impact on network resources and bandwidth usage. This does not mean that WINS does not generate any network traffic—just that the traffic is more organized and efficient. The amount of network traffic generated by WINS clients to a WINS server is minimal and should not have a negative impact in most network environments.

WINS server information can be entered manually into the TCP/IP configuration on a system, or it can be supplied via DHCP. If the WINS server addresses change and the client configuration is being performed manually, each system needs to be reconfigured with the new WINS server addresses. If you are using DHCP, you need to update only the DHCP scope with the new information.

Removing WINS from a network increases the amount of broadcast traffic and can potentially limit browsing to a single segment unless another method of resolution (such as the use of the statically maintained LMHOSTS file) is in place.

Adding, modifying, or removing DNS

As previously mentioned, the function of DNS is to resolve hostnames to IP addresses. Without such a service, network users would have to identify a remote system by its IP address rather than by its easy-to-remember hostname.

Name resolution can be provided dynamically by a DNS server, or it can be accomplished statically, using the HOSTS file on the client system. If you are using a DNS server, the IP address of the DNS server is required. DNS server addresses can be entered manually, or they can be supplied through a DHCP server.

Review and test yourself

The following sections provide you with the opportunity to review what you learned in this chapter and to test yourself.

The facts

For the exam, don't forget these important concepts:

➤ When presented with a troubleshooting scenario, consider the following procedure:

  1. Establish what the symptoms are.

  2. Identify the affected areas.

  3. Establish what has changed.

  4. Select the most probable cause.

5. Implement a solution.

6. Test the results.

7. Recognize the potential effects of the solution.

8. Document the solution.

➤ The central device, hubs or switches, provide a single point of failure.

➤ Hubs and switches provide LEDs that provide information regarding the port status.

➤ A physical ring topology uses a single length of cable interconnecting all computers and forming a loop. If there is a break in the cable, all systems on the network will be unable to access the network.

➤ The MSAU on a logical ring topology represents a single point of failure. If all devices are unable to access the network, it may be that the MSAU is faulty.

➤ Verify that the cabling and connectors meet the correct specifications.

➤ All NICs on the ring network must operate at the same speed.

➤ When connecting MSAUs in a ring network, ensure that the ring in and ring out configuration is properly set.

➤ A bus topology must be continuous. A break in the cable at any point will render the entire segment unusable.

➤ The cable used on a bus network has two distinct physical endpoints.

➤ The addition, removal, or failure of a device on the network might prevent the entire network from functioning.

➤ Some types of wireless communications require a point-to-point direct line-of-sight connection. If something is blocking this line of site such as a building, the transmissions may fail.

Key terms

➤ Topology

➤ Bus

➤ Star

➤ Ring

➤ Mesh

➤ Wireless

➤ Protocol

➤ Authentication

➤ Permissions

➤ Media

➤ Interference

➤ Attenuation

➤ EMI

➤ Segment

➤ NetBEUI

➤ Hub

➤ Switch

➤ MSAU

➤ Termination

Practice exam

Question 1

Which of the following should you consider when troubleshooting wiring problems? (Choose the three best answers.)

❏ A. The distance between devices

❏ B. Interference

❏ C. Atmospheric conditions

❏ D. Connectors

The correct answers are A, B, and D. When you're troubleshooting a wiring problem, you should consider the distance between devices, interference such as crosstalk and EMI, and the connection points. Answer C is not correct because bound media (that is, cables) are not affected by atmospheric conditions.

Question 2

A user calls you complaining that he is unable to access an application that he uses for accounting. The application runs on the local computer but the data files are stored on a remote Windows 2000 file server. The network uses TCP/IP and a DHCP server. What is your next step in the troubleshooting process?

○ A. Check the server logs

○ B. Verify that the user is logged on correctly

○ C. Log on to the system using the administration account

○ D. Establish what has changed

The correct answer is D. Before implementing a solution to a problem it is a troubleshooting best practice to first identify what has changed. In this scenario, the administrator would need to gather more information from the user to help isolate the problem and determine why he cannot access the accounting program. Although all of the answers provided may also be done, they would typically be done after gathering more information from the user.

Question 3

A user calls to tell you that after a lunch break she cannot log on to the network. The user's workstation is a Windows 2000 system with a 10BaseT network connection. The user was able to log on before lunch, and then she logged off before she left. What should you ask the user to check first?

- ○ A. Is the network cable securely plugged in to the back of the workstation?
- ○ B. Are you using the right password?
- ○ C. Is the Caps Lock key off?
- ○ D. Are you using the right username?

The correct answer is C. Windows 2000 systems use case-sensitive passwords. When a user enters a password, if the Caps Lock key is on and the user doesn't realize it, the password will be entered in the wrong case. All the other troubleshooting steps are valid, but you would perform Answer A first.

Question 4

You are troubleshooting a problem with a bus topology network. Users are reporting that they are sometimes unable to access the network, but it is fine at other times. Which of the following might you consider? (Choose the two best answers.)

- ❑ A. Faulty hubs or switch
- ❑ B. Improper or faulty termination
- ❑ C. Improper grounding
- ❑ D. Cable lengths in excess of 100 meters

The correct answers are B and C. A bus network must have a terminator at each physical end of the bus. It must also be grounded at one end. Improper grounding or faulty termination can lead to random network problems such as those described. Answer A is not correct because 10Base2 networks do not use hubs or switches. 10Base2 has a maximum cable length of 185 meters; therefore, Answer D is not valid either.

Question 5

A user in the sales department calls you and complains that she is unable to log onto the server and use the accounting software. All members of the sales department have access to the application and the user has worked with the software before. Two other users in the sales department claim they can access the server with no difficulty. Which of the following would be your next likely step in the troubleshooting process?

○ A. Check the user's access permissions

○ B. Verify that the accounting software is running on the server

○ C. Verify network settings on the workstation

○ D. Verify the user's logon information

The correct answer is D. If the user did not log on correctly it may be that she is unable to access resources on the server. Answer A is invalid, as the user had previously used the accounting software and therefore had sufficient rights to do so. Answer B is invalid as other users from the sales department can still access the accounting program. Answer C is a valid troubleshooting step in this scenario but only after more obvious solutions, such as correct logon information, has been verified.

Question 6

A user calls you to report that he is experiencing problems accessing a file on the server. Upon quizzing the user, you determine that he has not accessed the file before. Which of the following should be your next troubleshooting step?

○ A. Set the file permission so that the user can access the file.

○ B. Reset the user's password.

○ C. Reboot the server to reinitialize the permissions set.

○ D. Determine whether the user should have access to the file.

The correct answer is D. If a user is attempting to access a file that he has not accessed before, the first step before granting access to that file is to first determine whether the user should have access to that file. If it is determined that the user should have access to the file, the appropriate settings can be adjusted.

Question 7

> You are troubleshooting a network problem. The network is a star topology. There are four segments on the network: **sales**, **marketing**, **admin**, and **research**. Several users from the **admin** department call you reporting problems accessing the server. Where are you most likely to look for the source of the problem?
>
> ○ A. The users' workstations
>
> ○ B. The server
>
> ○ C. The switch that services the **admin** segment
>
> ○ D. The switch that services the **sales** segment

The correct answer is C. In this scenario, the common denominator is that all of the users reporting a problem are connected to the same network switch. Therefore, this would be the first place to look for a problem. Because there is more than one user with a problem, looking at their workstations is not the best troubleshooting step. Because you have not received any other calls from other departments, it is unlikely that there is a problem with the server. Because no users from the sales dept have reported a problem, there is unlikely to be a problem with the sales section of the network.

Question 8

> Which of the following need to be verified when troubleshooting client connectivity errors? (Check the three best answers.)
>
> ❑ A. Protocol configurations
>
> ❑ B. Authentication
>
> ❑ C. Logon permissions
>
> ❑ D. File permissions

The correct answers are A, B, and C. Client connectivity problems are normally due to authentication problems, but they can also be attributed to the protocol configuration on the workstation and logon permissions. File permissions do not represent a valid troubleshooting step when verifying client connectivity.

Question 9

A user calls to inform you that he is unable to print. Upon questioning, you determine that the user has just been moved from the second floor to the third floor. What is the most likely explanation of the problem?

○ A. The user is still printing to the printer on the second floor.

○ B. The printer is not working.

○ C. The printer drivers need to be reloaded on the workstation.

○ D. The print drivers have become corrupt.

The correct answer is A. Sometimes the solution to a problem is not technical at all, and instead just requires a little common sense. The other answers are all possible problems, but are less likely to be the cause.

Question 10

A user is having problems logging on to the server. Each time she tries, she receives a **server not found** message. No other users have reported a problem. Which of the following are possible explanations to the problem? (Check the two best answers.)

❑ A. The protocol configuration on the workstation is incorrect.

❑ B. Caps Lock is on.

❑ C. The cable has become disconnected from the user's workstation.

❑ D. The server is down.

The correct answers are A and C. The information provided indicates that this user is the only one who is experiencing a problem. Therefore, it is likely that the configuration of the workstation or the physical connectivity is to blame. The server not found error message would appear before she entered any user information. If she entered the wrong password and the server was found, she would receive an invalid password message. Because only a single user has reported a problem, it is unlikely that the server is down. Therefore, it is unlikely that answer D is correct.

Want to know more?

Haugdahl, J.Scott. *Network Analysis and Troubleshooting*. Addison-Wesley Publishing, 2000.

Sheldon, Thomas. *McGraw-Hill's Encyclopedia of Networking and Telecommunications*. McGraw-Hill Professional Publishing, 2001.

Habraken, Joe. *Absolute Beginners Guide to Networking, Third Edition*. Que Publishing, 2001.

Tulloch, Mitch. *Microsoft Encyclopedia of Networking* (with CD-ROM). Microsoft Press, 2000.

Practice Exam 1

This exam consists of 60 questions that reflect the material covered in this book. The questions are representative of the types of questions you should expect to see on the Network+ exam; however, they are not intended to match exactly what is on the exam.

Some of the questions require that you deduce the best possible answer. Often, you are asked to identify the best course of action to take in a given situation. You must read the questions carefully and thoroughly before you attempt to answer them. It is strongly recommended that you treat this exam as if it were the actual exam. When you take it, time yourself, read carefully, and answer all the questions to the best of your ability.

The answers to all the questions appear in the section following the exam. Check your letter answers against those in the answers section, and then read the explanations provided. You might also want to return to the chapters in the book to review the material associated with any incorrect answers.

Question 1

Which layer of the OSI model is responsible for placing the signal on the network media?

○ A. Physical

○ B. Data-link

○ C. MAC

○ D. LLC

Question 2

As system administrator, you have been asked to install a NetWare 5.x server system on your network. You have 20 Windows 98 workstations and four Linux systems that are used as clients. Which of the following can you install on the Windows 98 systems to allow you to connect to the NetWare server? (Choose the two best answers.)

❑ A. Novell Client for Windows 95/98

❑ B. Microsoft Client for NetWare Networks

❑ C. Novell CAFS Client

❑ D. Nothing, as long as TCP/IP is the default protocol

Question 3

You are a network administrator managing a midsized network that uses a NetWare print server, a Windows application server, and a Linux firewall server. One of your servers loses network connectivity; you type **ifconfig** at the command line to determine whether the server has a valid IP address. Which server has lost connectivity?

○ A. The firewall server.

○ B. The print server.

○ C. The application server.

○ D. **ifconfig** is not a valid command on any of these platforms.

Question 4

You are managing a network that uses both a Unix server and a Windows 2000 server. Which of the following protocols can you use to transfer files between the two servers?

○ A. Telnet

○ B. PPP

○ C. FTP

○ D. PPTP

Question 5

You have been called by a user who complains that access to a Web page is very slow. What utility can you use to find the bottleneck?

○ A. **ping**

○ B. Telnet

○ C. **tracert**

○ D. **nbtstat**

Question 6

During a busy administrative week, you install a new virus suite in your network of 55 computers, a new RAID array in one of the servers, and a new office suite on 25 of the computer systems. After all the updates, you are experiencing system errors throughout the entire network. Which of the following would you do to help isolate the problem?

○ A. Disable the RAID array

○ B. Uninstall the office suite

○ C. Check the virus suite vendor's Web site for system patches or service packs

○ D. Reinstall the virus software

Question 7

What utility do you use to check the IP configuration on a Windows 95 or Windows 98 workstation?

- ○ A. **netstat**
- ○ B. **winipcfg**
- ○ C. **ping**
- ○ D. **ipconfig**

Question 8

When a system running TCP/IP receives a data packet, which of the following does it use to determine which service to forward the packet to?

- ○ A. Port number
- ○ B. Packet ID number
- ○ C. Data IP number
- ○ D. IP protocol service type

Question 9

Which of the following backup methods clears the archive bit? (Choose the two best answers.)

- ❑ A. Differential
- ❑ B. Sequential
- ❑ C. Full
- ❑ D. Incremental

Question 10

You are troubleshooting a server connectivity problem on your network—a Windows 95 system is having trouble connecting to a Windows 2000 Server. Which of the following commands would you use to display per-protocol statistics on the workstation system?

○ A. **arp -a**

○ B. **arp -A**

○ C. **nbtstat -s**

○ D. **nbtstat -S**

○ E. **netstat -s**

Question 11

You are working as a network administrator on a Unix system. The system uses dynamic name resolution. What is used to dynamically resolve a hostname on a Unix server?

○ A. IPX

○ B. ARP

○ C. DNS

○ D. **LMHOSTS**

Question 12

During the night, one of your servers powers down. Upon reboot, print services do not load. Which of the following would be the first step in the troubleshooting process?

○ A. Examine the server log files

○ B. Reboot the server

○ C. Reinstall the printer

○ D. Reinstall the printer software

Question 13

> Which of the following technologies uses Category 5 cable?
>
> ○ A. 100BaseTX
> ○ B. Fiber-optic
> ○ C. 10Base5
> ○ D. 10Base2

Question 14

> Which of the following utilities can be used to view the current protocol connections on a system?
>
> ○ A. **ping**
> ○ B. **netstat**
> ○ C. Telnet
> ○ D. **tracert**

Question 15

> Which of the following protocols are part of the TCP/IP protocol suite? (Choose the three best answers.)
>
> ❑ A. AFP
> ❑ B. FTP
> ❑ C. DHCP
> ❑ D. HTTP
> ❑ E. NCP

Question 16

> Which of the following are connectionless protocols? (Choose the three best answers.)
>
> ❑ A. IP
> ❑ B. SPX
> ❑ C. IPX
> ❑ D. UDP

Question 17

Which of the following networking standards specifies a maximum segment length of 100 meters?

- ○ A.   10Base2
- ○ B.   10Base5
- ○ C.   10BaseYX
- ○ D.   10BaseT

Question 18

After several passwords have been compromised in your organization, you have been asked to implement a networkwide password policy. Which of the following represents the most practical and secure password policy?

- ○ A.   Daily password changes
- ○ B.   Weekly password changes
- ○ C.   Monthly password changes
- ○ D.   Password changes only after an account has been compromised

Question 19

You are experiencing a problem with a workstation and want to **ping** the local host. Which of the following are valid ways to check your local TCP/IP connection? (Choose the two best answers.)

- ❑ A.   **ping host**
- ❑ B.   **ping localhost**
- ❑ C.   **ping 127.0.0.1**
- ❑ D.   **ping 127.0.0.0**

Question 20

Which of the following network devices operates at the physical layer of the OSI model?

○ A. Router

○ B. Hub

○ C. Bridge

○ D. NIC

Question 21

You have been asked to implement a RAID solution on one of your company's servers. You have two hard disks and two hard disk controllers. Which of the following RAID levels could you implement? (Choose the three best answers.)

❑ A. RAID 0

❑ B. RAID 1

❑ C. Disk duplexing

❑ D. RAID 10

❑ E. RAID 5

Question 22

Which of the following represents a Class B IP address?

○ A. **191.23.21.54**

○ B. **125.123.123.2**

○ C. **24.67.118.67**

○ D. **255.255.255.0**

Question 23

What utility would produce the following output?

```
Proto  Local Address        Foreign Address            State
TCP    laptop:1028          LAPTOP:0                   LISTENING
TCP    laptop:1031          LAPTOP:0                   LISTENING
TCP    laptop:1093          LAPTOP:0                   LISTENING
TCP    laptop:50000         LAPTOP:0                   LISTENING
TCP    laptop:5000          LAPTOP:0                   LISTENING
TCP    laptop:1031          n218.audiogalaxy.com:ftp   ESTABLISHED
TCP    laptop:1319          h24-67-184-65.ok.shawcable.net:nbsess
```

- ○ A. **netstat**
- ○ B. **nbtstat**
- ○ C. **ping**
- ○ D. **tracert -R**

Question 24

You have been called in to troubleshoot a problem with a newly installed email application. Internal users are able to communicate with each other via email, but neither incoming nor outgoing Internet email is working. You suspect a problem with the port-blocking configuration of the firewall system that protects the Internet connection. Which of the following ports would you allow to cure the problems with the email? (Choose the two best answers.)

- ❑ A. 20
- ❑ B. 25
- ❑ C. 80
- ❑ D. 110
- ❑ E. 443

Question 25

What is the default subnet mask for a Class B network?

- ○ A. **255.255.255.224**
- ○ B. **255.255.255.0**
- ○ C. **127.0.0.1**
- ○ D. **255.255.0.0**

Question 26

At which OSI layer does TCP operate?

○ A. Network

○ B. Transport

○ C. Session

○ D. Presentation

Question 27

What is the basic purpose of a firewall system?

○ A. It provides a single point of access to the Internet.

○ B. It caches commonly used Web pages, thereby reducing the bandwidth demands on an Internet connection.

○ C. It allows hostnames to be resolved to IP addresses.

○ D. It protects one network from another by acting as an intermediary system.

Question 28

Email and FTP work at which layer of the OSI model?

○ A. Application

○ B. Session

○ C. Presentation

○ D. User

Question 29

You have been tasked with installing five new Windows 98 client systems, including the Novell Client software. Which pieces of information will you need during the Novell Client install to configure the connection to the NetWare server? (Choose the two best answers.)

❑ A. Target NDS replica name

❑ B. NDS tree name

❑ C. Username

❑ D. The context in which the user resides

❑ E. Password

❑ F. Domain name

Question 30

While reviewing the security logs for your server, you notice that a user on the Internet has attempted to access your internal mail server. Although it appears that the user's attempts were unsuccessful, you are very concerned about the possibility that your systems may be compromised. Which of the following solutions are you most likely to implement?

○ A. A more secure password policy

○ B. A firewall system at the connection point to the Internet

○ C. File-level encryption

○ D. Kerberos authentication

Question 31

Which of the following pieces of information is not likely to be supplied via DHCP?

○ A. IP address

○ B. NetBIOS computer name

○ C. Subnet mask

○ D. Default gateway

Question 32

While troubleshooting a network connectivity problem, you notice that the network card in your system is operating at 10Mbps in half-duplex mode. At what speed is the network link operating?

○ A. 2.5Mbps

○ B. 5Mbps

○ C. 10Mbps

○ D. 11Mbps

Question 33

Which of the following is a valid IPv6 address?

○ A. **42DE:7E55:63F2:21AA:CBD4:D773**

○ B. **42CD:7E55:63F2:21GA:CBD4:D773:CC21:554F**

○ C. **42DE:7E55:63F2:21AA**

○ D. **42DE:7E55:63F2:21AA:CBD4:D773:CC21:554F**

Question 34

While troubleshooting a network connectivity problem on a Windows 2000 Server, you need to view a list of the IP addresses that have been resolved to MAC addresses. Which of the following commands would you use to do this?

○ A. **arp -a**

○ B. **nbtstat -a**

○ C. **arp -d**

○ D. **arp -s**

Question 35

Which of the following statements best describes RAID 5?

- ○ A. A RAID 5 array consists of at least two drives. Parity information is written across both drives to provide fault tolerance.
- ○ B. A RAID 5 array consists of at least three drives and distributes parity information across all the drives in the array.
- ○ C. A RAID 5 array consists of at least three drives and stores the parity information on a single drive.
- ○ D. A RAID 5 array consists of at least four drives. The first and last drives in the array are used to store parity information.

Question 36

Which of the following IEEE specifications does CSMA/CD relate to?

- ○ A. 802.11b
- ○ B. 802.2
- ○ C. 802.5
- ○ D. 802.3

Question 37

While you are troubleshooting a sporadic network connectivity problem on a Windows 2000 system, a fellow technician suggests that you run the **ping -t** command. What is the purpose of this command?

- ○ A. It shows the route taken by a packet to reach the destination host.
- ○ B. It shows the time, in seconds, that the packet takes to reach the destination.
- ○ C. It allows the number of **ping** messages to be specific.
- ○ D. It **ping**s the remote host continually until it is stopped.

Question 38

Which of the following statements best describes NAS?

○ A. It provides address-translation services to protect the identity of client systems.

○ B. It refers to a storage device that is attached to a host system such as a server.

○ C. It refers to a storage device that is attached directly to the network media.

○ D. It refers to a small, dedicated network of storage devices.

○ E. It is a directory services system used on NetWare networks.

○ F. It provides a mechanism for users to access areas of a hard disk on a Linux system.

Question 39

What type of physical topology is shown in the following diagram?

○ A. Hierarchical star

○ B. Ring

○ C. Star

○ D. Mesh

Question 40

A remote user calls you to report a problem she is having connecting to the corporate network over her DSL connection. The user is able to connect to the Internet and browse Web pages, but she can't connect to the corporate remote access gateway. Which of the following troubleshooting steps would you perform first?

○ A. Check the corporate remote access gateway to see if it is running and operating correctly

○ B. Have the user reboot her system

○ C. Have the user reconfigure the IP address on her system to one of the address ranges used on the internal corporate network, and then try again

○ D. Have the user power cycle the DSL modem and try again

Question 41

By using network monitoring tools, you determine that your 10Base2 network is suffering performance degradation from too many collisions. Which of the following devices could you use to divide up the network and so reduce the number of collisions?

○ A. Ethernet switch

○ B. Source-route bridge

○ C. MSAU

○ D. Transparent bridge

Question 42

What command would generate the following output?

```
7    60 ms   30 ms    40 ms   home-gw.st6wa.ip.att.net [192.205.32.249]
8    30 ms   40 ms    30 ms   gbr3-p40.st6wa.ip.att.net [12.123.44.130]
9    50 ms   50 ms    60 ms   gbr4-p10.sffca.ip.att.net [12.122.2.61]
10   60 ms   60 ms    60 ms   gbr3-p10.la2ca.ip.att.net [12.122.2.169]
11   90 ms   60 ms    70 ms   gbr6-p60.la2ca.ip.att.net [12.122.5.97]
```

○ A. **ipconfig**

○ B. **netstat**

○ C. **ping**

○ D. **tracert**

Question 43

Your manager has asked you to implement security on your peer-to-peer network. Which of the following security models offers the highest level of security for this type of network?

○ A. Share level

○ B. User level

○ C. Password level

○ D. Layered

Question 44

You are working on a Linux system and are having problems **ping**ing a remote system by its hostname. DNS resolution is not configured for the system. What file might you look in to begin troubleshooting the resolution problem?

○ A. **RESOLV**

○ B. **STATICDNS**

○ C. **PASSWD**

○ D. **HOSTS**

Question 45

You are tasked with specifying a way to connect two buildings across a parking lot. The distance between the two buildings is 78 meters. An underground wiring duct exists between the two buildings, although there are concerns about using it because it also houses high-voltage electrical cables. The budget for the project is very tight, but your manager still wants you to specify the most suitable solution. Which of the following cable types would you recommend?

○ A. Fiber-optic

○ B. UTP

○ C. Thin coax

○ D. STP

Question 46

You are attempting to configure a client's email program. The user can receive mail but is unable to send any. In the mail server configuration screen of the mail application, you notice that the Type of Outgoing Mail Server field is blank. This explains why the client is unable to send mail. Which of the following protocols are you most likely to enter as a value in the Type of Outgoing Mail Server field?

- O A. NMP
- O B. POP3
- O C. SMTP
- O D. IMAP

Question 47

A user calls to inform you that she can't access the Internet from her system. When you visit the user, you run the **ipconfig /all** utility and see the following information. What is the most likely reason the user is having problems accessing the Internet?

```
C:\>ipconfig /all

Windows 2000 IP Configuration
    Host Name . . . . . . . . . . . : LAPTOP
    Primary DNS Suffix  . . . . . . :
    Node Type . . . . . . . . . . . : Broadcast
    IP Routing Enabled. . . . . . . : No
    WINS Proxy Enabled. . . . . . . : No

Ethernet adapter Local Area Connection:
    Connection-specific DNS Suffix  . :
    Description . . . . . . . . . . : Intel 8255x-based PCI Ethernet
    Physical Address. . . . . . . . : 00-D0-59-09-07-51
    DHCP Enabled. . . . . . . . . . : No
    IP Address. . . . . . . . . . . : 192.168.2.1
    Subnet Mask . . . . . . . . . . : 255.255.255.0
    Default Gateway . . . . . . . . :
    DNS Servers . . . . . . . . . . : 192.168.2.10
                                      192.168.2.20
```

- O A. The system is on a different subnet than the DNS servers.
- O B. DHCP is not enabled.
- O C. The subnet mask is incorrect.
- O D. The default gateway setting is not configured.

Question 48

Your ISP account manager suggests that it might be appropriate for you to install a DNS server internally. Which of the following functions does the DNS server provide?

○ A. It performs network address translation services.

○ B. It streamlines the resolution of NetBIOS names to IP addresses.

○ C. It allows some hostname-to-IP address resolutions to occur internally.

○ D. It allows users to retrieve Internet Web pages more quickly.

Question 49

Which of the following is not one of the private address ranges?

○ A. **192.168.x.x**

○ B. **10.x.x.x**

○ C. **172.16.x.x**

○ D. **224.181.x.x**

Question 50

Which of the following is a valid MAC address?

○ A. **00:D0:59:09:07:51**

○ B. **00:D0:59**

○ C. **192.168.2.1**

○ D. **00FE:56FE:230F:CDA2:00EB:32EC**

○ E. **00:DG:59:09:07:51**

Question 51

If you contacted IANA, what would you most likely be trying to do?

○ A. Get a new telephone number

○ B. Get an IP address to connect a system to a public network

○ C. Get an Internet domain name reassigned

○ D. Get an IP address to connect a system to a private network

Question 52

Which of the following technologies can be implemented on a switch to create multiple separate networks?

○ A. Proxy

○ B. Subnet masking

○ C. NAS

○ D. VLAN

Question 53

Which of the following protocols are responsible for network addressing? (Choose the two best answers.)

❑ A. IP

❑ B. SPX

❑ C. IPX

❑ D. TCP

Question 54

You are configuring a new NAS system. The configuration utility gives you the option to choose what application-level protocol you want to use with the system. Which of the following protocols are you likely to choose? (Choose the two best answers.)

❑ A. NCP

❑ B. SMB

❑ C. TCP

❑ D. NFS

Question 55

For many years, the design department and the marketing department have operated separate networks. The design department uses AppleTalk, and the marketing department uses Token Ring. Now, the two departments have decided that they want to be able to access files from each other's servers. What network device or service would you implement to facilitate this?

○ A. Gateway

○ B. Source-route bridge

○ C. Router

○ D. Transparent bridge

Question 56

Which of the following connectors would you use when working with fiber-optic cable? (Choose the two best answers.)

❏ A. RJ-11

❏ B. SC

❏ C. RJ-45

❏ D. ST

❏ E. BNC

❏ F. Vampire tap

Question 57

Which of the following is not a commonly implemented feature of a firewall system?

○ A. NAT

○ B. Packet filtering

○ C. Proxy

○ D. NAS

Question 58

You are the network administrator for a Token Ring network. A NIC in a system fails, and you replace it with a new one. However, the system is still unable to connect to the network. What is the most likely cause of the problem?

○ A. The NIC is set to the wrong ring speed.

○ B. The NIC is a 100Mbps card, and the ring is configured for only 10Mbps.

○ C. The NIC is set to full-duplex, and the ring is running at only half-duplex.

○ D. The NIC is faulty.

Question 59

You have enabled HTTPS because of concerns about the security of your Web server application, which runs on a Web server system in the DMZ of your corporate network. However, remote users are now unable to connect to the application. Which of the following is the most likely reason for the problem?

○ A. Port 80 is being blocked on the corporate firewall.

○ B. Port 443 is being blocked on the corporate firewall.

○ C. Remote users need to enable HTTPS support in their Web browsers.

○ D. Port 110 is being blocked on the corporate firewall.

Question 60

Which of the following is a valid Class A IP address?

○ A. 124.254.254.254

○ B. 127.0.0.1

○ C. 128.16.200.12

○ D. 131.17.25.200

Answers to exam questions

1. **A.** The physical layer of the OSI seven-layer model is responsible for placing the signal on the network media. The data-link layer (Answer B) is responsible for physical addressing and media access. MAC and LLC (Answers C and D) are sublayers of the data-link layer.

2. **A, B.** The Microsoft Client for NetWare Networks or the Novell Client for Windows 95/98 can be installed on the Windows 98 systems to facilitate connectivity. There is no such thing as the Novell CAFS client (Answer C). Although TCP/IP can be used to connect to certain versions of Novell NetWare, client software is needed unless NetWare 6 is being used (Answer D).

3. **A.** The `ifconfig` command is used on a Linux system to determine the IP configuration of the system. With NetWare you use the `config` command to obtain information about network addresses. On a Windows 2000 system, the `ipconfig` command is used to view the networking configuration including the IP address. `ifconfig` can be used on Unix/Linux platforms to view the networking configuration.

4. **C.** FTP can be used to transfer files between Windows and Unix systems. FTP is part of the TCP/IP protocol suite and is platform independent. The Telnet utility is used to open a virtual terminal session on a remote host (Answer A). PPP is used to establish communications over a serial link; thus, Answer B is incorrect. PPTP is used to establish a secure link over a public network such as the Internet (Answer D).

5. **C.** `tracert` is a Windows command that can be used to display the full path between two systems, including the number of hops between the systems. The `ping` utility (Answer A) can be used to test connectivity between two devices, but it only reports the time taken for the round trip; it does not give information about the time it takes to complete each hop in the route. The Telnet utility (Answer B) is used to open a virtual terminal session on a remote host. The `nbtstat` command (Answer D) is used to view statistical information about the NetBIOS status of a system.

6. **C.** Because the system errors are networkwide, it is likely that the cause of the problem in this scenario lies with the virus suite because it is installed on all computers. To troubleshoot such a problem, it would be a good idea to check for patches or updates on the vendor's Web site. A problem with a RAID array (Answer A) would affect only the server in which it is installed, not the entire network. Because the

office suite (Answer B) was installed on only some of the systems, it can be eliminated as a problem because all the systems are affected. The virus software (Answer D) appears to be the cause of the problem, but re-installing it is unlikely to help.

7. **B.** On Windows client-based systems such as Windows 95, Windows 98, and Windows Me, the `winipcfg` utility can be used to verify the TCP/IP configuration of the system. The same command does not work on Windows server systems. The `netstat` utility (Answer A) is used to view protocol statistics information. The `ping` utility (Answer C) is used to test the connectivity between two systems on a TCP/IP network. The `ipconfig` utility (Answer D) is used to view the TCP/IP configuration on a Windows NT or Windows 2000 system.

8. **A.** The service to which a data packet is destined is determined by the port number to which it is sent. Answers B, C, and D are not valid.

9. **C, D.** Both the full and incremental backup methods clear the archive bit, to indicate which data does and does not need to be backed up. In a differential backup (Answer A), the archive bit is not cleared. Sequential (Answer B) is not a type of backup.

10. **E.** The `netstat -s` command can be used to display per-protocol statistics. The `arp` command (Answers A and B) is used to view a list of the IP address-to-MAC address resolutions performed by the system. The `nbtstat` utility (Answers C and D) is used to view protocol statistics for the NetBIOS protocol.

11. **C.** DNS is used on Unix-based systems to resolve hostnames. IPX (Answer A) is a network-layer connectionless protocol. ARP (Answer B) resolves IP addresses to MAC addresses. The `LMHOSTS` file (Answer D) is used on Windows systems to resolve NetBIOS names to IP addresses.

12. **A.** In this scenario your first step is to gather information by examining the server log files. When you have that information, you can proceed with the rest of the troubleshooting process. Rebooting the server (Answer B) is unlikely to cure the problem. Before you reinstall the printer (Answer C) or printer software (Answer D), you should examine the log files to see if there are any problems reported in the server log files.

13. **A.** 100BaseTX uses Category 5 cable. Fiber-optic (Answer B) is a type of cable. 10Base5 (Answer C) is an Ethernet networking standard that uses thick coaxial cable. 10Base2 (Answer D) is an Ethernet networking standard that uses thin coaxial cable.

14. B. The `netstat -a` command can be used to display the current connections and listening ports. The `ping` utility (Answer A) is used to test connectivity between two devices on a TCP/IP network. Telnet (Answer C) is an application-level protocol that allows a virtual terminal session on a remote host. The `tracert` utility (Answer D) allows a path to be traced between two hosts.

15. B, C, D. FTP, DHCP, and HTTP are all protocols in the TCP/IP protocol suite. AFP (Answer A) is part of the AppleTalk protocol suite. NCP (Answer E) is part of the IPX/SPX protocol suite.

16. A, C, D. UDP, IPX, and IP are all connectionless protocols. SPX (Answer B) is a connection-oriented protocol.

17. D. 10BaseT has a maximum segment length of 100 meters. The maximum length of a 10Base2 segment (Answer A) is 185 meters. The maximum length of a 10Base5 segment (Answer B) is 500 meters. Answer C is not a valid networking standard.

18. C. Changing passwords too frequently is not practical, and changing them too infrequently represents a security risk. Monthly password changing is adequate for most environments. Changing passwords too frequently (Answers A and B) can cause problems because users might have problems remembering passwords and so use passwords that are too similar to one another. Although passwords should be changed if they are compromised, they should also be changed periodically, making Answer D incorrect.

19. B, C. To verify the IP configuration on a local computer system, you can either `ping` the local host or the IP address `127.0.0.1`. The default hostname for a system is `localhost`, not `host`, which means Answer A is incorrect. Answer D is not correct as this is the network address for the Class A loopback address, not a valid node loopback address.

20. B. A network hub operates at the physical layer of the OSI model. A router (Answer A) operates at the network layer of the OSI model. A bridge (Answer C) operates at the data-link layer of the OSI model. A NIC (Answer D) operates at the data-link layer of the OSI model.

21. A, B, C. With two hard disks and two controllers, you can implement RAID 0, RAID 1, and disk duplexing. RAID 5 (disk striping with parity; Answer E) requires a minimum of three disks to be implemented. RAID 10 (Answer D) is a combination of RAID 1 (disk mirroring) and RAID 0 (disk striping). RAID 10 requires a minimum of four disks.

22. A. The first octet of a Class B address must be in the range 128 to 191. Answers A and B represent Class A addresses. Class A addresses run from 1 to 126. Answer D is not a valid IP address.

23. A. The netstat utility can be used to display protocol statistics and TCP/IP network connections. The nbtstat utility (Answer B) shows statistical information about the NetBIOS over TCP/IP connections. The ping utility (Answer C) is used to test the connectivity between two devices on a TCP/IP network. The tracert utility (Answer D) traces the path between two hosts on a TCP/IP network.

24. B, D. TCP/IP port 25 is used by SMTP. TCP/IP port 110 is used by POP3. Because SMTP is used to send mail and POP3 is used to retrieve mail, port 25 and port 110 are the two ports that would need to be allowed for incoming and outgoing Internet email. TCP/IP port 21 (Answer A) is used by FTP. TCP/IP port 80 (Answer C) is used by HTTP. TCP/IP port 443 (Answer E) is used by HTTPS.

25. D. The default subnet mask for a Class B network is 255.255.0.0. Answer A is incorrect because it is not the default subnet mask for a Class B network. Answer B is not the default subnet mask for a Class B network. Answer C is the local loopback address.

26. B. TCP operates at the transport layer of the OSI model. Answers A, C, and D are all incorrect; TCP does not operate at the network layer.

27. D. The purpose of the firewall system is to protect one network from another. One of the most common places to use a firewall is to protect a private network from a public one such as the Internet. Answer A is incorrect because although a firewall can provide a single point of access, that is not its primary purpose. Answer B more accurately describes the function of a proxy server. Answer C describes the function of a DNS server.

28. A. Both email and FTP work at the application layer of the OSI model. Email and FTP are application-layer protocols, not session-layer protocols. User (Answer D) is not a layer of the OSI model.

29. B, D. To configure the client software, you need to have the context and the NDS tree name. The username and password are not needed during the client configuration, but they are necessary to actually log on. Answer A is incorrect because you do not need to specify the target NDS replica to connect to a NetWare server. The username (Answer C) is needed only when the user actually wants to authenticate to the server. The password (Answer E) is needed only when the user actually wants to authenticate to the server. A domain name (Answer F) does not need to be specified in order to connect to a NetWare server.

30. B. To prevent unauthorized access to a private network from the Internet, you can use a firewall server to restrict outside access. Implementing a more secure password policy (Answer A) is a good idea, but it is not the best choice of those available. Implementing a file-level encryption system (Answer C) is a good idea, but it is not the best choice of those available. Kerberos (Answer D) is an authentication system, not a method to prevent unauthorized access to the system.

31. B. The NetBIOS computer name is not supplied to client systems by a DHCP server. The IP address (Answer A) is one of the pieces of information provided by DHCP. The subnet mask (Answer C) is one of the pieces of information provided by DHCP. The default gateway (Answer D) is one of the pieces of information supplied by DHCP.

32. C. Because the NIC is functioning at half-duplex 10Mbps, the transfer rate is 10Mbps. None of the other answers are correct.

33. D. IPv6 uses a 128-bit address, which is expressed as eight octet pairs in hexadecimal format, separated by colons. Because it is hexadecimal, only numbers and the letters A through F can be used. An IPv6 address is composed of eight hexadecimal octets. Only numbers and the letters A through F can be used.

34. A. The `arp -a` command is used to display the IP addresses that have been resolved to MAC addresses. The `nbtstat` command (Answer B) is used to view protocol statistics for NetBIOS connections. `arp -d` (Answer C) is not a valid command. The `arp -s` command (Answer D) allows you to add static entries to the ARP cache.

35. B. A RAID 5 array consists of at least three hard disks and stripes parity information across all disks in the array. RAID 5 (disk striping with parity; Answer A) requires at least three drives. The parity information is stored in a stripe across all three drives in the array (Answer B). RAID 5 requires only three drives which makes Answer D incorrect.

36. D. CSMA/CD relates to the IEEE specification 802.3. The 802.11b (Answer A) standard describes wireless LAN networking. The 802.2 (Answer B) standard defines the media access methods for various networking standards. The 802.5 (Answer C) standard defines Token Ring networking.

37. D. The `ping -t` command is used to send continuous `ping` requests to a remote system. The `ping` request will continue until it is manually stopped. The trace route utility (Answer A) performs this task. The `ping` command (Answer B) shows the amount of time a packet takes to complete the round trip from the host to the destination. Answer C is incorrect because the `ping` command with the `-n` switch performs this task.

38. C. NAS is a storage device that attaches directly to the network media. DAS attaches to a server. Answer A describes NAT. Answer B describes DAS. Answer D describes a SAN, Answer E describes NDS, and Answer F describes NFS.

39. A. The diagram in the question shows a hierarchical star topology. The difference between a hierarchical star and a regular star topology is that hierarchical is a layered architecture. Answers B, C, and D are all incorrect. The figure does not represent any of these network types.

40. A. In this scenario, you would first check the remote access gateway to see if it is running and operating correctly. Because the user can browse Web pages, this is not a connectivity problem. Answer B is incorrect because although rebooting the system might help, the system appears to be working correctly, and rebooting it is unlikely to cure the problem. The IP address configuration appears to be working because the user is able to access Web pages and so Answer C is incorrect. The Internet connection appears to be working, so cycling the power on the DSL modem, as described in Answer D, is unlikely to help.

41. D. A transparent bridge is a device that can be used to divide an Ethernet network to reduce collisions. Switches can also be used, but the network in the question is a 10Base2 network and uses coaxial cable rather than twisted-pair cable. Ethernet switches (Answer A) can be used only on networks that are created with twisted-pair cable. 10Base2 is a networking standard that uses thin coaxial cable. A source-route bridge (Answer B) is used on Token Ring networks. 10Base2 is an Ethernet networking standard. An MSAU (Answer C) is used on Token Ring networks. 10Base2 is an Ethernet networking standard.

42. D. The output displayed in this question is from the Windows tracert utility. Answers A, B and C are all incorrect. These utilities produce output that is different from the output shown.

43. B. User-level security is more secure than share-level security and requires a user to provide a login ID, usually a username and password combination to access network resources. Answer A is incorrect because share-level security is not as secure as user-level security. Answers C and D are not accepted terms for describing levels of security.

44. D. The HOSTS file is used to manually configure hostname resolution, and if there is a problem with hostname resolution, entries in this file must be checked. Answers A and B are incorrect because files are not used on a Linux system. Answer C is incorrect because the PASSWD file is used to store user account information.

45. **A.** Fiber-optic cable provides the most resistance to EMI and therefore is often used in environments where there is a risk of interference. Although it is inexpensive, UTP (Answer B) cable has very low resistance to EMI. Therefore, it should not be run near high-voltage electric cables. Thin coax (Answer C) has low resistance to EMI. Therefore, it should not be run near high-voltage electric cables. STP (Answer D) has a good level of resistance to EMI, but it is still not as resistant as fiber-optic. Not factoring in the cost, fiber-optic is the most suitable solution.

46. **C.** SMTP is used for sending email. Answer A is not a valid answer. Answers B and D are incorrect because POP3 and IMAP are email retrieval protocols, not protocols for sending email.

47. **D.** The most likely cause of the problem is that the default gateway is not configured. Answer A is incorrect because from the output it appears that the DNS servers are on the same subnet as this system. Answer B does not apply because addressing is configured statically, so there is no DHCP service. This is not a problem, however. Answer C is incorrect because the subnet mask is the correct default subnet mask for a Class C network.

48. **C.** DNS allows hostname resolutions to occur internally. In most cases companies use a DNS server provided by the ISP. In some cases, however, it might be appropriate to have a DNS server on the internal network. Answer A is incorrect as NAT is normally a function of firewall or proxy servers. Answer B describes the purpose of a WINS server. Answer D describes the function of a proxy server.

49. **D.** Private address ranges are designed for use on private networks. The ranges are `192.168.X.X`, `10.X.X.X`, and `172.16.X.X–172.32.X.X`. Answers A, B, and C are all valid private IP address ranges.

50. **A.** The MAC address is a 6-byte address expressed in six pairs of hexadecimal values. Because it is hexadecimal, only the letters A through F and numbers can be used. Answer B is incorrect because MAC addresses are expressed as six hexadecimal pairs. Answer C shows an example of an IPv4 address. Answer D shows an example of an IPv6 address. Answer E is incorrect because MAC addresses are expressed in hexadecimal; therefore, only the letters A through F and numbers can be used.

51. **B.** IANA is responsible for assigning IP addresses for systems on public networks—specifically, the Internet. Answer A is incorrect. IANA is responsible for assigning IP addresses for use on public networks (such as the Internet). Answer C is incorrect because domain names are administered by domain registry organizations. Answer D is incorrect because you don't need to apply for a network address for use on a private network.

52. D. A VLAN is implemented on a switch to create multiple separate networks. A proxy server (Answer A) is used to control access to the Internet. Subnet masking (Answer B) is not a valid method of creating separate networks. NAS (Answer C) describes storage devices that are attached directly to the network media.

53. A, C. IP and IPX are responsible for network addressing. Answers B and D are incorrect because SPX and TCP are transport-layer protocols and so are not responsible for network addressing.

54. B, D. The protocols used by NAS are SMB and NFS. NCP (Answer A) is part of the IPX/SPX protocol suite. It is responsible for providing access to network services. TCP (Answer C) is a connection-oriented transport protocol.

55. A. A gateway is used to translate between networks that use dissimilar protocols. In this question, it is used to translate between an AppleTalk network and a Token Ring network. A source-route bridge (Answer B) is used on Token Ring networks. A router (Answer C) is used to connect two networks. Strictly speaking, a router does not perform translation tasks, although the gateway functionality can be implemented on some routers. A transparent bridge (Answer D) is used to segregate Ethernet networks.

56. B, D. Fiber-optic cable can use either SC or ST type connectors. RJ-11 connectors (Answer A) are associated with telephone cable, RJ-45 (Answer C) connectors are associated with UTP cable, and BNC connectors (Answer E) are associated with thin coaxial cable.

57. D. A firewall can provide several services to the network, including NAT, proxy services, and packet filtering. NAS is not a function of a firewall server. Answers A, B, and C are all incorrect because NAT, packet filtering, and proxy functionality are all commonly implemented on firewall systems.

58. A. When a new NIC is installed on a Token Ring network, the speed of the card has to be set to match the speed used by the network. Answer B is incorrect because Token Ring networks operate at either 4Mbps or 16Mbps. Answer C is incorrect because full-duplex connections are not used on Token Ring networks. Answer D is incorrect because, although it is possible, a faulty card is not the most likely answer.

59. B. The most likely explanation is that port 443, the HTTPS default port, is being blocked by a corporate firewall. Port 80 (Answer A) is used by HTTP. All modern Web browsers support HTTPS automatically; therefore, Answer C is incorrect. Port 110 (Answer D) is used by POP3.

60. A. Class A subnets use the range 1 to 126 for the value of the first octet. Answer B is the loopback address, which allows the IP stack functionality to be tested. Answers C and D are both addresses in the Class B range (128–191).

Practice Exam 2

This exam consists of 60 questions that reflect the material covered in this book. The questions are representative of the types of questions you should expect to see on the Network+ exam; however, they are not intended to match exactly what is on the exam.

Some of the questions require that you deduce the best possible answer. Often, you are asked to identify the best course of action to take in a given situation. You must read the questions carefully and thoroughly before you attempt to answer them. It is strongly recommended that you treat this as if it were the actual exam. When you take it, time yourself, read carefully, and answer all the questions to the best of your ability.

The answers to all the questions appear in the section following the exam. Check your letter answers against those in the answers section, and then read the explanations provided. You might also want to return to the chapters in the book to review the material associated with any incorrect answers.

Question 1

As system administrator, you have been asked to implement name resolution on your network. The network uses both Windows and Unix systems. Which of the following are you most likely to use?

- ○ A. LMHOSTS
- ○ B. DNS
- ○ C. WINS
- ○ D. DHCP

Question 2

You are attempting to connect an Apple workstation to an existing TCP/IP network. The Apple system was previously used on a peer-to-peer network using the AppleTalk protocol. When the system is connected to your network, it cannot connect to the server. Which of the following could you do to connect the Apple workstation?

- ○ A. Install the AppleTalk protocol on the server
- ○ B. Install the TCP/IP protocol on the workstation
- ○ C. Install NetBEUI on the workstation
- ○ D. Install TCP/IP on the server

Question 3

You have been employed by a small company to implement a fault-tolerant hard disk configuration. You have purchased four 40GB hard disks and intend on installing RAID 5 on the server. What is the storage capacity of the RAID solution?

- ○ A. 120GB
- ○ B. 40GB
- ○ C. 80GB
- ○ D. 160GB

Question 4

You have been called in to troubleshoot a small network. The network uses TCP/IP and statically assigned IP information. You add a new workstation to the network, which can connect to the local network but not to a server on a remote network. Which of the following is most likely the cause of the problem?

○ A. Incorrect IP address

○ B. Incorrect default gateway

○ C. DHCP server is unavailable

○ D. Duplicate IP addresses are being used

Question 5

You have been employed to configure a 10Base2 network. Which of the following technologies would you use? (Choose two.)

❑ A. UTP

❑ B. STP

❑ C. T-connectors

❑ D. RJ-11 connectors

❑ E. RG-58 cable

Question 6

You are working as an administrator in a network using NetWare, Windows, and Unix servers. You need to assign user permissions on the Unix and Windows systems. Which of the following permissions are available on the Windows server but not on the Unix server?

○ A. Read

○ B. Write

○ C. Execute

○ D. Change

Question 7

You have just installed a new Windows 2000 server on your network. When first logging onto the system, which of the following information is required to log on?

○ A. Username

○ B. Password

○ C. Context

○ D. Administrator's username

Question 8

Which of the following types of topologies offers the greatest amount of redundancy?

○ A. Star

○ B. Bus

○ C. Ring

○ D. Mesh

Question 9

You need to install a network printer and require the printers MAC address to finish the installation. Which of the following represents a valid MAC address?

○ A. **192.168.2.13**

○ B. **0x00007856**

○ C. **00:04:e2:1c:7b:5a**

○ D. **56g78:00h6:1415**

Question 10

You have been called in to replace a faulty ST connector. Which of the following media types are you working with?

○ A. RG-58

○ B. RG-62

○ C. Single mode fiber

○ D. SCSI

Question 11

One of the network devices used on your network forwards packets only to an intended port. Which of the following devices does this describe?

○ A. Hub

○ B. Switch

○ C. Gateway

○ D. PPP

Question 12

You are setting up a wide area network between two school campuses and decide to use BRI ISDN. What is the maximum throughput of your connection?

○ A. 64Kbps

○ B. 128Kbps

○ C. 128Mbps

○ D. 64Mbps

Question 13

You are troubleshooting a 10Base2 network and suspect that the maximum cable length has been exceeded. What is the maximum length of a 10Base2 network segment?

○ A. 25 meters

○ B. 100 meters

○ C. 185 meters

○ D. 500 meters

Question 14

You have been given the task of installing Samba on a Linux server. What services does this product provide?

○ A. Web server services

○ B. Thin client services

○ C. File and print services

○ D. Proxy server services

Question 15

What is the maximum cable length of a 10BaseT network?

○ A. 185 meters

○ B. 500 meters

○ C. 100 meters

○ D. 50 meters

Question 16

A user on your network can send data packets within the local subnet but cannot send packets beyond the local subnet. Which of the following is likely the problem?

○ A. Invalid permissions

○ B. Incorrect gateway information

○ C. No DNS server installed

○ D. No WINS server installed

Question 17

A number of users have called to report printing problems. Upon investigation, you trace the problem to a network printer connected to a server system. You arrive at the printer to find that it is connected on-line and appears to perform a test print without any problems. You check the network connectivity and that seems to be okay as well. Which of the following troubleshooting steps would you perform next?

○ A. Examine the log files on the server to determine whether there are any printing-related events.

○ B. Reboot the server that acts as the print server.

○ C. Remove and reinstall the printer drivers.

○ D. Change the network cable that connects the printer to the network.

Question 18

You are experiencing problems with the network connectivity of a Windows 2000 system, and you suspect that there might be a problem with an incorrect route in the routing table. Which of the following TCP/IP utilities can you use to view the routing table? (Choose the two best answers.)

- ❑ A. **tracert**
- ❑ B. **nbstat**
- ❑ C. **route**
- ❑ D. **netstat**
- ❑ E. **ping**

Question 19

Which of the following services provides name resolution services for FQDNs?

- ◯ A. DNS
- ◯ B. DHCP
- ◯ C. WINS
- ◯ D. ARP
- ◯ E. NTP

Question 20

You are installing a 100BaseFX network and need to purchase connectors. Which of the following might you purchase? (Choose two.)

- ❑ A. RJ-45
- ❑ B. ST
- ❑ C. BNC
- ❑ D. SC

Question 21

When designing a network, you have been asked to select a cable that offers the most resistance to crosstalk. Which of the following are you likely to choose?

○ A. Multi-mode fiber-optic

○ B. Shielded twisted pair

○ C. UTP

○ D. Shielded mesh

Question 22

Which of the following are considered disaster recovery measures?

○ A. Backups

○ B. UPS

○ C. RAID 5

○ D. Off-site data storage

Question 23

Which command produces the following output?

```
Interface: 24.77.218.58 --- 0x2
  Internet Address      Physical Address       Type
  24.77.216.1           00-00-77-99-a4-4c      dynamic
```

○ A. **arp**

○ B. **tracert**

○ C. **ipconfig**

○ D. **netinf**

Question 24

A user with a newly created user account cannot access an application on the network, yet other users can. Which of the following troubleshooting steps are you likely to perform first?

○ A. Delete the application and re-install it.

○ B. Delete the user account and recreate it.

○ C. Change the password of the new user account.

○ D. Check the file permissions for the new user account.

Question 25

As part of a network upgrade, you have installed a router on your network creating two networks. Now, workstations on one side of the router cannot access workstations on the other side of the router. Which of the following configuration changes would you need to make to the workstations to enable them to see devices on the other network?

○ A. Change the IP address assignments on one side of the router so that the router is on a different IP network from the other one.

○ B. Update the default gateway information on all systems so that they use the newly installed router as the gateway.

○ C. Update the default gateway information on all systems so that they use a workstation on the other network as the default gateway.

○ D. Make sure that the IP address assignments on all network workstations are the same.

Question 26

Which type of cable should be used in a 100BaseT network?

○ A. RG-58

○ B. Category 4 UTP

○ C. Category 5 UTP

○ D. Multimode fiber

Question 27

Which of the following network types is easiest to add new nodes to?

○ A. Bus

○ B. Ring

○ C. Star

○ D. Mesh

Question 28

You are the administrator for a network that uses TCP/IP. You are using a single registered class C network address. You want to continue to use it, because many of your systems are accessed from outside sources, but you also want to create more networks so that you can manage traffic and security more effectively. Which of the following strategies would help you achieve this?

○ A. Implement a **127.x.x.x** addressing system throughout the network.

○ B. Use reverse proxy.

○ C. Use subnetting.

○ D. Use private addressing.

Question 29

Placing a node on which of the following types of networks would require that you obtained an address from IANA?

○ A. Private network

○ B. Public network

○ C. Ethernet network

○ D. WAN

Question 30

You are implementing a new network. From the network specifications, you learn that you will be using the 1000BaseCX standard. What type of cable will you be using?

○ A. Multimode fiber

○ B. STP

○ C. Single mode fiber

○ D. CoreXtended fiber

Question 31

Which of the following network protocols can recover from lost or corrupted packets in a network transmission?

○ A. L2TP

○ B. TCP

○ C. IPX

○ D. ARP

Question 32

A colleague decided to close all unused ports on the corporate firewall to further secure the network from intruders. The ports that were open were 25, 80, 110 and 53. Your colleague knew that 25 and 110 are required for email, and that 80 is used for non-secure Web browsing, so he decided to close 53, as he didn't think it was necessary. Which network service is now not available?

○ A. Secure HTTP

○ B. FTP

○ C. Telnet

○ D. DNS

Question 33

You are working on a Linux system and you suspect that there may be a problem with the TCP/IP configuration. Which of the following commands would you use to view the network card configuration of the system?

- ○ A. **config**
- ○ B. **ipconfig**
- ○ C. **winipcfg**
- ○ D. **ifconfig**

Question 34

Your manager has asked you to implement a fault-tolerant disk solution on your server. You have two 30GB hard disks and two controllers, so you decide to implement RAID 1. After the installation, your manager asks you how much storage space is now available for storing data. What do you tell her?

- ○ A. 30GB
- ○ B. 40GB
- ○ C. 60GB
- ○ D. 120GB

Question 35

Which of the following statements best describes PRI ISDN?

- ○ A. PRI ISDN uses 128B channels and 2D channels.
- ○ B. PRI ISDN uses 23B channels and 1D channel.
- ○ C. PRI ISDN uses 2B and 1D channel.
- ○ D. PRI ISDN uses 23D channels and 1B channel.

Question 36

Which of the following user security models would you use if you were looking for the highest levels of security on your network? (Choose two.)

❏ A. User-administered security

❏ B. User-level security

❏ C. Share-level security

❏ D. Centrally administered security

Question 37

A remote user calls you because he cannot dial in to the remote server. He says that the modem dials the number and negotiates the connection but then the line is dropped. Which two of the following troubleshooting steps are you likely to try first?

❏ A. Change the modem IRQ assignments.

❏ B. Run a remote diagnostic on the remote access server's modem.

❏ C. Ask the user to verify that the username and password are correct.

❏ D. Ask the user to verify that he is dialing the correct system.

Question 38

At which layer of the OSI model does a NIC operate?

○ A. Physical

○ B. Network

○ C. Data-link

○ D. Transport

Question 39

You are implementing a 100BaseT network. Which logical topology does the network use?

○ A. Ring

○ B. Star

○ C. Mesh

○ D. Bus

Question 40

Consider the following output:

```
Proto Local AddressForeign Address          State
TCP    laptop:2848   MEDIASERVICES1:1755     ESTABLISHED
TCP    laptop:1833   www.dollarhost.com:80   ESTABLISHED
TCP    laptop:2858   194.70.58.241:80        ESTABLISHED
TCP    laptop:2860   194.70.58.241:80        ESTABLISHED
TCP    laptop:2354   www.dollarhost.com:80   ESTABLISHED
TCP    laptop:2361   www.dollarhost.com:80   ESTABLISHED
TCP    laptop:1114   www.dollarhost.com:80   ESTABLISHED
TCP    laptop:1959   www.dollarhost.com:80   ESTABLISHED
TCP    laptop:1960   www.dollarhost.com:80   ESTABLISHED
TCP    laptop:1963   www.dollarhost.com:80   ESTABLISHED
TCP    laptop:2870   localhost:8431          TIME_WAIT
TCP    laptop:8431   localhost:2862          TIME_WAIT
TCP    laptop:8431   localhost:2863          TIME_WAIT
TCP    laptop:8431   localhost:2867          TIME_WAIT
TCP    laptop:8431   localhost:2872          TIME_WAIT
```

Which of the following commands produces this output?

○ A. **arp**

○ B. **netstat**

○ C. **nbtstat**

○ D. **tracert**

Question 41

Which of the following security protocols is protocol-independent?

○ A. IPSec

○ B. L2TP

○ C. SLIP

○ D. SSL

Question 42

You are attempting to troubleshoot a remote connectivity problem for a user. Although the modem seems to be working properly within the computer, you cannot get the modem to dial a number. Working within a terminal software application, you attempt to communicate directly with the modem. From within the terminal application, which command would you issue to reset the modem?

○ A. ATD

○ B. ATI3

○ C. ATZ

○ D. ATH

Question 43

Which of the following protocols maps layer 2 addresses to layer 3 addresses on a TCP/IP network?

○ A. ARPA

○ B. ARP

○ C. AARP

○ D. RARP

Question 44

Which of the following is not a type of Digital Subscriber Line (DSL) technology?

○ A. VHDSL

○ B. RADSL

○ C. ADSL

○ D. XTDSL

Question 45

Which of the following WAN technologies offers speeds as high as 2.4Gbps?

- ○ A. X.25
- ○ B. Frame relay
- ○ C. SONET
- ○ D. ATM

Question 46

Which of the following is a reason to implement a proxy server?

- ○ A. To centrally control Internet access
- ○ B. To protect the internal network from intruders
- ○ C. To provide NAT services
- ○ D. To provide automatic IP addressing on the network

Question 47

Consider the following output:

```
    Name                Type         Status
 - - - - - - - - - - - - - - - - - - - - - - - - - - - - - - - -
 LAPTOP        <00>   UNIQUE      Registered
 KCS           <00>   GROUP       Registered
 LAPTOP        <03>   UNIQUE      Registered
```

Which of the following commands would produce this output?

- ○ A. **nbtstat**
- ○ B. **netstat**
- ○ C. **ifconfig**
- ○ D. **arp**

Question 48

Which of the following is a valid class C address that could be assigned to a workstation on the network?

○ A. **200.200.200.200**

○ B. **200.200.200.255**

○ C. **143.67.151.17**

○ D. **203.16.42.0**

Question 49

At which layer of the OSI model is flow control performed?

○ A. Network

○ B. Transport

○ C. Session

○ D. Data-link

Question 50

Which of the following statements is true of IMAP?

○ A. IMAP is more secure than POP.

○ B. IMAP is used for sending as well as receiving email.

○ C. IMAP can only be used for sending mail.

○ D. IMAP uses port 110.

Question 51

You are implementing a new network that will use 100BaseT with switches configured for full duplex. What is the maximum throughput that will be possible between two devices on the network?

○ A. 10Mbps

○ B. 20Mbps

○ C. 200Mbps

○ D. 100Mbps

Question 52

Your manager has asked you to implement a RAID 5 fault-tolerant disk solution using four 40GB disks. He now wants to know how much data storage capacity will be lost by the implementation. What do you tell him?

○ A. 10GB

○ B. 20GB

○ C. 40GB

○ D. 120GB

Question 53

A user calls you from a conference room. He needs to connect to the corporate RAS server, but the modem in his system is reporting a "no dial tone" error. When he plugs the telephone back in to the phone socket, he gets a dial tone and is able to dial out successfully. What is the most likely cause of the problem?

○ A. The phone line in the room is analog.

○ B. The phone line in the room is faulty.

○ C. The modem is faulty.

○ D. The phone line in the room is digital.

Question 54

Which of the following is not a valid file permission on a Windows 2000 system?

○ A. Read

○ B. Attribute

○ C. Execute

○ D. Write

Question 55

Which of the following utilities would you use to view the TCP connections that have been established between two systems?

- A. **netstat**
- B. **nbtstat**
- C. **tracert**
- D. **ipconfig**

Question 56

Which of the following authentication systems uses tickets as part of its authentication process?

- A. HTTPS
- B. POP3
- C. Kerberos
- D. SSL

Question 57

On an AppleTalk network, what is the function of AARP?

- A. It is a distance-vector routing protocol.
- B. It allows the resolution of AppleTalk addresses to MAC addresses.
- C. It allows the resolution of MAC addresses to AppleTalk addresses.
- D. It is a link-state routing protocol.

Question 58

Which term describes the process of using parts of the node address range of an IP address as the network ID?

- A. Subnetting
- B. Supernetting
- C. Subnet masking
- D. Super routing

Question 59

You are configuring a router. According to the manual, you need a transceiver to connect to the LAN ports of the router. What kind of physical interface does the router have?

○ A. AUI

○ B. MSAU

○ C. RJ-11

○ D. BNC

Question 60

In a hardware loopback plug, which wire numbers are connected? (Choose the two best answers.)

❏ A. 3 and 5

❏ B. 1 and 3

❏ C. 1 and 2

❏ D. 3 and 4

❏ E. 2 and 6

Answers to exam questions

1. B. DNS is used to provide hostname to IP address resolution on Windows and Unix systems. A is wrong because the LMHOSTS file is used to resolve NetBIOS names to IP address. Answer C is wrong because WINS resolves NetBIOS names to IP addresses. D is wrong because DHCP is used to automatically assign IP information to clients' systems.

2. A and B. To communicate on a network, the server and the client must use the same protocol. In this scenario, installing AppleTalk on the server or TCP/IP on the server would allow the client to access the server. C is wrong because Apple systems do not use the NetBEUI protocol. D is wrong because TCP/IP is already installed on the server; to communicate on the network, the client must also have TCP/IP installed.

3. A. RAID 5 reserves the equivalent space of one partition in the array for parity information. In this scenario, there are four 40GB hard disks. With one reserved for parity, you have 120GB of actual data storage.

4. B. To connect to systems on a remote network, the default gateway has to be correctly assigned. If this address is entered manually, the number may have been incorrectly entered.

Answer A is incorrect. Because the system is able to connect to the local network, this indicates that the actual address is correctly assigned. Answer C is incorrect because IP addresses are statically assigned. Answer D is incorrect, because duplicate addresses will prevent the system from being able to log onto the network.

5. C and E. 10Base2 networks use BNC connectors including T-connectors and RG-58 cable (Thinnet coaxial cable). None of the other technologies are used in 10Base2 networks.

6. D. The change permission is available on Windows-based server systems but not on Unix systems. All the other permissions are available on both platforms.

7. A and B. When logging on to a Windows server, all that is required is a valid username and password. C is incorrect because a context is associated with logging onto a NetWare network. D is wrong because you can log on using the Administrator's username, but this is not required.

8. D. In a mesh topology, each device is connected directly to every other device on the network. Such a structure requires that each device have at least two network connections. The mesh topology is not commonly implemented. All other network configurations do not offer the same level of redundancy as a true mesh network.

9. **C.** A MAC address contains six hexadecimal number sets. The first three sets represent the manufacturer's code, whereas the last three identify the unique station ID. A is wrong because the number represents a valid internal IP address. Neither C nor D are valid numbers.

10. **C.** ST connectors are a twist-type connector used with fiber-optic media. A is wrong because RG-58 (thin coax) uses BNC type connectors. B is incorrect because RG-62 (thick coax) uses vampire types AUI connectors. D is wrong because SCSI cables use a variety of connector types, none of which include ST connectors.

11. **B.** A switch is more efficient than a hub as it forwards data only to intended ports. A is incorrect because a hub directs data packets to all devices connected to the hub. C and D are wrong because these are not network devices.

12. **B.** BRI ISDN uses two 64Kbps data channels. Combined, BRI ISDN offers a total of 128Mbps transfer rate. All of the other answers are invalid.

13. **C.** 10Base2 is an Ethernet network standard implemented using thin coaxial cable. The maximum length of a segment is 185 meters. A is incorrect. B describes 10BaseT. D describes 10Base5.

14. **C.** Samba is a product that provides file and print services to Windows-based clients. A is wrong because Web server services are offered through a variety of products. Samba is not one of them. B is incorrect because Samba does not offer thin client services. D is incorrect because proxy server services are offered through a variety of products. Samba is not one of them.

15. **C.** 10BaseT networks use UTP media, which have maximum distance of 100 meters.

    A is not correct because 185 meters is the distance limitation of thin coax media used on 10Base2 networks. B is wrong because 500 meters is the distance limitation of thick coaxial media used with 10Base5 networks. D is wrong because 50 meters is not a valid cable distance.

16. **B.** If the gateway information is not correctly set, the data packets cannot get beyond the local subnet. The other options are not going to prevent the user from transmitting data to remote hosts.

17. **A.** Log files often record information about errors that can be vital to the troubleshooting process. It is also a step that has little or no impact on network services. B is wrong because rebooting the server is a last-resort troubleshooting step. C is incorrect because removing and reinstalling

the printer drivers may be a valid step, but it would not be the first choice of those listed. D is wrong because changing the network cable may be a valid troubleshooting step, but because it has been verified that the network connectivity is working, this should not be necessary.

18. C and D. Both the route and the netstat commands can be used to view the routing table on a Windows 2000 system. A is wrong because the tracert utility is used to track the route a packet takes between two destinations. B is incorrect because the nbtstat command is used to view statistical information for NetBIOS connections. E isn't correct because the ping utility is used to test network connectivity.

19. A. The Domain Name Service system (DNS) resolves Fully Qualified Domain Names (FQDNs) to IP addresses. B is wrong because the Dynamic Host Configuration Protocol (DHCP) provides automatic IP address assignment. C is wrong because the Windows Internet Naming Service (WINS) provides NetBIOS computer name to IP address resolution. D is wrong because the Address Resolution Protocol (ARP) resolves IP addresses to MAC addresses. E is wrong because the Network Time Protocol (NTP) facilitates the communication of time information between systems.

20. B and D. 100BaseFX networks use fiber media, which can use either SC or ST connectors. A is wrong because RJ-45 connectors are used with UTP media. C is incorrect because BNC connectors are used with thin coax media on 10Base2 networks.

21. A. Unlike copper-based media, fiber-optic media is resistant to crosstalk, as it uses light transmissions. B is wrong because STP offers greater resistance to crosstalk than regular UTP, but is not as resistant as fiber-optic cable. C is incorrect because UTP cable is more susceptible to crosstalk than either STP or fiber-optic. D is wrong because shielded mesh is not a type of cable.

22. A and D. Both backups and off-site data storage are considered disaster recovery measures. B is wrong because a UPS is considered a fault-tolerant measure, not a disaster recovery measure. C is wrong because RAID 5 is considered a fault-tolerant measure, not a disaster recovery measure.

23. A. The output is from the ARP -a command, which shows information related to IP address to MAC address resolutions. B is wrong because the tracert command displays the route a packet takes between two points. The output from the command is different from that shown in the example. C is incorrect because the ipconfig command displays the network configuration of a system. The output from the command is different from that shown in the example. D is wrong because there is no such command as `netinf`.

24. D. The problem is most likely related to incorrectly set file permissions, so this is the best course of action. A is wrong because this is unlikely to be the problem as other users are able to access the application without a problem. B is incorrect because although this may be a solution to the problem, this would not the first thing to try. C is wrong because if the user is able to log on, changing the password is unlikely to have any effect.

25. A and B. The devices on one side of the router need to be configured with a different IP network address than when the network was a single segment. Also, the default gateway information on all systems will need to be updated to use the newly installed router as the default gateway. C is wrong because the default gateway address should be the address of the router, not another workstation on the network. D is incorrect because for systems to communicate on an IP network, all devices must be assigned a unique IP address. Assigning systems the same address will cause address conflicts, thus resulting in none of the systems being able to communicate.

26. C. 100BaseT is implemented using a minimum of category 5 UTP cable. A is wrong because RG-58 is a type of coaxial cable with a maximum speed of 10Mbps. B is incorrect because Category 4 UTP cable is not intended for use on a 100BaseT network. D is wrong because multimode fiber is used in fiber-optic networks. The 100BaseT standard defines 100Mbps networking using UTP cable.

27. C. Each node on a star network uses its own cable, which makes it easy to add users without disrupting current ones. Adding a node to a bus network can sometimes involve breaking the segment, which makes it inaccessible to all other nodes on the network. This makes Answer A incorrect. Answer B is incorrect because a true ring network model would require that the ring be broken to add a new device. Answer D is incorrect because a mesh topology requires that every device be connected to every other device on the network. It is, therefore, quite difficult to expand a mesh network.

28. C. Subnetting allows you to create more than one network from a single network address by manipulating the subnet mask to create more network addresses. A is wrong because the `127.x.x.x` address range is reserved for TCP/IP loopback functionality and cannot be used as an addressing scheme. B is incorrect because reverse proxy is used when a proxy server protects another server (normally a Web server), which responds to requests from users on the other side of the proxy server. D is wrong because private addressing may well solve the issues of security and traffic management, but without also using reverse proxy, systems on the internal network aren't available to outside users.

29. **B.** The Internet Assigned Numbers Authority (IANA) manages the address assignments for public networks such as the Internet. A is wrong because on a private network, you can use any addressing scheme that is compatible with your network. C is incorrect because an Ethernet network can be either private or public. It does not, directly, need an IANA assigned addressing scheme. D is wrong because a WAN can be either private or public. It does not, directly, need an IANA assigned addressing scheme.

30. **B.** The 1000BaseCX standard specifies Gigabit Ethernet over STP cabling. A is wrong because 1000BaseSX and 1000BaseLX specifies Gigabit Ethernet over two types of multimode fiber. C is incorrect because single mode fiber-optic cable is used with the 100BaseFX standard. D is wrong because there is no such thing as CoreXtended fiber-optic cable.

31. **B.** TCP is a connection-oriented protocol, so it can recover from failed transmissions. A is wrong because L2TP is used in remote access connections. C is incorrect because IPX is a connectionless transport protocol and so cannot recover from lost packets. D is incorrect because ARP is part of the TCP/IP protocol suite that resolves IP addresses to MAC addresses.

32. **D.** The DNS service uses port 53. A is wrong because secure HTTP uses port 443. B is incorrect because FTP uses port 21. C is wrong because Telnet uses port 23.

33. **D.** On a Linux system, the `ifconfig` command shows the network card configuration. A is wrong because the `config` command shows the network configuration on a NetWare server. B is incorrect because the `ipconfig` command shows the network configuration information on a Windows system. C is wrong because the `winipcfg` command shows the network configuration information on a certain Windows systems such as Windows 95/98.

34. **A.** In a RAID 1 scenario (disk mirroring), one disk carries an exact copy of the other. Therefore, the total volume of one disk will be lost to redundancy. All of the other answers are incorrect.

35. B. Primary Rate ISDN (PRI) uses 23 B channels for carrying data, and 1 D channel for carrying signaling information. C is incorrect because this statement describes Basic Rate ISDN (BR). D is wrong because PRI uses 23 B channels and 1 D channel.

36. B and D. The most secure security model commonly implemented on networks is user-level security that is administered centrally. A is wrong because user administered security is normally associated with peer-to-peer networks and is not robust as there is more than one person administering security. C is wrong because share-level security is not as secure as user-level security.

37. C and D. In most cases, you should try the simplest solutions first. Information such as the username and password should be verified before any reconfiguration is attempted. A is wrong because if the modem is dialing the remote system and getting a response, it is most likely working correctly. B is incorrect because running a remote diagnostic on the modem is a valid troubleshooting step, but you should first verify that the correct connection information is being used.

38. C. Although it provides the physical connection to the network, an NIC is considered a data-link device. A, B, and D are wrong because a NIC is not said to operate at any of these layers.

39. D. The 100BaseT standard defines an Ethernet network using twisted pair cable, which would be configured in a physical star configuration. However, even in a star configuration, an Ethernet network still uses a logical bus topology.

40. B. The output shown is from the `netstat` command from a Windows-based system. A, C, and D are wrong because all of these commands produce a different output from that shown.

41. B. L2TP is a data-link layer protocol and so operates independently of upper layer protocols. A is wrong because IPSec is a security protocol used on TCP/IP networks. C is incorrect because SLIP is a dial-up protocol, not a security protocol. D is wrong because SSL is a security protocol used on TCP/IP networks.

42. C. The Hayes AT command set provides commands that allow you to communicate directly with the modem The `ATZ` command is used to reset the modem. A is wrong because the `ATD` command is used to dial a number. B is incorrect because the `ATI` command is used to retrieve information from the modem. The `ATI3` command shows the manufacturer and model of the modem. D is wrong because the `ATH` command is used to hang up a connection.

43. D. A layer 2 address is a MAC address. A layer 3 address is a software-configured protocol address. Because a normal resolution is considered to be a layer-3-to-layer-2 resolution, the resolution the other way is considered a reverse resolution. On a TCP/IP network, such a resolution is performed by the Reverse Address Resolution Protocol (RARP). A is wrong because ARPA is not an address resolution protocol. B is incorrect because the address resolution protocol (ARP) resolves layer 3 addresses to layer 2 addresses. C is wrong because the AppleTalk address resolution protocol is used, on AppleTalk networks, to resolve AppleTalk addresses to MAC addresses.

44. D. XTDSL is not a recognized form of DSL. A is wrong because Very High Bit Rate DSL (VHDSL) is a recognized version of DSL. B is wrong because Rate Adaptive DSL (RADSL) is a recognized version of DSL. C is wrong because Asymmetric DSL (ADSL) is a recognized, and arguably the most popular, version of DSL.

45. C. Currently SONET is the only one of these technologies that offers speeds as high as 2.4Gbps. A is wrong because X.25 has a maximum speed of 56Kbps. B is incorrect because Frame Relay has a maximum speed of 1.544Mbps. D is wrong because ATM has a maximum speed of 622Mbps.

46. A and C. A proxy server serves as a centralized point for Internet access, thus making it easy to control a user's Internet use. Also, the proxy server provides network address translation services as requests are sent out to the Internet using the address of the external interface of the proxy server, not the system that sent it. B is wrong because this statement describes the function of a firewall. Although some proxy servers also offer firewalling functionality, they are separate operations. D is incorrect because this statement describes the function of DHCP.

47. A. The output shown is from an `nbtstat` command running on a Windows system. B, C, and D are wrong because all of these commands produce different output from that shown.

48. A. Although it looks odd, this is a valid class C address that could be assigned to a system on the network. B is the broadcast address of the network `200.200.200.0`. C is incorrect because it represents a valid class B address. D is wrong because it is the network address for the network `203.16.42`.

49. B. Flow control occurs at the transport layer of the OSI model. A, C, and D are wrong because flow control does not occur at any of these layers.

50. A. IMAP is more secure than POP because it sends passwords encrypted. B and C are wrong because IMAP is used only for retrieving email. D is wrong because IMAP uses port 143. POP uses port 110.

51. C. 100BaseT is a network standard that runs at 100Mbps. A full-duplex configuration in a switched environment gives a maximum throughput between two devices of 200Mbps. A is wrong because this would be the maximum speed of a 10BaseT network in half-duplex mode. B is incorrect because this would be the maximum speed of a 10BaseT network in full-duplex mode. D is wrong because this would be the maximum speed of a 100BaseT network in half-duplex mode.

52. C. In a RAID 5 implementation, the space equal to the size of one disk in the array is lost to the storage of parity information. D describes the amount of space available for the storage of data, not the amount of space lost to the storage of parity information.

53. D. Most modern phone systems are digital, and therefore, regular analog modems that require analog lines will not work. A is incorrect because, if the phone line in the room were analog, the modem would probably work. B is incorrect because the phone line in the room is not faulty because the user can call you to report the problem. C is incorrect because if the modem can report a "no dial tone" error, it is most likely working correctly.

54. B. The attribute file permission is not a valid NTFS file permission. A, C, and D are all valid file permissions on a Windows 2000 system.

55. A. The `netstat` utility allows you to view the TCP/IP connections between two systems. The `nbtstat` utility (Answer B) is used to see the status of NetBIOS over TCP/IP connections. The `tracert` utility (Answer C) is used to track the path that a packet of data takes between two hosts. The `ipconfig` utility (Answer D) is used to view the IP addressing configuration information on a system.

56. C. The Kerberos authentication system uses tickets as part of the authentication process. HTTPS (Answer A) is an implementation of SSL. It does not use tickets. POP3 (Answer B) is an email retrieval protocol. SSL (Answer D) does not use tickets.

57. B. AARP is used to map the AppleTalk addresses to both Ethernet and Token Ring physical addresses. The distance-vector routing protocol used on AppleTalk networks is RMTP, which makes answer A incorrect. C is incorrect because AARP resolves AppleTalk addresses to MAC addresses—not the other way around. AARP is not a link-state routing protocol.

58. A. The term *subnetting* refers to the process of using parts of the node address range for network addressing purposes. *Supernetting* (Answer B) refers to the process of borrowing parts of the network address portion of an assigned address to be used for node addressing. *Subnet masking* (Answer C) describes the process of applying a subnet mask to an address. Answer D is not a valid term.

59. A. An AUI port is typically used to connect an external transceiver to a device such as a router. An MSAU (Answer B) is a type of network device used on Token Ring networks. RJ-11 (Answer C) is a connector type associated with telephone cable. BNC (Answer D) is a type of network connector used on coaxial networks.

60. B, E. A hardware loopback plug connects the 2 and 6 wires and 1 and 3 wires to simulate a live network connection. Answers A, C, and D are not correct for the cable in a hardware loopback adapter.

What's on the CD-ROM

This appendix is a brief rundown of what you'll find on the CD-ROM that comes with this book. For a more detailed description of the *PrepLogic Practice Tests, Preview Edition* exam simulation software, see Appendix B, "Using *PrepLogic, Preview Edition* Software." In addition to the *PrepLogic Practice Tests, Preview Edition*, the CD-ROM includes the electronic version of the book in Portable Document Format (PDF), several utility and application programs, and a complete listing of test objectives and where they are covered in the book. Finally, a pointer list to online pointers and references are added to this CD. You will need a computer with Internet access and a relatively recent browser installed to use this feature.

PrepLogic Practice Tests, Preview Edition

PrepLogic is a leading provider of certification training tools. Trusted by certification students worldwide, we believe PrepLogic is the best practice exam software available. In addition to providing a means of evaluating your knowledge of the Exam Cram material, *PrepLogic Practice Tests, Preview Edition* features several innovations that help you to improve your mastery of the subject matter.

For example, the practice tests allow you to check your score by exam area or domain to determine which topics you need to study more. Another feature allows you to obtain immediate feedback on your responses in the form of explanations for the correct and incorrect answers.

PrepLogic Practice Tests, Preview Edition exhibits most of the full functionality of the *Premium Edition* but offers only a fraction of the total questions. To get the complete set of practice questions and exam functionality, visit PrepLogic.com and order the *Premium Edition* for this and other challenging exam titles.

Again, for a more detailed description of the *PrepLogic Practice Tests, Preview Edition* features, see Appendix B.

Exclusive Electronic Version of Text

The CD-ROM also contains the electronic version of this book in Portable Document Format (PDF). The electronic version comes complete with all figures as they appear in the book. You will find that the search capabilities of the reader comes in handy for study and review purposes.

Easy Access to Online Pointers and References

The Suggested Reading section at the end of each chapter in this Exam Cram contains numerous pointers to Web sites, newsgroups, mailing lists, and other online resources. To make this material as easy to use as possible, we include all this information in an HTML document entitled "Online Pointers" on the CD. Open this document in your favorite Web browser to find links you can follow through any Internet connection to access these resources directly.

Using the *PrepLogic Practice Tests, Preview Edition* Software

This Exam Cram includes a special version of PrepLogic Practice Tests—a revolutionary test engine designed to give you the best in certification exam preparation. PrepLogic offers sample and practice exams for many of today's most in-demand and challenging technical certifications. This special *Preview Edition* is included with this book as a tool to use in assessing your knowledge of the Training Guide material, while also providing you with the experience of taking an electronic exam.

This appendix describes in detail what *PrepLogic Practice Tests, Preview Edition* is, how it works, and what it can do to help you prepare for the exam. Note that although the *Preview Edition* includes all the test simulation functions of the complete, retail version, it contains only a single practice test. The *Premium Edition*, available at PrepLogic.com, contains the complete set of challenging practice exams designed to optimize your learning experience.

Exam Simulation

One of the main functions of *PrepLogic Practice Tests, Preview Edition* is exam simulation. To prepare you to take the actual vendor certification exam, PrepLogic is designed to offer the most effective exam simulation available.

Question Quality

The questions provided in the *PrepLogic Practice Tests, Preview Edition* are written to the highest standards of technical accuracy. The questions tap the content of the Exam Cram chapters and help you to review and assess your knowledge before you take the actual exam.

Interface Design

The *PrepLogic Practice Tests, Preview Edition* exam simulation interface provides you with the experience of taking an electronic exam. This enables you to effectively prepare yourself for taking the actual exam by making the test experience a familiar one. Using this test simulation can help to eliminate the sense of surprise or anxiety you might experience in the testing center because you will already be acquainted with computerized testing.

Effective Learning Environment

The *PrepLogic Practice Tests, Preview Edition* interface provides a learning environment that not only tests you through the computer, but also teaches the material you need to know to pass the certification exam. Each question comes with a detailed explanation of the correct answer and often provides reasons the other options are incorrect. This information helps to reinforce the knowledge you already have and also provides practical information you can use on the job.

Software Requirements

PrepLogic Practice Tests requires a computer with the following:

➤ Microsoft Windows 98, Windows Me, Windows NT 4.0, Windows 2000, or Windows XP

➤ A 166 MHz or faster processor is recommended

➤ A minimum of 32MB of RAM

➤ As with any Windows application, the more memory, the better your performance

➤ 10MB of hard drive space

Installing *PrepLogic Practice Tests, Preview Edition*

Install *PrepLogic Practice Tests, Preview Edition* by running the setup program on the *PrepLogic Practice Tests, Preview Edition* CD. Follow these instructions to install the software on your computer.

1. Insert the CD into your CD-ROM drive. The Autorun feature of Windows should launch the software. If you have Autorun disabled, click the Start button and select Run. Go to the root directory of the CD and select setup.exe. Click Open, and then click OK.

2. The Installation Wizard copies the *PrepLogic Practice Tests, Preview Edition* files to your hard drive; adds *PrepLogic Practice Tests, Preview Edition* to your Desktop and Program menu; and installs test engine components to the appropriate system folders.

Removing *PrepLogic Practice Tests, Preview Edition* from Your Computer

If you elect to remove the *PrepLogic Practice Tests,, Preview Edition* product from your computer, an uninstall process has been included to ensure that it is removed from your system safely and completely. Follow these instructions to remove PrepLogic Practice Tests, Preview Edition from your computer:

1. Select Start, Settings, Control Panel.

2. Double-click the Add/Remove Programs icon.

3. You are presented with a list of software currently installed on your computer. Select the appropriate *PrepLogic Practice Tests, Preview Edition* title you wish to remove. Click the Add/Remove button. The software is then removed from you computer.

Using *PrepLogic Practice Tests, Preview Edition*

PrepLogic is designed to be user friendly and intuitive. Because the software has a smooth learning curve, your time is maximized, as you will start practicing almost immediately. *PrepLogic Practice Tests, Preview Edition* has two major modes of study: Practice Test and Flash Review.

Using Practice Test mode, you can develop your test-taking abilities, as well as your knowledge through the use of the Show Answer option. While you are taking the test, you can reveal the answers along with a detailed explanation of why the given answers are right or wrong. This gives you the ability to better understand the material presented.

Flash Review is designed to reinforce exam topics rather than quiz you. In this mode, you will be shown a series of questions, but no answer choices. Instead, you will be given a button that reveals the correct answer to the question and a full explanation for that answer.

Starting a Practice Test Mode Session

Practice Test mode enables you to control the exam experience in ways that actual certification exams do not allow:

➤ **Enable Show Answer Button**—Activates the Show Answer button, allowing you to view the correct answer(s) and a full explanation for each question during the exam. When not enabled, you must wait until after your exam has been graded to view the correct answer(s) and explanation(s).

➤ **Enable Item Review Button**—Activates the Item Review button, allowing you to view your answer choices, marked questions, and facilitating navigation between questions.

➤ **Randomize Choices**—Randomize answer choices from one exam session to the next; makes memorizing question choices more difficult, therefore keeping questions fresh and challenging longer.

To begin studying in Practice Test mode, click the Practice Test radio button from the main exam customization screen. This will enable the options detailed above.

To your left, you are presented with the options of selecting the pre-configured Practice Test or creating your own Custom Test. The pre-configured test has a fixed time limit and number of questions. Custom Tests allow you to configure the time limit and the number of questions in your exam.

The *Preview Edition* included with this book includes a single pre-configured Practice Test. Get the compete set of challenging PrepLogic Practice Tests at PrepLogic.com and make certain you're ready for the big exam.

Click the Begin Exam button to begin your exam.

Starting a Flash Review Mode Session

Flash Review mode provides you with an easy way to reinforce topics covered in the practice questions. To begin studying in Flash Review mode, click the Flash Review radio button from the main exam customization screen. Select either the pre-configured Practice Test or create your own Custom Test.

Click the Best Exam button to begin your Flash Review of the exam questions.

Standard *PrepLogic Practice Tests, Preview Edition* Options

The following list describes the function of each of the buttons you see. Depending on the options, some of the buttons will be grayed out and inaccessible or missing completely. Buttons that are accessible are active. The buttons are as follows:

➤ **Exhibit**—This button is visible if an exhibit is provided to support the question. An exhibit is an image that provides supplemental information necessary to answer the question.

➤ **Item Review**—This button leaves the question window and opens the Item Review screen. From this screen you will see all questions, your answers, and your marked items. You will also see correct answers listed here when appropriate.

➤ **Show Answer**—This option displays the correct answer with an explanation of why it is correct. If you select this option, the current question is not scored.

➤ **Mark Item**—Check this box to tag a question you need to review further. You can view and navigate your Marked Items by clicking the Item Review button (if enabled). When grading your exam, you will be notified if you have marked items remaining.

➤ **Previous Item**—This option allows you to view the previous question.

➤ **Next Item**—This option allows you to view the next question.

➤ **Grade Exam**—When you have completed your exam, click this button to end your exam and view your detailed score report. If you have unanswered or marked items remaining you will be asked if you would like to continue taking your exam or view your exam report.

Time Remaining

If the test is timed, the time remaining is displayed on the upper right corner of the application screen. It counts down the minutes and seconds remaining to complete the test. If you run out of time, you will be asked if you want to continue taking the test or if you want to end your exam.

Your Examination Score Report

The Examination Score Report screen appears when the Practice Test mode ends—as the result of time expiration, completion of all questions, or your decision to terminate early.

This screen provides you with a graphical display of your test score with a breakdown of scores by topic domain. The graphical display at the top of the screen compares your overall score with the PrepLogic Exam Competency Score.

The PrepLogic Exam Competency Score reflects the level of subject competency required to pass this vendor's exam. While this score does not directly translate to a passing score, consistently matching or exceeding this score does suggest you possess the knowledge to pass the actual vendor exam.

Review Your Exam

From Your Score Report screen, you can review the exam that you just completed by clicking on the View Items button. Navigate through the items viewing the questions, your answers, the correct answers, and the explanations for those answers. You can return to your score report by clicking the View Items button.

Get More Exams

Each *PrepLogic Practice Tests, Preview Edition* that accompanies your Exam Cram contains a single PrepLogic Practice Test. Certification students worldwide trust PrepLogic Practice Tests to help them pass their IT certification exams the first time. Purchase the *Premium Edition* of PrepLogic Practice Tests and get the entire set of all new challenging Practice Tests for this exam. PrepLogic Practice Tests—Because You Want to Pass the First Time.

Contacting PrepLogic

If you would like to contact PrepLogic for any reason, including information about our extensive line of certification practice tests, we invite you to do so. Please contact us online at `http://www.preplogic.com`.

Customer Service

If you have a damaged product and need a replacement or refund, please call the following phone number:

800-858-7674

Product Suggestions and Comments

We value your input! Please email your suggestions and comments to the following address:

`feedback@preplogic.com`

License Agreement

YOU MUST AGREE TO THE TERMS AND CONDITIONS OUT-
LINED IN THE END USER LICENSE AGREEMENT ("EULA")
PRESENTED TO YOU DURING THE INSTALLATION PROCESS.
IF YOU DO NOT AGREE TO THESE TERMS DO NOT INSTALL
THE SOFTWARE.

Glossary

Numbers and Symbols

10Base2

The IEEE 802.3 specification for Ethernet at 10Mbps over thin coaxial cable. The maximum length of a 10Base2 segment is 185 meters (that is, 607 feet).

10Base5

The IEEE 802.3 specification for 10Mbps Ethernet using thick coaxial cable. The maximum length of a 10Base5 segment is 500 meters (that is, 1,640 feet).

10BaseT

The IEEE 802.3 specification for running Ethernet at 10Mbps over twisted-pair cabling. The maximum length of a 10BaseT segment is 100 meters (that is, 330 feet).

100BaseFX

The IEEE 802.3 specification for running Fast Ethernet at 100Mbps over fiber-optic cable. The maximum length of a 100BaseFX segment is 2000 meters (6,561 feet), in full duplex mode.

100BaseT

The IEEE 802.3 specification for running Ethernet at 100Mbps over twisted-pair cabling. The maximum length of a 100BaseT segment is 100 meters (that is, 330 feet).

100BaseT4

The IEEE specification that allows the use of Fast Ethernet (100Mbps) technology over existing Category 3 and Category 4 wiring, using all four pairs of wires. The maximum length of a 100BaseT4 segment is 100 meters (that is, 330 feet).

100BaseTX

The IEEE 802.3u specification, also known as Fast Ethernet, for running Ethernet at 100Mbps over STP or UTP. The maximum length of a 100BaseTX segment is 100 meters (that is, 330 feet).

100BaseVG-AnyLAN

The IEEE 802.12 specification that allows data transmissions of 100Mbps over Category 3 cable, using all sets of wires. VG in 100BaseVG-AnyLAN stands for voice grade because of its capability to be used over voice-grade cable. The maximum length of a 100BaseVG-AnyLAN segment is 100 meters (330 feet) on Category 3 cable, 150 meters (492 feet) on Category 5 cable, and 2000 meters (6,561 feet) on fiber-optic cable.

1000BaseX
The IEEE 802.3z specification, also known as Gigabit Ethernet, that defines standards for data transmissions of 1000Mbps (1Gbps).

A
ACK
The acknowledgment message sent between two hosts during a TCP session.

ACL (access control list)
The list of trustees assigned to a file or directory. A trustee can be any object that is available to the security subsystem.

Active Directory
An X.500-compliant directory services system created by Microsoft for use on Windows 2000 networks.

active hub
A hub that has power supplied to it for the purposes of regenerating the signals that pass through it.

active termination
A termination system used on a SCSI bus. Unlike passive termination, which uses voltage resistors, active termination uses voltage regulators to create the termination voltage.

address
A set of numbers, usually expressed in binary format, used to identify and locate a resource or device on a network.

administrator
A person who is responsible for the control and security of the user accounts, resources, and data on a network.

Administrator account
In a Windows NT system, the default account that has rights to access everything and to assign rights to other users on the network. Unlike other user accounts, the Administrator account cannot be deleted.

ADSL (Asymmetric Digital Subscriber Line)
A service that transmits digital voice and data over existing (analog) phone lines.

ANSI (American National Standards Institute)
An organization that publishes standards for communications, programming languages, and networking.

antivirus software

A type of software that detects and removes virus programs.

anycast address

An address that is used in ATM for shared multiple-end systems. An anycast address allows a frame to be sent to specific groups of hosts (rather than to all hosts, as with simple broadcasting).

application layer

Layer 7 of the OSI model, which provides support for end users and for application programs that are using network resources.

Application log

A log that is located in Windows NT/2000 Event Viewer and provides information on events that occur within an application.

archive bit

A flag that is set on a file after it has been created or altered. Some backup methods reset the flag to indicate that it has been backed up.

ARCnet (Attached Resource Computer Network)

A token-bus LAN technology used in the 1970s and 1980s.

ARP (Address Resolution Protocol)

A protocol in the TCP/IP protocol suite that is used to resolve IP addresses to MAC addresses.

ARP table

A table of entries used by ARP to store resolved ARP requests. Entries can also be stored manually.

array

A group of devices arranged in a fault-tolerant configuration. *See also* RAID.

ATM (Asynchronous Transfer Mode)

A high-speed WAN technology that uses fixed cells of 53 bytes each.

attenuation

The loss of signal that is experienced as data is transmitted across network media.

AUI (attachment unit interface)

An IEEE 802.3-specified interface that is used between a MAU and an NIC.

AUI connector

A 15-pin D-type connector that is sometimes used with Ethernet connections.

authentication

The process by which a user's identity is validated on a network. The most common authentication method is a username and password combination.

B

B (bearer) channel

In ISDN, the channel that carries the data. *See also* D channel.

backbone

A network segment that acts as a trunk between other network segments. Backbones are typically high-bandwidth implementations such as fiber-optic cable.

backup schedule

A document or another plan that defines the point at which backups are made, what backups are made, and what data is backed up.

bandwidth

The rated throughput capacity of a given network protocol or medium.

baseband

A term applied to any media that is capable of carrying only a single data signal at a time. *Compare with* broadband.

baseline

A measurement of performance of a device or system for the purposes of future comparison. Baselining is a common server administration task.

baud rate

The speed or rate of signal transfer. The word *baud* is derived from the name of French telegraphy expert J. M. Baudot.

BDC (backup domain controller)

A Windows NT server that provides a backup of the PDC's user, group, and security information. *See also* PDC.

binary

A base-2 numbering system that is used in digital signaling. It uses only the numbers 1 and 0.

Bindery

The name of the user account information database on NetWare servers up to and including NetWare 3.x.

binding

The process of associating a protocol and an NIC.

biometrics

The science and technology of measuring and analyzing biological data. Biometrics is increasingly being used for security purposes, to analyze and compare characteristics such as voice patterns, retina patterns, and hand measurements.

BIOS (Basic Input/Output System)

A basic set of instructions that a device needs to operate.

bit

An electronic digit used in the binary numbering system. Bit is a contraction of the terms *binary* and *digit*.

blackout

A total loss of electrical power.

Blue Screen of Death

The term for the blue-screen STOP errors that occur and halt the system in Windows NT and Windows 2000.

BNC (British Naval Connector)

A T-shaped connector that is used to connect a device to a thin coaxial Ethernet network.

bound media

A term used to describe any media that have physical constraints, such as coaxial, fiber-optic, and twisted pair. *Compare with* unbound media.

boundless media

See unbound media.

BRI (Basic Rate Interface)

An ISDN digital communications line that consists of three independent channels: two B channels, each at 64Kbps, and one D channel, at 16Kbps. ISDN BRI is often referred to as 2B+D. *See also* ISDN, PRI.

bridge

A device that connects and passes packets between two network segments that use the same communications protocol. Bridges operate at the data-link layer of the OSI model. A bridge filters, forwards, or floods an incoming frame based on the MAC address of that frame.

bridging address table

A list of MAC addresses that a bridge keeps and uses when it receives packets. The bridge uses the bridging address table to determine which segment the destination address is on before it sends the packet to the next interface or drops the packet (if it is on the same segment as the sending node).

broadband

A communications strategy that uses analog signaling over multiple communications channels.

broadcast

A packet delivery system in which a copy of a packet is given to all hosts attached to the network.

broadcast storm

An undesirable condition in which broadcasts become so numerous as to bog down the flow of data across the network.

brouter

A device that can be used to combine the benefits of both routers and bridges. Its common use is to route routable protocols at the network layer of the OSI model and to bridge nonroutable protocols at the data-link layer.

brownout

A short-term decrease in the voltage level, usually caused by the startup demands of other electrical devices.

buffer

An area of memory in a device that is used to store data before it is forwarded to another device or location.

bus

A path that is used by electrical signals to travel between the CPU and the attached hardware.

bus mastering

A bus accessing method in which the NIC takes control of the bus in order to send data through the bus directly to the system memory, bypassing the CPU.

bus topology

A linear LAN architecture in which all devices are connected to a common cable, referred to as a bus or backbone.

byte

A set of bits (usually 8 bits) that operate as a unit to signify a character.

C

cable modem

A device that provides Internet access over cable television lines.

cable tester

A device that is used to check for electrical continuity along a length of cable. *Cable tester* is a generic term that can be applied to devices such as volt/ohm meters and TDRs.

caching-only server

A type of DNS server that operates the same way as secondary servers except that a zone transfer does not take place when the caching-only server is started.

carrier

A signal that carries data. The carrier signal is modulated to create peaks and troughs, which represent binary bits.

CDDI (Copper Distributed Data Interface)

An implementation of the FDDI standard that uses copper cable rather than optical cable.

Centronics connector

A connector that uses teeth that snap into place to secure the connector.

change control

A process in which a detailed record of every change made to the network is documented.

channel

A communications path that is used for data transmission.

checksum

A basic method of error checking that involves calculating the sum of bits in a section of data and then embedding the result in the packet. When the packet reaches the destination, the calculation is performed again, to make sure the value is still the same.

CIDR (classless interdomain routing)

A technique that allows multiple addresses to be consolidated into a single entry.

circuit switching

A method of sending data between two parties, in which a dedicated circuit is created at the beginning of the conversation and broken at the end. All data transported during the session travels over the same path, or circuit.

Class A network

A TCP/IP network that uses addresses from 1 to 126 and supports up to 126 subnets with 16,777,214 unique hosts each.

Class B network

A TCP/IP network that uses addresses from 128 to 191 and supports up to 16,384 subnets with 65,534 unique hosts each.

Class C network

A TCP/IP network that uses addresses from 192 to 223 and supports up to 2,097,152 subnets with 254 unique hosts each.

client

A node that uses the services from another node on a network.

client/server networking

A networking architecture in which front-end, or client, nodes request and process data stored by the back-end, or server, node.

clustering

A technology that allows two or more computers to act as a single system to provide improved fault tolerance and load balancing.

coaxial cable

A data cable, commonly referred to as *coax*, that is made of a solid copper core that is insulated and surrounded by braided metal and covered with a thick plastic or rubber covering. Coax is the standard cable used in cable television and in older bus topology networks.

CONFIG

A command that is used on a NetWare server to see basic information such as the server name, NDS information, and the details of network interface configurations.

collision

The result of two frames transmitting simultaneously on an Ethernet network and colliding, thereby destroying both frames.

collision domain

A segment of an Ethernet network that is between managing nodes, where only one packet can be transmitted at any given time. Switches, bridges, and routers can be used to segment a network into separate collision domains.

collision light

An LED on networking equipment that flashes to indicate a collision on the network. A collision light can be used to determine whether the network is experiencing a large number of collisions.

COM port (communication port)

A connection through which serial devices and a computer's motherboard can communicate. A COM port requires standard configuration information, such as an IRQ, an I/O address, and a COM port number.

communication

The transfer of information between nodes on a network.

concentrator

Any device that acts as a connectivity point on a network.

connectionless communication

Packet transfer in which delivery is not guaranteed.

connection-oriented communication

Packet transfer in which delivery is guaranteed.

connectivity

The linking of nodes on a network in order for communication to take place.

copy backup

Normally, a backup of the entire hard drive. A copy backup is similar to a full backup, except the copy backup does not alter the state of the archive bits on files.

cost

A value that is used to encourage or discourage the use of a certain route through a network. Routes that are to be discouraged are assigned a higher cost, and those that are to be encouraged are assigned a lower cost. *See also* metric.

cracker

A person who attempts to break software code or gain access to a system to which he or she is not authorized. *See also* hacker.

cracking

The process of attempting to break software code, normally to defeat copyright protection or alter the software's functioning. Also the process of attempting to gain unauthorized access to a computer system. *See also* hacking.

CRC (cyclical redundancy check)

A method used to check for errors in packets that have been transferred across a network. A computation bit is added to the packet and recalculated at the destination, to determine whether the entire content of the packet has been transferred correctly.

crimper

A tool that is used to join connectors to the ends of network cables.

crossover cable

A UTP cable in which the 1 and 3 wires and the 2 and 6 wires are crossed for the purposes of placing the transmit line of one device on the receive line of the other. Crossover cables can be used to directly connect two devices—for example, two computer systems—or as a means to expand networks that use devices such as hubs or switches.

crosstalk

Electronic interference that is caused when two wires are too close to each other.

CSMA/CA (carrier-sense multiple-access with collision avoidance)

A contention media access method that uses collision-avoidance techniques.

CSMA/CD (carrier-sense multiple-access with collision detection)

A contention media access method that uses collision-detection and retransmission techniques.

CSU (channel service unit)

A network communications device used to connect to the digital equipment lines of the common carrier, usually over a dedicated line or Frame Relay. A CSU is used in conjunction with a DSU.

cut-through packet switching

A switching method that does not copy the entire packet into the switch buffers. Instead, the destination address is captured into the switch, the route to the destination node is determined, and the packet is quickly sent out the corresponding port. Cut-through packet switching maintains a low latency.

D

D (delta) channel

The channel used on ISDN to communicate signaling and other related information. Use of the D channel leaves the B channels free for data communication. *See also* B channel.

D-shell connector

A connector that is shaped like a letter D and uses pins and sockets to establish connections between peripheral devices, using serial or parallel ports. The number that follows *DB* in the name of a D connector is the number of pins used for connectivity; for example, a DB-9 connector has 9 pins and a DB-25 connector has 25 pins.

daemon

A service or process that runs on a Unix or Linux server.

DAS (dual attached station)

A device on an FDDI network that is connected to both rings. *Compare with* SAS.

DAT (digital audio tape)

A tape recording technology that uses the helical scan recording method. This technology has been used in videotape recorders and VCRs since the 1950s.

Data field

In a frame, the field or section that contains the data.

datagram

An information grouping that is transmitted as a unit at the network layer. *See also* packet.

data-link layer

Layer 2 of the OSI model, which is above the physical layer. Data comes off the cable, goes through the physical layer, and goes into the data-link layer. The data-link layer has two distinct sublayers: MAC and LLC.

DB-9

A 9-pin connector that is used for serial port or parallel port connection between PCs and peripheral devices.

DB-25

A 25-pin connector that is used for serial port or parallel port connection between PCs and peripheral devices.

DDNS (dynamic DNS)

A form of DNS that allows systems to register and deregister themselves with the DNS system dynamically. This is in contrast with the conventional DNS system, in which entries must be made manually.

DDS (digital data storage)

A format for storing computer data on a DAT. DDS-formatted tapes can be read by either a DDS or DAT drive. The original DDS standard specified a 4mm tape cartridge with a capacity of 1.3GB. Subsequent implementations of DDS have taken the capacity to 40GB with compression.

dedicated line

A dedicated circuit that is used in WANs to provide a constant connection between two points.

default gateway

Normally, a router or a multi-homed computer to which packets are sent when they are destined for a host on a different network.

Delete or Erase

A right given to users that allows them to delete a file or files in a directory or to delete a directory.

demarcation point

The point at which communication lines enter a customer's premises. Sometimes shortened to simply "demarc."

destination address

The network address to which the frame is being sent. In a packet, this address is encapsulated in a field of the packet so that all nodes know where the frame is being sent.

DHCP (Dynamic Host Configuration Protocol)

A protocol that provides dynamic IP addressing to workstations on the network.

dial-up networking

Refers to the connection of a remote node to a network using POTS.

differential backup

A backup of only the data that has been created or changed since the previous full backup. In a differential backup, the state of the archive bits is not altered.

directory services

The organization of the accounts and resources directory to help network devices locate service providers. Examples of directory services systems include Novell eDirectory and Microsoft Active Directory.

disaster recovery plan

A plan for implementing duplicate computer services in the event of a natural disaster, a human-made disaster, or another catastrophe. A disaster recovery plan includes off-site backups and procedures to activate information systems in alternative locations.

disk duplexing

A fault-tolerant standard based on RAID 1 that uses disk mirroring with dual disk controllers.

disk mirroring

A fault-tolerant standard that is defined as RAID 1 and mirrors data between two disks to create an exact copy.

disk striping

An implementation of RAID in which data is distributed across multiple disks in a stripe. Some striping implementations provide performance improvements (RAID 0), whereas others provide fault tolerance (RAID 5).

distance-vector routing

A type of routing in which a router uses broadcasts to inform neighboring routers on the network of the routes it knows about. *Compare with* link-state routing.

DIX (Digital, Intel, and Xerox)

A type of 15-pin connector that is used to connect to network media.

DLT (digital linear tape)

A high-performance and high-capacity tape backup system that offers capacities up to 220GB with compression.

DMA (direct memory access)

The process of transferring data directly into memory at high speeds, bypassing the CPU and incurring no processor overhead.

DNS (Domain Name Service)

A system used to translate domain names, such as www.quepublishing.com, into IP addresses, such as 165.193.123.44. DNS uses a hierarchical namespace that allows the database of hostname-to-IP address mappings to be distributed across multiple servers.

domain

A logical group of computers in a Windows NT/2000 network. Also, a section of the DNS namespace.

domain name server

A server that runs application software that allows the server to perform a role associated with the DNS service.

DoS (Denial of Service) attack

A type of hacking attack in which the target system is overwhelmed with requests for service, resulting in it not being able to service any requests—legitimate or otherwise.

downtime

A period of time during which a computer system or network is unavailable. This might be due to scheduled maintenance or to hardware or software failure.

drive mapping

A process through which an alias makes a network path appear as if it were a local drive.

DSL (Digital Subscriber Line)

A public network technology that delivers high bandwidth over conventional copper wiring over limited distances.

DSU (data service unit)

A network communications device that formats and controls data for transmission over digital lines. A DSU is used in conjunction with a CSU.

DTE (data terminal equipment)

A device used at the user end of a user network interface that serves as a data source, a destination, or both. DTE devices include computers, protocol translators, and multiplexers.

dumb terminal

A keyboard/monitor combination that allows access to a multiuser system but provides no processing or storage at the local level.

duplexing

In RAID, a RAID 1 mirror set in which each drive is connected to a separate controller to eliminate the single point of failure that the controller created.

dynamic routing

A routing system that allows routing information to be communicated between devices automatically and can recognize changes in the network topology and update routing tables accordingly. *Compare with* static routing.

dynamic window

A flow control mechanism that prevents the sender of data from overwhelming the receiver. The amount of data that can be buffered in a dynamic window varies in size, hence its name.

E

eDirectory

A standards-compliant directory services system created by Novell. eDirectory was originally implemented as NDS in versions of NetWare up to 5.0.

EIA (Electronic Industries Association)

A group that specifies electrical transmission standards.

EISA (Extended Industry Standard Architecture)

The successor to the ISA standard. EISA provides a 32-bit bus interface that is used in PCs.

EMI (electromagnetic interference)

External interference of electromagnetic signals that causes a reduction of data integrity and increased error rates in a transmission medium.

encapsulation

A technique that is used by layered protocols in which a layer adds header information to the protocol data unit from the layer above.

encryption

The modification of data for security purposes prior to transmission so that it is not comprehendable without the decoding method.

ERD (emergency repair disk)

A floppy disk that contains security files and resource configurations that are used for recovery when a Windows NT/2000 operating system becomes corrupt.

ESD (electrostatic discharge)

A condition that is created when two objects of dissimilar electrical charge come into contact with each other. The result is that a charge from the object with the higher electrical charge discharges itself into the object with the lower-level charge. This discharge can be extremely harmful to computer components and circuit boards.

Ethernet

The most common LAN technology. Ethernet can be implemented using coaxial, twisted-pair, or fiber-optic cable. Ethernet uses the CSMA/CD media access method and has various implementation standards.

Event Viewer

A troubleshooting tool that is available in both Windows NT and Windows 2000 systems. On

Windows NT, the Event Viewer provides three logs that record system information: the System log, the Security log, and the Application log. More logs are included in the Windows 2000 version.

EXT2

The default file system used in Linux systems.

F

failover

The automatic switching from one device or system to another. Servers can be configured in a failover configuration so that if the primary server fails, the secondary server takes over automatically.

Fast Ethernet

The IEEE 802.3 specification for data transfers of up to 100Mbps over twisted-pair cable. *See also* 100BaseFX, 100BaseTX, 100BaseT, and 100BaseT4.

fault tolerance

The capability of a component or system to endure a failure.

FDDI (Fiber Distributed Data Interface)

A high-speed data transfer technology that is designed to extend the capabilities of existing LANs by using a dual-ring topology and a token-passing access method.

FDM (Frequency-Division Multiplexing)

A technology that divides the output channel into multiple smaller-bandwidth channels, each of which uses a different frequency range.

fiber-optic cable

Also known as fiber optics or optical fiber, a physical medium that is capable of conducting modulated light transmissions. Compared with other transmission media, fiber-optic cable is more expensive, but it is not susceptible to EMI or crosstalk, and it is capable of very high data rates.

fibre channel

A technology that defines full gigabit-per-second data transfer over fiber-optic cable.

firewall

A program, system, device, or group of devices that acts as a barrier between one network and another. Firewalls are configured to allow certain types of traffic to pass while blocking others.

FireWire

A high-speed serial bus technology that allows up to 63 devices to be connected to a system. FireWire provides sufficient bandwidth for multimedia operations and supports hot swapping and multiple speeds on the same bus.

fixed wireless

A technology that provides data communication capabilities between two fixed locations. Fixed wireless can be used as a private networking method but is also becoming increasingly common as an Internet access method.

flow control

A method of controlling the amount of data that is transmitted within a given period of time. There are different types of flow control. *See also* dynamic window, static window.

FQDN (fully qualified domain name)

The entire domain name that specifies the name of the computer as well as the domain in which it resides and the top-level DNS domain (for example, www.quepublishing.com).

fragment-free switching

A fast-packet-switching method that uses the first 64 bytes of a frame to determine whether the frame is corrupted. If this first part is intact, the frame is forwarded.

frame

A grouping of information that is transmitted as a unit across the network at the data-link layer of the OSI model.

FCS (Frame Check Sequence) field

A field of a packet that holds a CRC value to ensure that all the frame's data arrives intact.

Frame Length field

In a data frame, the field that specifies the length of a frame.

Frame Relay

A high-speed data-link layer switching protocol that is used across multiple virtual circuits of a common carrier to give the end user the appearance of a dedicated line.

Frame Type field

In a data frame, the field that names the protocol that is being sent in the frame.

frequency

The number of cycles of an alternating current signal over a unit of time. Frequency is expressed in Hertz.

FTP (File Transfer Protocol)

A protocol that provides for the transfer of files between two systems. FTP is part of the TCP/IP protocol suite.

full backup

A backup in which files, regardless of whether they have been changed, are copied to the backup media. In a full backup, the archive bits of the files are reset.

full-duplex

A system in which data is transmitted in two directions simultaneously. *Compare with* half-duplex.

G

gateway

A hardware or software solution that enables communications between two dissimilar networking systems or protocols. A gateway can operate at any layer of the OSI model.

Gb (gigabit)

1 billion bits or 1000Mb.

Gbps (gigabits per second)

The throughput of a given network medium in terms of 1 billion bps.

GFS (Grandfather-Father-Son)

A backup strategy of maintaining backups on a daily, weekly, and monthly schedule. Backups are made on a five-day or seven-day schedule. A full backup is performed at least once a week. On all other days full, incremental, or differential backups (or no backups at all) are performed. The daily incremental, or differential, backups are known as the *son*. The *father* is the last full backup in the week (the weekly backup). The *grandfather* is the last full backup of the month (the monthly backup).

Gigabit Ethernet

The IEEE 802.3z specification that defines standards for data transmissions of 1Gbps. *See also* 1000BaseX.

guaranteed flow control

A method of flow control in which the sending and receiving hosts agree on a rate of data transmission. After the rate is determined, the communication takes place at the guaranteed rate until the sender is finished. No buffering takes place at the receiver.

H

hacker

A person who carries out hacking on a computer software program. *See also* cracker.

hacking

The process of deconstructing computer software in an effort to understand how it works and to improve it. *See also* cracking.

half-duplex

A connection in which data is transmitted in both directions, but not simultaneously. *Compare with* full-duplex.

handshake

The initial communication between two data communication devices, during which they agree on protocol and transfer rules for the session.

hardware address

The hardware-encoded MAC address that is burned into every NIC.

hardware loopback

A device that is plugged into an interface for the purposes of simulating a network connection and thus enabling the interface to be tested as if it is operating while connected.

High-Speed Token Ring

A version of Token Ring that has a maximum speed of 100Mbps. This is in contrast with other Token Ring standards, which have maximum speeds of 4Mbps or 16Mbps.

hop

The means by which routing protocols determine the shortest way to reach a given destination. Each router constitutes one hop; so if a router is four hops away from another router, there are three routers, or hops, between itself and the destination. In some cases, the final step is also counted as a hop.

host

Any computer system on a network. In the Unix world, any device that is assigned an IP address.

host ID

An identifier that is used to uniquely identify a client or resource on a network.

hostname

A name that is assigned to a system for the purposes of identifying it on the network in a more user-friendly manner than by the network address.

HOSTS file

A text file that contains hostname-to-IP address mappings. All commonly used platforms accommodate static name resolution using the HOSTS file.

hot site

A disaster-recovery term used to describe a site that can be immediately functional in the event of a disaster at the primary site.

hot spare

In a RAID configuration, a drive that sits idle until another drive in the RAID array fails, at which point the hot spare takes over the role of the failed drive.

hot swap

The removal and replacement of a component in a system while the power is still on and the system is functioning.

HSSI (High Speed Serial Interface)

The network standard for high-speed serial communications over WAN links. It includes Frame Relay, T1, T3, E1, and ISDN.

HTTP (Hypertext Transfer Protocol)

A protocol used by Web browsers to transfer pages and files from the remote node to the user's computer.

HTTPS (Hypertext Transfer Protocol Secure)

A protocol that performs the same function as HTTP but does so over an encrypted link, ensuring the confidentiality of any data that is uploaded or downloaded. Also referred to as S-HTTP.

hub

A hardware device that acts as a connection point on a network that uses twisted-pair cable. Also known as a concentrator or a multiport repeater.

HyperTerminal

A Windows-based communications program that allows users to establish host/shell access to a remote system.

I

IANA (Internet Assigned Numbers Authority)

An organization that is responsible for IP addresses, domain names, and protocol parameters. Some functions of IANA, such as domain name assignment, have been devolved into other organizations.

ICMP (Internet Control Message Protocol)

A network-layer Internet protocol documented in RFC 792 that reports errors and provides other information relevant to IP packet processing. Utilities such as `ping` and `tracert` use functionality provided by ICMP.

IDE (Integrated Drive Electronics)

The most common type of disk drive used in PCs today. In these devices, the controller is integrated into the device.

IEEE (Institute of Electrical and Electronics Engineers)

A professional organization that develops standards for networking and communications.

IEEE 802.1

A standard that defines the OSI model's physical and data-link layers. This standard allows two IEEE LAN stations to communicate over a LAN or WAN and is often referred to as the internetworking standard.

IEEE 802.2

A standard that defines the LLC sublayer of the data-link layer for the entire series of protocols covered by the 802.x standards. This standard specifies the adding of header fields, which tell the receiving host which upper layer sent the information.

IEEE 802.3

A standard that specifies physical-layer attributes, such as signaling types, data rates, and topologies, as well as the media access method used. It also defines specifications for the implementation of the physical layer and the MAC sublayer of the data-link layer, using CSMA/CD. This standard also includes the original specifications for Fast Ethernet.

IEEE 802.4

A standard that defines how production machines should communicate and establishes a common protocol for use in connecting these machines together. It also defines specifications for the implementation of the physical layer and the MAC sublayer of the data-link layer, using Token Ring access over a bus topology.

IEEE 802.5

A standard that is used to define Token Ring; however, it does not specify a particular topology or transmission medium. It provides specifications for the implementation of the physical layer and the

MAC sublayer of the data-link layer, using a token-passing media-access method on a ring topology.

IEEE 802.6

A standard that defines the distributed queue dual bus technology to transfer high-speed data between nodes. It provides specifications for the implementation of MANs.

IEEE 802.7

A standard that defines the design, installation, and testing of broadband-based communications and related physical media connectivity.

IEEE 802.8

A standard that defines a group, called the Fiber Optic Technical Advisory Group, that advises the other 802 standard committees on various fiber-optic technologies and standards.

IEEE 802.9

A standard that defines the integration of voice and data transmissions using isochronous Ethernet.

IEEE 802.10

A standard that focuses on security issues by defining a standard method for protocols and services to exchange data securely by using encryption mechanisms.

IEEE 802.11

A standard that defines the implementation of wireless technologies, such as infrared and spread-spectrum radio.

IEEE 802.11b

An extension to the IEEE 802.11 standard that defines wireless access for local area networking.

IEEE 802.12

A standard that defines 100BaseVG-AnyLAN, which uses a 1Gbps signaling rate and a special media access method that allows 100Mbps data traffic over voice-grade cable.

IETF (Internet Engineering Task Force)

A group of research volunteers that is responsible for specifying the protocols used on the Internet and for specifying the architecture of the Internet.

ifconfig

A command used on Linux, Unix, and OS/2 systems to obtain configuration for and configure network interfaces.

IMAP (Internet Message Access Protocol)

A protocol that allows email to be retrieved from a remote server. It is part of the TCP/IP protocol suite and is similar in operation to POP but offers more functionality.

incremental backup

A backup of only files that have been created or changed since the last backup. In an incremental backup, the archive bit is cleared to indicate that a file has been backed up.

infrared

A wireless data communication method that uses light pulses in the infrared range as a carrier signal.

inherited rights

The file system or directory access rights that are valid at a given point as a result of those rights being assigned at a higher level in the directory structure.

intelligent hub/switch

A hub or switch that contains some management or monitoring capability.

intelligent UPS

A UPS that has associated software for monitoring and managing the power that is provided to the system. In order for information to be passed between the UPS and the system, the UPS and system must be connected, which is normally achieved through a serial or USB connection.

interface

A device, such as a card or a plug, that connects pieces of hardware with a computer so that information can be moved from place to place (for example, between computers and printers, hard disks, and other devices, or between two or more nodes on a network). Also, the part of an application or operating system that the user sees.

interference

Anything that can compromise the quality of a signal. On bound media, crosstalk and EMI are examples of interference. In wireless environments, atmospheric conditions that degrade the quality of a signal would be considered interference.

internal IPX address

A unique eight-digit hexadecimal number that is used to identify a server running IPX/SPX. It is usually generated at random when the server is installed.

internal loopback address

Functionality built into the TCP/IP protocol stack that allows one to verify the correct functioning of the stack by pinging any address in the 127.x.x.x range, except the network address (127.0.0.0) or the broadcast address (127.255.255.255). The address 127.0.0.1 is most commonly used.

Internet domain name

The name of an area of the DNS namespace The Internet domain name is normally expressed along with the high-level domain to which it belongs (for example, comptia.org).

Internet layer

In the TCP/IP architectural model, the layer that is responsible for addressing, packaging, and routing functions. Protocols that operate at this layer are responsible for encapsulating packets into Internet datagrams. All necessary routing algorithms are run here.

internetwork

A group of networks that are connected by routers or other connectivity devices so that the networks function as one network.

intrusion detection

The process or procedures that provide a warning of successful or failed unauthorized access to a system.

I/O (input/output)

An operation in which data is either entered into a computer or taken out of a computer.

IP (Internet Protocol)

A network-layer protocol, documented in RFC 791, that offers a connectionless internetwork service. IP provides features for addressing, packet fragmentation and reassembly, type-of-service specification, and security.

IP address

The unique address used to identify the network number and node address of a device that is connected to a TCP/IP network.

ipconfig

A Windows NT/2000 command that provides information about the configuration of the TCP/IP parameters, including the IP address.

IPSec (IP Security)

A protocol that is used to provide strong security standards for encryption and authentication on VPNs.

IPv6 (Internet Protocol version 6)

The new version of IP, which has a larger range of usable addresses than the current version of IP, IPv4, and enhanced security.

IPX (Internetwork Packet Exchange)

A network-layer protocol that is usually used by Novell's NetWare. IPX provides connectionless communication, supporting packet sizes up to 64KB.

IPX/SPX (Internetwork Packet Exchange/Sequenced Packet Exchange)

The default protocol used in NetWare networks. It is a combination of IPX, to provide addressing, and SPX, to provide guaranteed delivery for IPX. IPX/SPX is similar to its counterpart, TCP/IP.

IPX address

The unique address used to identify a node in a network.

IRQ (interrupt request)

A number assigned to a device in a computer that determines the priority and path in communications between a device and the CPU.

IRTF (Internet Research Task Force)

The research arm of the Internet Architecture Board that performs research in the areas of Internet protocols, applications, architecture, and technology.

ISA (Industry Standard Architecture)

The standard of the older, more common, 8-bit and 16-bit bus and card architectures.

ISDN (Integrated Services Digital Network)

An internationally adopted standard for end-to-end digital communications over the PSTN that permits telephone networks to carry data, voice, and other source traffic.

ISDN terminal adapter

A device that enables communication over an ISDN link.

ISO (International Organization for Standardization)

A voluntary organization founded in 1946 that is responsible for creating international standards in many areas, including communications and computers.

ISP (Internet service provider)

A company or an organization that provides facilities for clients to access the Internet.

J

jumpered (or jumpering)

Refers to the physical placement of shorting connectors on a board or card.

jumperless

A term used to describe devices that are configured via a software utility rather than by physical jumpers on the circuit board.

Devices are increasingly moving away from jumpered configuration and toward jumperless configuration.

K

Kb (kilobit)

1,000 bits.

KB (kilobyte)

1,000 bytes.

kernel

The core of an operating system. The kernel provides basic functions and services for all other parts of the operating system, including the interface with which the user interacts.

L

L2F (Layer 2 Forwarding Protocol)

A VPN protocol designed to work in conjunction with the PPP to support authentication standards, such as Terminal Access Controller Access Control System (TACACS+) and Remote Authentication Dial-In User Service RADIUS), for secure transmissions over the Internet.

L2TP (Layer 2 Tunneling Protocol)

A dial-up VPN protocol that defines its own tunneling protocol and works with the advanced security methods of IPSec. L2TP allows PPP sessions to be tunneled across an arbitrary medium to a home gateway at an ISP or a corporation.

LAN (local area network)

A group of connected computers located in a single geographic area—usually a building or campus—that share data and services.

laser printer

A type of printer that uses electrophotography as the means of printing images on paper.

latency

The delay induced by a piece of equipment or device that is used to transfer data.

learning bridge

A bridge that builds its own bridging address table rather than requiring someone to enter information manually. Most modern bridges are learning bridges. Also called a smart bridge.

legacy

An older computer system or technology.

line conditioner

A device used to stabilize the flow of power to the connected component. Also known as a power conditioner or voltage regulator.

link light

An LED on a networking device such as a hub, switch, or NIC. The illumination of the link light indicates that, at a hardware level, the connection is complete and functioning.

link-state routing

A dynamic routing method in which routers tell neighboring routers of their existence through packets called link-state advertisements (LSAs). By interpreting the information in these packets, routers are able to create maps of the entire network. *Compare with* distance-vector routing.

Linux

A Unix-like operating system kernel that was created by Linus Torvalds. Linux is distributed under an open-source license agreement, as are many of the applications and services that run on it.

LLC (logical link control) layer

A sublayer of the data-link layer of the OSI model. The LLC layer provides an interface for the network-layer protocols and the MAC sublayer.

LMHOSTS file

A text file that contains a list of NetBIOS hostname-to-IP address mappings used in TCP/IP name resolution.

logical addressing scheme

The addressing method used in providing manually assigned node addressing.

logical topology

The appearance of the network to the devices that use it, even if in physical terms the layout of the network is different. *See also* physical topology.

loop

A continuous circle that a packet takes through a series of nodes in a network until it eventually times out.

loopback plug

A device used for loopback testing.

loopback testing

A troubleshooting method in which the output and input wires are crossed or shorted in a manner that allows all outgoing data to be routed back into the card.

LTO (Linear Tape Open)

An open standard that allows both high storage capacity and fast data access in tape backup systems. LTO is implemented in two forms: Ultrium and Accelis.

M

MAC (Media Access Control) address

A six-octet number that uniquely identifies a host on a network. It is a unique number that is burned into the network interface.

MAC layer

In the OSI model, the lower of the two sublayers of the data-link layer. It is defined by the IEEE as being responsible for interaction with the physical layer.

mainframe system

A large computer network in which the central computer handles all the data processing and storage; only the results that are requested are sent to the requesting nodes.

MAN (metropolitan area network)

A network that spans a defined geographical location, such as a city or suburb.

master name server

The supplying name server that has authority in a DNS zone.

MAU (media access unit)

A transceiver that is specified in IEEE 802.3. Not to be confused with a Token Ring multistation access unit, which is abbreviated MSAU.

Mb (megabit)

1 million bits. Used to rate transmission transfer speeds.

MB (megabyte)

1 million bytes. Usually refers to file size.

Mbps (megabits per second)

The number of millions of bits that can travel across a given medium in a second. Used as a measurement for the bandwidth of network media.

MDI (medium-dependent interface)

A type of port found on Ethernet networking devices, such as hubs and switches, in which the wiring is straight through. MDI ports are sometimes referred to as uplink ports and are intended for use as connectivity points to other hubs and switches.

MDI-X (medium-dependent interface crossed)

A type of port found on Ethernet networking devices in which the wiring is crossed so that the transmit line of one device becomes the receive line of the other. MDI-X is used to connect hubs and switches to client computers.

memory address

The label assigned to define the location in memory where information is stored. Usually expressed in binary.

message

A portion of information that is sent from one node to another. Messages are created at the upper layers of the OSI model.

metric

A value that can be assigned to a route to encourage or discourage the use of the route. *See also* cost.

MIB (Management Information Base)

A data set that defines the criteria that can be retrieved and set on a device, using SNMP.

microsegmentation

The process of using switches to divide a network into smaller segments.

microwaves

Very short radio waves that are used to transmit data.

mirroring

A fault-tolerant technique in which an exact duplicate of data on one volume is created on another. Mirroring is defined as RAID 1. *See* RAID.

modem (modulator-demodulator)

A device used to modulate and demodulate the signals that pass through it. It converts the direct current pulses of the serial digital code from the controller into the analog signals that are compatible with the telephone network.

MSAU (multistation access unit)

A hub that is used in an IBM Token Ring network. It organizes the connected nodes into an internal ring and uses the RI and RO connectors to expand to other MSAUs on the network. Sometimes referred to as MAU.

MTBF (mean time between failure)

The amount of time, normally expressed in hours, that represents the average amount of time a component will function before it fails.

MTTF (mean time to fix)

The amount of time it normally takes to fix a problem or swap out a component.

multicast

A single-packet transmission from one sender to a specific group of destination nodes.

multihomed

A term used to refer to a device that has more than one network interface.

multiplatform

A term used to refer to a programming language, technology, or protocol that runs on different types of CPUs or operating systems.

multiplexing

A method of transmitting multiple logical signals across the same channel at the same time.

multiprocessor

A term that refers to the use of multiple processors in a single system.

multitasking

The running of several programs simultaneously. In actuality, during multitasking the processor is sharing its time between the programs, and it only appears as if they are running concurrently.

multithreading

A form of multitasking in which the different tasks that appear to be running concurrently are coming from the same application rather than from different applications.

N

name server

A server that contains a databases of name resolution information used to resolve network names to network addresses.

NAS (network attached storage)

A storage device, such as a disk drive or CD-ROM, that is connected directly to the network medium rather than to a server or another system.

NAT (Network Address Translation)

A standard that enables the translation of IP addresses used on one network to a different IP address that is acceptable for use on another network. This translation allows multiple systems to access an external network, such as the Internet, through a single IP address.

NBNS (NetBIOS name server)

A central server that provides name resolution for NetBIOS names to IP addresses.

nbtstat

A Windows operating system command-line utility that displays protocol statistics and current TCP/IP connections using NetBIOS over TCP/IP (NBT).

NCP (NetWare Core Protocol)

A protocol that provides a method for hosts to make calls to a NetWare server for services and network resources. NCP is part of the IPX/SPX protocol suite.

NDIS (Network Driver Interface Specification)

A specification for NIC drivers that allows multiple protocols to be bound to a single network interface.

NDS (Novell Directory Services)

A standards-compliant directory services system implemented by Novell in NetWare 4.x. NDS has since been renamed eDirectory.

NetBEUI (NetBIOS Extended User Interface)

A nonroutable, Microsoft-proprietary networking protocol designed for use in small networks.

NetBIOS (Network Basic Input/Output System)

A software application that allows different applications to communicate between computers on a LAN.

netstat

A Windows operating system command-line utility that displays protocol statistics and current TCP/IP network connections.

NLM (NetWare loadable module)

A service or process that runs on a NetWare server.

NLSP (NetWare Link State Protocol)

A link-state routing protocol that is used on networks that use Novell's IPX/SPX protocol suite.

network card

See NIC.

network ID

The part of a TCP/IP address that specifies the network portion of the IP address. The network ID is determined by the class of the address, which in turn is determined by the subnet mask used.

network interface layer

The bottom layer of the TCP/IP architectural model, which is responsible for sending and receiving frames.

network layer

Layer 3 of the OSI model, which is where routing that is based on node addresses (that is, IP or IPX addresses) occurs.

network operating system

An operating system that runs on the servers on a network. Network operating systems include NetWare, Unix, Windows NT, and Windows 2000.

newsgroup

A discussion group that focuses on a specific topic and is made up of a collection of messages posted to an Internet site. Newsgroups are useful resources for support personnel.

NIC (network interface card)

A hardware component that serves as the interface, or connecting component, between a network and the node. It has a transceiver, a MAC address, and a physical connector for the network cable. Also known as a network adapter or a network card.

NIS (Network Information Services)

The user, group, and security information database that is utilized in a Unix internetwork.

NMS (Network Management System)

An application that acts as a central management point for network management. Most NMS systems use SNMP to communicate with network devices.

NMTP (Network News Transfer Protocol)

An Internet protocol that controls how news articles are to be queried, distributed, and posted.

noise

Another name for EMI. *See* EMI.

NTP (Network Time Protocol)

A protocol used to communicate time synchronization information between devices on the network. NTP is part of the TCP/IP protocol suite.

O

ODI (Open Data-Link Interface)

Heavily used drivers in both Novell and AppleTalk networks that allow multiple protocols to be bound to an NIC. This enables the card to be used by multiple operating systems. Similar to NDIS.

operating system

The main computer program that manages and integrates all the applications running on a computer.

OSI (Open Systems Interconnect) reference model

A seven-layer model that was created by the ISO to standardize and explain the interactions of networking protocols.

OSPF (Open Shortest Path First)

A link-state routing protocol used on TCP/IP networks. *Compare with* distance-vector routing.

P

packet filtering

A firewall method in which each packet that attempts to pass through the firewall is examined to determine its contents. The packet is then allowed to pass or it is blocked, as appropriate.

packet sniffer

A device or an application that allows data to be copied from the network and analyzed. In legitimate applications, it is a useful network troubleshooting tool.

passive hub

A hub that has no power and therefore does not regenerate the signals it receives. *Compare with* active hub.

passive termination

A SCSI bus terminator that uses a terminating resistor pack that is placed at the end of the bus. This resistor relies on the interface card to provide it with a consistent level of power.

password

A set of characters that is used with a username to authenticate a user on a network and to provide the user with rights and permissions to files and resources.

patch

A fix for a bug in a software application. Patches can be downloaded from the Internet to correct errors or security problems in software applications.

patch cable

A cable, normally twisted-pair, that is used to connect two devices. Strictly speaking, a patch cable is the cable that connects a port on a hub or switch to the patch panel, but today people commonly use the term to refer to any cable connection.

patch panel

A device in which the cables used in coaxial or twisted-pair networks converge and are connected. The patch panel is usually in a central location.

PCAnywhere

A software program that allows users to gain control of a computer remotely.

PCI (Peripheral Component Interconnect)

A relatively new high-speed bus designed for Pentium systems.

PCMCIA (Personal Computer Memory Card International Association)

An industry group that was organized in 1989 to promote standards for credit card–sized devices such as memory cards, modems, and network cards. Almost all laptop computers today have multiple PCMCIA slots. PCMCIA cards are now generally referred to simply as PC cards.

PDC (primary domain controller)

In a Windows NT network, the server that acts as the main repository for the user, group, and security information of the domain. *See also* BDC.

peer-to-peer networking

A network environment that does not have dedicated servers, where communication occurs between similarly capable network nodes that act as both clients and servers.

permissions

Authorization provided to users that allows them to access objects on a network. The network administrators generally assign permissions. *Permissions* is slightly different from but often used with *rights*.

physical address

The MAC address on every NIC. The physical address cannot be changed.

physical layer

Layer 1 of the OSI model, where all physical connectivity is defined.

physical topology

The actual physical layout of the network. Common physical topologies include star, bus, and ring. *Compare with* logical topology.

PING

A TCP/IP protocol stack utility that works with ICMP and uses echo requests and replies to test connectivity to other systems.

plenum

The space between the structural ceiling and a drop-down ceiling that is commonly used for heating, ventilation, and air-conditioning systems as well as for running network cables. Network cables placed in this space must have a fire-retardant coating, which gives rise to the term "plenum rated."

plug and play

An architecture designed to allow hardware devices to be detected by the operating system and for the driver to be automatically loaded.

polling

The media-access method for transmitting data in which a controlling device is used to contact each node to determine whether it has data to send.

POP (point-of-presence)

The physical location where a long-distance carrier or a cellular provider interfaces with the network of the local exchange carrier or local telephone company.

POP (Post Office Protocol)

A protocol that is part of the TCP/IP protocol suite and is used for retrieving mail stored on a remote server. The most commonly used version of POP is POP3.

port

In physical networking terms, a socket on a networking device that allows other devices to be connected. In software terms, a port is the entry point into an application, a system, or a protocol stack.

port mirroring

A process by which two ports on a device, such as a switch, are configured to receive the same information. Port mirroring is useful in troubleshooting scenarios.

POTS (plain old telephone system)

The current analog public telephone system. *See also* PSTN.

PPP (Point-to-Point Protocol)

A common dial-up networking protocol that includes provisions for security and protocol negotiation and provides host-to-network and switch-to-switch connections for one or more user sessions. It is the common modem connection used for Internet dial-up.

PPTP (Point-to-Point Tunneling Protocol)

A protocol that encapsulates private network data in IP packets. These packets are transmitted over synchronous and asynchronous circuits to hide the underlying routing and switching infrastructure of the Internet from both senders and receivers.

presentation layer

Layer 6 of the OSI model, which prepares information to be used by the application layer.

PRI (Primary Rate Interface)

A high-level network interface standard for use with ISDN. PRI is defined as having a rate of 1.544Mbps, and it consists of a single 64Kbps D channel plus 23 T1 B channels for voice or data. *See also* BRI, ISDN.

primary name server

The DNS server that offers zone data from files that are stored locally on the machine.

private network

A network to which access is limited, restricted, or controlled. Most corporate networks are private networks. *Compare with* public network.

proprietary

A standard or specification that is created by a single manufacturer, vendor, or other private enterprise.

protocol

A set of rules or standards that control data transmission and other interactions between networks, computers, peripheral devices, and operating systems.

Protocol Identification field

In a frame, a 5-byte field used to identify to the destination node the protocol that is being used in the data transmission.

protocol suite

Two or more protocols that work together, such as TCP and IP or IPX and SPX. Also known as a protocol stack.

proxy

A device, an application, or a service that acts as an intermediary between two hosts on a network, eliminating the ability for direct communication.

proxy server

A server that acts as a go-between for a workstation and the Internet. A proxy server typically provides an increased level of security, caching, and administrative control.

PSTN (public switched telephone network)

A term that refers to all the telephone networks and services in the world. The same as POTS, PSTN refers to the world's collection of interconnected public telephone networks that are both commercial and government owned. All the PSTN is digital, except the connection between local exchanges and customers (which is called the local loop or last mile), which remains analog.

public network

A network, such as the Internet, to which anyone can connect with the most minimal of restrictions. *Compare with* private network.

punchdown block

A set of ports that are connected to the network ports throughout a building. Connections to networking equipment, such as hubs or switches, are established at the punchdown block.

punchdown tool

A hand tool that enables the connection of twisted-pair wires to wiring equipment such as a patch panel.

PVC (permanent virtual circuit)

A logical path that is established between two locations in a packet-switching network. A PVC is similar to a dedicated line and is known as a *permanent virtual connection* in ATM terminology. (Note that private virtual circuits are also called PVCs.)

PVC (private virtual circuit)

A circuit that provides a logical connection between locations through a Frame Relay/ATM cloud (for example, a company with three branch offices, where each location physically connects to the Frame Relay provider's network through a series of switches). To end users, the three branch offices appear to be directly connected to each other, and the PVC appears to be an unbroken circuit. (Note that permanent virtual circuits are also called PVCs.)

R

RAID (Redundant Arrays of Inexpensive Disks)

A method of storing data on multiple hard drives, allowing the overlapping of I/O operations. Depending on the level of RAID, there are either fault-tolerant or performance advantages.

RAID 0

A RAID configuration that employs data striping but lacks redundancy because there is no parity information recorded (*see* RAID 5). As a result, RAID 0 offers no fault tolerance, but it does offer increased performance.

RAID 1

A fault-tolerant method that uses disk mirroring to duplicate the information stored on a disk.

RAID 2

A fault-tolerant method that uses disk striping with error correction.

RAID 3

A fault-tolerant method that uses disk striping with a single disk for parity.

RAID 4

A fault-tolerant method that uses disk striping with a single disk for parity. Striping is done across the disks in blocks.

RAID 5

A fault-tolerant method that uses disk striping with distributed parity. Striping is done across the disks in blocks.

RAID 10

Also referred to as RAID 1/0, a RAID configuration in which stripe sets (RAID 0) are mirrored (RAID 1). This combination provides the fault-tolerant aspects of RAID 1 and the performance advantages of RAID 0.

RARP (Reverse Address Resolution Protocol)

A protocol, part of the TCP/IP protocol suite, that resolves MAC addresses to IP addresses. Its relative ARP resolves IP addresses to MAC addresses.

RAS (Remote Access Service)

A Windows NT/2000 service that allows access to the network through dial-up connections.

read-only

An assigned right that allows the user to open a file and look at the contents or to execute the file if it is an application. The user cannot change the file or delete it.

read-write

An assigned right that allows the user to open, change, or execute a file. The user cannot delete a read-write file in some network operating systems, but can in others. The user can create new files in the directory if he or she is granted read-write permissions to a directory.

remote control

In networking, having physical control of a remote computer through software such as PCAnywhere or Microsoft Systems Management Server.

remote node

A node or computer that is connected to a network through a dial-up connection. Dialing in to the Internet from home is an example of the remote node concept.

repeater

A device that regenerates and retransmits signals on a network. Repeaters are usually used to strengthen signals going long distances.

resolver

A system that is requesting the resolution of a name to an IP address. This term can be applied to both DNS and WINS clients.

resource conflict

A problem that occurs when multiple devices are using the same IRQ or I/O address at the same time, usually causing the devices to fail and the program to halt.

restore

To copy data from backup media to a server. The opposite of back up.

RFC (Request for Comments)

The process by which standards relating to the Internet, the TCP/IP protocol suite, and associated technologies are created, commented on, and approved.

RG-58

A designation for the coaxial cable used in thin coaxial networks that operate on the Ethernet standard.

RI (ring in)

A connector that is used in an IBM Token Ring network on an MSAU to expand to other MSAUs on the network. The counterpart to the RO, the RI on the MSAU connects to the medium to accept the token from the ring.

rights

An authorization provided to users that allows them to perform certain tasks. The network administrator generally assigns rights. Slightly different from but often used with the term *permissions*.

RIP (Routing Information Protocol)

A protocol that uses hop count as a routing metric to control the direction and flow of packets between routers on an internetwork. There are versions of RIP for use on both TCP/IP- and IPX/SPX-based networks.

RJ-11 connector

A connector that is used with telephone systems and can have either four or six conductors. A red/green pair of wires is used for voice and data; a black/white pair is used for low-voltage signals.

RJ-45 connector

An Ethernet cable connector that is used with twisted-pair cable and can support eight conductors for four pairs of wires.

RO (ring out)

A connector used in an IBM Token Ring network on an MSAU to expand to other MSAUs on the network. The counterpart to the RI, the RO on the MSAU connects to the medium to send the token out to the ring.

root

The top level of a file system or a directory services structure. Also, the name of the default administrative account on Unix and Linux systems.

route

The entire path between two nodes on a network.

router

A device that works at the network layer of the OSI model to control the flow of data between two or more network segments.

RS-232

A communications standard that defines the flow of serial communications and the particular functions assigned to the wires in a serial cable.

S

sag

A momentary drop in the voltage provided by a power source.

SAP (service access point)

A field in a frame that tells the receiving host which protocol the frame is intended for.

SAP (Service Advertising Protocol)

A NetWare protocol that is used on an IPX network. SAP maintains server information tables, listing each service that has been advertised to it, and provides this information to any nodes that attempt to locate a service.

SAP (Service Advertising Protocol) agent

A router or another node on an IPX network that maintains a server information table. This table lists each service that has been advertised to it and provides this information to any nodes that attempt to locate a service.

SAS (Single Attached Station)

In an FDDI system, a device that is attached to only one of the two rings. *Compare with* DAS.

SCSI (Small Computer System Interface)

A technology defined by a set of standards originally published by ANSI for use with devices on a bus known as a SCSI bus.

SCSI-1

The first set of ANSI standards for small computer systems that called for up to seven devices, known as targets, to be connected to a computer known as an initiator.

SCSI-2

The second set of ANSI standards for small computer systems, published in 1994. An upgrade to the SCSI-1 standard, SCSI-2 provides a synchronous data transfer rate of 2.5Mbps to 10Mbps for an 8-bit data bus and 5Mbps to 20Mbps for a 16-bit (or *wide*) bus.

SCSI-3

The SCSI standard most widely used today. SCSI-3 splits the 400-plus pages of documents used to describe SCSI-2 into a series of smaller documents. SCSI-3 does not define any particular performance or transfer rate but rather is a set of documents that define the architecture of the updated SCSI specification.

SCSI bus

The high-speed channel between the SCSI devices on a chain. The SCSI bus architecture contains a multithreaded I/O interface that can process multiple I/O requests at the same time.

SCSI bus termination

The use of a set of electrical resistors called terminators at the extreme ends of the SCSI bus to reflect the electrical impulses being transmitted across the bus.

SCSI ID

A number ranging from 0 to 15 that is assigned to a SCSI device to identify the device and its priority when two or more devices are competing for the right to send data on the bus.

secondary name server

A type of DNS server that gets its zone data from another DNS name server that has authority in that zone.

Security log

A log located in the Windows NT 4/2000 Event Viewer that provides information on audit events that the administrator has determined to be security related. These events include logons, attempts to log on, attempts to access areas that are denied, and attempts to log on outside normal hours.

security policy

In general terms, a written policy that defines the rules and regulations pertaining to the security of company data and the use of computer systems. More specifically, the policy configuration on a server system or a firewall that defines the security parameters for a system.

segment
A physical section of a network. Also, a unit of data that is smaller than a packet.

server
A network node that fulfills service requests for clients. Usually referred to by the type of service it performs, such as file server, communications server, or print server.

server-based application
An application that is run from a network share rather than from a copy installed on a local computer.

server-based networking
A network operating system that is dedicated to providing services to workstations, or clients. *See also* client/server networking.

service pack
A software update that fixes multiple known problems and in some cases provides additional functionality to an application or operating system.

session
A dialogue between two computers.

session layer
Layer 5 of the OSI model, which establishes, manages, and terminates sessions between applications on different nodes.

shared system
The infrastructure component that is routed directly into the backbone of an internetwork for optimal systems access. It provides connectivity to servers and other shared systems.

shell
An interface, graphical or otherwise, that enables the functionality of an operating system.

SLIP (Serial Line Internet Protocol)
A protocol that uses encapsulation to allow TCP/IP to be transmitted over asynchronous lines, such as standard telephone lines. Previously used for most Internet access, SLIP has been largely replaced by PPP because of SLIP's lack of error-checking capabilities.

SMDS (Switched Multimegabit Data Service)
The physical-layer implementation for data transmission over public lines at speeds between 1.544Mbps (T1) and 44.736Mbps, using cell relay and fixed-length cells. Defined in IEEE 802.6.

SMP (symmetrical multiprocessing)
The utilization of multiple processors on a single system.

SMTP (Simple Mail Transfer Protocol)
An Internet protocol that is used for the transfer of messages and attachments.

SNAP (Subnetwork Access Protocol)

An Internet protocol that specifies a standard method of encapsulating IP datagrams and ARP messages on a network.

SNMP (Simple Network Management Protocol)

A protocol that provides network devices with a method to monitor and control network devices; manage configurations, statistics collection, performance, and security; and report network management information to a management console. SNMP is part of the TCP/IP protocol suite.

SNMP agent

A software component that allows a device to communicate with, and be contacted by, an SNMP management system.

SNMP trap

An SNMP utility that sends an alarm to notify the administrator that something within the network activity differs from the established threshold, as defined by the administrator.

socket

A logical interprocess communications mechanism through which a program communicates with another program or with a network.

socket identifier

An 8-bit number used to identify the socket and is used by IPX when it needs to address a packet to a particular process running on a server. The developers and designers of services and protocols usually assign socket identifiers. A socket identifier is also known as a socket number.

SONET (Synchronous Optical Network)

A U.S. standard for data transmission that operates at speeds up to 2.4Gbps over optical networks referred to as OC-x, where x is the level.

source address

The address of the host that sent the frame. The source address is contained in the frame so the destination node knows who sent the data.

source-route bridge

A bridge that is used in source-route bridging to send a packet to the destination node through the route specified by the sending node.

spike

An instantaneous, dramatic increase in the voltage output to a device. Spikes are responsible for much of the damage that is done to network hardware components.

SPX (Sequenced Packet Exchange)

A protocol that is used in conjunction with IPX when guaranteed delivery is required. SPX is used mainly in NetWare network environments.

SSL (Secure Sockets Layer)

A method of securely transmitting information to and receiving information from a remote Web site. SSL is implemented through the HTTPS.

STA (Spanning Tree Algorithm)

A standard that is defined by IEEE 802.1 as part of STP to eliminate loops in an internetwork with multiple paths.

static IP address

An IP address that is assigned to a network device manually, as opposed to dynamically via DHCP.

static routing

A routing method in which all routes must be entered into a device manually and in which no route information is exchanged between routing devices on the network. *Compare with* dynamic routing.

static window

A mechanism used in flow control that prevents the sender of data from overwhelming the receiver. The amount of data that can be buffered in a static window is configured dynamically by the protocol.

station IPX address

A 12-digit number that is used to uniquely identify each device on an IPX network.

storage area network

A subnetwork of storage devices, usually found on high-speed networks and shared by all servers on a network.

store-and-forward

A fast-packet-switching method that produces a higher latency than other switching methods because the entire contents of the packet are copied into the onboard buffers of the switch. CRC calculations are performed before the packet can be passed on to the destination address.

STP (shielded twisted-pair)

Twisted-pair network cable that has shielding to insulate the cable from EMI.

STP (Spanning Tree Protocol)

A protocol that was developed to eliminate the loops caused by the multiple paths in an internetwork. STP is defined in IEEE 802.1.

subdomain

A privately controlled segment of the DNS namespace that exists under other segments of the namespace as a division of the main domain.

subnet

A logical division of a network, based on the address to which all the devices on the network are assigned.

subnet mask

A 32-bit address that is used to mask, or screen, a portion of an IP address to differentiate the part of the address that designates the network and the part that designates the host from one another.

subnetting

The process of dividing an assigned IP address range into smaller clusters of hosts.

supernetting

The process of aggregating IP network addresses and using them as a single network address range.

Supervisor account

In a NetWare network, a default account that has rights to access everything and to assign rights to other users on the network.

surge

A voltage increase that is less dramatic than that of a spike but can last a lot longer. Sometimes referred to as a swell. The opposite of brownout.

surge protector

An inexpensive and simple device that is placed between a power outlet and a network component to protect the component from spikes and surges. Also known as a surge suppresser.

SVC (switched virtual circuit)

A virtual circuit that is established dynamically on demand to form a dedicated link and is then broken when transmission is complete. Known as a switched virtual connection in ATM terminology.

switch

A Layer 2 networking device that is used in twisted-pair networks. A switch forwards frames based on destination addresses.

SYN

A message that is sent to initiate a TCP session between two devices.

synchronous transmission

A digital signal transmission method that uses a precise clocking method and a predefined number of bits sent at a constant rate.

System log

A log that is located in the Windows NT 4/2000 Event Viewer that provides information on events logged by Windows NT/2000 system components. These events include driver failures, device conflicts, read/write errors, timeouts, and bad block errors.

T

T-line

A digital communication line used in WANs. Commonly used T designations are T1 and T3. It is also possible to use only part of a T1 line, which then becomes known as *fractional T1*.

TCP (Transmission Control Protocol)

A connection-oriented, reliable data transmission communication service that operates at the transport layer of the OSI model. TCP is part of the TCP/IP protocol suite.

TCP/IP (Transmission Control Protocol/Internet Protocol)

A suite of protocols that includes TCP and IP. TCP/IP was originally designed for use on large internetworks but has now become the de facto protocol for networks of all sizes.

TCP/IP socket

A socket, or connection to an endpoint, that is used in TCP/IP communication transmissions.

TDI (Transport Driver Interface)

A kernel-mode network interface that is exposed at the upper edge of all Windows NT transport protocol stacks. The highest-level protocol driver in every such stack supports the TDI interface for still higher-level kernel-mode network clients.

TDR (time-domain reflectometer)

A device that is used to test copper cables to determine whether and where a break is on the cable. For optical cables, an optical TDR is used.

Telnet

A standard terminal emulation protocol in the TCP/IP protocol stack. Telnet is used to perform terminal emulation over TCP/IP via remote terminal connections, enabling users to log in to remote systems and use resources as if they were connected to a local system.

Terminal Services

A service provided in Windows 2000 and as an add-on in Windows NT that allows clients to connect to the server as if it were a multiuser operating system. All the

processing for the client session is performed on the server, with only screen updates and user input being transmitted across the network connection.

TFTP (Trivial File Transfer Protocol)

A simplified version of FTP that allows file transfers but does not offer any security or file management capabilities.

Thick Ethernet

The IEEE 802.3 standard 10Base5, which describes Ethernet networking using thick coaxial cabling.

thick coaxial

The thick cable most commonly used as the backbone of a coaxial network. It is approximately .375 inches in diameter.

thin client

An application that is run from a back-end server system such as Microsoft Terminal Services. The processing tasks are all performed at the terminal server rather than on the client.

Thin Ethernet

The 802.3 standard 10Base2, which describes Ethernet networking using thin coaxial cabling.

thin coaxial

Cable that is thinner than thick coaxial cable but still about .25 inches in diameter. It is commonly used in older bus topologies.

TIA (Telecommunications Industry Association)

An organization that, along with EIA, develops standards for telecommunications technologies.

token

A frame that provides controlling information. In a Token Ring network, the node that possesses the token is the one that is allowed to transmit next.

Token Ring

An IBM-proprietary token-passing LAN topology defined by IEEE standard 802.5. It operates at either 4Mbps or 16Mbps, in a star topology.

Token Ring adapter

Traditionally, an ISA or a Microchannel device with 4Mbps or 16Mbps transfer capability that is used to connect nodes to a Token Ring network.

tone generator

A device that is used with a tone locator to locate and diagnose problems with twisted-pair cabling.

topology

The shape or layout of a physical network and the flow of data through the network. *See also* logical topology, physical topology.

trace route

A function of the TCP/IP protocol suite, implemented in utilities such as traceroute and tracert, that allows the entire path of a packet to be tracked between source and destination hosts. It is used as a troubleshooting tool.

transmit

To send data using light, electronic, or electric signals. In networking, this is usually done in the form of digital signals composed of bits.

transparent bridging

A situation in which the bridges on a network tell each other which ports on the bridge should be opened and closed, which ports should be forwarding packets, and which ports should be blocking packets—all without the assistance of any other device.

transport layer

Layer 4 of the OSI model, which controls the flow of information.

TTL (time to live)

A value that is assigned to a packet of data to prevent it from moving around the network indefinitely. The TTL value is decremented each time the packet crosses a router, until it reaches 0, at which point it is removed from the network.

twisted-pair

A type of cable that uses multiple twisted pairs of copper wire.

U

UART (Universal Asynchronous Receiver/Transmitter)

A chip that is responsible for communications carried over a serial port; it converts between data bits and serial bits.

UDP (User Datagram Protocol)

A communications protocol that provides connectionless, unreliable communications services and operates at the transport layer of the OSI model. It requires a network-layer protocol such as IP to guide it to the destination host.

unbound media (or boundless media)

A term used to describe any media that do not have physical constraints. Examples of unbound media include infrared, wireless, and microwave. *Compare with* bound media.

UNC (Universal Naming Convention)

An industry naming standard for computers and resources that provides a common syntax that should work in most systems, including Windows, Unix, and NetWare. An example of a UNC name is `\\servername\sharename`.

unicast

A network communication that is directed at a single network node. Unicast is the standard method of communication on a network.

UPS (uninterruptible power supply)

A system that provides protection against power surges and power outages. During blackouts, a UPS gives you time to shut down the network before the temporary power interruption becomes permanent. A UPS is also referred to as battery backup.

uptime

The amount of time that a device has been on and operating.

URL (uniform resource locator)

A name used to identify a site and subsequently a page on the Internet. An example of a URL is `www.quepublishing.com/products`.

USB (universal serial bus)

A type of interface between a computer system and peripheral devices. The USB interface allows you to add or remove devices without shutting down the computer. USB supports up to 127 devices.

user account

An account that an end user uses when logging in to a network. It contains the rights and permissions assigned to the user.

UTP (unshielded twisted-pair)

A type of cable that uses multiple twisted pairs of copper wire in a casing that does not provide much protection from EMI. The most common network cable in Ethernet networks, UTP is rated in categories including Category 1 through Category 5, as well as Category 5e and Category 6.

V

virtual memory

A process for paging or swapping from memory to disk that is used to increase the amount of RAM available to a system.

virus

A software program that is designed specifically to affect a system or network adversely. A virus is usually designed to be passed on to other systems with which it comes in contact.

VLAN (virtual LAN)

A group of devices that are located on one or more different LAN segments, whose configuration is based on logical instead of physical connections so that they can communicate as if they were attached to the same physical connection.

volume set

Multiple disks or partitions of disks that have been configured to read as one drive.

VPN (virtual private network)

A network that uses a public network, such as the Internet, as a backbone to connect two or more private networks. A VPN provides users with the equivalent of a private network in terms of security. VPNs can also be used as a means of establishing secure remote connectivity between a remote system and another network.

W

WAN (wide area network)

A data communications network that serves users across a broad geographical area. WANs often use transmission devices, such as modems or CSUs/DSUs, to carry signals over leased lines or over common carrier lines.

WAP (wireless access point)

A network device that offers connectivity between wireless clients and (usually) a wired portion of the network.

Web server

A server that runs an application and makes the contents of certain directories on that server, or other servers, available to clients for download via a protocol such as HTTP.

WiFi

A voluntary standard that manufacturers can adhere to, which aims to create compatibility between wireless (802.11b) devices.

window flow control

A flow control method in which the receiving host buffers the data it receives and holds it in the buffer until it can be processed. After the data is processed, an acknowledgment is sent to the sender. *See also* dynamic window, static window.

Windows NT Diagnostics

A troubleshooting tool that is provided in Windows NT and Windows 2000 that helps you diagnose hardware and driver problems. It provides a graphical database of system devices and resources that is similar to the Device Manager in Windows 95 and 98.

WINS (Windows Internet Name Service)

A NetBIOS name-to-IP address resolution program that is available in the Windows NT and Windows 2000 operating systems.

WINS database
A dynamically built database of NetBIOS names and IP addresses that is used by WINS.

wire crimper
A tool that is used to create networking cables. The type of wire crimping tool used depends on the cable being made.

wireless networking
Networking that uses any unbound media, such as infrared, microwave, or radio waves.

workstation
A client computer on a network that does not offer any services of its own but uses the services of the servers on the network.

Z

zone
A logical grouping of network devices in an AppleTalk network. Also, an area of the DNS namespace.

zone transfer
The passing of DNS information from one name server to a secondary name server.

Index

DHCP (Dynamic Host Configuration Protocol), 108, 187-188
    reconfiguring, 302-303
    removing, 303
    scopes, 107
dial-up access (remote networks), 144-145
dialog modes
    full-duplex, 27, 53
    half-duplex, 26
    simplex, 26
differential backups, 209
direct sequence modulation, 34
disaster recovery, 212
    differential backups, 209
    full backups, 208-209
    incremental backups, 210
    tape rotation backups, 211
disk duplexing, 202
disk mirroring, 201
disk striping with parity. *See* RAID 5 fault tolerance
distance vector routing protocols, 59-60
distributed computing networks, 5
DNS (Domain Name Service), 84
    ping command, 252
    protocol, 108
    servers, 186, 304
DSL (Digital Subscriber Line), 142, 265-267
dynamic routing environments, 59-60

E

e-Directory (Novell). *See* NDS (Novell Directory Services)
EAP (Extensible Authentication Protocol), 136
EFS (Encrypting File Systems), Windows 2000 network operating system, 164
EMI (electromagnetic interference), 27-29
encryption, 138, 231
    3DES, 233
    DES, 232
    IPSec, 232
    packet sniffing, 232
    presentation layer (OSI reference model), 79
    public key encryption
        PGP, 233
        SSL (Secure Sockets Layer) protocol, 140

error control (LLC standards), 12
error messages (ping command), 248-250
Ethernet
    CSMA/CD (Carrier Sense Multiple Access with Collision Detection), 12-14
    IEEE 802.3 network standards, 12-13
        10Base2 standards, 39
        10Base5 standards, 39-40
        10BaseT standards, 40
        fast Ethernet standards, 41-42
        Gigabit Ethernet standards, 42-43
    PC connections, 183
    PPPoE (Point-to-Point Protocol over Ethernet), 143
    switches, 53, 57
exam simulation interface, PrepLogic Practice Tests, 378
Examination Score Report, 382
Expired TTL (Time to Leave) error message (ping command), 250

F

failover configuration, stand-by servers, 205
fast Ethernet standards, 41-42
FAT (File Allocation Tables), Windows NT 4 network operating system, 159
fault tolerance
    hard disks, 200-204
    servers, 205-206
    UPS (Uninterruptable Power Supplies), 207-208
FDDI (Fiber Distributed Data Interface) networks, 14, 130-131
FDM (Frequency Division-Multiplexing), 26
fiber connectors, 37
fiber-optic cable, 28, 32-33
firewalls, 224-226
flow control, 78
FPNW (File and Print Services for NetWare), 173
FragmentFree-switching environments, 54
frame relay, 132
frequency hopping, 34
FTP (File Transfer Protocol), 101
full backups, 208-209
full-duplex dialog mode, 27, 53

How can we make this index more useful? Email us at indexes@quepublishing.com

X